KATHAK

KATHAK
The Dance of Storytellers

RACHNA RAMYA

EDITED BY PAMELA ADELMAN

NIYOGI
BOOKS

Published by
NIYOGI BOOKS
Block D, Building No. 77,
Okhla Industrial Area, Phase-I,
New Delhi-110 020, INDIA
Tel: 91-11-26816301, 26818960
Email: niyogibooks@gmail.com
Website: www.niyogibooksindia.com

Text © Rachna Ramya
Photographs © As mentioned in the Illustration Credits on pp. 337–42

Editor: Sukanya Sur
Design: Misha Oberoi

ISBN: 978-93-86906-88-5
Publication: 2019

Printed at: Niyogi Offset Pvt. Ltd., New Delhi, India

To Pandit Rajendra Kumar Gangani
Guru Dr Maya Rao
Vidushi Sandhya Desai

and

To my mother Dr Kamla Kanodia
You all have given me thousands of reasons to celebrate life
You all are my blessings

Contents

Transliteration of Key Words

Most of the Sanskrit and Hindi words in the text are written in the way they are pronounced. However, some of the key words used in the text have peculiar pronunciations that can be best written using mixed Greek/Coptic diacritical marks.

Key Word	Transliteration	Key Word	Transliteration
Aamad	Āmad	Nataraja	Natrāja
Aharya	Āh‾arya	Natwar	Natvar
Ang	Anga	Natya	Nāya
Angika	Āngika	Nritya	Nritya
Avartan	Āvartan	Nrtta	Nrtta
Baant	Bānt	*Natyashastra*	*Nāyaśāstra*
Barabar ki laya	Barābar ki laya	Nayak	Nāyaka
Bhava	Bhāva	Nayika	Nāyikā
Chaal	Cāl	Padhant	Padhant
Chakkar	Cakkar	Prakar	Prakār
Chala	Cāla	Raas Leela	Rāslīlā
Desi	Desī	Radha	Rādhā
Gharana	Gharānā	Raga	Rāga
Ghungru	Ghungru	Sadhana	Sādhanā
Jati	Jāti	Salami	Salāmī
Katha	Kathā	Sangeet	Sangīta
Khali	Khālī	Satvik	Sāttvika
Khandani	Khāndānī	Sawal-jawab	Sawāl-jawāb
Krishna	Ka	Shakti	Śakti
Kriya	Kriyā	Shloka	Ślokā
Lasya	Lāsya	Sum	Sama
Laykari	Layakarī	Tala	Tāla
Lehra	Lehrā	Tali	Tālī
Margi	Mārgi	Tandava	Tāndava
Matra	Mātrā	Tarana	Tarānā
Mudra	Mudrā	Tatkar	Tatkār

That	Thāt	Upang	Upānga
Theka	Thekā	Vachik	Vācika
Tihai	Tihaī	Vadya	Vādya
Thumri	Thumrī	Vandana	Vandāna
Tukda	Tukda	Vibhag	Vibhāg

Transliteration of *Bols*

Key *Bols*	Transliteration
Aa	Ā
Dha	Dhā
Dhage	Dhāge
Dhalang	Dhalānˈg
Dhikita	Dhikita
Digdig	Diga-diga
Gadigina	Gadigīna
KaTa	Katā
Kirdha	Kirdhā
Na	Nā
Ta	Tā
Taghanna	Ta-gha-nna
Taka	Taka
Takita	Takita
TaT	Ta-Ta
Tete	Tete
Thai	Theī
Tho	Thō
Tig	Tig
Tin	Tin
Traka	Tra-ka
Tram	Trām
Tunna	Tun-na

Preface

THE ANCIENT SEERS OF INDIA explored the fundamental truth of life by contemplating the ultimate nature of the Supreme Self. They acquired the intuitive knowledge and wisdom to deepen their communion with the Divine through meditation, yoga, and various arts. Their comprehension of the Absolute Truth formed the bedrock of classical Indian music and dance. All Indian arts take us within, where divine expressions can be felt and experienced through the principle of unity. The integrated purpose is greater than the sum of its parts. All paradoxes and contradictions of human emotions transcend in the glorious light of arts that allow us to tap into our authentic source.

Through centuries, India endured many social, political, and economic setbacks and obstacles as a result of foreign invasions and occupations. But the ironclad chain of Indian arts remained unbroken, because the arts of India graciously invited others to witness its beauty and truth with its boundless capacity for acceptance. Indian arts became a haven for all who were weary from division and destruction.

Like other Indian art forms, Kathak dance was shaped and evolved over millennia through a multitude of influences, such as the Mughal invasion in the early tenth century, the Bhakti Movement, the system of patronage, and various cross-cultural exchanges throughout India. *Kathak: The Dance of Storytellers* explores both the philosophical and practical aspects of Kathak dance, including its origin, development, schools, techniques, and music. Kathak, the dance of North India, originated more than 2,000 years ago as a form of storytelling. At that time, the storytellers staged performances on religious and mythological folk tales through the media of dance, drama, and music. The first few chapters offer an appraisal of this compelling dance style from artistic, cultural, and historical perspectives, explaining how Bharata Muni's *Natyashastra*, an ancient treatise on dramatic arts, inspired many significant aspects of Kathak. No modern-day performing art styles of India can be fully appreciated without the reference point of *Natyashastra*. Therefore, various concepts of *Natyashastra* are related throughout the book, informing Kathak's phases of development from an ancient art form to the current Kathak style. Emerging from the traditions of ancient *kathakar*s, Kathak during the Mughal era was influenced by the Bhakti Movement and found its place both in the devotional performances of the Raas Leelas and in the passion-infused artistic atmosphere of the Mughal courts. Reverence for Kathak declined during the British Raj, and the dance form suffered greatly from being labelled as a nautch dance—a dance style purely for sensual pleasures. Kathak in independent India regained its repute and became the classical dance of North India.

There are chapters which focus on aesthetics and expressional philosophies in Kathak, and the characterization of heroes and heroines. The aesthetic model of *rasa* and *bhava* are explored in depth in the chapter '*Rasa* and *Bhava*', which are the elements that transform ordinary experiences into artistic ones. The ultimate goal of Indian arts is to evoke *rasa* in the hearts of the viewer and the performer. Brief explanations of the inner state of consciousness, such as *bhutas* (five elements), *gunas* (fundamental universal nature), *doshas* (physiological energies), *koshas* (mystical sheaths of being), and *siddhis* (spiritual powers) are provided to enhance the reader's understanding of the nature of *rasa*. This chapter also explains the *bhava* or the internal intent and its categories, which help in creating the nine fundamental *rasas*. The chapter ends with the philosophy of *sadharanikaran* or the universalization of a *rasa* and its purpose in dance. *Natyashastra's sadharanikaran* is compared with Aristotle's Rhetoric for a better understanding of the concept. The *rasa* theory provided by Bharata Muni is also compared with the works of other Sanskrit scholars. Chapters '*Abhinaya*', 'Three Facets of *Abhinaya*', and '*Nayak* and *Nayika Bhed*' explore the facets of *abhinaya* (the art of expressions) and throw light on how these categories of *abhinaya* are employed in Kathak dance. The chapters also include the four *vrittis* or styles of expressions that account for the different dimensions of human behaviour. *Abhinaya* is expressed by *nayaks* and *nayikas*, the archetypal male and female characters in Indian arts. These characterizations are determined through *nayak-nayika-bhed*, which is based on age, temperament, action, situation, class, emotions, and the inherent disposition of a character. *Vesh-bhusha* (clothing and accessories) used by a character either to reveal or conceal a character's personality is also examined. The section on characterization concludes with the notion that many modern-day Kathak dancers avoid the concept of stereotypical *nayika-bhed* in order to elevate the status of women in arts.

Kathak is a rhythm-oriented dance form. Therefore, chapters '*Tala* and *Laya*: Musical Time in Kathak', '*Laykari*', 'Ways of Resolving a Composition on *Sum*', '*Nrtta*: Rhythmic Interpretation through Body Movements' are devoted to the musical time/interplay of rhythm—rhythmic execution through footwork and body movements in Kathak. Most of this subject matter is supported with musical notations of compositions from the Kathak repertoire. *Tala* and *laya* are discussed in detail in these chapters. The nature of the ancient Indian rhythmic system, which was based on the ideas of *chhand* and *laya* (the metrical modes) that imbued the recitation of Vedic chants, is the basis of the modern-day *tala* system. *Tala*s provide the rhythmic laws of Indian music based on stresses, form, regularity, accents, intonation, duration, length, and continuity of the rhythmic patterns. The medieval concept of the *dus pran of tala*s (ten life forces of *tala*s) determines the nature, arrangement, mood, and magnitude of rhythmic cycles. Although not practised precisely today, they remain important as profound influences on the characteristics of the modern-day *tala* system. The components of *tala* and the concept and performance of *laya* in Kathak are explained with examples, using musical notations. *Tala* is not merely a rhythmic structure to measure time; it also assists in evoking *rasa* during a performance. The aesthetic value of rhythms depends on many factors, such as *laykari* and the ways of resolving compositions. *Laykari* is the performance of captivating variations and patterns in tempo. The presentation of *laykari* is a stimulating aspect of Kathak dance. The way in which compositions conclude on *sum* (the first beat of a *tala*) facilitates the dynamic *laykari* of a composition. *Tihai* is one of the most important ways to resolve a composition. This section of the book gives considerable attention to the art of creating *tihai*, a triadic structure and a cadential configuration that creates a sense of conclusion. The rules and the aesthetic functions of *tihai* have been discussed. Types of *tihai*s, including atypical and exceptional varieties, are explained with their mathematical equations. Many exceptional and unique compositions that are performed only by the masters of Kathak are notated here. Creating designs of sound imagery through footwork is one of the most dazzling aspects of Kathak. A lot of *laykari* in Kathak is performed through intricate footwork. The book covers different *kriya*s or actions of footwork in Kathak. There are suggestions provided with notated examples to strengthen both a dancer's footwork and rhythmic interpretation. The rhythmic repertoire of Kathak falls under the category of *nrtta* or the art of pure dance. There are many repertoires in Kathak that entail *laykari* through engaging body movements and are performed in different tempos. The varieties of *laykari* are described with examples from Kathak repertoire using musical notations, which can be practically followed by the readers.

The book further delves into the use of Kathak repertoire to express an idea or a story, essential principles and techniques of Kathak, its schools and major artists, the format of a Kathak performance, Kathak repertoire, the application of music in Kathak, the importance of conscientious training, and the system of practice through the lens of theory and application.

A FEW PRACTICAL NOTES FOR READING THIS BOOK

Terminology The use of dance terminologies and philosophical vocabulary was anticipated in this book. Most of these terms are from Sanskrit, Hindi, and Arabic languages, or from some North Indian dialects. Transliterating the words from another language to English was sometimes challenging. The spelling of words from Sanskrit language was particularly complicated because Sanskrit is written in Devanagari script—a writing system that uses syllabary. In Sanskrit, a word is composed of one or many consonants and symbols, followed by a vowel sound. Also, when a word ends in a consonant, it shares a syllable with the subsequent word. Sometimes a word ends with a consonant and a symbol, where the symbol represents an intended vowel. This is why the English spelling of Sanskrit words is somewhat problematic. I have spelled the Sanskrit and Hindi words in a way that they represent the way they are spoken. There may be spelling differences in the text of this book and the quotes cited from other books; nonetheless, the subject matter being discussed is not diluted. In the beginning of the book, I have also included the diacritical marks of some key words that are used commonly in the field of Kathak dance. However, Sanskrit and Hindi words are not transliterated in the body of the text so that it is less cumbersome for the readers.

Notation The examples and notations for the *tihai*s and footwork compositions are given in a *tala* called *teental*. *Teental* is used because it is the most employed *tala* in classical Indian music and dance. It is a symmetrical *tala* and its sixteen beats are divided evenly, making it a balanced *tala* to handle. This *tala* can also be subdivided and compounded easily, and the sixteen-beat cycle in slow speed gives ample opportunities to a dancer to improvise in one cycle.

Examples for the compositional repertoire in the chapter 'Rhythmic Interpretation through Body Movements' are not given since these compositions have specific body movements that can only be learned from instruction by a competent guru. There are examples, notations, and mathematical equations for the execution of various *laykari*s and for creating *tihai*s. The *nrtta* aspect of Kathak, which uses only footwork, is also supported by examples and musical notations.

In many dance compositions, both the capital 'T' and small 't' are used to differentiate between their pronunciations. The capital 'T' is pronounced with a 'hard' sound, as in the English word 'tea', where the tip of the tongue touches the back of the upper middle teeth. The small 't' in compositional examples is pronounced more softly, as in the English word 'tambourine'.

Nataraja and Natwar: The Cultural Perspective

INDIAN DANCE FORMS are fundamentally linked with Indian philosophy and spirituality. The Indian rishis, or the ancient seers, saw dance as a manifestation of the Divine. For them, dance was a vehicle that helped humankind journey towards the Absolute. It was a channel that could undeniably deepen people's relationships with themselves and the universe. Even today, Indian dancers view dance as a law of action and reaction in which the body acts in response to the splendour of the natural world. Consequently, dance becomes more abstract, non-materialistic, and formless in nature. It invariably leads both the dancer and the observer to a sacred experience.

NATARAJA: THE LORD OF INDIAN DANCE

Indian dances are associated with the Hindu philosophy of the 'cycle of life'—creation, preservation, and destruction. According to Indian mythology, the cosmic dancer Lord Shiva, through His divine dance, destroys the decayed universe in order for Brahma, the Lord of Creation, to begin the process of a new creation. Therefore, Lord Shiva is also called Nataraja or the Lord of Dance. The picturesque presentation of Nataraja is symbolic and has much cultural, artistic, and spiritual significance. During the Chola Dynasty in South India (ninth century to thirteenth century CE), artists created and developed the dynamic visual form of Nataraja as a series of exquisite bronze sculptures. Even in contemporary times, this iconic representation of Lord Shiva holds a significant place in Indian arts and signifies many different aspects of His disposition and attributes. In this visual interpretation, He is depicted as dancing in ecstasy to the cosmic rhythm of creation. In His matted locks, He holds the personification of the holy river Ganges, which cascades down to earth to provide life and fertility to all beings. Shiva's hair becomes dishevelled during His rapturous dance, symbolizing the movement of wind, which, in its subtle form, is the breath of life.

The statue of Nataraja rests on a lotus pedestal, symbolizing an awakening of consciousness. The ring of fire that surrounds Him connotes the manifest universe, an endless cycle of birth and death. The dancing Shiva is stepping with His right leg on Apasmara Purusha, who is a personification of illusion and ignorance, and His raised left leg symbolizes the triumph over materialistic bondages. The Nataraja statue illustrates Shiva with four hands, since He is perceived to be the ruler of four cardinal directions. His upper right hand holds a *damaru*, an hourglass-shaped drum of creation on which He plays the rhythm of the universe. Shiva's *damaru* has two distinct heads, which are perceived as soul and body. These two heads are connected vertically by a narrow neck, denoting the dissociation between the body and soul. With Shiva's dancing, the *damaru* vibrates and brings the cosmic sound of Om into being. In Hinduism, the sacred and eternal sound 'Om' is made up of three letters—A, U, and M. The letter 'A' signifies the state of consciousness; 'U' is the state of dreaming consciousness; and the letter 'M' represents the state of undifferentiated consciousness, where every aspect of creation becomes one. As Shiva's dance reaches a crescendo, the two separate aspects of *damaru* start to merge, forming a shape resembling a star of illumination. Shiva's upper left hand holds *agni*, the fire of dissolution of form: 'The balance of the two hands represents the dynamic balance of creation and destruction in the world, accentuated further by the Dancer's calm and detached face in the centre of the two hands, in which the polarity of creation and destruction is dissolved and transcended.'[1]

Shiva's lower right hand is in *abhaya* position, which means 'fearlessness'. His lower left hand points to His raised leg, which indicates liberation from worldly subjections. The two cobras around Shiva's waist symbolize kundalini. According to *Yogasastra*, kundalini is a dormant corporeal energy at the base of the

[1] Fritjof Capra, *The Tao of Physics: An Exploration of the Parallels between Modern Physics and Eastern Mysticism* (Massachusetts, USA: Shambhala Publications, 1991), 3rd edition, p. 244.

human spine, which can be awakened through the practice of meditation and other esoteric disciplines. The crescent moon adorns His forehead and the fierce cobras coil around His neck in a subdued state. The crescent moon represents the passage of time ruled by Shiva. The cobras coiled around Shiva's neck represent triumph over egoism. The tiger-skin loincloth is His attire and signifies Shiva's power to subdue untamed minds. Finally, His third eye represents divine knowledge and insight—His power to perceive beyond the illusions of the material world.

Ananda Natanam, the cosmic dance of Shiva

Attributes of Nataraja

Shiva's cosmic dance embodies His five cosmic actions: *shristi, sthiti, tirobhava, anugraha,* and *samhara*. *Shristi* signifies the creation of the manifest and the unmanifest worlds, where Shiva as a creator penetrates all existence with His pure consciousness. In the state of *sthiti*, He preserves and sustains the universe. Through *tirobhava*, Shiva veils His shaktis or powers that permeate every aspect of existence, creating the world of maya or illusion. Shiva possesses five ultimate powers known as *chit shakti* (pure consciousness), *anand shakti* (blissful state), *ichcha shakti* (willpower), *jnana shakti* (absolute knowledge), and *kriya shakti* (dynamic energy). Maya is also an aspect of His shakti. Shakti is recognized as Shiva's eternal consort. Through *tirobhava*, Shiva conceals His pure powers and uses maya to create ignorance and illusion in order to nourish the idea that only after experiencing the oppositions and contradictions, life becomes whole. Through *anugraha*, Shiva reveals His knowledge and truth, which are the sources of liberation. Shiva's *samhara* represents dissolution. Shiva as a destroyer extracts all cosmic energy and restores it within Himself. *Samhara* also denotes Shiva's temporary retreat in order to create the universe anew. Shiva destroys the universe only so that it can be renewed and the embodied souls can be liberated.

Tandava Nritya

In the altered state of samadhi or superconsciousness, Shiva is *nirguna* or unmanifest and formless. It is His *saguna* or manifest state when He becomes Nataraja and performs His divine dance—Tandava. Shiva's five actions that are the principles of eternal forces are exemplified through His Tandava dance. It arouses the dormant energies that finally recreate the world. His dance is the cause of all movements within the universe and represents the cosmic cycles of creation and destruction, which are the basis of the continual cycle of life and death. Shiva's dynamic and energetic dance takes place at the centre of the universe, which lies within our hearts.

Sharangdeva (1210–1247 CE), in his revered musicological text *Sangeet Ratnakara*, indicates that Shiva's assistant Tandu, also known as Nandishwar, instructed the art of Tandava dance to Sage Bharata. Tandu also taught Bharata the Lasya dance performed by Parvati, the counterpart of Shiva. Subsequently, Bharata Muni taught the art of dance to his sons and disciples.

The accuracy of this legend is debatable; still it is probable that dance in ancient India started with the Shaivite tradition, a sect of Hinduism. In his *Natyashastra*, Bharata has discussed about 32 *anghara*s and 108 *karana*s that he claims to be derived from the Tandava and Lasya dances. *Karana*s are the basic dance postures, and the combinations of *karana*s create *anghara*s. The combination of feet and hand postures and movements are very important in *karana*s because, according to ancient texts, Shiva's foot movements initiate the rotation of the earth, and His hand movements commence the activities of celestial objects. Bharata in *Natyashastra* refers to Tandava dance as brought to earth by Tandu Muni.

Rechaka Angharashchah pindibandhasthaiva cha
Srishta bhagwata dattastandate munaye tada
Tenapi hi tatah samyagganabhandsamanvitah
Nritta prayog srishto yah sa tandava iti smritah[2]
[Translation: Lord Shiva taught *anghara*s, *rechaka*s (the movements of hands), and *pindibandh*s (the patterns for group compositions) to Tandu Muni.

---

[2] Prem Dave, *Kathak Nritya Parampara* (Jaipur: Panchsheel Prakashan, 2004), p. 11.

Tandu Muni consequently added musical elements from instrumental and vocal music to these movements and named this dance style, the Tandava.]

Tandava dance is vigorous in nature and reflects the masculine powers of Shiva. Many different types of Tandava dance are referred to in ancient scriptures. Most of His dances take place at *shamashan*, or the cremation ground, symbolizing the obstinate ego burned down to ashes. In one specific form, Shiva smears the ashes of *shamashan* on His body. Shiva's Samhara Tandava is the dance of dissolution. It transpires when Shiva opens His third eye, and the entire universe is consumed by a fierce fire in order to regenerate itself. The dance that Shiva performed after annihilating the arrogant demon Tripurasur is called Tripur Tandava. In the performance of Tripur Tandava, the moksha or emancipation of the soul is given importance as a subject matter. Shiva performs Kalika Tandava with Mahakali, the Hindu Goddess of Time and Death. In Kalika Tandava, emphasis is given to the ultimate liberation of the soul after it experiences the sufferings of this world in 8.4 million birth cycles. Sandhya Tandava is when Shiva's dance graces the time of dusk and is performed in front of His consort Parvati, also known as Gauri. In scriptures, the beautiful description of Sandhya Tandava is offered, according to which Shiva performs Sandhya Tandava in front of Parvati, who sits on a throne studded with precious jewels. Saraswati, the Goddess of Knowledge, accompanies Him on Her veena or lute; Indra, the Lord of Heaven, is on flute; Brahma, the Creator of the World, keeps the rhythm, while Vishnu, the Preserver of the World, accompanies Him on His drum; and the other gods and deities become His devoted spectators. Shiva dedicates His Gauri Tandava to His consort Gauri. Uma Tandava is the dance of Shiva's grief after the death of His wife Uma, another name for Goddess Parvati. During this dance, a grief-stricken Shiva lifts the dead body of Uma, the Mountain Goddess, on His shoulders and dances. During the Uma Tandava and Gauri Tandava, Shiva assumes the form of Bhairav, the fierce and enraged god. In Rudra Tandava, Shiva strikes Yama, the God of Death. Finally, the Anand Tandava is Shiva's dance of bliss. Coomaraswamy elaborates:

> An essential significance of Siva's [sic] dance is threefold: First, it is the image of his rhythmic play as the source of all movement within the cosmos, which is represented by the arch: Secondly the purpose of His dance is to release the

countless souls of men from the snare of illusion: Thirdly, the place of the dance, Chidambaram, the center of the universe, is within the heart.[3]

Shiva performs different types of Tandavas at different occasions, and each episode has an inherent philosophical meaning that is directly linked to human life.

Lasya Nritya

Shiva's Tandava is complimented by the Lasya dance performed by His consort, Goddess Parvati. Lasya is expressed through graceful, delicate, and tantalizing movements. According to mythology, Parvati performed Lasya with pride and joy at Her husband's victory after Shiva killed the demon Tripurasur. Lasya derives from the word *lasana*, meaning 'luster'. Lasya's charming and poised movements gleam with beauty. Bharata in *Natyashastra* does not mention the Lasya Nritya; however, he uses the words *sukumar prayoga* or the approaches for this delicate dance: '*Lasya* is not defined in *Natyasastra*....In *Natyasastra*, Bharata mentioned "Sukumara Prayoga" merely as the essence of *Lasya*, being the main feature of the dance of Parvati, but the nature of the "*Sukumara Prayoga*" was not elaborated.'[4]

Three main types of Lasya are prevalent in Kathak. In Visham Lasya, movements perpendicular to the body are performed, followed by a vertically opposite angle. In Vikar Lasya, techniques and expressions are performed together. In Laghu Lasya, different body movements are performed with elegance.

From a philosophical perspective, Shiva is considered 'consciousness' and Parvati as Shakti is considered 'energy'. Together, they symbolize the masculine and feminine forces of nature respectively. Shiva and Parvati are also referred to as 'purusha' and 'prakriti' or 'consciousness' and 'nature'. Prakriti is the divine manifestation of purusha. Parvati as prakriti depicts movement, change, and energy, whereas Shiva as purusha is unchangeable and infinite. Purusha and prakriti are also the two halves of primordial energy hidden within all of humankind, which strive for union and purity. And when this unity occurs,

[3] Saskia Kersenboom, 'Ananda's Tandava: "The Dance of Shiva" Reconsidered', The Free Library by Farlex, Marg, A Magazine of the Arts, 1 March 2011, https://www.thefreelibrary.com/Ananda's+Tandava%3A+%22The+Dance+of+Shiva%22+reconsidered.-a0253862093 (accessed on 12 April 2018).

[4] 'A General Introduction to Lasya and Dance Traditions', p. 9, http://shodhganga.inflibnet.ac.in/bitstream/10603/25592/9/09_chapter%201.pdf (accessed on 12 April 2018).

the process of creation is activated. Separately, Shiva and Shakti are incomplete—Shiva represents the unmanifest and Shakti signifies the manifest. Indian dances honour this concept of Shiva and Shakti. The basis of all Indian classical dances is the dissolution of this duality of Shiva and Shakti and treading on the path of unity and creation by merging the masculine and feminine forces of the universe.

Shiva and Parvati (Sas Bahu Temple, Eklingji, India)

The picturesque representation of Nataraja has fascinated metaphysicists and the classical physicists equally. According to the pioneering historian and philosopher Ananda Coomaraswamy:

> In the night of *Brahman*, Nature is inert, and cannot dance till Shiva wills it: He rises from His rapture, and dancing sends through inert matter pulsing waves of awakening sound, and lo! Matter also dances, appearing as a glory round about Him. Dancing, He sustains its manifold phenomena. In the fullness of time, still dancing, He destroys all forms and names by fire and gives new rest. This is poetry, but nonetheless science.[5]

Dr Fritjof Capra (1 February 1939), an Austrian-born physicist, connects Nataraja's dance with modern physics. He first discusses this idea in his article titled 'The Dance of Shiva: The Hindu View of Matter in the Light of Modern Physics', which was published in 1972. Later, in his book *The Tao of Physics*, he again emphasizes the parallels between Shiva's dance and modern science: 'Modern physics has shown that the rhythm of creation and destruction is not

---

[5] Capra, *The Tao of Physics*, p. 242.

only manifest in the turn of the seasons and in the birth and death of all living creatures, but is also the very essence of inorganic matter....For the modern physicists, then, Shiva's dance is the dance of subatomic matter.' [6]

The Indian government presented the statue of Nataraja to CERN, the European Center for Research in Particle Physics, in Geneva on 8 June 2004. This statue of dancing Shiva is over 6 feet high and is placed at the building's entrance. Beside the statue is a special plaque inscribed with both Sri Ananda K. Coomaraswamy and Fritjof Capra's quotes about the significance of Shiva's cosmic dance. The text of the plaque includes the following quotes:

> Ananda K. Coomaraswamy, seeing beyond the unsurpassed rhythm, beauty, power and grace of the Nataraja, once wrote of it: 'It is the clearest image of the activity of God which any art or religion can boast of.'

> It is indeed as Capra concluded: 'Hundreds of years ago, Indian artists created visual images of dancing Shiva in a beautiful series of bronzes. In our time, physicists have used the most advanced technology to portray the patterns of the cosmic dance. The metaphor of the cosmic dance thus unifies ancient mythology, religious art and modern physics.'[7]

Shiva's mystical dance has profoundly inspired the arts and philosophy of India, and it continues to be the source of spirituality that is inseparable from the arts.

NATWAR: THE LORD OF KATHAK DANCE

Shiva is the Lord of Dissolution, and Krishna, as an incarnation of Vishnu, is the Preserver of the Universe. Shiva is the Nataraja and the lord of all Indian dances. Lord Krishna as Natwar is the lord of Kathak dance, and is revered for His leelas or divine plays. Shiva and Krishna represent contrasting aspects of the same ultimate supreme power. Shiva's dance is aggressive, vigorous, and even violent. Krishna's dance is graceful, lyrical, and always alluring.

....

[6] Capra, *The Tao of Physics*, pp. 244–45.

[7] Fritjof Capra, 'Shiva's Cosmic Dance at CERN', 20 June 2004, http://www.fritjofcapra.net/shivas-cosmic-dance-at-cern/ (accessed on 12 April 2018).

Krishna dancing with *gopis*

On the night of the full moon in autumn, Krishna plays His enchanting flute. *Gopi*s, the maidens of Braj, are mesmerized by His magical music, and their hearts get established in the divine love of the beautiful blue god, Krishna.

Drenched with Krishna's absolute and mystical love, they arrive in the middle of a lush forest, where a charming Krishna waits for them to dance raas with Him. Krishna multiplies Himself by many by using His maya, the cosmic illusion suggesting that the material world is real. He dances with each *gopi* in a circle, performing the dance of Divine Love. In the centre of the circle, He dances with His mysterious lover, Radha. Their Raas Leela reaches the state of blissful trance, where all dualities disappear. Time is suspended for the duration of one night of Brahma, approximately 4.32 billion years, and the *gopi*s, the souls, merge with Krishna, the universe.

Krishna's mythic raas bequeathed Him the title 'Natwar'—one who is the supreme artist of performing arts. Krishna's leelas are the central laws of the universe and have inspired artists since ancient times. By the eleventh century CE, the Vaishnava Bhakti sect was established all over North India, which propagated the spiritual and devotional aspects of life by surrendering oneself to an unconditional love for Krishna. The Vaishnavites perceived Krishna as the Supreme God, rather than just as an incarnation on earth.

Kathak dance, which at one point was also referred to as the Natwari Nritya, has taken its inspiration from Krishna's legends. The earliest Kathaks were the *kathakar*s or the storytellers, who recited stories of Vishnu and His incarnations through the medium of performing arts. *Mahabharata* (between the eight and ninth century BCE), the world's longest epic poem written in Sanskrit, casts Krishna as its main character. In *Mahabharata*, there are various allusions

Krishna playing the flute

to Kathak dance. Later, Kathak became very inspired by the Raas Leelas that evolved as a musical theatre form in North India. Swami Sri Uddhavaghamanda Devacharya in the early fifteenth century CE started the formal performance of Raas Leelas in Vrindavan, India. At that time, many saint-poets wrote beautiful devotional poetry and songs in praise of Krishna and Radha. Krishna's love for His supreme lover Radha signifies the meeting of the soul with God. It is believed that Krishna captivates the universe, and the Supreme Goddess Radha captivates Krishna. Radha-Krishna became the Shakti-Shiva aspect of the devotional philosophy of Vaishnavites.

Even though Kathak was nurtured mainly in the Mughal courts of India, the lyrical expressions of the Vaishnavite saint-poets became an integral part of Kathak repertoire. Krishna in literature, folk theatre, arts, and Kathak is portrayed in many ways. Krishna is depicted as a naughty child, a cherished son, an admired brother, a diligent cowherd, a charming lover, a charismatic prankster, a courageous warrior, a daring charioteer, a devoted disciple, a sharp politician, and a grand guru. These are the role playings in which the ever-omnipresent and omniscient divine hero Krishna engages while performing His leelas on earth.

The miraculous stories associated with Lord Krishna fascinated the Kathak dancers. As a divine child, Krishna is revered for His playfulness. The striking and charming child Krishna is depicted in poems, paintings, and sculptures as a small, crawling, or dancing child playing with friends, exotic birds, and magnificent peacocks, performing incredible miracles, slaying demons, and stealing butter. Upon the birth of Krishna, the earth blossomed, the rivers filled themselves to their brims, and cool breeze started to blow through lush forests. The skies became dark and it rained incessantly until Krishna was safely transported to a secure place from the brutal Kansa's prison, where His mother and father were in shackles.

As a baby, Krishna killed Putana, the rakshasi (demoness) who tried to kill Him by feeding her poisonous milk to Him. In His youth, Krishna is depicted as a brilliant flute player, dancer, and a divine lover. Krishna, a mischievous butter thief in His teenage years, became a saviour and rescued his villagers from many evils and tribulations. Among these stories, Krishna taming the ferocious serpent Kaliya is one of the most favoured stories for Kathak dancers. After a long, arduous battle with the vicious Kaliya, Krishna supposedly danced Kathak in Tandava style on the hood of the serpent. He also lifted the entire Govardhan Mountain on His right pinky, under which the drowning villagers could be sheltered and saved from Indra's wrath that transpired in heavy hammering rainstorms.

During His teenage years, Krishna's personality took on many facets: romantic, playful, mischevious, and heroic. Krishna, who had a dark complexion, fell in love with fair Radha, whose face had a golden hue. When He danced with Her, it looked like lightning among the clouds. Krishna also played many pranks on the maidens of the village. For instance, as the *gopi*s walked back home after fetching water from the river, carrying it in clay pots balanced on their heads, Krishna threw stones at the pots, breaking the pots and thus drenching the *gopi*s with water. In another instance, Krishna hid the *gopi*s' clothes while they bathed in the river. Later, Krishna, the warrior, overthrew the tyrant monarch Kansa and seized the throne of the Vrisni kingdom.

In His adult years, Krishna is portrayed as a diplomat, a prince, and an undaunted warrior, who imparts the philosophical knowledge of Bhagavadgita to His great archer and warrior devotee Arjuna, who was also a Pandava prince. He helped Pandavas in fighting the mythic epic *Dharma Yuddha* or the righteous war of the Kurukshetra on the day of the solar eclipse and the night of the new moon. In this war, Krishna served as a guide and a charioteer to Arjuna. At the commencement of the war, when Arjuna became weak after seeing the

Young Krishna on swing (left)
Yashoda adorning Krishna with ornaments (right)

Krishna stealing butter

opposing party comprised of his close relatives, Krishna revealed to him His *vishwarupa* or the supreme form of Vishnu. Krishna, in His *vishwarupa* avatar, imparted the absolute philosophical knowledge to Arjuna for him to experience self-realization. This knowledge is safeguarded in the form of the sacred Bhagavadgita. In His *vishwarupa*, Krishna has a cosmic form where all beings of the earth are a part of Him. His many arms hold various weapons, including a *shankh* (conch shell), *gada* (mace), a sword called *nandaka*, and his discus-like weapon *sudarshan chakra*. His many heads touch the sky and His feet cover the earth. The universe resides within Him, and He is beyond all space and time.

Krishna lifting Govardhan Mountain

The *Dharma Yuddha* is symbolic of the internal battle between the mundane and the spiritual aspects of human nature. Krishna's *shankh* is the symbol of five elements, namely earth, air, fire, water, and ether. *Aum*, the primordial sound of the universe, is the sound produced from His *shankh*. The *sudarshan chakra* represents the wheel of life. His *gada* symbolizes the eternal force of the cosmos. The lotus flower held by Krishna's *vishwarupa* form symbolizes wholesomeness and cosmic perfection. Krishna's flute has been interpreted in many ways. Through His divine music, He draws his devotees. The flute has to be hollow in order to produce music. The

Krishna on Kaliya Naag

Pandit Rajendra Gangani in Krishna pose (left)

Pandit Rajendra Gangani in Nataraja pose (right)

hollowness of the flute represents the human mind, which is symbolic of the transcended ego. Krishna holds the egoless minds in His hands and plays His divine music through them. Krishna wears a peacock feather on His forehead, which represents magnificence and knowledge. In Krishna's *tribhangi* standing position, His body bends at three places: the neck, waist, and ankles. The Kathak dance form has adopted this *tribhangi* position in its dances:

> Krishna's personality is clearly a syncretic one, though the different elements are not easily separated. Vasudeva-Krishna, a Vrishni prince who was presumably also a religious leader, was elevated to the godhead by the 5th century BCE. The cowherd Krishna is obviously the god of a pastoral community that turned away from the Indra-dominated Vedic religion. The Krishna who emerged from the blending of these ideologies was ultimately identified with the supreme god Vishnu-Narayana and, hence, considered his avatar. His cult preserved distinctive traits, chief among them an exploration of the analogies between divine love and human love. Thus, Krishna's youthful dalliances with

the *gopis* are interpreted as symbolic of the loving interplay between God and the human soul. The rich variety of legends associated with Krishna's life led to an abundance of representation in painting and sculpture.[8]

Krishna as the source of creation is *ishvara*. Supreme consciousness and the material world is prakriti or His energy. Krishna as omniscient and omnipresent is eternal and transcends space and time. He resides both independent of and within all *jivas* (living entities):

> The concept of space divides the individual objects from one another. If there is no space in between them all objects will come together so closely that they will become one single entity. In this mass of things there will certainly be different shapes and forms of all things at one and the same place and time. This is the picture of the Universal or Cosmic Man, the vision of the world viewed from a mind wherein there is no concept of time and space.[9]

The wholesome depiction of Krishna through His leelas and through His divinity is beautifully portrayed in performing, visual, and literary arts. The legends of Krishna are filled with mysterious situations and heartfelt human emotions. Kathak has taken all the aesthetics and emotions that the character of Krishna had to provide and has become inseparable from the Krishna theme. The Nataraja philosophy is also woven into Kathak, which makes Kathak a more wholesome dance form. It sensibly and beautifully intermingles the vigour of Nataraja and the mesmerizing charm of Natwar. Bound with two different philosophical sides, the river of Kathak has flowed uninterrupted for centuries.

---

[8] Krishnan, 'Krishna, Human Manifestation of God', Wednesday, 13 June 2007, http://blog1gk.blogspot.com/2007/06/krishna-human-manifestation-of-god.html (accessed on 12 April 2018).

[9] T.N. Sethumadhavan, 'Bhagavad Gita–Chap 11 (Part-1) Vishwaroopa Darshana Yogah—Yoga of the Vision of the Universal Form', May 2011, http://www.esamskriti.com/essay-chapters/Bhagavad-Gita--Chap-11-(Part-1)-Vishwaroopa-Darshana-Yogah--Yoga-of-the-Vision-of-the-Universal-Form-1.aspx (accessed on 12 April 2018).

Bharata's *Natyashastra*

NATYASHASTRA, WRITTEN BY BHARATA MUNI, is one of the most comprehensive treatises on the dramatic arts and stagecraft. It is presumed to be written between the second century BCE and the eighth century CE. The word *natya* in *Natyashastra* broadly encompasses the arts of dance, drama, music, and poetry, and covers all aspects of these art forms. This all-inclusive text of the dramatic arts is given an exalted status of the *Pancham Veda* or the fifth Veda. The Vedas are the four ancient sacred texts of India and considered as the earliest literary documents of the Indo-Aryan civilization. The word Veda means 'highest wisdom' or 'divine vision'. The texts were given this name because it is believed that they were directly imparted to humans during their meditative state by the gods. The content of the Vedas reflects all aspects of human existence, including, but not limited to, spiritual and philosophical doctrines, social and domestic principles, astronomy, physiology, literature, arts, medicine and healing, and mathematics. *Natyashastra* lies outside the realm of the four Vedas and deals with the literary interpretations, artistic principles, and stagecraft in detail, yet it is as great as the Vedas in its scope.

NATYASHASTRA'S AUTHORSHIP

Natyashastra may have been conceived even earlier than the second century BCE. All Indian sacred texts were passed on orally; there was seldom any written transmission of ideas. The knowledge contained in *Natyashastra* was probably preserved and passed on from generation to generation through precise mnemonic techniques as collective memory. It is therefore very likely that the concepts presented in this manual were conceived much earlier than when they were written as a volume. Likewise, there are differing opinions about both the authorship and the time of conception of this sacred treatise on dramatic arts.

Natyashastra is so vast in its content that many find it nearly impossible to believe that it is the work of a solitary author. Many scholars have speculated that Bharata was an artistic community who collectively formulated the text of *Natyashastra* over a long period of time. According to renowned dramatist and scholar Sri Adya Rangacharya:

> Even a cursory reading of the text would show that this is the work neither of one man nor of one time; as a matter of fact if Bharata were an authority on drama, here in this book other subjects like music and dancing are given so much importance, that it is strange that the book is called *Natyashastra*. On the other hand, it seems as if someone later on tried to bring in one volume all the available information on the various arts.[1]

Sri Rangacharya's argument is noteworthy. The enormity of this text does make one doubt that it is a work of a single author. At the same time, in his argument, Sri Rangacharya does not take into account that Indian arts have always been all-inclusive in nature. In Indian culture, music and dance have been integral parts of drama. Therefore, their detailed inclusion in *Natyashastra* is not at all surprising.

According to some ancient Indian dictionaries and thesauruses, the word 'Bharata' is a synonym of the word *nata*, which means an actor or an artiste. Amarasimha (around 380 CE), in his Sanskrit thesaurus *Amarakosha*, presents many synonyms for *nata*. There were only minute differences in their performance:

Shilalinastu Shailusha Jayajivah Krishashvinah,
Bharata ityapi natah charanastu kushilavah.[2]
[Translation: The words *shilali*, *shailashu*, *jayajiva*, *krishashvi*, *bharata*, *nata*, *charan*, and *kushilava* were all synonyms for *nata*.]

---

[1] Adya Rangacharya, *Introduction to Bharata's Natyasastra* (New Delhi: Munshiram Manoharlal Publishers Pvt. Ltd., 1966), p. 1.
[2] Thakur Jaideva Singh, *Bharatiya Sangeet ka Itihaas* (Calcutta: Sangeet Research Academy, 1994), p. 280.

Considering that the word 'Bharata' was used interchangeably with *nata*, it is possible that Bharata was a community of actors and performers who collectively wrote *Natyashastra*. The stylistic differences at many places in the text give the impression that many different authors have contributed to this book. Most of the book is written in a poetic form, but there are also places where the language has no formal metrical structure. In the first chapter of *Natyashastra*, Bharata specifies that he imparted the knowledge of *natya* to his hundred *putra*s or sons. He even provides the names of all his *putra*s. In ancient India, bona fide disciples were given the exalted status of *manasputra*s or sons born out of the guru's mind. The interpreters of *Amarakosha* have alleged that Bharata's hundred disciples were also believed to be Bharata's sons, and formed a clan of *nata*s. It is very likely that these disciples added their views to the text later. Since many scholars have interpreted the *Natyashastra*, today there are various versions of this text. Apparently, these scholars also modified the *Natyashastra* during their analytical commentary of the manuscript, which may explain the stylistic differences in the text.

This is why many insist that the stylistic differences in the text do not disprove the single authorship theory. They believe that the structural flow of *Natyashastra* is so flawless that it can only be the work of one author. According to Dr Kapila Vatsyayan, one of the leading modern scholars of classical Indian arts:

> [A] close reading of the text makes it clear that the work reflects a unity of purpose and that it was the product of a single integrated vision, perhaps also of a single author. There are complexities, but no contradictions. Many subjects deal *[sic]* with in the earlier chapters can only be understood by the perusal of later chapters and vice versa. Indeed the author claims at many places that a particular sub-theme will be dealt with later, or that the chapters which come early in the sequence are in fact a condensation of details discussed later....[I]t could not have been the work of several authors over a long period of time. This will be obvious when the structure of the Natyasastra is analysed.[3]

Abhinavagupta's (950 CE–1016 CE) *Abhinavabharati* is considered to be one of the most comprehensive commentaries on *Natyashastra*. Abhinavagupta refuted the

---

[3] Kapila Vatsyayan, *Bharata: The Natyasastra* (New Delhi: Sahitya Akademi, 1996), pp. 6, 7.

theory of multiple authorship. He alleged that the structural organization of subject matter and the consistency of philosophical and aesthetic ideas in *Natyashastra* prove that it was written by one author. Looking at the flow and the subject matter of *Natyashastra*, Abhinavagupta finds it quite evident that the structure of the text is well thought-out and the contents are skilfully organized. The sequential and logical order of information in *Natyashastra* influences the relationship among the ideas successfully.

Regardless of the dissension about the authorship and time period of this text, scholars and critics unanimously agree that the *Natyashastra* is undoubtedly the most complete and one of the most significant treatises on the Indian dramatic arts.

Myth–Reality Axis

India is a country where myth and reality are interwoven in such a fascinating manner that even common perceptions of the physical world are elevated to a spiritual and metaphysical appreciation of human experiences. The *Natyashastra* is no exception to this myth-reality axis. According to *Natyashastra*, dramatic art was a great gift to humankind from God. After the end of the Golden Age, which was governed by the gods and when humanity experienced ultimate fulfilment and spiritual perfection, the Silver Age began. During the Silver Age, humankind started to experience the first signs of suffering and troubles. Along with other gods, Indra, the Leader of the Gods and the Ruler of Heaven, approached Brahma, the Creator, with His concerns for the humans. He asked Brahma to find a way to save them from their sufferings in order to reinstate the Golden Age. Brahma immersed Himself in deep contemplation and envisioned the art of *natya* during His meditative state. Later, Brahma imparted the knowledge of *natya* to a sage— Bharata—who taught it to his one hundred sons. The knowledge that Bharata received from Brahma was later documented in the book *Natyashastra*.

The myth around the creation of *natya* merely suggests the reality of how art is perceived in India. The fact that, for Indians, art is the means to attain a state of spiritual perfection is symbolically accentuated by the myth of God as Brahma creating the art of *natya*. And because of this notion, there is also a universal conciliation between all art forms. This is why the subject of theatre is elaborated in so much details and with such immense reverence in *Natyashastra* that it considers drama as an inclusive art form that effortlessly integrates music, dance, poetics, aesthetics, and other related art forms considered sacred in nature. For Bharata, *natya* in its truest form was divine and all-encompassing. The *Natyashastra* was written ages ago, but the reverence embedded in it for divinity still inspires the dramatic arts of India. For Indian artists, their aesthetic consciousness emerges from the sacred experiences of life, which in turn affect them and their art at deeper, spiritual levels.

Thirty-six Chapters of *Natyashastra*

The text of *Natyashastra* is written in the archaic language of Sanskrit, and it consists of 6,000 poetic verses spreading over thirty-six chapters. The manuscript with 6,000 verses is believed to be a condensed version of the original text, which comprised of 12,000 verses. Some commentaries on *Natyashastra* have thirty-seven chapters. The text material is the same in different commentaries of this manuscript. The text focuses on many topics in detail, such as the origin of theatre, the description of the playhouse and the stage, aesthetics, sentiments and emotional states, stage movements, styles and types of plays, playwriting, rules of prosody and morphology, metrical patterns, diction, the use of languages, intonation, plot, costume and make-up, dramatic criticism, audience, producer, dance, vocal music, instrumental music, time measures, types of characters, and distribution of roles. The subject matter is discussed brilliantly through the lens of aesthetics, philosophy, psychology, and theology. The entire text is written in a dialogue form, where Bharata Muni imparts his knowledge of dramaturgy to interested sages.

In the first chapter of *Natyashastra*, Bharata Muni provides a detailed inquiry into the origin of *natya* and its first performance. He also advises to invoke the presiding deities of *natyagraha* or theatre-auditorium before starting the performance. The second chapter deals with the rules and models of the theatre architecture—different shapes and sizes of the auditorium, a table of measurement units, preference of their locations and positions, and methods of constructing a stage. In the third chapter, Bharata describes the elaborate rituals to purify the performance space and to invoke the gods in order to protect the performance from obstacles.

The elements of the Tandava dance performed by Lord Shiva are provided in the fourth chapter. In this section, a detailed explanation of 108 *karana*s or the combined positions and movements of hands and feet, 32 *anghara*s or the groupings of particular *karana*s, and other types of dance movements are offered. The essentials of *angika abhinaya* or the expressions through body movements are laid out in this chapter. *Angika abhinaya* is discussed further in chapters eight through fourteen, where Bharata exhaustively sheds light on all aspects of body expressions, such as movements of the minor limbs of the body, expressions through hand gestures, movements of major limbs of the body, performance of *chari*s or extended foot movement, and *mandala*s or the combinations of *chari*s. The thirteenth chapter describes different kinds of stage walks and gaits for characterization, as well as sitting and sleeping postures to convey a character's disposition. A substantial portion of *Natyashastra* is devoted to the *angika abhinaya*, which has greatly influenced and shaped the nature of body movements in the dances of India.

The fourth chapter of *Natyashastra* covers some aspects of *angika abhinaya*, but it mainly includes the styles, productions, and nature of a play. In the fifth chapter, Bharata elaborates upon *purvarang* or the preliminary rituals that are carried out before the commencement of a performance.

The sixth and the seventh chapters are related to the philosophy of art and the concepts in terms of the nature and ultimate purpose of art, how art is interpreted and conveyed, and how art universalizes an emotion. Bharata proposes the theory of *rasa* and *bhava*. *Rasa* is the exalted mental state evoked in a viewer of a performance as a result of *bhava*s or sentiments produced by a performer. Bharata's aesthetic theory of *rasa* and *bhava* has become the criterion for Indian poetry and performing arts.

Chapters fifteen through twenty-two contain the components of *vachika abhinaya*, that is, expression through vocal or verbal representation. In these chapters, Bharata describes the significance of words and language in *natya*, different poetic concepts, and the pattern of rhythm and sounds used in poetry. He also defines ten different kinds of plays along with their structure, styles, and the techniques of plotting. A foundation of rhythmic system of music and dance is laid in chapter sixteen, where Bharata discusses the metrical patterns of poetry. The chapters on *vachika abhinaya* are important, since the expressional repertoire of dance, where a dancer depicts words of poetry, falls under the category of *vachika abhinaya*.

Chapter twenty-two of *Natyashastra* is about *aharya abhinaya* and contains the information on make-up, costume, ornamentation, and stage properties in a performance. Chapter twenty-three starts with the description of *samanya abhinaya*, where words, emotions, and physical gestures are compatible with one another. Bharata discusses the various schemes of characterization towards the end of this chapter and extends the subject matter to chapters twenty-four and twenty-five. Chapter twenty-six outlines the methods for making a production successful.

Chapters twenty-eight to thirty-two delve exhaustively into the musical aspect of production. In these chapters, Bharata discusses the types of musical instruments, the musical notes and patterns in vocal music, microtones, the characteristics of songs, rhythmic patterns, and musical time. Chapters thirty-three to thirty-five contain information on the types of characters, distribution of major and minor acting roles, types of production, and the qualifications of the other members of a production. In the concluding chapter, Bharata once again links a mythological story with the origin of theatre and the creation of *Natyashastra*, and declares that people who appreciate the art of *natya* realize the blessed state of the gods.

In the thirty-six chapters of *Natyashastra*, Bharata has considered every single aspect of *natya*. The treatise is undoubtedly an authority on Indian dramatic arts. It has set an unprecedented standard in the world of performing arts. There has been no other scripture on dramatic arts in India that has not taken its inspiration from *Natyashastra*. This text has also brought *natya* to an exalted spiritual level. For Indian musicians and dancers who are inspired to this day by the tenets of *Natyashastra*, a performance is a sacred act, and the practice of music and dance has a metaphysical purpose which goes far beyond the mundane.

Classical Dance Styles of India

INDIA HAS ENDURED VARIOUS foreign rules and has gone through many historical, economical, political, and social transformations over the centuries. As a result, the country has also enjoyed the rich blending of cultures and art forms, making its ancient land one of the most culturally diverse countries in the world. Many exquisite forms of dance emerged in different regions of India, corresponding to the local traditions. Sangeet Natak Akademi, a national-level organization set up by the government of India, dedicated to preserving and supporting the performing arts, has granted classical status to eight Indian dance forms. The criterion for being regarded as classical is the particular dance style's adherence to the guiding principles laid down in *Natyashastra*.

MARGI NRITYA: SYSTEMATIC CODIFICATION OF DANCE

Since ancient times, Indian music and dance have been broadly categorized as *margi* and *desi*. Margi literally means 'adopting a path'. Margi music and dance are regulated by the systematic rules prescribed in ancient scriptures. Codification of margi arts is not merely for the sake of practising technicalities, but for the attainment of specific internal qualities that facilitate one's philosophical and spiritual endeavours through the arts. According to Sharangdeva, 'which guides to salvation is margi' (*Sangeet Ratnakara*, thirteenth century). Conversely, the word desi means 'of a region'. Therefore, desi music and dance belong to the tradition of a particular region and are performed for entertainment and celebratory functions. Phillip Zarrilli quotes Nair and Paniker: 'The concepts of margi and desi styles as applied to arts such as music and dance have been enunciated in India from ancient times. While the desi style is bound by space and time, with consequent

Pandit Rajendra Gangani with Sharmila Sharma

limitations in aesthetics, margi transcends space and time to provide lasting and boundless rapture.'[1]

Today, the terms Shastriya Nritya for classical dance and Lok Nritya for regional dance are used, which connote the same meaning as margi and desi.

The eight Shastriya dance forms recognized by Sangeet Natak Akademi are Bharatnatyam, Kathak, Kathakali, Kuchipudi, Manipuri, Mohiniattam, Odissi, and Sattriya.

EIGHT CLASSICAL DANCE FORMS OF INDIA

Bharatnatyam, one of the most popular South Indian classical dance forms, was developed and has been nurtured in the state of Tamil Nadu. The source of the name of this dance form is attributed to Sage Bharata, the author of *Natyashastra*. Bharatnatyam faithfully adheres to many principles and ideas of *Natyashastra*. It is also speculated that the word Bharata has originated from the root words 'bha', 'ra', and 'ta', where the syllable 'bha' means *bhava* or mood, 'ra' represents raga or melody, and 'ta' implies *tala* or rhythm. As an important component of temple rituals, Dasi Attam, the dance performed by the devadasis (devotees of the Divine), is the core inspiration and even the foundation of today's Bharatnatyam. In South India, the Maratha rulers of the seventeenth century CE coined the term Sadir Natyam, and with this new idiom, Dasi Attam travelled

[1] Phillip Zarrilli, *Kathakali Dance-Drama: Where Gods and Demons Come to Play* (London: Routledge, 11 New Fetter Lane, 2000), p. 35.

from the temples to the court. The royal patrons supported the Sadir dance. Bharatnatyam took inspiration from both Dasi Attam and the Sadir Natyam, but it evolved into its present form in the eighteenth century CE due to the efforts of the four brothers who came to be known as the Thanjavur Quartet. The brothers Chinnayya, Ponnayya, Vadivelu, and Sivanandam were renowned for their unprecedented contributions to the development of Bharatnatyam. During the British colonial rule, all Indian dance forms suffered degradation, as they were falsely perceived as explicitly provocative and vulgar through the Western lens of artistic sensibility and morality. Bharatnatyam was no exception and experienced its decline during the British Raj. E. Krishna Iyer, a lawyer and a dance student, started the Bharatnatyam revival movement in the early 1920s. Later, such devoted dancers as Rukmini Devi Arundale and Balasaraswati revitalized the dance form. Today, Bharatnatyam is one of the leading dance forms of India. The *nattuvanar* or the dance master keeps the rhythm using hand cymbals. The Bharatnatyam repertoire includes *alarippu, jathiswaram, shabdam, varnam, padam*, and *thillana*. The dancers usually conclude their performances with *mangalam*. The debut performance of a dancer is called an *arangetram*. The music of Bharatnatyam is based on Carnatic sangeet, the classical music of South India. The main instruments used are mridangam, veena, flute, and violin. The major styles of this dance form are Pandanallur, Vazhuvoor, Thanjavur, Mysore, and Kanchipuram. This exquisite dance form is known for its beautiful stances, perfect body alignment, geometrical movement patterns, intricate rhythmic footwork, and mesmerizing facial expressions.

Kuchipudi dance form acquired its name from a small village called Kuchipudi in the Krishna district of Andhra Pradesh. The resident Brahmins in this area practised this traditional dance for many centuries. Kuchipudi essentially was structured as *yakshagana*, a traditional theatre form, and was performed exclusively by men who played female characters by dressing up as women. These performers sang, danced, and even spoke dialogues and possessed sophisticated knowledge of Sanskrit sacred texts. The court accounts of Karnata Empire or Vijayanagara Empire (sixteenth to seventeenth centuries CE) confirm that dance dramas by the performers of Kuchipudi village were performed in the royal courts and these dancers also received royal patronage. Later, in the seventeenth century, Tirtha Narayanayati, a follower of the Advaita philosophy, wrote dance dramas with embedded dance syllables, which became the foundation for the present-day Kuchipudi dance. During the twentieth century, Guru Vedantam

A dancer portraying a facial expression in Bharatnatyam (left)
An expressive pose in Kuchipudi dance by Yashoda Thakur (right)

Lakshminarayana Shastri revolutionized Kuchipudi by teaching it to devadasis. In 1955, two Kuchipudi dancers, Mohana and Samanti, performed Kuchipudi at the National Dance Festival in Mumbai. Their dance was appreciated as Kuchipudi Bharatnatyam. By 1959, through the tenacious efforts of Guru Vempati Chinna Satyam, Kuchipudi acquired its independent identity and was recognized as a classical dance style, and an institutionalized training for Kuchipudi became a requirement for the Kuchipudi dancers. Today, Kuchipudi is acknowledged as a full-fledged classical dance form and is known for its rich solo repertoire. The repertoire of Kuchipudi includes both *kalapa* and *yakshagana*. In *kalapa*, the theme revolves around a single episode or a character, whereas in *yakshagana*, an entire story with many characters is portrayed. *Tarangam* is a fascinating piece in Kuchipudi, wherein the performer dances on the rim of a brass plate and executes complex rhythms.

Odissi, referred to as Odra-Magadhi in Bharata's *Natyshastra*, is one of the most sensuous and poetic dance forms in which the dance becomes synonymous with movable sculptures. This dance style, indigenous to the state of Odisha, is considered as the oldest surviving dance form of India on the basis of archeological relics found in the caves of Udayagiri and Khandagiri from the time of Emperor Kharavela, dating back to the second century BCE. The Shaivite, Vaishnavite, and Shakta temples from the second century through the tenth century CE have exquisite sculptures of dancing yoginis, gods, and celestial musicians in Odissi dance poses. Konark Sun Temple, built in the thirteenth century CE, has a *natya* mandap or 'the hall of dance' adorned with rich dancing sculptures and carvings, which are an inspiration for Odissi dancers even today. Diverse traditions of East Indian dancing have shaped the art of Odissi. For centuries, *mahari*s were the ones who kept the art of Odissi alive. *Mahari*s were the devadasis in the Jagannath temple, where their dance became an essential component of daily rituals. The great ruler of Eastern Ganga Dynasty, King Anantavarman Chodaganga Deva, built the famous Jagannatha temple in Puri, Odisha, in the late eleventh century CE.

*Mahari*s were adept dancers who danced to mantras and other Sanskrit texts. Later, their dance was inspired by the imaginative literature of the twelfth century—*Gita Govinda*, written by the poet Jayadeva. The *mahari*s became *nartaki*s or 'qualified dancers' after they were employed by the royal courts. Vaishnavas, the followers of Lord Vishnu, did not approve of women dancing; so a group of male dancers called Gotipuas dressed as female dancers and were trained by *mahari*s. Consequently, the Gotipua tradition became an emerging commercial theatre-dance style in the sixteenth century CE. The *mahari* tradition declined by the end of that century due to the political and social turmoils that Odisha faced during the Mughal, Maratha, and British occupations.

In seventeenth century, Sri Maheswara Mohapatra authored a manual on the techniques of Odissi dance entitled *Abhinaya Chandrika*. However, the revival and restructuring of Odissi took place mainly in the twentieth century. An Oriya poet, playwright, and dramatist named Kalicharan Pattanayak is credited with identifying the dance form as Odissi. This dance form was revitalized and shaped into modern-day Odissi by the great maestros of the dance, such as Pankaj Charan Das, Kelucharan Mohapatra, Deba Prasad Das, Mayadhar Raut, Harekrushna Behera, Priyambada Mohanty Hejmadi, Sanjukta Panigrahi, and Indrani Rahman. Today, Odissi has adapted the rules of formal stage presentation and has become one of the major classical dance forms. Solo Odissi repertoire includes *manglacharan*, *batu nritya*, *pallavi*, *abhinaya*, and *moksha*.

Odissi style emphasizes *tribhangi*, the simultaneous flexion of the body at three places. Besides *tribhangi*, there are many other *bhanga*s or body positions integrated in this dance

Nandini Ghosal performing Odissi at the Coffman Memorial Union in the University

form. The basic square stance of Odissi is *chauka*. Odissi performance is based on Odissi music. *Veena* (lute), *mardala* (drums), *venu* (flute), and *kartala* (hand cymbals) are some of the main instruments used in Odissi dance.

One of the oldest theatre forms in the world, and known for its elaborate make-up and highly stylized gestures, Kathakali originated in the south-western Indian coastal state of Kerala. The word *katha* means 'story', and *kali* means 'drama'. Kathakali has emerged from the folk theatre traditions of Kerala, in which dancers enact an entire story through dance, drama, mime, and music. The roots of Kathakali are believed to be in *Krishnanattam*, created by Manavedan Raja, a ruler of the sixteenth century CE. *Krishnanattam* was written in Sanskrit and portrayed the glories of Lord Krishna. At the same time, out of rivalry, Kottarakkara Thampuran, the ruler of Kottarakkara, created *Ramanattam*, written in Malayalam, in which Lord Rama's magnificent life was depicted. Later on, *Ramanattam* was titled *Attakatha*, which acquired the title Kathakali by the end of the seventeenth century CE. Kathakali incorporated other traditional art and ritualistic forms along with martial arts into its movement vocabulary. The International Centre for Kathakali in New Delhi is dedicated to the colossal work of popularizing Kathakali, and it is attributed with inspiring Kathakali dancers to perform many new themes outside of traditional stories. These themes include Greek mythology, European classics, and Shakespeare's plays. Traditionally, Kathakali productions were presented in open-air theatres, lasting for the entire night in front of a sole *kalivilakku* or dance lamp. Contemporary Kathakali performances have been modified to be presented on the proscenium stage, and the entire performance lasts for two to three hours.

Padmashree Guru Chengannur is one of the most renowned artists of Kathakali, whose efforts to propagate Kathakali as a classical art form is truly admirable. The Kathakali training is very rigorous and focuses on developing mental faculties, physical skills, and stamina. The training methods are rooted in *kalaripayattu*, the ancient martial art of Kerala. Dancers undergo strenuous training in order to achieve mastery of their major and minor limbs, body flexibility, and muscle control. Kathakali is mainly a male-oriented dance form; however, women have made significant entry into Kathakali since the 1970s. The costume and make-up of Kathakali set the dancers apart from the mortal world and transport the audience to the realm of mysteries. Dancers paint their faces with different colours for distinctive characterizations. For example, green signifies noble and virtuous characters, red is used for evil characters, black is used for forest dwellers, and yellow-gold is used for female characters. The dancers also use large headdresses and exaggerate their facial contours with a paste of rice and lime. Kathakali style is known as *sampradayam*. Each *sampradayam* has its own way of presentation, where they differ from each other in movement quality, choreographic principles, body and hand positions, and originating villages, among other factors. The three leading *sampradayam*s are Vettathu, Kalladikkodan, and Kaplingadu. The orchestra of Kathakali includes a lead singer called *ponnani*, and his follower, *singidi*. They both use *chengila*, a gong made of bells, and *ilathalam*, a pair of cymbals. The style of singing is called *sopaanam*. The percussion instruments used are *chenda* and *maddalam*. In

Divya Nedungadi, Mohiniyattam

traditional Kathakali performances enacted in the villages of Kerala, the drummers start playing a few hours before the performance starts, which serves as publicity for the show. Another interesting aspect of Kathakali is that the actors and dancers never use dialogue. All expressions are conveyed through hand gestures, facial expressions, and rhythmic body movements.

Mostly performed as solo art by women, Mohiniattam is a captivating dance form from Kerala. This poetic, sensual, and suggestive dance form has the poise and elegance of Bharatnatyam and the vitality of Kathakali. But, unlike other classical dances of India, Mohiniattam did not flourish in the temples and, therefore, does not have a strong religious orientation. The word Mohiniattam is a synthesis of two words—*mohini* and *attam*. *Mohini* means an 'enchantress' and *attam* means 'elegant body movements'. Therefore, the word Mohiniattam literally means 'the dance of an enchantress'.

According to Indian mythology, Lord Vishnu assumed the form of Mohini twice by transforming Himself into a beautiful woman. Once, He disguised Himself as Mohini to entice the asuras or the demons, so that they could not get hold of amrit or the nectar of immortality acquired during the churning of the milky ocean. Lord Vishnu also took the avatar of Mohini to aid Lord

K G Vasudevan Nair, Kalamandalam

Shiva in destroying a very powerful demon, Bhasmasur. Bhasmasur's infatuation with Mohini became his destruction. There are indications that Mohiniattam was performed as early as the eighteenth century. But it was actually popularized in the nineteenth century by King Swathi Thirunal of the state of Travancore, who was a great scholar and poet. King Swathi Thirunal is credited with many poetic compositions and musical arrangements, created especially to accompany Mohiniattam. After King Swathi Thirunal's rule, Mohiniattam experienced a decline in popularity. Later, in the twentieth century, the great Malayalam poet Vallathol established the Kerala Kalamandalam, an institute for Kerala dances, and revived Mohiniattam. In the latter part of the twentieth century, Smt. Kalamandalam Kalyanikutty Amma made immeasurable contributions towards shaping Mohiniattam into its current form. Mohiniattam's lyrics are in a language called Manipravalam, which is a fusion of Sanskrit and Malayalam. The rhythmic variations in the vocal music of this dance form are known as *chollu*. The percussion instruments include mridangam, *maddalam*, cymbals, and an hourglass-shaped drum, *edakka*. Mohiniattam dancers always wear white or off-white costumes. Some of the popular repertoires of Mohiniattam are *varnam*, *padam*, *saptam*, *cholkettu*, *jathiswaram*, and *thillana*.

Known for its elegant and delicate ripple-like movements, Manipuri is a devotional dance form from a state in north-east India called Manipur. The word Manipur means 'the land of jewels'. Situated in the Purbanchal area, where the Eastern Himalayan peaks end, Manipur has an interesting mix of various religious traditions. The Meitei community of Manipur practised their own ancient religion and rituals. The Krishna Bhakti or the Vaishnavite tradition emerged in that area during the fifteenth century. Even though the indigenous community of Manipur valley is mentioned in legends as *gandharva* (skilled musicians and dancers), it was not until the fifteenth century when the highly spiritual Manipuri dance form took shape in the temples of Manipur as a result of the Krishna Bhakti tradition. Krishna's Raas Leelas became the central theme of Manipuri dance.

Bimbavati Devi performing Manipuri dance

The term 'raas' or 'rasa' means aesthetics, and 'leela' means an act or dance. In Hindu philosophy, Raas Leela is defined as the dance of divine love, where the theme of the dance is woven around the sublime and transcendental love story of two Hindu deities, Radha and Krishna. The Raas Leelas were customarily performed in the precincts of the Hindu temples. King Bhagyachandra in the eighteenth century codified the Manipuri dance style and created three different types of Raas Leelas—Maha Rasa, Basant Rasa, and Kunj Rasa. These raas dances were performed at the Sri Sri Govindji temple in Imphal. The dancers wore *kumil*, an elaborate costume designed by the king. An important text entitled *The Govindasangeet Lila Vilasa*, which lays down the fundamentals of dance, is also credited to him. King Bhagyachandra created Achouba Bhangi Pareng dance, an added repertoire of Manipuri dance. In the nineteenth century, King Gambhir Singh created two more *pareng*s which were in Tandava style. He called these *pareng*s the Goshtha Bhangi Pareng and the Goshtha Vrindaban Pareng. King Chandra Kirti Singh, who ruled after King Gambhir Singh, was an exceptional drummer. He added two more *pareng*s—Vrindaban Bhangi Pareng and Khrumba Bhangi Pareng—to the Manipuri dance repertoire in Lasya style. King Chandrakirti Singh also composed sixty-four *pung cholom*s, which are drum dances. In 1919, Nobel Prize Laureate Rabindranath Tagore popularized this dance form by bringing some eminent gurus of Manipuri dance to his university town Shantiniketan to teach, choreograph, and perform. Subsequently, many other gurus moved to Shantiniketan and other dance centres of India to establish Manipuri as an important style of Indian dancing. The Raas Leelas in Manipuri dances are a highly evolved and stylized form of dance dramas. The lyrics of Manipuri dance are taken from the classical poetry of Jayadeva, Vidyapati, Chandidas, Govindadas, Gyandas, and other eminent poets. A singer always accompanies the dance. The musical accompaniment consists of a double-headed drum called the *pung*, cymbals such as *kartala* and *manjira*, flute, and stringed instruments called *pena* and *esraj*. Unlike other classical dances of India, Manipuri dancers do not wear ankle bells. Foot movements are light, subtle, and soft. Even during vigorous foot movements, the dancer's feet touch the ground lightly with the ball of the foot. Body movements are circular, lyrical, and delicate, so as to convey the devotional and transcendental dispositions of this highly spiritual dance form.

Krishnakahi Kashyap performing
Sattriya dance

Sattriya, a deeply devotional dance form from the state of Assam, was recognized as a classical dance by Sangeet Natak Akademi in the year 2000. The term *sattra* means 'monastery'. Sattriya, a traditional theatre tradition, evolved in the Vaishnava monasteries of Assam in the fifteenth century. Srimanta Sankardev, a great Vaishnavite saint, poet, and social reformer, founded neo-Vaishnavism, which unified various different sects. During Sankardev's congregational gatherings, the *bhokot*s (male monks) of the monastery performed *ankiya naat*, one-act plays conceived by Sankardev as their prayers to Lord Krishna. Sankardev, along with his disciples, composed Ojapali songs and dances to incorporate them into *ankiya naat*. The performance of *ankiya naat* included dance, song, puppetry, masks, dialogues, and other stagecraft. At that time, it remained largely a male-dominated art form. Until the second half of the twentieth century, Sattriya remained inside the closed walls of monasteries and their performances adhered to strict disciplines and rituals. The stories revolved around Hindu mythology. In the latter half of the twentieth century, Sattriya dance made its way to the outside world. Finally, in the year 2000, it was recognized as a classical dance form. Today, both male and female dancers perform Sattriya, and contemporary stories have become a part of Sattriya performances. Now, Sattriya is staged both as a solo and group dance. Sattriya dance is mostly accompanied by a drum called a *khol*, cymbals, violin, and flute. Some of the Sattriya repertoires are *apsara nritya, behar nritya, chali nritya, dasavatara nritya, manchok nritya, natua nritya, rasa nritya, sutradhara, rajaghariya chali nritya, gosai prabesh, bar prabesh, gopi prabesh, jhumura,* and *nadu bhangi.*

Kathak is a North Indian classical dance form of India that originated more than 2000 years ago. The name Kathak is derived from the Sanskrit root word katha, which means 'story'. *Kathakar*s were the storytellers who conveyed the stories from ancient Hindu scriptures through the medium of dance, drama, song, or mime. During the Mughal rule in India, Kathak moved from the temples to the royal courts and became a sophisticated chamber dance. Under the patronage of royalty, Kathak developed as an intricate art form with emphasis on the mastery of complex rhythmic patterns, mnemonic *bol*s or syllables, stylized mime, and dynamic pirouettes. Kathak is the only classical dance form of India that was influenced both by the Vaishnavite Bhakti Movement of the fifteenth and sixteenth centuries and the Persian and Central Asian cultural philosophies prevalent in the royal courts of the Mughal era. This book is devoted to the ancient art form of Kathak dance.

The Origin and History
of Kathak Dance

THE ORIGIN OF 2000-YEAR-OLD KATHAK DANCE can best be traced by using the etymological and comparative linguistics methods, through which a very clear picture of Kathak's antiquity and how it was regarded in the earlier periods of its history can be deciphered. The word Kathak originates from the root word *katha*. In Sanskrit, the word *katha* has been used in many different contexts, both as a noun and a verb, depending on the intended meaning. As Bandlamudi explains:

> The closest translation for the Sanskrit word Katha is 'story', but this English word tends to convert the 'active verb' into a 'passive noun'. Etymologically, the word Katha is derived from the Sanskrit root 'Kath', which means 'to converse with, to tell, relate, narrate, speak out, explain' (Monier Williams 1899, A Sanskrit-English dictionary) and Katha, therefore, best translates as an act of storying or telling, which includes the tellers, the tales, and the listeners. The dialogical angle is fundamental to the Katha activity.[1]

The term *katha* is spread all over the ancient Indian texts connoting different meanings, such as narration, topic, words, conversation, description, incident, information, intention, message, discussion, incident, story, and policy. However, *katha* has been most widely used in reference to the art of

---

[1] Lakshmi Bandlamudi, *Dialogics of Self, The Mahabharata and Culture: The History of Understanding and Understanding of History* (UK and USA: Anthem Press, 2010), p. 121.

storytelling. In the dictionary of the Pali language, the liturgical Prakrit language of Theravada Buddhism, the word *kathako* means a 'discourse' or 'sermon'. In ancient texts in Prakrit language, the word Kathak is explicitly used to describe the dancers. The following verse describes how the *shringar* (exquisite) dance of the Kathaks in exaltation of God's glory pleased Lord Adinath, when performed during a very auspicious time in the month of Margashirsha (ninth lunar month in the Hindu calendar) in the *shukla-paksha nakshatra* (the period of waxing moon) to the north-west of Varanasi situated on the banks of the river Ganges:

> *maggasirasuddhapakkhe nakkhhate varanaseeye nayareeyeuttarpuratthime*
> *diseebhage gangaye mahanadeeye tate savvokathako bhingarnatenam teese stuti*
> *kayam yehi raya adinaho bhavenam passayi*[2]

The aforementioned text was written in the fourth century BCE in a Prakrit language called Ashokan Brahmi, which predates the *Natyashastra*.

In Nepali ancient texts, Kathak refers to an interpreter. In the ancient sacred book of Jainism—*Kalpa Sūtra*—the word *kahub* is used to denote the same meaning as Kathak, *kathiko*, or *kathika*. In early Jain texts, the word *kathaka* is used as *kahaga*, which means the performing artists. *Abhidhan Rajendra*, a Jain dictionary, mentions the word *kahaga* as the one who narrates a story brilliantly.

Maharshi Panini (fourth century BCE), who is known for setting the linguistic standards for classical Sanskrit, mentioned the word Kathak in his colossal work *Ashtadhyayi*. According to Panini, the word Kathak originated from the root word *katthya*, which means 'to convey'. Later, in another of his noteworthy works *Siddhanta Kaumudi*, Panini used a sutra or an aphorism *kathadibhyasthak*, which means the one who is well versed in storytelling.

A few of the eighteen Puranas, the sacred texts of Hinduism that were composed from the fourth century BCE to 1000 CE, also define the word Kathak. In *Brahma Purana*, Kathak alludes to actors, dancers, and musicians. The Purana reference dictionary also uses the word *charan* for Kathak. *Padma Purana* describes *charan* as the one who tells the story of the gods through music.

The *Ramayana* and the *Mahabharata*, the two great ancient epic poems of India, mention the word Kathak in the context of dancers, musicians, actors, and

---

[2] Shovana Narayan, 'Forgotten Page of History', *Spectrum, The Tribune*, 28 September 2008.

Kathak pose, author: Pradeep Adwani

storytellers. Saint Valmiki in his *Ramayana* very clearly describes a class of people who were skilled in the art of storytelling and were called *kushilav*s. He especially accentuates this point in the chapter where Lava and Kusa, the two sons of Lord Rama, recite the story of *Ramayana*.

The ancient Indian epic poem *Mahabharata*, believed to have been conceived between the ninth century BCE and the fourth century CE, culminated into the longest epic poem in the world with 100,000 two-line stanzas. Kathak appears in a few places in the text here. In the 'Adi Parva' of *Mahabharata*, Kathaks are described as storytellers. The stanza from the *Mahabharata* that follows articulates how the *kathakar*s accompanied the kings to the forest and pleasingly narrated the divine stories along with their dancing and singing.

In his book *Amarakosha*, Amarasimha mentions that *charan* and *kushilav*s were two other titles for *kathakar*s. However, some ancient texts, including Chanakya's *Arthashastra* (350–283 BCE), have described *kushilav*s more as musicians and instrumentalists. In his *Kamasutra*, Vatsyayana (400–200 BCE), who lived during approximately the same time period as Chanakya, has depicted *kushilav*s dancing at the Saraswati Bhavan. It may seem contradictory that the same term is used for two different activities during the same time period by

Dr Maya Rao

two different authors. It all makes perfect sense, however, if we look at how Indians have always taken an integrated approach towards arts and other facets of life. For ancient Indians, dance, drama, music, singing, storytelling, and other art forms were interconnected. No separation existed between them, and all art forms shared the same philosophy of arts as a means to attain spiritual heights. This is evident in how the word sangeet (music) is defined by ancient and medieval scholars. In one of the most comprehensive musicological texts of the thirteenth century *Sangeet Ratnakara*, the great scholar Sharangdeva defines sangeet as *gitam vadyam tatha nrityam trayam sangeetmuchyate*—sangeet or music is the combination of vocal music, instrumental music, and dance.

Many literary texts and dictionaries that were written between the seventh and fourteenth centuries CE use the word Kathak to describe storytellers, dancers, and actors. Banabhatta, an eminent Sanskrit writer (seventh century CE), also mentions the word Kathak in his work *Harshacharita*, a biography of Emperor Harsha. Sarala Das, a fifteenth-century poet and scholar of Oriya literature, uses the word Kathak in the 'Anusasana Parva' of his own version of *Mahabharata*, which he wrote during the reign of Kapileswar, the famous Gajapati king of Odisha. *Siddhanta Kaumudi*, a commentary on Panini's work by Bhattoji Dikshita in early seventeenth century CE, *Shabdartha Chintamani*, written by Chidambara Kavi around the same time, and early dictionaries such as *Vachaspatyam Kosha* and *Sabdakalpadruma* also describe Kathak as a storytelling art form, which combined various other performing art forms.

Given this ample evidence, it can be concluded that Kathak dance indeed was an art of storytelling in India, which profoundly influenced the modern-day Kathak dance. Even today, all Kathak dancers firmly believe in the maxim: *Kathan Kare so Kathak Kahave*—Kathak is the one who articulates a story. Most likely,

Kathak dance originated from the ancient art of storytelling, where Kathaks, *kathikas*, *vyasas*, or *kathavaachaks* transmitted knowledge and wisdom through their entertaining storytelling skills, which integrated dance, drama, literature, and music. Historically, the *katha* or the act of storytelling, which was didactic in nature, was frequently followed by a *pravachan* or discourse. According to Projesh Banerji:

> One of the peculiarities of the social organization in India has been that certain professions become hereditary to certain sections of the people; and, it has been so especially in the fields of arts like dance, drama, and music. The Kathak has been known for the centuries as a community of dancers and musicians, which is settled in several regions. It is quite likely that the dance also came to be named as Kathak by virtue of its association with this community. An important point should be noted here that the Kathak Brahmins are invariably called Maharajas, meaning great kings. They were regarded not only great in Kathak dancing and playing on percussion instruments but also much superior human beings than the ordinary folks, and were held in high esteem.[3]

The following verse from *Bhavishya Purana* states how the Kathaks were held in high esteem and regarded as Brahmins, the highest echelon of the social divisions, and were considered priestly and spiritual. In *Bhavishya Purana*, the word Kathak was used as one of the four jatis or the categories of Brahmins. The four jatis were *bhojak*, *kathak*, *shivavipra*, and *suryavipra*.

> Jatibhedashcha chatvaron bhojakah kathakstatha
> Shivaviprah suryaviprashchaturthaha paripathayate.[4]

In the extensive Hindi dictionary *Hindi Shabdasagar*, which is a compilation of three decades of work by Hindi scholars published between 1922 and 1929, the word Kathak is given several meanings: a storyteller, the one who studies Puranas; an actor, one who explains the synopsis of a play; a narrator; a dance style; a social caste that indulges in singing; a percussionist; and a dancer.

---

[3] Projesh Banerji, *Kathak Dance through Ages* (New Delhi: Cosmos Publications, 1982), p.11.
[4] Prem Dave, *Kathak Nritya Parampara* (Jaipur: Panchsheel Prakashan, 2004), p. 18.

Archeological evidence also suggests that Kathak was indeed performed during ancient times. In 1922, archeologists excavated the ruins of Harappa and Mohenjodaro, which are believed to be two of the earliest major urban settlements built around 2600 BCE. Scholars have found similarities between Kathak stances and the poses of the bronze dancing statues unearthed in these excavations.

In ancient scriptures, there is a description of a dance form called Chalit Nritya. The gaits that were used in Chalit Nritya have many similarities with Kathak. Chalit Nritya was depicted in some of the paintings found in Ajanta Caves. The Ajanta Caves in Maharashtra, India, date back to approximately the second century BCE and are considered the masterpiece of Buddhist religious art. The dancing poses in these paintings resemble the stances of Kathak dance. In fact, the term *chal* from the word *chalit* is used in a repertoire of Kathak called *gat*. The exact time when these postures of Chalit Nritya were added to the Ajanta Caves is difficult to determine. However, many more artistically exquisite caves were added between the fifth and sixth centuries CE during the Gupta period. It seems more plausible that the poses resembling Kathak were added during the same period. Kalidas was a great classical Sanskrit author and scholar during the Gupta period. In his play *Vikramorvasiyam*, Kalidas mentions the Chalit Nritya as being performed in the heavens.

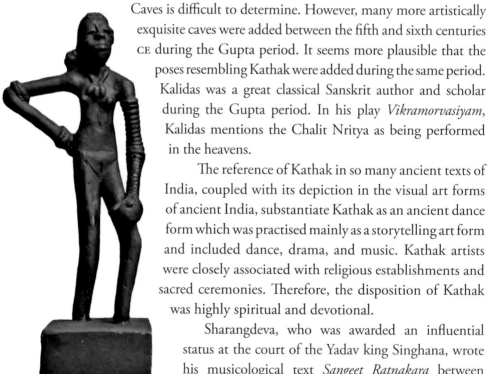

Replica of 'Dancing Girl' of Mohenjodaro at Chhatrapati Shivaji Maharaj Vastu Sangrahalaya in Mumbai

The reference of Kathak in so many ancient texts of India, coupled with its depiction in the visual art forms of ancient India, substantiate Kathak as an ancient dance form which was practised mainly as a storytelling art form and included dance, drama, and music. Kathak artists were closely associated with religious establishments and sacred ceremonies. Therefore, the disposition of Kathak was highly spiritual and devotional.

Sharangdeva, who was awarded an influential status at the court of the Yadav king Singhana, wrote his musicological text *Sangeet Ratnakara* between 1210–1247 CE. *Sangeet Ratnakara* is regarded as one of the most comprehensive texts on musicology after Bharata's *Natyashastra*. There are seven chapters in *Sangeet Ratnakara*. While the first six chapters deal with different aspects of vocal and instrumental music, the seventh and the last chapter titled 'Nartanadhyaya' expounds on the art of dance. This chapter attests to the fact that, by the thirteenth century, a more specific and explicit form of Kathak had transpired. The following verse from *Sangeet Ratnakara* defines Kathaks as charming and soft-spoken connoisseurs, who are experts in revelation of characters, skilful in creating poems, and who belong to a good lineage:

> *Kathaka Bandinshchaatra Vidyavantah Priyamvada*
> *Prashansakushalshachaanye chaturah sarvamaatushu.*[5]

KATHAK DURING THE MUGHAL ERA

The topography of India changed considerably during the tenth-century invasions, which in turn modified the social, cultural, economic, political, psychological, philosophical, and artistic notions. The invasions took place after Muhammad Ghori from the Ghor district of Afghanistan defeated Prithviraj Chauhan, an emperor of the Hindu Chauhan Dynasty, and captured Delhi in 1192. At that time, the Delhi Sultanate was established, where the Muslim dynasties of Turkish and Pashtun or Afghani origins ruled India during 1210–1526. The Afghani Lodi Dynasty (1451–1526), which was the last dynasty of Delhi Sultanate, was replaced by the dynamic and powerful Mughal Dynasty. Although both the Delhi Sultanate and the Mughal Empire were established by Muslim rulers, they were two different regimes that ruled India at two different time periods. Kathak started to take a more definite shape during the time of Delhi Sultanate, but it gained status as a well-defined dance form during the reign of the Mughal Dynasty. The Mughal Dynasty played a major role in elevating the status of Kathak as a vital and independent dance form.

During this time, Kathak took its inspiration from the great Bhakti Movement, which developed in central and northern India. The followers of this movement opposed the daunting caste hierarchy and the rigid structures and rituals of Hinduism, as well as the unyielding Islamic religious impositions.

---

[5] Laxmi Narayan Garg, *Kathak Nritya* (Hathras: Sangeet Karyalaya, 1994), p. 28.

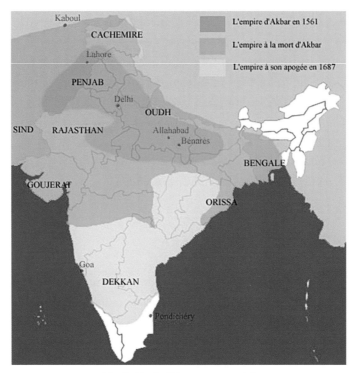

Mughal India [Map not to scale]

The Bhakti Movement

The Bhakti Movement was the path of love, devotion, and surrender. By making the heart the central point of human existence, the followers of the Bhakti Movement believed in loving devotion and found it a simple and undemanding way to attain union with the Supreme. The Bhakti Movement mainly embraced the Vaishnava philosophy, which arose from Hinduism. At the same time, the movement was also inspired by Sufism, which had emerged as the mystical dimension and extraction of Islam. Bhakti seekers worshipped different manifestations of one Supreme Being, but their purpose was the same and they all went through the same spiritual experiences. Initially, poetry became the most gratifying medium of expression for the bhakti seekers, which gradually seeped into all other art forms of India. The Bhakti period, which spanned from the fourteenth century to the seventeenth century CE, was set apart by the rise in vernacular devotional literature.

Kabir Das, the great Bhakti poet from the fourteenth century, described the path of bhakti beautifully in the following verse:

The bhakti path winds in a delicate way. On this path there is no asking and no not asking. The ego simply disappears the moment you touch him. The joy of looking for him is so immense that you just dive in, and coast around like a fish in the water. If anyone needs a head, the lover leaps up to offer his.[6]

According to the saint-poet Kabir Das, the ego simply disappears as soon as the soul surrenders itself to the lover, who, as the spiritual essence and the ultimate truth, is beyond this material world.

About a century before Kabir, the Sufi poet Jalal ad-Din Muhammad Rumi from Persia was delving into similar spiritual practices and experiences. Rumi became absolutely absorbed in the Divine, whom he spoke of as his lover:

Return to home, O friend of mine—
A place has been made ready in my heart
Pillows and fine carpets cover the marble floor
And incense burns in its holder
Your chair is ready; no one has sat there
Lest the shape you left behind be erased
No one has drunk from goblets
Nor eaten from plates since your going away
Everything is as you left it—
Even the dust is undisturbed.[7]

The devotional and romanticized poetry of this era with lyrical and delicate sentiments influenced all facets of Indian arts. Integration between the Hindu and Islamic arts and culture became the premise upon which Kathak flourished as an independent dance form. Even though Kathak incorporated in it the mystical qualities of Nirguna Bhakti, where God is not limited by materialistic forms or worldly attributes, it is predominantly inclined towards Vaishnava Bhakti. Different incarnations of Lord Vishnu are revered in Vaishnava Bhakti. Lord Krishna, the eighth incarnation of Lord Vishnu, became the protagonist of Kathak dance.

---

[6] Poet Seers, 'Bhakti Poets', site developed by members of the Sri Chinmoy Centre, http://www.poetseers.org/poets/bhakti-poets/ (accessed on 13 April 2018).
[7] Nigel Watts, *The Way of Love* (London: Thorsons, 1999), p. 110.

Even before the Bhakti Movement started, *kathakar*s, who were also called *granthika*s, portrayed the stories of Lord Vishnu through the medium of performing arts. Since Krishna was identified as an incarnation of Vishnu, a rich Krishna-theatre tradition emerged in Mathura, Uttar Pradesh, which is presumed to be the birthplace of Lord Krishna. However, it was during the Bhakti Movement when Kathak became a full-fledged dance form and Krishna became the central theme of Kathak repertoire. Swami Haridas, a great Krishna devotee who was also a great poet and musician (circa 1480 CE), is known for dancing in front of the statue of Lord Krishna. In states of spiritual trance, Swami Haridas composed many songs that inspired both the Bhakti Movement and the performing arts of India. Many musicians and Kathak dancers of his time trained under him and became inspired by the Krishna theme that they devotedly expressed through their arts.

Madhura Bhakti

One of the ancient texts of India *Srimad Bhagavata Maha Purana* mentions nine different kinds of bhakti, among which *atma-nivedana* or absolute self-surrender to God is considered the highest path.

Madhura Bhakti (euphoric devotion) is one of the principal characteristics of *atma-nivedana*, which brings a devotee closest to God, his supreme lover. The concept of Madhura Bhakti became the fertile ground for the literary framework of Vaishnavite literature, which in turn influenced the expressive aspects of the art of Kathak tremendously. Madhura Bhakti is associated with Hinduism, and more specifically with Saguna Bhakti, where God is imagined as a form, having a certain appearance. But the essence of Madhura Bhakti is a sentiment full of passion and surrender, which can also be experienced in Sufi poetry. Kathak dancers of medieval India were obviously attracted to the feelings of this passion and surrender. Perhaps, this is the reason that Kathak developed as one of the most romanticized and passionate classical dance forms of India.

Ashta-Chaapkars

Vallabhacharya (1479–1531 CE) was the proponent of Shuddhadvaita or Monism. Shuddhadvaita is a non-dualistic philosophy, according to which all existing things and experiences can be explained in terms of one single reality or a single source. For Vallabhacharya, Lord Krishna was that one single reality and the Absolute. He also placed great emphasis on *pushti* (grace) and *bhakti* (devotion).

The eight disciples of Vallabhacharya were called *ashta-chaap* poets. These *ashta-chaap* poets were Surdas, Krishnadas, Paramanand, Kumbhandas, Chaturbhuj, Nand Das, Cheetswami, and Govindadas. The devotion of these *ashta-chaap* poets was so ethereal that they experienced the transcendental realm within the mundane world.

> Shri Krishna brought Suradas water when he was thirsty, threw pebbles at Govindadas, stole dairy products with Chatrabhujadas, and engaged in a cooking contest with Kumbhanadas. Through these and other lilas, the Ashta Chhap's worldly existence became thoroughly divine. These poets' love for Krishna was not conditioned by fear. Nor did their devotion, in this stage of fulfillment, depend upon knowing Krishna's greatness. They were not concerned with any philosophical debates concerning the nature of the Supreme reality: it was experienced. All philosophical contradictions were resolved in the abode of sweetness.[8]

These poets did not only produce a wealth of lyrical poems, but they were also musicians and their poems were meant to be sung. Music and dance have always been so intertwined in Indian culture that the poems composed by the *ashta-chaap* poets also made their way to the art of dance, thus strengthening the bhakti elements in Kathak. To this day, the poignant and soulful poems of these *ashta-chaap* poets are an integral part of Kathak repertoire. According to some scholars, the *ashta-chaap* poets were also competent dancers. They used the Kathak dance terminology, expressions, and vocabulary in their poems. In her book *Kathak Nritya Parampara*, Dr Prem Dave illustrates this point by giving the following examples that clearly have used the idioms of Kathak dance:

> *Nritatti sudhang ang, rang, sang radhika*
> *Gidi gidi ta tat thai thai raas rangini* (Krishnadas).[9]

[*Gidi gidi ta tat thai thai* are the rhythmic sounds created by the Kathak dancers.]

---

[8] Shyamdas, 'The Ashta Chaap Poets and their Bhava', excerpt from *Krishna's Inner Circle: The Ashta Chhap Poets* by Shyamdas, http://shyamdas.com/2010/07/01/the-ashta-chaap-poets-and-their-bhava-2/ (accessed on 13 April 2018).
[9] Dave, *Kathak Nritya Parampara*, p. 29.

In the earlier poem, Lord Krishna is dancing raas with His consort Radhika. Raas Leela tradition of Kathak was very popular in the temples of India at that time. The following examples by Kumbhandas and Cheetswami integrate the Kathak vocalizations and terminology beautifully with poetry.

Urap tirap tandava kare
Ta thai rachi ughati taan (Kumbhandas)

Gid gidta, gid gid ta
Tat tat tat tat tat thai thai gati lino (Cheetswami)[10]

In the previous poem, *urap tirap* are expressions taken from Kathak terminology, which mean a leap and slanted movement respectively in dance. The 'Tandava ang' is a feature of Kathak, where more vigorous and energetic movements are performed. *Gid gidta, gid gid ta, tat tat tat tat tat thai thai* are the rhythmic sounds used in Kathak. The word *gati* comes from the Kathak repertoire *gat-nikas*.

A fifteenth-century saint-poet and musician Surdas was one of the most renowned *ashta-chaap* poets. It is believed that he composed one lakh poems, out of which only 8,000 remain in existence. These songs are compiled in his books *Sur Sagar*, *Sur Saravali*, and *Sahitya Lahri*. Surdas was born blind, but his writings about Krishna's life are so vivacious that it seems as if he had eyewitnessed all the events portrayed in his poems. The following poem of Surdas depicts Lord Krishna divinely dancing on the hood of the overpowered Kaliya Naga, a multi-headed venomous serpent:

Tandava gati mundane par nirtat ban maali
Pum pum pum patakat, fun fun fun funan upar
Bin bin bin binati karat, naag vadhu aali
Sun sun sun sunkadik, nun nun nun naradadi
Gan gan gan gandharva sabhi det Tali
Surdas prabhu ki bani, kin kin kin kinhu na jani
Chan chan chan charan dharat, abhaya bhayo kali.[11]

---

[10] Dave, *Kathak Nritya Parampara*, p. 30.
[11] Ibid.

Surdas has used sound devices in the given poem in order to reinforce the meaning and to evoke images of Krishna's dancing. He has especially used some mnemonic sounds to create an emotional response. It is believed that when Krishna danced on the hood of Kaliya Naga, various mnemonic sounds or *bols* originated from His divine feet, which became the essential elements of Kathak dance. These *bols* are called *natwari bols*, based on one of Krishna's names, Natwar. Indeed, many great dancers of the past called Kathak the Natwari Nritya.

Even though Kathak was associated with the legends of Krishna for thousands of years, it is evident that the Bhakti Movement influenced the art of Kathak immensely and profoundly.

Raas Leela and Kathak

Raas Leela emerged as a component of the traditional storytelling art of Krishna's life, where Lord Krishna dances with Radha and other maidens during the exquisite night of a splendid full moon in the lush forests of Vrindavan. The word *raas*, derived from the Sanskrit word *rasa*, means aesthetics. The word *leela* connotes the divine act or divine play, and is considered as the nature of supreme consciousness where it transforms into the manifest world. According to some legends, Krishna with His divine powers extends that one night of the full moon to the length of one night of Brahma, a Vedic cyclical time in Hinduism which lasts for approximately 4.32 billion years. The Raas Leela is performed in a *mandala* or circular formation. The divine lovers Radha and Krishna occupy the centre of the circle. During this dance, Krishna multiplies His form to dance with every *gopi*. Each *gopi* represents an individual soul, and Raas Leela signifies the soul's spiritual longing to immerse itself in the divine dance created by God Himself.

Raas Leela performance was originated by Swami Sri Uddhavaghamanda Devacharya in the early fifteenth century CE in Vrindavan in the Mathura district. He belonged to Nimbarka Sampradaya, which is one of the four authorized schools of Vaishnavism, a major tradition within Hinduism. His guru Swami Harivyasa Devacharya reflected on the *Yugala Shataka*, a book of songs composed by his own guru Shribhatta Devacharya. This book is considered the first Vani book in the Braj language compiled during the fourteenth century CE, and the songs in this book describe the eternal spiritual dwelling of Radha Krishna. Swami Uddhavaghamanda learned the songs from his guru and trained his disciples to enact the Raas Leela episodes of the songs for an engaging visual presentation.

Raas Leela of Lord Krishna

According to many scholars, Raas Leela had a great impact on Kathak. Some even postulate that Kathak as a dance form originated from Raas Leela. Some others go as far as to infer that Raas Leela appropriated the movements and expressions of the ancient *kathakar*s, who later became Kathak dancers.

> The emergence of Raslila *[sic]*, mainly in the Braj region (Mathura in Western U.P.) was an important development. It combined in itself music, dance and the narrative. Dance in Raslila *[sic]*, however, was mainly an extension of the basic mime and gestures of the Kathakars or story-tellers which blended easily with the existing traditional dance.[12]

However, there are many scholars who feel that Kathak and Raas Leela developed independent of each other, although they did influence one another in a significant way, since they both were the by-products of Vaishnavite philosophy and grew around the same time in roughly the same geographic area. According to Reginald Massey:

[12] Centre for Cultural Resources and Training, http://ccrtindia.gov.in/kathak.php (accessed on 13 April 2018).

There is much speculation as to whether Ras Lila, which is a folk art, has borrowed from the classical style of North India. Certainly there are many points of similarities between the two, but these may have arisen because both deal with the same Vaishnavite themes, although Kathak by no means is restricted to these. Bhava in the mime of Ras Lila, like that of Kathak, is natural although not as developed. Again this resemblance may exist because both grew roughly in the same geographical area. The kavita torah in Kathak and the kavita with dance boles in Ras Lila are examples of this. Now, while it is difficult to state categorically that the Ras Lila borrowed from Kathak, it is quite possible, since both dances were at their peak at the same time, that certain elements from Kathak, mainly the gaths, permeated into the Ras Lila through the influence of the professional Kathak dancers, so numerous and poplular at that time.[13]

Whatever the arguments, it cannot be denied that the character of the Supreme Godhead Krishna played the central role in the development of Kathak from ancient times and even after the Bhakti era, inspired by the Bhakti Movement. Kathak took inspiration from other poets besides the *ashta-chaap* ones, such as the imminent poets of medieval India—Jayadeva, Nand Das, Paramanand Das, Meerabai, and Vidyapati. Kathak was both impacted and influenced by the poetic literature of the Bhakti era.

Kathak in Mughal Courts

During the Mughal era, Kathak was brought to the Mughal courts where it went through vital modifications and, as a result, transformed into a full-fledged classical dance form. The artistic sensibilities of the Mughal rulers, along with new musical styles and innovative musical instruments, added a whole new vocabulary to Kathak's existing expressions. Intricate footwork and dazzling spins, combined with the presentation of delicate expressions, shifted the theme of Kathak from devotionalism to romanticism.

The sophisticated and stylish environment of the courts trickled down to the art of Kathak, which provided Kathak more aesthetic and sensual dimensions. The Mughal period has the legacy of having multiracial and multireligious

[13] Reginald Massey, *India's Kathak Dance: Past, Present, Future* (New Delhi: Abhinav Publications, 1999), p. 62.

societies. During this era, the distinctive artistic and aesthetic characteristics of both the Indian and Persian cultures were ingeniously commingled in North Indian arts, which enriched and enhanced the performance of Kathak dance.

The concluding stage of the Delhi Sultanate, from 1300 CE to 1800 CE, is believed to be decisive in the development of Indian arts, particularly the North Indian visual, literary, and performing arts, since the Mughal emperors mainly occupied the North Indian territories. During the rule of Alauddin Khalji (1296–1316) in Delhi, his court musician and scholar Amir Khusrow contributed significantly to the musical and literary arts of North India. Amir Khusrow was a spiritual disciple of an eminent mystic Nizamuddin Auliya and was himself a great scholar, Sufi musician, and poet. He wrote his poems primarily in Persian and Hindavi languages. Hindavi derived its vast vocabulary from Arabic, Persian, Sanskrit, a North Indian dialect Khariboli, and a Turkish language Chagatai. The origin of Hindavi language is controversial, but there is no doubt that Amir Khusrow made this language popular through his highly evolved literature. A substantial number of Kathak vocabularies have stemmed from the Hindavi language. He also wrote *ghazals*, a poetic form that consists of rhyming couplets which subtly idealize life, love, pain, togetherness, and separation in a piercing and tantalizing manner. The sentiments of *ghazals* and Sufi bhakti, in a way, became the backdrop for Kathak, making it a romanticized dance form. Henceforth, performing the lyrics of *ghazals* through bodily and facial expressions became a key component of Kathak repertoire.

Amir Khusrow is also credited for introducing Persian, Arabic, and Turkish elements of music into Indian classical music. The result was a magnificent musical fusion of both Indian and Persian cultures, which gave birth to *khyal* and *tarana* styles of music. The word *khyal* is derived from a Persian word, meaning 'imagination' or 'idea'. At that time, *dhrupad* was one of the oldest forms of Hindustani classical music, and was the customary performance of Indian music. *Dhrupad* was highly systematized and sombre in nature, whereas *khyal* delivered a subtle, free-flowing, and fluid presentation with greater application of musical embellishments and ornamentations. *Khyal* is presented in two parts—*bada khyal* and *chota khyal*. In *bada khyal*, the main emotion of a raga or the modal scale is explored in slow tempo in order to develop and establish that particular raga. However, *chota khyal* is sung in medium tempo and is slowly brought to the crescendo, where the audience is left in a state of heightened emotion. The core presentation of Kathak is somewhat analogous to

Amir Khusrow surrounded by young men. Miniature from a manuscript of Majlis Al-Usshak by Husayn Bayqarah

the nature of *khyal* style, where, like the *bada khyal*, the dancer introduces the movements of minor and major limbs slowly and develops it fully to create the mood of the performance. And then, just like *chota khyal*, Kathak, in the later part of its performance, is executed in medium and fast tempos. The footwork of Kathak to create crescendo is very comparable to the *tans* in *khyal gayaki* style. One can clearly see the influence of graceful and elegant *khyal gayaki* on Kathak dance. Similarly, Amir Khusrow's introduction of *tarana* also had an effect on Kathak. *Tarana* actually became a part of Kathak repertoire. *Tarana* is sung and danced in fast tempo and uses the syllables of Sanskrit, Arabic, and Persian phonemes along with the rhythmic syllables of tabla, pakhawaj, and sitar.

Amir Khusrow also felt the need for appropriate instruments to suitably accompany the *khyal gayaki*. He is credited for inventing the sitar, a stringed instrument, and tabla, a percussion instrument. It is believed that both sitar and tabla were the adaptations of ancient Indian instruments veena and pakhawaj respectively. Both sitar and tabla became, and remain, the preferred accompaniments for a Kathak performance, further cementing Amir Khusrow's legacy as an artistic visionary in the development of Kathak.

The golden era of Kathak is considered to have begun under the third and, perhaps, the greatest ruler of the Mughal Dynasty, Akbar the Great (1542–1605). According to Paris Franz, 'Akbar's patronage of the arts was an aspect of government, in an age where cultural grandeur reinforced the regime's legitimacy.'[14]

---

[14] Paris Franz, Decoded = {Past}, 'The Emperor Akbar: Mughal Patron of the Arts', 13 Sep. 2013, http://decodedpast.com/the-emperor-akbar-mughal-patron-of-the-arts/ (accessed on 13 April 2018).

Akbar and Tansen visit Swami Haridas in Vrindavan. Swami Haridas is to the right, playing the lute; Akbar is to the left, dressed as a common man; Tansen is in the middle, listening to Haridas. Jaipur-Kishangarh mixed style, 1750

Under Akbar's patronage, the most impressive features of Hindu and Muslim traditions were amalgamated, giving birth to an integrated and sophisticated Indo-Islamic art and culture. Akbar's library consisted of over 24,000 volumes written in Sanskrit, Persian, Greek, Latin, and Arabic. Numerous artists, poets, musicians, dancers, scholars, calligraphers, architects, painters, and craftsmen adorned his court. According to the *Ain-i-Akbari*, a sixteenth-century detailed document written by Abu'l-Fazl ibn Mubarak, there was a famous Kathak dancer in his court known as Vallabhdas.

After Akbar, his son Emperor Jahangir (1569–1627) became known for his patronage of arts. During his rule, a unique style of Mughal miniature painting developed and thrived. Jahangir himself was an artist and owned an atelier. Mughal miniature painting is characterized by attention to small details—geometrical and intricate patterns, lush tones and colours, epic subject matter, strong, linear, two-dimensional perspective, great energy, and a romantic portrayal of nature. These characteristics can be observed in all North Indian art forms of that time, including Kathak. Kathak also developed as a linear dance form as opposed to other circular Indian classical dance styles. Just like the miniature paintings of that time, Kathak also depicted stories in a romanticized manner with great energy and vitality.

The seventeenth century witnessed the rule of Jahangir's son—Emperor Shah Jahan (1592–1666)—who is known for his love for architecture. Shah Jahan built many prominent monuments, among which the magnificent Taj Mahal stands out as one of the finest structures of Mughal dynasty. The unique design patterns of the Mughal miniature paintings can be seen in the decorative elements of Taj Mahal. These decorative, intricate, and vibrant designs can be witnessed in all North Indian art forms that were inspired by the Indo-Persian influences, whether it be the fine arts such as dance, music, painting, and poetry, or the craftsmanship in architectural structures, ornamental carpets, brilliantly decorated utensils, fine jewellery designs, Kashmiri woodwork, and tapestries. The designs created by the artists of this time were geometrical in nature.

> A great contribution has been made by the Moghals to the art of India, and that in the art of geometrical designs and patterns in every branch....This art of geometrical designs may be explained in the way that more of finer and nicer designs and patterns within patterns, and the designs within designs, very often most intricate ones, were introduced in every art, so much so that no space in broad structure were allowed. These geometrical designs made the art more beautiful and attractive....The modern system of Kathak in which more of intricate time measurements are shown, is obviously the product of this Indo-Persian cultural fusion. There are doubles, four times, eight times, and more and more speed with every kind of fractional measurements.[15]

However, after the reign of Shah Jahan, Kathak and other North Indian art forms experienced a significant decline in their development and expansion. Shah Jahan's son Aurangzeb (1618–1707) fervently opposed the practice of arts. He was an orthodox Muslim and discarded his grandfather Akbar's ideas of secularism. It is reported that Aurangzeb ordered the burial of all musical instruments and banned painters and paintings. During his time, Kathak dancers went back to their rural homes and villages in hiding. They were treated as social outcasts. During Aurangzeb's reign, arts did not receive royal encouragement or royal patronage. Nevertheless, a painting in gouache is in existence from his time in which two girls are dancing Kathak. At present, this painting is located at the Musée de l'Orangerie in Paris, France. On 21 March 1995, the United Kingdom issued a stamp of this painting in a booklet form with nine other stamps in the series.[16]

---

[15] Banerji, *Kathak Dance through Ages*, pp. 19–20.
[16] 'Girls performing a Kathak Dance' (Aurangzeb period), United Kingdom of Great Britain and Northern Ireland, http://colnect.com/en/stamps/stamp/3453-Girls_performing_a_Kathak_Dance_Aurangzeb_period-Greetings_Stamps_-_Art-United_Kingdom_of_Great_Britain_Northern_Ireland (accessed on 18 April 2018).

Many traditionalists assume that tradition opposes and resists experimentation. In the case of North Indian music and dance, this presumption does not hold true. During the Mughal period, Kathak proved its progressive penchant by adopting new movement vocabulary and disposition of Mughal arts while still keeping the integrity of its pedigree. In this era, the main elements and characteristics of Kathak dance were developed. The use of footwork, spins, intricate rhythmic displays, and angular movements became the signature trademark of Kathak. The devotional Kathak dancers of temples became the entertainers in Mughal courts with lavish costumes, refined movement and rhythmic vocabulary, extraordinary aesthetics, improvisational aptitude, and technical genius. Kathak became a sensual art form, which leaned towards romanticism and, therefore, shifted its disposition of being a temple dance to a court dance.

During the period of Bhakti Movement, there was more emphasis on the emotional aspects of dance. Kathak became more of an art to display in the Mughal era. The lavish and grand environment of the Mughal courts attracted the artists of that time, where their attention turned to please the emperors and courtiers in order to receive expensive gifts, favours, and fame. *Nayika-bhed*, which is an archetypal classification of the romantic heroines and their relationship with the nayaks or the heroes, became a favourite subject to portray in dance for Kathak dancers. New vocabularies such as *ched-chad* and *kasak-masak* were developed to create suggestive sentiments and gestures. The passion and erotic elements became more dominant in Kathak. Notably, there were also Kathak dancers during this time who avoided the seduction of the luxurious lifestyle of the Mughal courts. They continued to practice the art of Kathak in its purest and unadulterated form. This is why, today, Kathak has retained both its traditional beauty and the Mughal era's progressive passion, making itself a complete dance form.

KATHAK DURING THE POST-MUGHAL PERIOD

By the seventeenth century, the Mughal empire began to crumble because of the European presence in India. After the decline of the powerful Mughal empire, the patronage for Kathak was sustained in the kingdoms of semi-autonomous Muslim rulers of the princely states, who were titled nawabs. Kathak also kept its identity at this time in the courts of Hindu rajas and the temples of North India. The gharanas or the various schools of Kathak were created during this period.

Contributions of Nawab Wajid Ali Shah

It was during the rule of Nawab Wajid Ali Shah (1822–1887) that Kathak regained its glory. Wajid Ali Shah was the nawab of Oudh, the region at the centre of present-day Uttar Pradesh. Wajid Ali Shah, during his rule from 1847 until 1856, carried all North Indian art forms to new heights through his generous patronage and artistic talents. Many scholars credit him for the revival of Kathak dance and securing its status as one of the major classical Indian dance styles. Wajid Ali Shah himself was an exceptional musician and dancer. He had studied Indian classical vocal music under some of the great masters of that time, such as Basit Khan, Jafar Khan, and Pyar Khan. He studied Kathak under the great gurus Thakur Prasad and Durga Prasad. Due to the uniquely creative efforts of Guru Thakur Prasad, the Lucknow school of Kathak came into existence. Under Wajid Ali Shah's patronage, the Lucknow style of Kathak dance prospered and was perfected. Bindadin Maharaj and Kalkadin Maharaj, the famous sons of Thakur Prasad ji, also graced the court of Wajid Ali Shah. The expressive Lucknow style became known for its *nazakat* or elegance, and *nafasat* or finesse. Wajid Ali Shah also choreographed dance dramas in Kathak style, which were called *raha*s, in which he himself danced. The *raha* probably was the Persian alteration of the dance style Raas Leela. His accompanying royal female dancers belonged to his *parikhana* or the dwelling of fairies, which consisted of hundreds of beautiful women who were given skilful training of music and dance by the expert teachers of that time. It is believed that Wajid Ali Shah created thirty-six different types of *raha*s, choreographed in Kathak style. He is also believed to have enhanced the status of *thumri*, a light classical genre of music. During his time, *thumri* became a significant repertoire of Kathak dance. Wajid Ali Shah's pseudonym was Qaiser, but he assumed the name Akhtarpiya for his *thumri* compositions. He also wrote many romanticized Urdu poems called *ghazal*s, which often depict the agony and rapture of unrequited love. In the court of Wajid Ali Shah, *ghazal*s also became the expressive repertoire of Kathak, where Kathak dancers expressed the sensual and delicate poetry of *ghazal*. Even in modern times, *thumri* and *ghazal* hold a significant place in the repertoire of Kathak.

Wajid Ali Shah's patronage to uplift the artistic endeavours of *twaif*s also facilitated enhancements in the art of Kathak. The *twaif* community was an artistic section of the feudal society of North India. They were the courtesans who excelled in arts, music, dance, and poetry, and professionally entertained their

Wajid Ali Shah, an engraving from 1872
(also published in the
Illustrated London News, 1857)

guests during their *mehfil*s or evening gatherings. These *twaif*s trained under the same gurus who taught music and dance in the courts. However, their presentation of Kathak differed from the Kathak presented in the courts, and incorporated more playful, enticing, and teasing movements. There was free exchange of artistic ideas between the royal artists and *twaif*s. Sometimes, skilled *twaif*s were called to teach in the courts. This freedom of interchange helped in merging the Kathak of two different communities, therefore consolidating the repertoire of Kathak. Kathak attained extraordinary levels of elegance and complexity under the patronage of the last nawab of the state of Oudh, Wajid Ali Shah. Unfortunately, the annexation of Oudh by the British in 1856 imposed very discouraging and damaging consequences on Kathak, and the decline of this dance form became inevitable for some time.

KATHAK DURING THE BRITISH RULE

British Raj, or the British rule, was instituted in the Indian subcontinent from 1858 to 1947. The Indian rebellion of 1857 by the soldiers, employed by the East India Company against the Company's rules, caught fire and intensified into civilian rebellion and other mutinies. The disorganization of the rebellion gave an opening to the British government to take control of the Company, an action that ultimately resulted in the establishment of British rule in India.

Kathak dance faced a major decline during the British Raj to the extent that the Kathak dancers faced social humiliation and disgrace:

The grandeur of Kathak eclipsed during this period. Apparently the predominantly oriental dance vocabulary of Kathak was misinterpreted by the Western mindset and it became an eye-sore, both literally and metaphorically, for the colonial perception of classical dance. Kathak was demeaned, demoted and even denounced as a lowly dance performed solely for the sensory pleasure of the kings. However, thanks to the herculean efforts of a few twaifs, among whom Gauhar Jaan was a leading light, Kathak somehow managed to survive British denunciation and remained alive, albeit in a fractured and fragmented form.[17]

The British annexed Oudh in 1856 and Wajid Ali Shah was exiled to Matiya Burj in Calcutta. All the kingdoms ruled by individual nawabs and rajas became princely states and were required to submit to the dominion of the British Crown. British authority had no interest in supporting the art of Kathak dance. A very few Kathak gurus were given royal patronage. Most of the royal dancers had to leave the courts and survive in poverty.

The *twaifs* were forced to become mere entertainers and they started to lose the artistic substance in their art in order to please the nouveau riche patrons, who were not sensible enough to appreciate arts for art's sake. These *twaifs* started to use more erotic elements in their dance, which cheapened the dance for the sophisticated elites. Many of these *twaifs* were ousted and were perceived as nautch girls by the British. The word 'nautch' was the distorted adaptation of the Hindi word *naach*, which means 'dancing'. Nautch was in practice during the late Mughal era too, but it was disgraced during the British Raj. Kathak performed by the *twaifs* was demoted to the dishonoured nautch dance and became the means of amusement for sahibs or the higher British officials and the zamindars or the native aristocrats.

A dinner in the community was usually followed by a nautch performance. So were other festive occasions, such as the celebration of a King Emperor's birthday and visits of dignitaries to civil and military stations. Nautch girls would also accompany the British army whenever it was on the move,

---

[17] Nupur Global Dance Academy, http://www.learnkathak.com/index.php?option=com_content&view=article&id=16&Itemid=14 (accessed 13 April 2018).

entertaining the soldiers on the way. At times they were also engaged to welcome arriving guests on the highways....Quite often, lonely men would send for nautch girls to entertain them in their own houses. Usually, groups of civilians or soldiers joined hands to hire nautch girls for an evening of amusement.[18]

Many journals, chronicles, and travel documents by the travellers at that time mention the nautch community. On reading these documents, one can decipher that the *nautchwalis* or the nautch dancers were mainly condemned for performing for a payment or for being patronized by the feudal rulers. Moreover, the nautch community was later subdivided into various classes due to subtle differences in the dance styles and living styles: *mirasi*, *bai*, *rumzani*, *domni*, *nariyal*, and *kheloni*. There were many misperceptions and misinterpretations about the nautch community:

A photograph of two dancing girls, by K L Brajbasi & Co., Patna, 1910

> It is surprising how a famous Indologist like E.B. Havel, who visited India towards the close of the 19th century, passed an unjust remark on Nautchwalis of Benaras. Probably, he had a biased view and did not study them properly. He observes, 'The dancing girls of Benaras are generally the unmarried daughters of the Kathak caste—the caste of professional musicians.' Havel did not know that the teachers in India call their disciples as sons and daughters, and obviously the Kathaks were the dance teachers of the professional dancing girls.[19]

....

[18] Pran Nevile, 'Nautch Girls: Sahibs Danced to Their Tune', Excerpted from Stories from the Raj: Sahibs, Memsahibs and Others, Indialog Publications, *Spectrum, The Tribune*, 25 July 2004, http://www.tribuneindia.com/2004/20040725/spectrum/main1.htm (accessed on 13 April 2018).

[19] Banerji, *Kathak Dance through Ages*, p. 48.

A Calcutta nautch dancer from Frederic Courtland Penfield, East of Suez

Studio portrait of a 'Mohammedan dancing girl', Jaipur, 1890

Nautch dance was not about erotic expressions and vulgar gestures, as perceived by many at that time. There were some sensible and unprejudiced viewers who observed the intricate techniques and appealing aesthetics of nautch dancers.

Charles Doyley in his *The European in India*, published in 1813, a very rare book now, gives the following account of a dancing woman of Lucknow.

It should be understood that the dancing women of India pique themselves entirely on the gracefulness of their positions and motions. They have no variety of steps, the feet being kept parallel and close, one foot advancing, or moving only a few inches, and the other always following it; this however, is done with remarkable exactness as to times which, on all occasions, is regulated by the instruments played by the men, attached to the set.[20]

Some others have also mentioned the perfect walking techniques and foot movements of nautch girls. These art lovers obviously noticed the precision and complexity of the dance form, which can only be achieved through dedicated training. The foot movement, body positioning, and aesthetics of the nautch dance were admired and observed by many scholars of that time and can be traced in today's Kathak performances.

The Anti-Nautch Movement

In the late nineteenth century, reformist groups that consisted mainly of Christian missionaries, doctors, journalists, and social workers began a social purity movement in colonial India and addressed the issues related to reforming the status of women, who were considered socially and morally inferior. In 1882, the first Anti-Nautch and Anti-Dedication Movement was instigated.

The 'scientific' basis of social purity was summed up by Max Nordau's (1849–1923) concept of 'degeneration'. According to this theory, a preoccupation with gambling, alcohol, sex, and the other vices as defined by the Christian churches, led to a decay of the central nervous system. Such decay in turn led to further indulgence and licentious behaviour, which again leads to further neurologic decay. According to the Lamarckian theory of evolution that was popular at the time, such 'degenerate' characteristics would be transmitted to the next generation. The cascading nature of degeneration would inevitably lead to a breakdown of all civil society. It was clear that in order to save society from this dire fate, it was essential that such vices be eliminated. Among the myriad of vices that society was prone to, the sexual vices were considered the most serious. The rising unacceptability of Indian dance and its practitioners is illustrated by an incident that occurred in 1890. Prince Albert visited India and was entertained to a traditional Indian dance. Visiting dignitaries had been entertained to traditional Indian dance for as long as anyone was aware; however this time things were little different [sic]. There were protests from

[20] Ibid., p. 49.

many quarters, especially from a Christian missionary by the name of Reverend J. Murdoch. He printed a number of publications strongly condemning these 'nautch parties' and called for all British to refrain from attending them.[21]

The Anti-Nautch Movement included the strengthening of the status of the North Indian *twaif*s, nautch girls, and the devadasis of South India. Devadasis were the dancers in the temples of South India and were considered married to the deities for their entire lives. Many of these devadasis were manipulated, controlled, and sexually exploited. According to some scholars, the Anti-Nautch Movement was inspired by the Social Purity Movement in Great Britain linked with the Puritan Movement. In 1892, an appeal started by the Hindu Social Reforms Association regarding the Anti-Nautch Movement was brought to the viceroy, the general governor of India, and the governor of Madras. The appeal did not make much progress and, later, some other organizations were established and their ideas made way to major publications.

> One publication from the Punjab Purity Association quotes the social reformer Keshab Chandra Sen as saying that the nautch girl was a hideous woman...hell in her eyes. In her breast is a vast ocean of poison. Round her comely waist dwell the furies of hell. Her hands are brandishing unseen daggers ever ready to strike unwary or wilful victims that fall in her way. Her blandishments are India's ruin. Alas! Her smile is India's death. Another example of the extreme zeal of many who pursued the Anti-Nautch Movement may be seen in the case of Miss Helen Tennant. She truly believed that it was her assignment from God to abolish dance girls. She came all the way from England to India for this purpose.[22]

It took a long time for the Anti-Nautch Movement to make a difference in uplifting the status of dancers. In 1905, when the Prince of Wales visited India, it

---

[21] David Courtney, 'The Tawaif, The Anti-Nautch movement, and the Development of North Indian Classical Music, Part 3 – Evolution of the Will to End the Tawaifs', https://chandrakantha.com/articles/tawaif/3_the_will.html (accessed on 19 April 2018).

[22] Courtney, 'The Tawaif, The Anti-Nautch movement, and the Development of North Indian Classical Music, Part 5 – The Anti-Nautch Movement', https://chandrakantha.com/articles/tawaif/5_anti_nautch_movement.html (accessed on 19 April 2018).

was decided not to organize an Indian dance reception for him. By 1920, the Anti-Nautch Movement reached its zenith. In 1934, the Bombay Devadasi Protection Act, the first legal initiative, was passed. India reclaimed its independence in 1947, and, in the same year, the Madras Devadasis Act outlawed devadasi tradition in much of southern India. By 1988, the devadasi system was outlawed throughout India, which greatly affected North Indian Kathak. As the Anti-Nautch Movement peaked, Kathak started to find a respectful place for itself by paving its way to a higher class of society. The dance performed by the *twaifs* was labelled as *mujra*, which was distinguished from the pure Kathak performed by the trained and talented artists. The Anti-Nautch Movement did provide the Indian dances their due respect, yet many dancers also suffered because of this movement. They had to endure the rejection of their profession that was their very livelihood.

It is certain that Kathak went through a period of decline during the British Raj, but the spirited and zealous practitioners of this art form kept the strong chain of Kathak unbroken. Despite social disgrace and lack of support, they devotedly preserved this ancient art form. Kathak, reduced merely to a dishonoured dance form by the feudalistic society of British Raj, later redeemed its glorious identity when it was welcomed by a more favourable social and political environment.

KATHAK IN INDEPENDENT INDIA

Various national and regional protests, campaigns, and lobby groups in India finally led India to its independence from the British imperial authority. Even though the authorization of the Indian Independence Act 1947 created the independent dominions of India and Pakistan, India remained the dominion of the Crown until 1950. The constitution of India was put into effect on 26 January 1950, which established the Republic of India. There was a great need to resolve the trauma that India's social and cultural environment had suffered from being under foreign rules for such a long time. From a psychological perspective, the restoration and revitalization of Indian arts and culture, which Indian society always perceived as a national honour and treasure, became imperative. The reclamation of India's rich heritage of all art forms, nurtured by Indians from ancient times, became symbolic of regaining of India's national identity.

The end of princely states in a politically independent India discontinued the royal patronage to Kathak dance to a great degree. Thus, the mantle of reviving

Kathak dance fell to urban institutions and rich benefactors. Courtesans and *twaifs* were replaced by middle-class artists, who practised, taught, and performed Kathak with much dedication. The public performance spaces replaced the courts and *kotha*s. All these changes brought a shift in the public perspective, and Kathak once again started to be seen as a revered dance form: 'The creation of national, "classical" music and dance genres was fundamental to this cultural repossession. Central to the revival was the need to link contemporary culture to an indigenous past, one that was, in Janet O'Shea's words, "pure, distinctive, and unaltered by colonial hybridity".'[23]

The first four dance forms to be recognized as India's classical art forms were Kathak, Bharatnatyam, Kathakali, and Manipuri dance styles. The *khandani* male Kathak dancers played a crucial role in the growth of Kathak. *Khandani* means the lineage of dancers through heredity. These *khandani* dancers had suffered greatly during the British Raj, and most of them had become the teachers of the *twaifs*. After independence, these professional *khandani* dancers became the torchbearers of Kathak. They became honoured gurus in Kathak schools and institutions founded in urban settings, where respectable men and women came for Kathak training.

The Sangeet Natak Akademi was the first academy of Indian performing arts established by the Republic of India on 31 May 1952. The Akademi's goals were to provide assistance to the government of India in the formulation and implementation of various programmes in the art field and to foster the cultural contacts between various regions in India, as well as between India and the world. The Sangeet Natak Akademi played a major role in the growth of Indian performing arts. The following speech was made by the first Minister of Education of independent India, Maulana Azad, at the inauguration of Sangeet Natak Akademi on 28 January 1953:

> India's precious heritage of music, drama and dance is one which we must cherish and develop. We must do so not only for our own sake but also as our contribution to the cultural heritage of mankind. Nowhere is it truer than in the field of art that to sustain means to create. Traditions cannot be preserved

[23] Margaret Walker, 'Revival and Reinvention in India's *Kathak* Dance', https://journals.lib.unb.ca/index.php/MC/article/view/20234/23336 (accessed on 19 April 2018).

Dancers: Abha Bhatnagar Roy, Prerna Shrimali, and Veronique Azan (standing from left to right); Bhaswati Mishra and Arjun Mishra (sitting). Photographer: Avinash Pasricha

Kathak Dance Drama 'Shavan Atah-Kim' by Kadamb.
Choreographer: Kumudini Lakhia

Saswati Sen

but can only be created afresh. It will be the aim of this Akademi to preserve our traditions by offering them an institutional form...[24]

One of the most important schools of Indian music and dance Shriram Bharatiya Kala Kendra was established in Delhi in 1955 and became a part of the Sangeet Natak Akademi in 1964. Kathak Kendra was the Kathak division of this institution, which was headed by a great *khandani* dancer Pandit Shambhu Maharaj, the nephew of Pandit Bindadin Maharaj, a celebrated dancer in the court of Oudh. Pandit Shambhu Maharaj was known for his expertise in the expressive aspects of Kathak. He revived *thumri*s and other expressive genres and added them to the Kathak repertoire. His disciples later took up the responsibility of expanding the field of Kathak and became great Kathak exponents. Pandit Shambhu Maharaj's brother Pandit Lachhu Maharaj settled in Bombay and also connected himself to Hindi cinema by becoming a choreographer. His remarkable efforts in the area of film choreography in Kathak style gave the much-needed popularity to Kathak. Both brothers were awarded the highest awards of Sangeet Natak Akademi. After Shambhu Maharaj passed away in 1970, his nephew Guru Birju Maharaj became the head of the faculty of Kathak Kendra. Pandit Birju Maharaj

[24] Sangeet Natak Akademi, http://sangeetnatak.gov.in/sna/introduction.php (accessed on 19 April 2018).

Pandit Rajendra Gangani

gave a new dimension to the Kathak solo dance style by popularizing the group performances of Kathak and making it popular even outside of India. Another Kathak Kendra was established in Lucknow in the state of Uttar Pradesh (UP) in 1973. Inspired by the UP government's initiative, the government of the state of Rajasthan established the Jaipur Kathak Kendra.

There were many other private organizations that contributed in preserving the North Indian arts and the art of Kathak:

Institutions such as the *Gandharva Mahavidyalaya* established in Delhi in 1939, the *'Jhankar'* precursor of the present day *Sriram Bharatiya Kala Kendra* in 1947 followed by *Sangeet Bharati, Triveni Kala Sangam* were among the few societies that sought to spread awareness about Indian classical music and dance. More importantly, in this effort, they patronised some of the legendary Kathak Gurus and maestros of the era such as Pandit Achhan Maharaj (Kathak), Pandit Shambhu Maharaj (Kathak), Guru Sunder Prasad (Kathak), Guru Purshottam Das (pakhawaj/mridanga), Naina Devi (vocal), Ustad Hafiz Ali Khan (sarod), Nasir Moinuddin Dagar and Nasir Aminuddin Dagar, popularly known as Dagar brothers (senior) for Dhrupad and later Pandit Birju Maharaj (Kathak), Kundanlal Gangani (Kathak), Pandit Tirath Ram Azad, Devi Lal and Siddheshwari Devi (thumri ang) to name a few, thus contributed their bit in the preservation and furtherance of Kathak and related art forms.[25]

Saswati Sen

The female disciples of these *khandani* Kathak masters brought Kathak to a highly regarded position and made it possible for girls and women from reputable families to train in Kathak and take it up as their profession. Later, these female dancers established their own Kathak schools in various cities of North India. Many dancers in India have devoted their lives to the preservation and promotion of this vibrant and magnificent dance form.

Kathak went through many trials and tribulations in the form of political and economic crises, traumatizing cultural exploitations, and foreign invasions that fractured India's social and cultural pride. But the 2,500-year-old Kathak lives on as an important art form today because of its impeccable flexibility to absorb other cultures in it. The practitioners of Kathak never relented. Today, the practice of Kathak has reached beyond the subcontinent of India. It has made its way through the seven seas and has become an important dance form in the global arena. No longer is it limited to the Brahmin *kathakar*s. It embraces anyone who has the artistic sensibilities and devotion for this dance form.

It can therefore be concluded that Kathak dance form with its oral tradition has had an unbroken continuity since 4th century BC. Weaving through contours of socio-political history and inter-cultural dynamics, Kathak exudes the fragrance not only of 2500 years of Indian history but more so of the last 1000 years of heritage, subtly capturing the natural beauty, innate solutions to historical cultural conflicts and unobtrusively imbibing the cultural diversity of this distinctive cross cultural fertilization, a unique

[25] Shovana Narayan, 'The Origin and Evaluation of Kathak in Delhi', *Yumpu*, https://www.yumpu.com/en/document/view/45426585/the-origin-and-evolution-of-kathak-in-delhi-delhi-heritage-city/8 (accessed on 13 April 2018).

contribution of Delhi....Thus, the dynamic Kathak dance form reflects Delhi's secular ethos of faith and belief in syncretism plurality. This tradition and legacy of the intangible Kathak heritage is being transmitted from generation to generation, and is being sustained and nurtured by the present day generations of Kathak artistes, responding to environment, honing and promoting human creativity with a sense of identity and continuity.[26]

In the words of Dr Maulana Azad, 'India's precious heritage of music, drama and dance is one which we must cherish and develop. We must do so not only for our own sake but also as our contribution to the cultural heritage of mankind.'[27]

[26] Shovana Narayan, 'Kinetics of Cultural Synthesis in Performing Arts', *Explore Rural India, Heritage and Development* 2(2) (2014), http://www.itrhd.com/magazine/volume2-issue2-july-2014.pdf (accessed on 13 April 2018).

[27] S. Sankaranarayanan, 'Sangeet Natak Akademi,' *Sruti: India's Premier Magazine for Performing Arts*, http://www.sruti.com/index.php?route=archives/heritage_details&hId=50 (accessed on 19 April 2018).

Rasa and *Bhava*

THE OBJECTIVE OF INDIAN CLASSICAL DANCE is to carry the performer and the viewer to a level where their ordinary experiences transcend—where they are both able to find pleasure in the extraordinary aesthetic and artistic experiences, which in turn uplift them emotionally, mentally, and spiritually. Therefore, the concept of *rasa* proposed by Bharata is still revered by dancers and dance theorists, as this theory facilitates the realization of this intention of transcendence of ordinary experiences through arts.

THE CONCEPT OF *RASA*

Rasa has been regarded as one of the most important aspects in the theory of Indian aesthetics. The word *rasa* can be literally translated as sap, juice, flavour, extract, nectar, or essence. In the realm of aesthetics, *rasa* is referred to as the emotional flavour created by artists and savoured by *rasika*s or the discerning viewers. *Rasa* is the quintessential essence produced by a work of art. Long before Bharata, the concept of *rasa* had been mentioned in the *Rig Veda*: 'Bharata himself mentions this fact that many holy beings and great scholars before him have contemplated on the enormity of *Rasa* theory—*Ete Hrishtou Rasa Prokta Druhinen Mahatmanah*' [Translation].[1]

In the *Rig Veda*, in the context of *rasa*, Rishi Agastya contemplates an omnipresent yet intangible essence—something that is present in everything, yet

---

[1] Ganapatichandra Gupta, *Sahityik Nibandh* (Allahabad: Lokbharti Prakashan, 1990), p. 73.

defies explanation. He uses the analogy of fragrance emanating from a flower, made of matter, yet, the existence of fragrance itself is inexplicable:

> Rasa is bestowed not made. Arguably the most important term in Indian art theory, rasa lays claim to several definitions. In its most obvious sense, rasa refers to the sap, juice of plants or extract. More composite connotations include the non-material essence of something or the 'best or finest part of it', like perfume which comes from matter but which is not so easy to describe or comprehend. Rasa also denotes taste and flavour, relating to consuming or handling either the physical object or taking in its non-physical properties that yield pleasure.[2]

Ayurveda, the ancient Indian holistic medicine system, also mentions *rasa*. In Ayurveda, *rasa* is the colourless fluid extracted from the digestive process. In *Rasayanshastra*, an ancient treatise on the art of chemistry, *rasa* is the study or the process through which different metals and substances are combined with herbs to treat ailments. *Rasa* here can be equated with the ancient Mediterranean and Western European art of alchemy, the mysterious process of transformation of matter such as lead transmuting into gold. The theory of alchemy was also applied to the human psyche, where the alteration in one's consciousness led from a mundane existence to a spiritual awakening. *Rasa* in the medical arena was defined as *raso vai saha*, meaning *rasa* in itself is divinity. In Indian aesthetics and Bharata's *Natyashastra*, *rasa* represents the mental and emotional state evoked by a work of art, which the audience savours. Therefore, in dance, *rasa* is an aesthetic experience of an emotion which the dancer induces in a *rasika*. Artists strive for creating *rasa* in their art, so that a connoisseur can relate to their artistic emotions by intuitively sensing the effect of that *rasa*, which in turn gives the feeling of ananda or absolute bliss to *rasika*s. Ananda is the main purpose of *rasa*.

The *patra* or the actor is an agent of *rasa*. In Sanskrit, the word *patra* also means 'container'. When used in the context of dramatic performance, *patra* implies that an actor is a container of delight.

Ancient scholars believed that *rasa* represented both the psychological and spiritual principles. They have assigned each *rasa* a corresponding deity, colour, and inner state of consciousness, namely *bhuta*, *guna*, *dosha*, *kosha*, and *siddhi*.

---

[2] 'Navrasa: An Embodiment of Indian Art', IHC Visual Arts Gallery, http://archive.is/XZ0hY (accessed on 19 April 2018).

This attempt to describe the emotional experiences in such a detailed way is a reflection of how the ancient Indian aestheticians perceived arts as a wholesome endeavour in harmony with the universal laws. Brief explanations of *bhuta*, *guna*, *dosha*, *kosha*, and *siddhi* will be useful in understanding the nature of emotions.

THE INNER STATES OF CONSCIOUSNESS

The inner states of consciousness, described in ancient Indian scriptures, constitute the fundamentals of human psyche, which correspond to the universal consciousness.

The *panch bhutas*, or five elements of nature, are *agni* (fire), *vayu* (air), *jal* (water), *prithvi* (earth), and *aakash* (ether). Each element corresponds to both cosmic principles and physical attributes. Fire corresponds to transformation, air to movement, water to the flow of life, earth to stability and structure, and ether to expansion. In the physical sense, fire relates to the metabolic system of the body; air relates to the nervous system and all the cell and tissue functions; water is linked to blood, plasma, and chemical energies of the body; earth is associated with bones, muscles, and skin; and ether is considered the root cause of all other elements and is associated with energy.

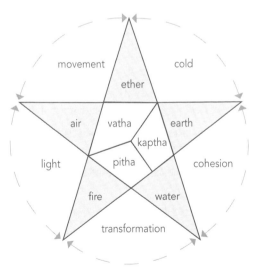

The three humours in Ayurveda and the five great elements that they are composed of. The colours used are arbitrary.

According to Indian philosophy, the human body is composed of these five elements, and after death, it yet again dissolves into these five elements. The ancient Indian scriptures on medicine state that these five elements are the building blocks of the entire cosmos. The five *bhutas* sustain life when they are in balance and harmony. An imbalance of any of these elements in body manifests as psychological disturbances.

Gunas are the fundamental operating tendencies of prakriti or universal nature. The three main *guna*s are *sattva, rajas,* and *tamas. Sattva guna* is the mode of pureness. The ultimate goal of our mind is to attain the state of *sattva,* so that it can stay in harmony with nature. *Sattva* is the quality of intelligence and integrity and promotes balance and stability. Light and radiant in nature, *sattva* possesses an upward motion of the body, mind, and soul. *Rajas guna* is the mode of change, energy, and activity. At an internal level, it provides stimulation and indulgence, but its external motion can disturb the existing equilibrium. *Tamas guna* is dark and heavy in nature. Its qualities are lethargy, selfishness, and darkness. Its downward motion causes ignorance, insensitivity, and delusion. *Tamas* is materialistic in nature and is activated by the subconscious mind.

*Dosha*s are the physiological energies that affect both the mental and physical processes. There are three *dosha*s—*vata, pitta, and kapha*—and they can be equated with the three *guna*s. *Dosha*s represent different types of mind-body relationships, and they express energies unique to themselves that comprise different physical, mental, and emotional qualities. Balanced *dosha*s have a positive impact on body and mind, whereas imbalanced *dosha*s cause a negative impact.

Vata dosha presides over all other *dosha*s; therefore, it can exhibit the qualities of all *guna*s. The qualities of *vata* are dry, subtle, and movable. It puts in order the functions of the nervous system and relates to the space and air elements. *Pitta dosha* is the energy related to digestion and metabolism. *Pitta dosha's* quality is heat and it is equated with *rajas guna*; it is related to the element of fire. The qualities of *pitta* are hot, oily, and moving. *Kapha dosha* relates to the element of earth. It is the energy connected with the body's fluid and lubrication properties. The qualities of *kapha* are cold, moist, sticky, and inert.

*Siddhi*s are the psychic powers acquired through spiritual practices. The word *siddhi* in Sanskrit means both perfection and accomplishment. Many scholars have regarded art as a spiritual practice and believe that the purpose of Indian arts is the communion of humankind with the Divine. Therefore, some have associated *siddhi*s with *rasa*s. However, correlating *rasa*s with *siddhi*s does not imply that the attainment of *rasa*s bestows *siddhi*s on an artist or the *rasika*. While engaging in a profound artistic experience, the mental states of the artist and the audience go through a process of transformation, wherein their experiences temporarily go beyond the normal range of perceptions. In that altered state of perception, an elevation in awareness takes place and the effect of different *rasa*s approaches the characteristics of *siddhi*s. In Indian scriptures, there is a mention of *ashta-siddhi* or eight *siddhi*s. These *siddhi*s are *anima, mahima, laghima,* *garima, prapti, prakamya, isitva,* and *vasitva.* They correspond to different psychic abilities, such as the ability to reduce the size of the body even to the size of an atom or expanding one's body to infinite size, becoming weightless or becoming infinitely heavy, unrestricted access to any place, realization of desires, power to create and control things, and subjugation of anything or everything. It is understandable why some have correlated *siddhi*s with *rasa*s. With the perfection of *rasa* transmission, a transformation in perception takes place and the dominant, emotional theme of a work of art can evoke the kind of imagination in an artist or a spectator that comes close to the direct experience from the attainment of a particular *siddhi.*

In ancient India, the mystics and philosophers saw humans as multidimensional beings. *Kosha*s are the mystical sheaths of being that create a field of energy and become the connector between the body, mind, and soul. It is a framework through which one can navigate the path to the self. The physical body is the outer edge from where the journey begins and ultimately finds its destination, which is the self. There are five *kosha*s (sheaths) in which consciousness exists: *annamaya, pranamaya, manomaya, vijnanmaya,* and *anandmaya.*

Annamaya kosha is related to the physical body and is a sheath of matter. The word *anna* literally means the 'nutritious substance that sustains life'. It is a tool for the consciousness to expand itself and to work through the physical self.

The word *prana* in *pranamaya kosha* means 'moving life force'. Breath is one of *prana*'s manifestations. Breath supplies energy to the body and is vital for survival. The *prana* or the vital forces permeate every part of the body, including every cell, and keep it energized and healthy. The *annamaya kosha* is the gross body, which is supported by the subtle energy force of *pranamaya kosha.*

Manomaya kosha, the mental sheath, includes the aspects of the mind such as ego, thoughts, and feelings, along with the five sensory organs. It is through the *manomaya kosha* that the world is perceived and information is processed.

Vijnanmaya kosha, the wisdom and knowledge sheath, provides discriminating powers along with willpower and motivation. It moves from the exoteric to esoteric concepts and lies deeper within.

As the name suggests, the *anandmaya kosha* is the sheath of bliss that lies at the core of all other surrounding sheaths. In ancient Indian scriptures, this sheath is also known as the 'causal body', which is the reservoir of all consciousness and intrinsic qualities accumulated from all previous lifetimes. The vibration of this sheath is the highest, and it facilitates the unfolding of consciousness and pure awareness. This is where the pure being is in its blissful state beyond all dualities. The realization of the self happens through *anandmaya kosha*, which is untouched by any outside forces and experiences a never-changing truth.

Humans shift through different *kosha*s throughout their existence, and thereby experience the physical, mental, emotional, psychological, and spiritual aspects of being. The physiological and psychological functions of *kosha*s do have a certain relationship with the *rasa*s that are experienced through arts, since *rasa*s have psychological and spiritual effects. Although each *rasa* has an assigned *kosha*, the ultimate goal of *rasa* is related to the *anandmaya kosha*, the sheath of bliss.

THE COMPONENTS OF *RASA*

The components of *rasa* determine how the *rasa* is created. *Rasa*s are created by complementary emotions called *bhava*s or internal intent and sentiment. Bharata Muni's reflection on *bhava*s confirms that he was not only a remarkable aesthetician and a great scholar of theatrical arts, but he also proficiently comprehended human psychology. He examined the human psyche in depth and observed different nuances of human emotions and sentiments. Bharata regarded the human psyche as *bhava-jagat* or the universe of sentiments. He also purported that *bhava* and *rasa* are reciprocally dependent. Bharata attributes the law of causality to *bhava* and concludes that *bhava* is the mental state that brings about an awareness of it in the consciousness of those experiencing it.

> Emotion, in Bharata's language, is bhâva (BHAH-vuh), which is the thing that Bharata associates with food and flavor. In Bharata's analogy, a person tastes the flavors of food, enjoys those flavors, and then feels a certain kind of pleasure. An audience member experiences—or tastes—the activity on the stage, including words, gestures, and also feelings or emotions, as though these things were the flavors of food. The audience member then feels pleasure in his or her experience. This last feeling of pleasure is what Bharata calls rasa.[3]

---

[3] David Mason, 'Introduction to Theatre in India: Rasa', http://www.yavanika.org/ theatreinindia/?page_id=446 (accessed on 13 April 2018).

According to *Natyashastra*, all *bhava*s fall into three categories: *sthayi, sanchari,* and *sattvika.*

Sthayi bhava is the permanent or pre-established state of mind in the human psyche. Humans have a certain inherent and instinctive nature, which comprises of fundamental and invariable sentiments and emotions. *Sthayi bhava* has staying power. It develops gradually and becomes enduring. Bharata lists the eight *sthayi bhava*s that inspire the eight *rasa*s:

> *Ratirhaashcha sokashcha krodhotsaahou bhayam tatha.*
> *Jugupsa vismayashreyati sthayibhavah prakirtita.*[4]

According to this verse, the *sthayi bhava*s are: *rati* (love), *haas* (mirth), *shoka* (sorrow), *krodha* (anger), *utsaha* (energy), *bhaya* (terror), *jugupsa* (disgust), and *vismaya* (astonishment). The resultant of these mental states are the eight *rasa*s: *shringar* (erotic), *hasya* (comic), *karuna* (pathetic), *raudra* (furious), *veera* (heroic), *bhayanaka* (terrible), *bibhatsa* (repulsive), and *adbhuta* (marvellous).

*Sanchari bhava*s are fleeting emotions, considered transient in nature, yet act as reinforcements of the permanent states. They appear like lightning and dissipate quickly. They reinforce the permanent states of human nature. They are a strong agitation of the feelings activated by experiencing love, fear, and other emotions, and are accompanied by certain physiological changes such as rapid heartbeat or trembling. There are thirty-three *sanchari bhava*s: *nirveda* (despondency), *glani* (despair), *sanka* (misgiving), *asuya* (envy), *mada* (intoxication), *shrama* (exhaustion), *alasya* (languor), *dainya* (helplessness), *chinta* (worry), *moha* (fervour), *smriti* (remembrance), *dhrti* (audacity), *vrida* (disgrace), *chapalata* (changeability), *harsha* (joy), *aavega* (agitation), *jadata* (shock), *garva* (conceit), *vishada* (anguish), *autsukya* (curiosity), *nidra* (sleep), *apasmara* (contortion), *supta* (reverie), *vibodha* (awakening), *aamarsha* (intolerance), *avahittha* (suppression), *ugrata* (fierceness), *mati* (knowledge), *vyaadhi* (ailment), *unmaad* (insanity), *marana* (bereavement), *trasa* (anxiety), and *vitarka* (disbelief).

The physical expression of an emotion is the *sattvika bhava. Sattvika bhava*s are a responsive manifestation of *sanchari* and *vyabhichari bhava*s:

---

[4] Babu Lal Shukla Sastri, *Natyashastra of Bharat Muni*, Part 1 (Varanasi: Chaukhambha Sanskrit Sansthan, 2009), p. 221.

Stambhah swedotha romancha swarbhedoth vepathuh
Vaivarnyamashru-pralaya ityashto Sattvikah smritah.[5]
[Translation: The eight *sattvika bhavas* are: *stambha* (petrification), *sveda* (perspiration), *romancha* (horripilation), *svarabheda* (change in voice), *vepathu* (trembling), *vaivarnya* (change in facial complexion), *ashru* (teary eyes), and *pralaya* (fainting).]

Bharata also categorized emotions based on their strongly motivating quality, their reaction to certain events or objects, the way they motivate certain kinds of behaviours, their consequences, and their complementary states. These emotions are called *vibhava*, *anubhava*, and *vyabhichari bhavas*. According to Bharata, a *rasa* is created when *vibhava*, *anubhava*, and *sanchari bhavas* are integrated.

Vibhavas are the catalysts and the motivating forces that give rise to emotions. They are *karanas* or determinants for a specific experience to be activated. *Vibhavas* fall into two categories: the *alamban vibhava* and the *uddipan vibhava*. The person or object that activates an emotion is called *alamban vibhava*. *Alamban vibhava* is directly accountable for the instigation of an emotion. For example, coming face to face with a tiger in a dense forest can activate the emotion of fear in a person. In this case, the tiger is the *alamban vibhava*. The external situation that escalates an emotional experience after an *alamban* is placed there is *uddipan vibhava*. *Uddipan* is an accessory to *alamban*. In this example, the dense forest is *uddipan*. Being in proximity with a tiger in a dark and thick forest can be terrifying. However, a caged tiger in a zoo does not really activate the emotion of fear. Therefore, a compatible and congenial outer situation is important for the intensification of an emotion. The person who experiences the rise of an emotion through *alamban* and *uddipan* is called the *ashraya*. The person who comes in proximity of the tiger in the dense forest is an *ashraya*.

Anubhava is an effect or a consequence. It is an expression through which the outcome of *vibhavas* becomes discernible. In the previous example of the tiger, the rapid heartbeats, sweating, and trembling of the person looking at the tiger are *anubhavas*.

A question arises regarding the difference between *anubhavas* and *sattvika bhavas*. Both *anubhavas* and *sattvika bhavas* are the physical reactions of a certain

---

[5] Sastri, *Natyashastra of Bharat Muni*, Part 1, p. 223.

emotion. However, the *sattvika bhava* is usually perceived when an emotional experience is at its height, extremely intensified. *Anubhava*s result from a particular triggering situation or a *vibhava* and are of only one kind. *Sattvika bhava*s can take place in different situations. For example, the *sattvika bhava ashru*, or teary eyes, can occur both when one is grief-stricken or tremendously blissful.

*Vyabhichari bhava*s, or surging emotions, are complementary and reciprocal emotional states, which are also transient in nature. They are influenced by the central emotional experience and arise as a corresponding disposition. In the earlier example of the tiger, the person goes through a state of panic on spotting the tiger. Experiencing panic is a *vyabhichari bhava*, which complements the emotion of fear. Bharata Muni has identified thirty-three *vyabhichari bhava*s: *nirveda* (indifference), *glani* (mental or physical fatigue), *sanka* (apprehension), *asuya* (insecurity), *mada* (intoxication), *srama* (exhaustion), *alasya* (lassitude), *dainya* (pity), *chinta* (anxiety), *moho* (delusion), *smrti* (recollection), *dhrti* (resoluteness), *vrida* (shame), *capalata* (impulsiveness), *harsa* (delight), *avega* (excitement), *jadata* (daze), *garva* (arrogance), *visada* (depression), *autsuka* (longing), *nidra* (sleep), *apasmara* (epilepsy), *supta* (dreaming), *vibodha* (awakening), *amarsa* (restrained anger), *avahittha* (deception), *ugrata* (ferocity), *mati* (analysis), *vyadhi* (sickness), *unmada* (temporary insanity), *marana* (death), *trasa* (panic), and *vitarka* (argumentativeness).

When the *sthayi bhava*s (dominant states) collaborate with other *bhava*s, *rasa* is produced.

NAV-RASA: THE NINE *RASA*S

Bharata indicated eight different kinds of *rasa*s, which, with the support of *bhava*s, create clear impressions on the minds of *rasika*s:

> *Shringarhasyakaruna Raudraveerbhayanakah,*
> *Bibhatsaadbhutsangyau chetyashtau natye rasah smritah.*[6]

Bharata's eight *rasa*s are *shringar* (erotic), *hasya* (humorous), *karuna* (pathetic), *raudra* (terrible), *veera* (heroic), *bhayanaka* (fearful), *vibhatsa* (odious), and

---
[6] Ibid., p. 218.

adbhuta (wonderous). The ninth *rasa*, the *shanta rasa* (peace), was added later by other classical aestheticians.

Shringar is also known as *rasa-raja* or the king of *rasa*s. It is the most revered *rasa* in Indian arts. According to Bharata, whatever is pure, sacred, and placid can be compared to *shringar rasa*. The word *shringar* derives from the root word *shringa* or 'zenith'. Therefore, the love that is the basis of *shringar rasa* is the state where human emotions exalt and reach their highest peak. *Shringar* means both love and adornment. This *rasa* elevates the mind, adorns it with beauty, and evokes the feeling of love. It is portrayed with exquisite imageries, immense passion, and heightened sensitivity in all Indian arts. *Kama* forms the foundation for *shringar rasa*. *Kama* refers to desire, passion, and the pleasures of life. The Hindu tradition defines four goals of life—*dharma* (virtuous life), *artha* (materially prosperous life), *kama* (fulfilment of desires), and *moksha* (the state of liberation). When *kama* is fulfilled without sacrificing *dharma* or *artha*, it is considered holistic and healthy. In ancient Indian literature, Kama Deva, the God of Love, is personified as a strikingly attractive god who appears with His sensual and beautiful consort Rati. The name Rati means 'to delight in'. Kama Deva's arrow, which He uses to pierce hearts, is dipped into the nectar of five flowers—red lotus for passion, *ashoka* flower for the state of emotional intoxication, jasmine for intense longing, blue lotus for the feeling of immobilization when the desired object is not achieved, and mango blossoms for the anguish created from the absence of the desired object. As Madana, Kama intoxicates the hearts with love; as Manmatha, He agitates the mind; as Kushumesu, He uses his arrow of flowers; and, as Pradyumna, He conquers all. The *shringar rasa* relies on *kama* or desire, and this desire for love and beauty is the central of the realm of the human heart.

> The Vedas recognize '*Kama*' that is 'desire' to be the first seed of the mind and hence it becomes the mind's powerful driving force. A realm of 'ananda', a charmed space, a sensuous journey, an aesthetic experience, an exalted state of '*madhurya*'—Shringar is an amalgam of all this. The beautiful moments enjoyed by lovers—the '*nayaka*' and '*nayaki*', their anguish, ecstasy, longing, jealousy, romantic dalliances, love-sports—romantic poetry resonates with all of these. 'Shringar' denotes not the shallow, baser excitement but is an exalted, aesthetic emotion resulting in a higher state of 'ananda' or bliss.[7]

[7] Ambika Ananth, 'Shringara—The Raja Rasa', issue 18 (March–April 2018), http://www.museindia.com/Home/AuthorContentDataView, *Muse India* (accessed on 13 April 2018).

There are two facets of *shringar rasa*: *samyoga* and *viyoga*. *Samyoga shringar* depicts meeting, togetherness, or union. *Viyoga shringar* represents separation. Both union and separation are two aspects of love. The separation of *shringar rasa* is light and ethereal in nature. *Shringar rasa* is portrayed beautifully in Kathak through the love stories of Radha and Krishna. Radha-Krishna stories and their eternal, ageless love have shaped Kathak, and *shringar rasa* is the central theme of Kathak dance form.

> *Sthayi bhava* or dominant emotion: *Rati* (love)
> Presiding deity: Vishnu in His Kama form
> Colour: Blue
> Dominant element: Water
> Dominant *dosha*: *Kapha*
> Dominant *guna*: *Rajas*
> Dominant *kosha*: *Manomaya kosha* (mind)
> Dominant *siddhi*: *Prapti* (attainment)

Hasya rasa expresses humour either by portraying a joyful or comic character or by amusing the audience by inducing laughter. The role of *vidushaka*s in Sanskrit drama was to amuse the audience with witty dialogues and actions, which in turn produced *hasya rasa*. *Vidushaka*s are the direct vehicle to express *hasya rasa*. Sometimes, the *hasya rasa* is evoked in an indirect manner through an event or a character capable of suggesting joy, mirth, laughter, and amusement: 'Humor—the second significant meaning of Hasya—is, however, linked to particular situations. The favorite subject of Humor is *maya*, the illusionary aspect of the universe, the eternal play of the opposites that is never the ultimate truth but merely a reflection of truth.'[8]

The contradictions and oppositions create paradoxes. At a deeper level, the paradoxes are ironic and unexpected, where the glimpse of truth can be seen. Going beyond these dualities and witnessing the whole truth carries the power of pure joy or *hasya*. Therefore, pure *hasya* comes from deep within. Subtle changes in the nature of laughter change the context and meanings. Six different kinds of laughter are analysed in *hasya rasa*. *Smita* or a soft smile, *hasita* or gentle laughter, *vihasita*

---

[8] Peter Marchand, *The Yoga of the Nine Emotions: The Tantric Practice of Rasa Sadhana* (Vermont, US: Destiny Books, 2006), p. 48.

or exposed laughter, *upahasita* or scornful laughter, *apahasita* or offensive laughter, and *atihasita* or rowdy laughter. *Hasya rasa* can be depicted as *atma-samuththa* or *para-samuththa*. *Atma-samuththa* is personal in nature, where the actor expresses amusement to oneself, whereas *para-samuththa* is shared and the actor makes others laugh. *Hasya rasa* is an important *rasa* used in Indian dance and dramas.

Sthayi bhava or dominant emotion: *Haas* (mirth)
Presiding deity: Pramatha
Colour: White
Dominant element: Fire
Dominant *dosha*: *Pitta*
Dominant *guna*: *Rajas*
Dominant *kosha*: *Manomaya kosha* (mind)
Dominant *siddhi*: *Vashitva* (subjugation of anything and everything)

Raudra rasa is expressed through fury and rage, which are at the high end of the emotional continuum. It is shown as aggression towards something or someone. In its milder form, *raudra rasa* manifests as anger, a more primary and natural emotional response. Wrath, anger, outrage, impudence, and fury are all different forms of *raudra rasa*. Violence and aggression are the main characteristics of *raudra rasa*. *Raudra rasa* is based on a Rigvedic deity Lord Rudra, whose name is literally translated as 'the howler'. Lord Rudra is the lord of storm and wind. In the *Rig Veda*, He is called the mightiest of the mighty. According to the scriptures, Lord Shiva Himself appeared as Rudra. Sometimes, the fury of nature, destructive weather patterns, and death are associated with Rudra. To evoke *raudra rasa*, the dancers and actors engage the audience with violent actions and behaviours. These actions differ depending on whether a wicked character or a virtuous character is being shown under the influence of *raudra rasa*. *Raudra rasa* in dance is always shown in combative scenes or the settings where conflicts or confrontations are depicted. Gnarling, scornful faces, red eyes, smacking hands, burning cheeks, eyebrow actions, hitting the palm with the fist, and sweating profusely are some of the *anubhava*s through which actors and dancers portray *raudra rasa*.

Sthayi bhava or dominant emotion: *Krodha* (anger)
Presiding deity: Rudra
Dominant element: Fire

Dominant *dosha*: *Pitta*
Dominant *guna*: *Rajas*
Dominant *kosha*: *Vijnanmayi* (ego)
Dominant *siddhi*: *Bhukti* (elevated material happiness)

Veera rasa is expressed through heroic actions and behaviours, where the characters are depicted as brave, confident, courageous, and fearless. These characters display willpower and valour in the face of threat and adversity. They even rise above the point of limitations and display moral and ethical courage. The characters portraying *veera rasa* are powerful and influential. Physical as well as mental capacities are important for the characters who are the agents of depicting *veera rasa*. Lord Rama, the central character of the epic poem *Ramayana*, is considered the model character for this *rasa*. His heroic stories, both in terms of physical prowess and mental and moral fortitude, are revered in all Indian art forms. The heroic characters are beneficent, benevolent, and free of obsessions or delusions. Greater good for all is the maxim for their enthusiastic, motivated, and brave actions. In mythological stories, the male characters of *veera rasa* also become the protagonists of *shringar rasa*. The hero's basic qualities are desirable for the characters of love stories. This is why the *veera rasa* and *shringar rasa* also become the root *rasa*s, and these root *rasa*s are the major emotions of most of Indian folklore, mythology, and love stories.

Sthayi bhava or dominant emotion: *Krodha* (anger)
Presiding deity: Indra (Ruler of Heaven, and god of lightning, thunder, and rain)
Dominant element: Water
Dominant *dosha*: *Kapha*
Dominant *guna*: *Rajas*
Dominant *kosha*: *Vijnanmayi* (ego)
Dominant *siddhi*: *Ishatattava* (power to rule)

Bhayanaka rasa is expressed through the actions and behaviours that portray fear. *Bhaya* or fear is a negative and unpleasant emotion that occurs in response to some perception of danger, a dreadful event, or a traumatic situation. Sometimes, *bhaya* is more future-oriented and is stimulated by some kind of perceived threat. The changes that occur in the brain and body because of extreme fear such as horror or terror produce the most immobilizing result in which the person is unable to act. There are many different kinds of fear, such as fear of one's own death, fear of the death of others, fear of the unknown, fear over one's well-being and safety, and fear of an authority figure. Yamaraja is the key deity associated with this *rasa*. Yamaraja, also known as Yama, is described as the God of Death in Vedic mythology. He is believed to be the first mortal who faced death. Therefore, He is considered the Ruler of the Departed. According to post-Vedic scriptures, He is also the Lord of Dharma or the principle of cosmic order.

Bhayanaka rasa is portrayed through different facial and body expressions, such as quivering, goosebumps, pale face, agitation, palpitations, paralysed stance, throbbing heart, dry mouth, nervous and anxious face, and trembling voice.

> *Sthayi bhava* or dominant emotion: *Bhaya* (terror)
> Presiding deity: Yama
> Colour: Black
> Dominant element: Air
> Dominant *dosha*: *Vata*
> Dominant *guna*: *Tamas*
> Dominant *kosha*: *Manomaya* (mind)
> Dominant *siddhi*: *Iccha* (Influence)

Karuna rasa is depicted through the behaviours and actions that represent pathos, sorrow, and sympathetic pity. This *rasa* portrays despair, melancholy, and emptiness. Suffering is the main origin of *karuna*. *Karuna* is a natural response to some kind of loss that brings about suffering in the human heart. *Karuna* also corresponds to the concern and empathy for the sufferings of others. *Karuna* as compassion motivates our desire to alleviate the pain of a person who is suffering. Varuna, one of the oldest Vedic deities, is the presiding deity of *karuna rasa*. As the god of celestial oceans and all water forms, Varuna is also considered the Lord of Moral Laws. He is compassionate and possesses a forgiving disposition towards those who contravene these moral laws. Suffering is emotional in nature. However, compassion is more rational in nature. Compassion is based on the notions of fairness, integrity, and morality. *Karuna rasa* is produced through different actions and behaviours, such as weeping and lamenting, dry mouth, limp body, loss of memory, comforting someone, or loss of speech.

Sthayi bhava or dominant emotion: *Karuna* (pathos)
Presiding deity: Varuna
Colour: Gray
Dominant element: Water
Dominant *dosha*: *Kapha*
Dominant *guna*: *Rajas*
Dominant *kosha*: *Vijnanmayi* (ego)
Dominant *siddhi*: *Mahima* (heaviness)

Bibhatsa rasa signifies disgust, aversion, and repugnance. This emotion is evoked by anyone and anything that is a source of something repulsive and offensive. The person experiencing this emotion feels revolted by highly repellent object or situation. Taste and smell senses are most readily stimulated by disgusting objects. Seeing something repulsive and hearing and touching something unpleasant also evokes *bibhatsa rasa*. Lord Shiva as Mahakala is the principal deity of *bibhatsa rasa*. He is the god who balances all contradictions and oppositions. In some scriptures, He is depicted in a form usually considered *bibhatsa*. His naked body is smeared with the ashes of *shamashan* or the cremation ground. *Shamashan* represents the end of the physical life cycle. Shiva's ash-smeared body symbolizes death and regeneration. *Bibhatsa rasa* is portrayed through different bodily and facial gestures, such as compressing the body inwards, spitting, narrowing the eyes, and clenching the nose.

Sthayi bhava or dominant emotion: *Bibhatsa* (disgust)
Presiding deity: Lord Shiva as Mahakala
Colour: Gray
Dominant element: Water
Dominant *dosha*: *Kapha*
Dominant *guna*: *Tamas*
Dominant *kosha*: *Manomaya* (mind)
Dominant *siddhi*: *Prakrama* (ability to assume any form)

Adbhuta rasa connotes the feelings of wonder, surprise, curiosity, and awe. These feelings of overpowering reverence and admiration are produced by something extremely influential, admirable, sublime, magical, or splendid. Sometimes, a sense of fear is also embedded in the feeling of wonderment. Anything divine and supernatural, something irresistibly beautiful, or simply something never witnessed or imagined before brings about the *adbhuta rasa. Adbhuta rasa* is always evoked by something unusual and beyond the mundane. The presiding deity of *adbhuta rasa* is Brahma. Brahma is the creator of the universe and all beings. He is also regarded as the Lord of Dharma or the cosmic order and laws. The creation of the four Vedas is attributed to Brahma. *Adbhuta rasa* is portrayed through actions and behaviours such as wide eyes, a bewildered face, tears, heaving a sigh, and words of praise.

> *Sthayi bhava* or dominant emotion: *Adbhuta* (wonder)
> Presiding deity: Brahma
> Colour: Gray
> Dominant element: Fire
> Dominant *dosha*: *Pitta*
> Dominant *guna*: *Rajas*
> Dominant *kosha*: *Manomaya* (mind)
> Dominant *siddhi*: *Laghima* (lightness)

Shanta rasa signifies the mental and emotional state of peace and tranquility. It is the harmonious state where there is freedom from any kind of trouble or disorder. *Shanta rasa* is characterized by the absence of fear, lack of violence, and freedom from conflicting feelings. *Shanta rasa* is being at peace in the face of disharmony, dissonance, and anxieties arising from fears. The feeling of *shanta* is a way of being. In the state of *shanta rasa*, one is free of all the stimulations caused by other emotions. The mind is completely still and calm. People who follow meditative paths strive all their lives to attain this clear and light state of mind. Therefore, many scholars argue that it should not be characterized as a *rasa*. Indeed, there is no mention of *shanta rasa* in *Natyashastra*. However, in all Indian dance forms, *shanta rasa* occupies a very important place. An enlightened character is often depicted through *shanta rasa*. Bhakti or devotion is an accessory of *shanta rasa*. Lord Vishnu, the Supreme God, who is omnipresent and omnipotent, is the presiding deity of *shanta rasa*. Along with Brahma and Shiva, Lord Vishnu forms the Trinity. There are three cosmic functions of creation: formation, preservation, and destruction. Lord Vishnu is the preserver or maintainer of the universe. In Indian scriptures, one of the ways He fulfils this responsibility is to reincarnate on earth whenever dharma or the principle of cosmic order is being threatened among people.

Sthayi bhava or dominant emotion: *Shanta* (peace)

Presiding deity: Vishnu

Colour: White

Dominant element: Air

Dominant *dosha*: *Vata*

Dominant *guna*: *Sattva*

Dominant *kosha: Anandmayi* (bliss)

Dominant *siddhi: Anima* (atomization)

Abhinavagupta made a reference of bhakti in his commentary of *Natyashastra* as an accessory sentiment of the *shanta rasa*. After the *shanta rasa* gained prominence and became established as an essential *rasa*, the need for branching out *bhakti rasa* from *shanta rasa* gained momentum among the artists and aestheticians. *Bhakti rasa* connotes the feelings of intense devotion and allegiance to the Supreme. There is no allusion to *bhakti rasa* in *Natyashastra*. However, with the inception of the bhakti period in the fourteenth century, many artists and scholars felt the need to include bhakti as one of the *rasa*s:

> The fusion of *rasa* theory and *bhakti* is widely attributed to Rupa Gosvami, a disciple of Caitanya, who is credited with two key texts examining emotional devotion—the *Bhaktirasamrtasindhu* ('River of the ImmorTala Nectar of the Experience of Devotion') and the *Ujjvalanilamani* ('The Effulgent Blazing Sapphire'). Emotional devotion begins with the 'ordinary' forms of love and desire felt by human beings, but the intention is to transform the ordinary into the sublime.[9]

On the path of bhakti, devotees go through three different stages: *vaidhi bhakti*, *raganuga bhakti*, and *ragatmika bhakti*. *Vaidhi bhakti* is preparation to embark on the journey of devotion. Under the guidance of a spiritual master, devotees carry out all the devotional and ritualistic instructions and apply them to purify their heart and mind. In *raganuga bhakti*, devotees passionately walk their journey. In this stage, the devotees do not follow the ritualistic practices. On the contrary, they are guided by their love for the Divine. Surrendering to

---

[9] Phil Hine, 'Rasa Theory', http://enfolding.org/wikis-4/tantra-wikiwikis-4tantra-wiki/tantra_essays/rasa-theory/ (accessed on 13 April 2018).

the Divine is the main purpose of *raganuga bhakti*. This juncture of the journey intersects five different mental and emotional states known as *rati*s. In *shanta rati*, the state of neutrality is achieved, where the devotees merely contemplate on the Divine. The feeling of servitude is achieved through *prita rati*, where the devotees engage themselves in serving God in various ways. *Vatsalya rati* is an affectionate love for God, where the devotees take care of God as a mother takes care of her child. In *preyo rati*, the feeling for the Divine takes the form of companionship and the devotee feels more intimate with the Divine. In *madhurya rati*, God becomes the beloved. *Ragatmika bhakti* is the final and the perfect stage of devotion, where the devotee experiences cosmic love for all beings. It is the stage of pure faith.

The *nav-rasa*s are the essence of all human emotions. Arts imitate life; therefore, their purpose is to simulate human emotions in a way that they touch the hearts of sympathetic *rasika*s:

> 'Na hi rasadrite kaschidarthah pravartate', Bharata Muni very emphatically states in the *Rasadhyaya* of *Natyashastra* that 'no meaningful idea is conveyed if the '*Rasa*' is not evoked.' Bharata says that Natya is the imitation of life (lokanukruti) wherein the various human emotions have to be dramatically glorified (bhavanukirtanam) so that the spectator is able to flavor the portrayed pleasure and pain (lokasya sukhaduhkha) as Natyarasa. This Rasa experience will entertain and enlighten the spectator who hence becomes the 'Rasika'.[10]

Lord Shiva's picturesque representation as the Lord of the Universe also describes Him as the source of *nav-rasa*s. *Nav-rasa*s are the expressions of Lord Shiva Himself. Lord Shiva's consort Parvati represents *shringar rasa*. The crescent moon on Shiva's forehead depicts *adbhuta rasa*. Shiva's blue throat symbolizes *karuna rasa* when He swallowed poison to save the world. The cobras intertwined with His body represent *bhayanaka rasa*. His body smeared with ashes from the cremation ground suggests *bibhatsa rasa*. Lord Shiva as a great destroyer represents *raudra rasa*. As the lord of all devas or demigods, Shiva becomes the symbol of *veera rasa*.

---

[10] Jayashree Rajagopal, 'Rasa Theory with Reference to Bharata's *Natyasastra*', http://www.shadjamadhyam.com/rasa_theory_with_reference_to_bharatas_natyashastra (accessed on 13 April 2018).

Shiva's *gana* army represents *hasya rasa*. And, in His deep meditative state, Shiva becomes the symbol of *shanta rasa*.

SADHARANIKARAN

The word *sadharanikaran* takes its root from *sadharan*, the Sanskrit term for generalization or universalization. *Sadharanikaran* in *Natyashastra* theorizes the idea of universalization of an emotion and how it becomes the channel of widespread appeal. The actors and dancers become the couriers of a particular emotion and universalize that emotion by pulling the audiences in the sphere of that emotion. Therefore, that particular emotion is experienced both by the actor and the spectators. The transmission of an emotion from actor to audience is the process of *sadharanikaran*. The purpose of *sadharanikaran* is to achieve *sahridayata* or unity and harmony amongst everyone present at a performance. 'Bharata muni *[sic]* describes sadharanikaran as that point in the climax of a drama when the audience becomes one with the actor who lives an experience through his/her acting on stage and starts simultaneously reliving the same experience.'[11]

Bharata Muni's *sadharanikaran* is often compared with Aristotle's rhetoric, which is an ancient Greek dissertation on the art of persuasion. Aristotle categorized his rhetoric as ethos, pathos, and logos. Ethos corresponds to the ethical appeal, where the readers get convinced by the disposition and credibility of the author or the speaker. Readers take the author's reputation into account, which in turn influences their way of thinking and feeling. Pathos appeals to the readers' emotions. The readers relate to the writer's thoughts and feelings, which affect their own emotions and imaginations, which in turn persuade the readers by pulling them emotionally to the subject matter. In logos, appeal is created through reasoning, where facts, arguments, logic, and the effectiveness of evidence befit the internal reliability of the message.

In Aristotle's rhetoric or communication model, persuasion is the central theme. The reader or the listener becomes merely the receiver and does not play any participatory role. In this model, the author becomes the figure of authority and strives to persuade. The author does not anticipate a response or

....

[11] Shiva Magar, 'Communication in Eastern and Western Perspectives', 16 December 2010, http://shivamagar.wordpress.com/2010/12/16/communication-in-eastern-and-western-perspectives/ (accessed on 13 April 2018).

feedback from the reader or the listener. However, in Bharata's *sadharanikaran* or communication model, both the audience and the actor participate actively. *Sadharanikaran* propagates not only the influence and authority of the actor, but its focal point is the convergence of the audience and actor, together creating and experiencing *sahridayata*, achieving the corresponding feelings and emotions.

VIEWS OF SCHOLARS OTHER THAN BHARATA

Many other arts scholars and practitioners who came after Bharata Muni also devoted themselves to profound deliberation on the *rasa* theory. The ninth *rasa*, the *shanta rasa*, was later added by these classical aestheticians. These eminent, ancient aestheticians had a very intellectual view towards arts. Bhatta Lollata perceived art as an imitation of reality, whereas Sri Sankuka perceived art as an allusion where things cannot be imitated, only inferred. Sri Sankuka's example of *Chitaraturaganyaya*, an analogy of an illustrated horse, is famous in this regard. He asserted that when viewers see a painting of a horse, they do not perceive it as an actual horse, but as a representation of a horse. This identification is the reason behind the aesthetic pleasure attained through the painting. Tauta Bhatta contradicted both Bhatta Lollata and Sri Sankuka, stressing that the nature of *rasa* is pleasure, and the aesthetic experience of art depends directly on the imagination of an aesthete. Actors put themselves in place of the characters that they are portraying; therefore, their feelings are just an assumption of how they would feel if they were that character. It is the spectators who, with their imaginations, identify with that character.

Abhinavagupta made an important contribution to the theory of *rasa*. He felt that the theory of aesthetics proposed by the scholars who preceded him were significant, but they all had certain limitations. He believed that the purpose of art is not only to evoke feelings. Art should also contain the suggestive power to produce various meanings. Accordingly, art encompasses in itself the literal meaning (*abhida*), symbolical meaning (*lakshana*), and the suggested meaning (*vyanjana*). Therefore, the purpose of *rasa* is to stir both the senses and the imagination of an aesthete. Herein lies the difference between the mundane and the aesthetical experience. In this theory, the spectator becomes an active participant and gets transported to the world of imagination while witnessing art. The aesthetic experience transcends the time-space notion, and the aesthete experiences something beyond this world, almost a feeling of universality, which Abhinavagupta called *alaukikatva*. During the experience of *alaukikatva*, the soul is no longer bound by the body and an aesthete's experience becomes very different from the mundane, especially in terms of the response that it induces, since that particular response creates a transformation of the aesthete's emotions into purely transcendental pleasure:

> According to him [Abhinavagupta] the pleasure one derives out of a real work of art is no less than divine pleasure. As one has to constantly struggle and detach oneself to reach the Almighty similarly a true connoisseur of arts has to learn to detach the work from its surroundings and happenings and view it independently, e.g. the feeling that might bring pain in real life is capable of causing pleasure in an art form. The great success of Greek tragedies can be attributed to the pleasure it aroused in the spectators and brought about the emotional Catharsis (purging out).[12]

Bharata's *rasa* theory developed into a well-established theory of aesthetics after different scholars during various times analysed and explored it further. To this day, *rasa* theory is considered one of the most important aspects of aesthetics in all art forms of India.

---

[12] Geetika Kaw Kher, 'A Glimpse into Abhinavagupta's Ideas on Aesthetics', http://shaivism.net/abhinavagupta/4.html (accessed on 13 April 2018).

Abhinaya

ABHINAYA IS NORMALLY DEFINED as an art of expression. However, it is much greater in its scope when viewed through the prism of dramatic arts. This word is derived from two Sanskrit root words—*abhi* and *ni*. The root word *abhi* means 'towards' and the suffix *ni* is to 'carry or guide'. Therefore, *abhinaya* leads the viewers towards the *rasa* or the essence of a performance. In the following verse, Bharata affirms that *abhinaya* is a vehicle through which a viewer experiences the poetic meaning and a particular emotion or sentiment associated with that meaning, which ultimately guides one towards bliss:

> Abhi-purvasya nin-dhatur-abhimukhyartha-nirnaye
> Yasbhaat Prayogam nayati tasmad-abhinayah smritah.[1]
> [Translation: The word abhinaya is a combination of two syllables—*abhi* and *ni*. It transports the audience towards the main purpose (experience of *rasa*).]

FOUR CATEGORIES OF *ABHINAYA*

Bharata also deliberates on the four categories of *abhinaya*: *angika* (*abhinaya* through bodily expressions), *vachik* (*abhinaya* through verbal expressions), *aharya* (*abhinaya* through costume and decor), and *sattvik* (*abhinaya* through mental state). In a dramatic representation, the four aspects are not independent of each other. Rather, they are interrelated and interdependent. Only the proficient

---

[1] Babu Lal Shukla Sastri, *Natyashastra of Bharat Muni*, Part 2 (Varanasi: Chaukhambha Sanskrit Sansthan, 2009), p. 4.

Pandit Rajendra Gangani

synthesis of all four aspects of *abhinaya* can lead the viewer towards a particular, intended sentiment.

Angika Abhinaya

In *angika abhinaya*, the meaning is communicated through the movements of the major and the minor limbs of the body—*ang*, *pratyang*, and *upang*.

There are two different approaches to convey *angika abhinaya*: *padarth abhinaya* and *vakyarth abhinaya*. In *padarth abhinaya*, the exact meaning of every word is acted; whereas in *vakyarth abhinaya*, the broad idea of a sentence, theme, or song is expressed. In Kathak dance, *vakyarth abhinaya* is expressed brilliantly, where a Kathak dancer expresses the general mood of a *thumri*. For example, in the lyric *ghir aayi badariya*, which literally translates to 'the sky is overcast', a Kathak dancer skilfully expresses the deeper meaning of the line by using the overcast sky as simile, metaphor, or analogy. The overcast sky can represent blue, dark Krishna, a distressed heart, or in any other way a dancer interprets it.

Bharata describes the *angika abhinaya* in detail, and includes every possible movement of body limbs, postures, and alignments expressed through *ang* (major limbs), *pratyang* (supporting limbs), and *upang* (minor limbs). There are six *ang*s or major limbs: *shira* (head), *hasta* (hands), *vaksha* (chest), *parshava* (hip), *kati* (sides), and *pada* (feet). When an *ang* moves, the *pratyang* and *upang* follow it. The movement of an *ang* is deliberately connected to the space on the stage. Bharata places more emphasis on the joints of the body than the muscles of the body:

Saswati Sen

The Indian understanding of the body was based on the *bhuta*s (elements) and their attributes. Anatomy placed emphasis on joints rather than muscles. A close analysis of the *Natyashastra* reveals the author's deep understanding of the function of joints and articulation of movements. He is keenly aware of weight and energy.[2]

Movements of *shira* (head) Bharata mentions thirteen different *shira* (head) movements in *Natyashastra*:

Akampita: The head is gradually raised and then slowly brought back to its normal position.

Kampita: Rapid movement of *akampita*. *Kampita* is basically a successive up and down movement of the head.

Dhuta: Head turning right or left in slow motion.

Vidhuta: Quick motion of *dhuta*.

Parivahita: Quick small shakes of the head.

Adhuta: Lifting the head once at an oblique angle.

Avadhuta: Pointing the head downward once.

Anchita: Arching the head downward to the side.

Nihanchita: The head is contracted to one side and, at the same time, both shoulders are raised slightly.

Paravritta: Turning of the head to either right or left to look at something rearward.

Utshipta: Head held high with an upward glance.

Adhogatam: Head tilting downward with eyes looking down.

Lolita: Circular movement of the head.

---

[2] Kapila Vatsyayan, *Bharata: The Natyasastra* (New Delhi: Sahitya Akademi, 1996), pp. 18–19.

Movements of *hasta* or *hasta* *mudra*s *Hasta mudra*s, the movements of hands, hold a significant place in Indian culture. In yoga and tantra, hand gestures relate to ritualistic and spiritual practices. In tantra, 108 hand gestures are used for various rituals. It is also believed that the mudras affect both the macrocosm and microcosm—the entire universe and the smaller structures contained within it. In yoga, there are twelve *hasta mudra*s used as psychic gestures for meditation. As

Uma Sharma

it is theorized in yoga, the *hasta mudra*s have energetic effects on the body and mind. This is why the symbolic application of *hasta mudra*s in Indian dance is so significant. The meaning of the dance is conveyed with suggestive hand gestures. While many hand gestures are used to convey important meanings in a dance performance, some are used for purely aesthetic appeal.

There are two types of hand gestures in Kathak dance: *asamyukta mudra* and *samyukta mudra*. Single-hand gestures are referred to as *asamyukta mudra*s, and the gestures created with the use of both hands are called the *samyukta mudra*s. Bharata describes twenty-four *asamyukta mudra*s. Later, in his book *Abhinaya Darpana*, Nandikeshvara added a few more mudras. All Indian classical dances use at least some of these twenty-four mudras. The *asamyukta* and *samyukta mudra*s are combined in various ways with the movements of the body and facial expressions to transform the context and meaning of a basic *hasta mudra*.

The names of twenty-four *asamyukta mudra*s, or one-hand gestures, mentioned in *Natyashastra* are: *pataka, tripataka, ardhapataka, kartarimukha, mayura, ardhchandra, arala, shukatunda, mushti, shikhara, kapittha, katakamukha, suchi, chandrakala, sarpashirsha, padmakosha, mirgshirsha, simhamukha, kangula, alpadma, chatura, bhramara, hamspaksha, samdansha, mukula, tamrachuda, trishula, ardhasuchi, vyagraha, palli,* and *kataka.* The names of the *samyukta mudra*s, both-hand gestures, are: *anjali, kapota, karkata, swastika, dola, pushpaputa, utsanga, shivalinga, kataka-vardhana, kartari-swastika, shakata, shankha, chakra,* *pasha, kilaka, samputa, matsya, kurma, varaha, garuda, nagabandha, khatava, bhairunda,* and *avahitta*.

Bharata also described the *hasta pracharas* (hand positions), *hasta rechakas* (arm movements combined with hand movements), and *hasta karanas* (ways to rotate the hands).

Movement of *vaksha* or chest Bharata has catalogued the following movements of the chest:

Sama: Chest held in upright position.

Abhugna: Caved-in or crouched chest, with the arms loosely held at the sides and the shoulders hunched down. *Abhugna* is used to convey negative emotions such as fear and sorrow.

Nirbhugna: Expansion of the chest. *Nirbhugna* is used to convey positive or uplifting emotions.

Prakampita: Shuddering of the chest. The *prakampita* chest movement is used to convey tense moments.

Udvahita: A raised and lifted chest.

Movements of *parshva* or sides There are five positions of sides mentioned in *Natyashastra*:

Nata: A slight twist of the side where the shoulder of that particular side is held slightly back and the hip on the same side appears arched.

Sammunnata: Simultaneously raising the side, hip, shoulder, and arm of one side of the body.

Prasarita: Outstretched sides.

Vivartita: Lower part of the spine is twisted.

Apasrita: The side is repositioned back while being in *vivartita* position.

Movements of *kati* or the hips

Chhinna Kati: Looking back while turning the sides.

Nivrtta Kati: Rotating the sides frontward.

Rechita Kati: Circling the sides.

Kampita Kati: Angular movements of sides in fast speed.

Udvahita Kati: Raising the sides gracefully.

Movements of *pada* or feet Bharata dedicated a considerable portion of *Natyashastra* to describing the foot positioning and movements. *Sthanaka* is a static standing position in which the feet are kept in a certain position on the floor. Bharata describes the following *sthanaka*s:

Udghattita: Striking of the heel on the floor while standing on the tips of the toes.
Sama: Neutral standing position, wherein the feet are facing forward.
Agratala-sanchara: Raising the heel while spreading out the big toe and curling other toes inward.
Anchita: Lifting the front part of the feet and keeping the toes in an unfolded position with the heel stable on the floor.
Kunchita: Curling the toes while raising the heel.

In addition to the six major limbs, *angika abhinaya* also includes the movements of different parts of the face and movements generated through the body. Bharata stipulates the functions of the eyes, eyeballs, eyelids, eyebrows, nose, cheeks, lips, and chin. The *drishti-bhed*, or movements of the eyes, are given much consideration in *Natyashastra*. There are thirty-six different varieties of eye movements in Indian dances. The first eight eye movements are the most important as they convey the eight *rasa*s. The next eight eye movements correspond to *sthayi bhava*s. The remaining twenty eye movements are used to express *sanchari bhava*s.

Bharata describes specific movements generated from one leg called *chari*s. In a *chari*, the foot, calf, thigh, and waist are harmoniously coordinated. Bharata mentions sixteen different types of *bhumi chari*s, which are earth-grounded steps in which a foot is planted on the floor and the movements are initiated with a drag, stomp, shuffle, crossing of the feet, or strike. In sixteen different *aakash chari*s, a foot is raised from the earth to initiate a movement, giving a sense of elevation.

The blending of foot movements and hand movements results in many different captivating arrangements and permutations called *karana*s. There are total of 108 *karana*s. The combination of two *karana*s is called a *matrika*. Three *karana*s combined is called a *khanda* or *kalapaka*. The combinations of four to nine *karana*s are called *anghara*s. There are thirty-two different *anghara*s.

Bharata also classifies the movements of nose, cheeks, lips, and chin under the *upang* section of *angika abhinaya*. The appropriate use of *upang*s is vital for effective *mukharaga* or facial expressions. The movements of the nose are determined by the various ways of using the nostrils. The nostrils can be used in six ways: normal positioning, quivering, cringing, holding breath, and inflating. Movements of the cheeks also have six varieties.

The cheeks can be kept in hollow, full-blown, inflated, pallid, throbbing, or normal positions. Likewise, the lips have six positions: bowed, trembling, lips extended sideways, squashed, biting lips, and pouting lips. The chin movements are achieved through the movements of lips and teeth. Different movements of the lips change the positions of the chin.

Ang, *pratyang*, and *upang* in *angika abhinaya* are interdependent. All body parts work through the nervous system; therefore, all body parts are linked together and depend on each other for proper functioning. None of these parts should be compromised and has to function together harmoniously.

Rohini Bhate

Indian dances use complex rhythmic footwork with refined movements of upper body parts along with facial expressions to express a theme, idea, or emotion. The *Natyashastra* offers a solid and detailed foundation of *angika abhinaya* for dancers to perfect their body movements and use them in a very specific manner. The movements described in *Natyashastra* are helpful to practice balance and coordination, since these movements easily facilitate the exercise of muscle and joint flexion and extension, abduction and adduction, elevation and depression, hyperextension, opposition, and rotation. These movements also aid in flexibility and agility.

Angika Abhinaya in Kathak

Kathak has changed significantly with time. Although the philosophy and aesthetics of theatre delineated in *Natyashastra* are still the essential driving forces in Kathak, the need for a new movement vocabulary was desperately needed to suit the mood of Kathak. The great maestros of different schools of Kathak created a new body movement vocabulary to augment the disposition of Kathak repertoire.

Kathak maestro Pandit Birju Maharaj (1938–), himself an institution, has made tremendous contributions to the art of Kathak by introducing aesthetically appealing movements and choreography. He has introduced a new vocabulary of hand gestures and hand movements to Kathak. He defined and illustrated these movements in his book *Ang Kavya*. The basic hand gestures and movements described in *Ang Kavya* are: *naman, utpatti, sthir, palat, urdhva hasta chakra, madhya hasta chakra, tala hasta, chakra, tala kona suchita, sumtala, aalingan, vyapti, ardhalingan*, and *pushpak*. Birju Maharaj ji makes the distinction between basic and ornamental hand gestures. Ornamental hand gestures that he has defined are *pravah, lava-shikha, thaap, swaagat, anjuri, matanga, umang, dhwaj, strota*, and *ardhaang*.

Since the early development of Kathak as a dance form, Kathak dancers have practised the movements of the hands and wrists described by Pandit Birju Maharaj. But categorizing these movements and ascribing proper names to them is enormously valuable for today's Kathak dancers. The Kathak vocabulary presented by Maharaj ji brings more clarity and organization to the language of Kathak.

The dexterity of graceful hand movements in Kathak is achieved by initiating the movements from the wrists. The *thaat* and *gat* repertoires of Kathak specifically use very involved wrist movements. Therefore, wrist movements are of particular importance in Kathak to give the feeling of weightlessness in movements and make them look enticingly fluid. Since most of the hand movements in Kathak originate from the wrist, Maharaj ji also mentions wrist movements in *Ang Kavya*:[3]

Chapal kalaas: Back and forth movement of one or both arms with sideways flips of the wrist.

Thirkan: Quick sideways twitches of wrists.

Jalbhramari: A circular wrist movement near the waist in which the wrist moves from inside to outside.

Mridang: *Mridang* is a cylindrical double-headed drum. In this movement, the wrists snap inwards as if striking both ends of the drum.

Jyoti: Outstretched hand with a curve in the elbow and upward-facing palms with the help of wrist, as if holding a platter.

....

[3] Pandit Birju Maharaj, *Ang Kavya* (New Delhi: Har-Anand Publications Pvt. Ltd., 2002).

Kavach: One hand crosses the body near the waistline with a slight bend in the wrist.

Palta: With palm facing up, the hand is brought up, the wrist turns fully, and comes back to the basic position.

Chanwar: Hands are brought up and palms face down. With the help of the wrists, the palms flip out gracefully.

Arpan: Both hands are outstretched and the palms face outward.

Ot: With the help of the wrists, palms are brought up to veil the face by the palm and the arm.

Meend: A circular movement of the wrists, arms, and torso in which the arms in a parallel position make a circle over the head.

Pandit Birju Maharaj also classified twelve *pada bhangima*s or feet positions in Kathak:

Sama: Neutral position of feet.

Angad: One foot in neutral position and the other foot pointing forward at a forty-five degree angle with the heels of both feet very close together.

Hanumat: One leg in a crossed position and raised.

Krishna: One foot crossed behind the opposite leg, with the crossed foot positioned on its toes.

Urdhva: Both feet lifted up with the support of the toes.

Adhar: A raised foot touching the calf muscles of the other leg.

Ardhaghat: One foot resting on its outer edge.

Uchang: One foot in 'T' position and lifted slightly up.

Tandava: One foot crosses another in a wide stance.

Lasya: One foot in neutral position and the other foot pointing forward in forty-five degree angle with the heels of both feet further apart than in the *angad* position.

Lalit: One foot crossed in front of the other foot and positioned on toes.

Udan: One foot in the back in a forward-walking position.

In addition to these movements identified by Birju Maharaj ji, many other movements of the eyes, chest, head, hips, and sides defined by Bharata are used in Kathak. With time, Kathak has developed its own specific vocabulary of movements.

Vachik Abhinaya

The word *vachik* is derived from the word *vachya*, which means 'that which is spoken'. In *vachik abhinaya*, an actor expresses through voice, language, tone, accent, dialogues, diction, or enunciation.

In Indian mantra meditation, every mantra has powers of both the *vachya shakti* and *vachak shakti*, where *vachya* refers to the meaning of the mantra and *vachak* refers to the locution of the mantra. *Vachak shakti* is the means to attain the *vachya shakti*. Bharata's explanation of *vachik abhinaya* is modelled after the ancient Indian tradition of mantra meditation. According to *Natyashastra*, *vachik abhinaya* is expression through speech. Dance is considered to be a non-verbal language, wherein the body becomes the main vehicle for a dancer's expressions. *Natyashastra* is a comprehensive treatise on theatrical arts, and *vachik abhinaya* is essentially an important part of a drama. Nevertheless, Indian dances are not devoid of *vachik abhinaya*. In *natya* or the dramatic aspect of Indian dances, *vachik abhinaya* is used ingeniously. Bharata defines *vachik abhinaya* in detail, encompassing all aspects of acting through voice:

> Bharata has discussed in detail the different '*vrttas*' or metres in poetry; the '*laksana*s' or figures of speech; the *guna*s and *dosa*s that is the strong and weak points of poetic writing as well as diction. According to Bharata, speech is the vocal representation of words and is the basic structure for building up drama. So, it is essential that this branch of expression should be very carefully used. *Angika, aharya* and *sattvika abhinaya*s interpret the speech. All *sastra*s or sciences are given form in words and are controlled by them. So, all knowledge is gained through word or speech. Therefore, there is nothing that is superior to speech and it is the basis of all activities.[4]

Vachik Abhinaya in Kathak

Vachik abhinaya is an important aspect in the performance of Kathak. In traditional Kathak performances, the performers sing the songs themselves and express the meaning of those songs through *abhinaya*. In *thumri* repertoire of

---

[4] C.S. Srinivas, 'Significance of *Rasa* and *Abhinaya* Techniques in Bharata's *Natyasastra*', *IOSR Journal of Humanities and Social Science* (IOSR-JHSS) 19, no. 5 (2014), Ver. IV, http://iosrjournals.org/iosr-jhss/papers/Vol19-issue5/Version-4/E019542529.pdf (accessed on 17 April 2018).

Kathak, the performer sings the same line over and over. By emphasizing different words or changing the intervals of the words, the performer expresses different meanings of the same line. Sometimes, the mere change in tone, notes, and pitch changes the meaning of the entire line. Pandit Shambhu Maharaj, one of the greatest Kathak masters, was widely recognized for his *thumri* performances in which he interpreted the same line in many different ways. Pandit Birju Maharaj similarly communicates many emotions through his interpretation of a single line of a *thumri*. When the Kathak dancers do not sing themselves, they still express *vachik abhinaya* on vocal accompaniment. It is not important to have a female voice accompaniment for a female dancer or vice versa, because the meaning of the poetry is more important and transcends the common notion of gender. Even when a Kathak dancer expresses a theme without words, the expressions are derived from the dancer's internal dialogues.

Aharya Abhinaya

Aharya abhinaya is expressed through costumes and adornments of the characters as well as the physical decor of the stage itself. The characters' appearances, coupled with the scenery and sets on the stage, create the mood and feelings even before the actors and dancers carry out any other types of *abhinaya*. Therefore, *aharya abhinaya* is considered the backdrop of a theatrical presentation against which the *angika*, *vachik*, and *sattvik abhinaya*s are performed. *Aharya abhinaya* is external in nature, but it provides a strong foundation for the internal expressions:

> The aim in dealing with an exclusive study of the Āhārya Abhinaya is threefold.
> 1. To bring out the importance given by Bhārata to Āhārya Abhinaya in Natya and its relevance for all times with cross-reference from other chapters.
> 2. To showcase the vast treasure of social history available in the chapter in the context of the different communities and class, religious orders and tribes, identifiable through their āhārya. 3. To establish the emotional impact of Āhārya. The rasa-realisation of a production is primarily kindled by the āhārya in the form of dress, colour of make-up, props and accessories, which become the vibhāva or determinant to establish the sthāyi bhāva to create Rasa. There is an instant communication of the character through the āhārya and a rapport beyond language and action is established with the spectator. The different perspectives of Aharya Abhinaya are dealt along with the four-fold classification of Pusta (model work of stage props and sets),

Niketa Patel—Moghul costume   Hetvi Desai—Kathak Jewellery

(*Aharya Abhinaya*)   (*Aharya Abhinaya*)

Alankära (decoration with ornaments and dress), Anga-racana (cosmetic painting of the body) and Sajjiva (life-like representation of birds, animals, and inanimate objects, giving the touch of realistic presentation). These again are with reference to Pravrtti (regional preferences), Dharmi style of presentation) Rasa (asthetic relish), deça (region), jäti (class or category) and avasthä (mental condition) of the character. Ähärya Abhinaya through ages has been studied in the thesis with literary, sculptural and pictorial Evidence.[5]

The costumes and adornments of an actor are referred to as *rangbhusha* in *Natyashastra*. Dance costumes are intended to complement the dance and, in traditional theatrical performances, they are designed according to gender, ethnicity, class, culture, mood, or the social status of a character. The aesthetically designed costumes also supplement in enhancing and accentuating the lines and movements created by a dancer's body. They engage the audience by becoming the means to relate to a dancer's vision. Similarly, jewellery and make-up play a significant role in theatre.

The decorations of the stage, including sets, scenery, and lighting, enhance a performance by creating ambience and are referred as *nepathya* in *Natyashastra*.

[5] Jayashree Rajagopalan, 'Aharya Abhinaya—A Study', http://www.jayashreerajagopalan. com/download/Synopsis_of_Thesis_Aharya_Abhinaya.pdf (accessed on 16 April 2018).

The stage setting literally sets the scenery in the space where the action is performed. Sets and scenery are planned in detail in order to suggest the time, history, culture, theme, and mood of a theatrical performance.

Aharya Abhinaya in Kathak

The costumes and ornamentation of modern Kathak are the products of the magnificent amalgamation of Mughal and Hindu cultures. However, it is important to examine the differences between the ancient, medieval, and modern costumes in order to fully comprehend the development of Kathak.

Since Kathak originated in the temples of India and developed with a strong influence of raas (traditional folk) dance, it is believed that in ancient times, the costuming of male dancers in Kathak was inspired by the *poshak* or the garments in which Lord Krishna's idols were dressed. Male dancers most likely wore *pitambar* or a yellow dhoti in a North Indian style, with an *uttariya* or a long, slender shawl. A dhoti is a rectangular piece of cloth, about five yards long, which is wrapped around the waist and the legs and is secured with a knot at the waist. The *uttariya* was tied around the waist or was wrapped around the neck. The forehead was adorned with tilak, marks created with sandalwood paste or red powder. Female dancers were garbed in the way the artists imagined Krishna's consort Radha's attire in their arts. They wore lehenga or a long skirt, choli or a short blouse, and a chunni or a veil. Both male and female dancers bedecked themselves from head to toe with stunning gold and silver jewellery.

Two different styles of costumes were used in medieval Kathak: Mugulkaleen style and Rajputkaleen style. Both of these styles are portrayed in the Mughal miniature paintings. Mugulkaleen costumes were inspired by the traditional Mughal formal dress and ornamentation. Both women and men wore churidar pyjamas, tight-fitting trousers. Female dancers wore a vibrant *angarkha* or *peshwaj* on top, which looked like a long frock

Rachna Ramya

Hetvi Desai, *Bhava*

with many pleats. On top of the *angarkha*, a short *koti* was worn that accentuated a dancer's form. Female dancers also used a dupatta or a veil. They adorned themselves with magnificent jewellery set in gold with Indian gemstones like *meena*, *kundan*, rubies, emeralds, and pearls. They also decorated their foreheads with *jhoomar* or *chapka*, a type of headdress introduced by the Mughal tradition. Male dancers wore a long sherwani or achkan over the churidar pyjama, which looked like a long coat made of velvety material. Sometimes, both the male and female dancers wore striking brocaded berets. Rajputkaleen costume was inspired from traditional Hindu attire. Female dancers dressed in a lehenga (long, frilled skirt), choli (blouse), churidar pyjama, and dupatta (scarf). Male dancers wore a kurta (long shirt) over their churidar pyjama. They also wore a decorated pagri (turban).

Modern-day Kathak dancers use the same Mugulkaleen and Rajputkaleen costumes. However, today's dancers are more minimalistic in their costume, avoiding too much jewellery or flashiness. Sometimes, Kathak dancers make special costumes for their choreographed pieces with a particular design and colour that caters to the theme and characterization of the choreographed piece. Spins and pirouettes are a very important part of Kathak technique, and the costumes are tailored to flare up during spins, enhancing their movements and making them more attractive to the audience. During the revival of Kathak dance, many female dancers wore the traditional garment of India, the sari. Saris are made from decorative fabric, typically six yards long, one end of which is pleated and wrapped around the waist and the other end draped over one shoulder. Saris are worn over a short blouse with a petticoat or a slip underneath. Kathak dancers ties the shoulder end of the sari around their waists for greater freedom of movement.

The make-up of Kathak is minimal. Kathak dancers use make-up only to accentuate their facial features, so that the expressions can be more visible in

Hemant Panwar and Vaishali Panwar

stage lights. They decorate their hair with *veni* or *gajra*, which are small garlands of jasmine flowers. Kathak dance performances do not typically use stage sets and scenery, unless the piece is theatrical and thematic in nature. Sometimes, the stage is decorated with fresh-cut flowers to give the performance a more traditional appearance. The fragrance of fresh-cut flowers also gratifies the senses of the performer and the audience, while adding to both the spiritual and entertainment aspects of a dance performance. In solo Kathak performances, little emphasis is given to lighting. Simple lights that make a dancer's face and body clearly visible are preferred. However, during the performance of a conceptual piece or choreographed pieces, dancers use sets and lighting depending upon the requirements of the story or the theme.

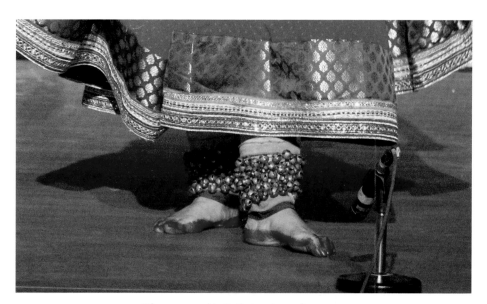

Ghungru used in Kathak solo performance

The jingling *ghungru*s are considered the most important part of *aharya abhinaya* in Kathak. These spherical bells, about two centimetres in diameter, are tied around the dancer's ankles. For Kathak dancers, *ghungru*s are both aesthetically appealing and musically indispensable. They play a vital role in supporting the music of Kathak. *Ghungru*s are worn in every classical dance style of India; however, the Kathak bells are significantly different from the bells worn in other dance forms. In other dance forms, fewer bells are worn and they are sewn over leather or a cloth strap. In Kathak, bells are strung together and each bell is held in place with a knot. Decorative and complex techniques of knotting that resemble the art of macramé are used to string the *ghungru*s together. There are usually 100 to 200 tiny bells on each string, depending on how much weight a dancer would want around the ankles. The heavier the string of *ghungru*s, the more difficult it is to control the movement and the sound. *Ghungru*s in Kathak help dancers develop strength in their lower body, and are worn just above the ankles. They are placed on the medial malleolus, the inner side of the ankle formed by the lower end of the tibia; and the lateral malleolus, the outer side of the ankle formed by the lower end of the fibula. The strings are laid over each other neatly, without leaving any space between them.

The *ghungru*s are made of copper or brass. The copper bell metal ore is a mixture of tin, copper, and stannite. Many Kathak dancers also have experimented with gold, bronze, or silver *ghungru*s. The bells have small iron balls inside them, which produce the sounds. Kathak dancers make many different sounds with their feet, and these various sounds also seem to alter the musical tones of *ghungru*s. Therefore, *ghungru*s play the role of a musical instrument for a Kathak dancer and accentuate the rhythmic aspects of this dance form. A Kathak dancer creates many intricate rhythmic sounds and has tremendous control over the use of these bells. Sometimes, a dancer can generate sound from one bell out of the many by controlling the movement of a single leg muscle. Kathak dancers are trained to amplify or reduce the volume of the *ghungru* jingle by using different motions of their feet. In Kathak, the ankle bells truly serve the role of a percussive instrument. *Natyashastra* specifies that the *ghungru*s should be ideally made of bronze, copper, or silver. They should be sweet-toned, pleasantly shaped, and elegant. They should be tied with an indigo string with a knot between the two *ghungru*s. Bharata does not overtly stipulate why the *ghungru*s should be tied with indigo string. By observing Bharata's disposition towards spirituality in theatrical arts, an assumption can be made that his suggestion of the colour indigo for *ghungru* strings is somehow linked with the value associated with the colour indigo in Indian spiritual practices. The ancient Indians associated the colour indigo with a deeper level of consciousness and the psychic faculties of intuition and perception. They believed that meditation on the colour indigo, which relates to the third eye chakra, promoted concentration, introspection, integrity, and balance in life. In modern days, most of the dancers wear bells strung in white cotton twine. Sometimes, the ends of the strings are decorated with tassels and trimmings. *Abhinaya Darpana*'s author Nandikeshvara discusses the functions of *kinkini* or the *ghungru*s. He suggests that the *ghungru*s should be made of *kansa* metal, which is a hard alloy. According to Nandikeshvara, each string of bells should have the same size and same shape of *ghungru*s and should be knotted with light loops. He also suggests that the *ghungru*s should be tied at the *angul* or the finger's ridge's distance, which is approximately half an inch in measurement.

There are two different types of *ghungru*s: moon-shaped and star-shaped. Moon-shaped *ghungru*s have one cut, and the star-shaped *ghungru*s have two cuts intersecting each other and making a cross-like sign. Most of the Kathak dancers use star-shaped *ghungru*s, since they have a sweeter and more pleasing sound.

The pitch of the *ghungru*s varies, depending on their metallic composition, size, and shape. Therefore, the *ghungru*s in Kathak are chosen very carefully where each *ghungru*'s sound is approximately matched with the sound of another

Ghungru

Pandit Rajendra Gangani

ghungru, so that the jingling of *ghungru*s, when strung together, sounds harmonious and in tune. The pitch of each *ghungru* in a string is difficult to match. Projesh Banerji in his book *Kathak Dance through Ages* mentions an experiment in this regard, which was conducted by Pandit Uday Shankar:

> While tuning up a big gong a pump of melted resin was stuck at the depression at the middle of the gong, and the amount of the secretion put in was regularized up to the point when the sound reaches the vibrating one of standing note. In the same way, the experiment was adopted in the case of all the ghungrus tied in the string by applying melted resin inside the bells. But it is an irksome task and every ghungrus has to be examined for producing the same pitch of sound. There is another problem with so many ghungrus that while dancing there is danger of further melting of the resin and consequently an out of tune sound.[6]

Kathak dancers touch the *ghungru*s to their head before wearing them and after taking them off. This signifies that the dancers have intense devotion for the *ghungru*s and that they come to revere *ghungru*s as living beings.

---

[6] Projesh Banerji, *Kathak Dance through Ages* (New Delhi: Cosmos Publications, 1982), p. 114.

Sattvik Abhinaya

Angika abhinaya represents emotions and theme through body movements, whereas *sattvik abhinaya* is the physical manifestation of emotional, psychological, and mental states. The word *sattva* means 'mind'. Therefore, in *sattvik abhinaya*, the mental and emotional states produce physical reactions, such as tears, perspiration, numbness, or goosebumps. *Sattvik abhinaya* is often confused with *angika abhinaya*, where the emotions are shown through the body; however, in *sattvik abhinaya*, a physical reaction is a consequence of a thought or an emotion. A person's body responds to thoughts and feelings. Therefore, *sattvik abhinaya* is a psychophysical experience.

Sattvik abhinaya is the representation of *sattva*, which, by and large, can be translated as temperaments or psychological states. Daniel Meyer-Dinkgräfe in his book *Approaches to Acting: Past and Present* mentions a few contemporary Indian scholars and their views on *sattva*:

> [Shveni Pandya] defines Sattva as 'the capability of an individual to bring into being the pleasures and pains experienced by others, making them his own. This capability applies to the author, the actor, and the spectator. [Minakshi] Dalal interprets Sattva similarly. Referring to Dhanika, a later Sanskrit theorist of drama and poetry, she states that Sattva 'is a mental condition which is highly sympathetic to joys and the sorrows of the others'...[G.K. Bhat] Bhat takes both the mental and the physical aspect into account when he defines Sattvik Abhinaya as a 'physical manifestation of a deep mental state'. Marasinghe defines Sattva as 'a certain law (dharma) which governs the expressions of the inner state of a person'.[7]

The modern behavioural and neurological sciences also support this notion. The body, with every thought and emotion, releases different types of chemical proteins called neuropeptides. Each variety of neuropeptide triggers a specific physiological effect. *Sattvik abhinaya* refers to the physiological effects that happen because of what modern scientists call the neuropeptide. These scientists study thoughts, emotions, feelings, and mood as separate phenomena. A thought is an idea, opinion, or arrangement of many ideas

---

[7] Daniel Meyer-Dinkgräfe, *Approaches to Acting: Past and Present* (New York: Bloomsbury Continuum, 2001), p. 106.

together, produced by thinking or formed by an occurrence in the mind. Emotion is the body's reaction to mind or thoughts. Feelings are subjective representations of emotions. The response part of an emotion is a private and exclusive experience for each individual. Moods are diffused affective states and last much longer than emotions. Emotions are more intense than moods and include a situation, perception, interpretation, and response to a particular situation. As Dr John Mayer states: 'Emotions operate on many levels. They have a physical aspect as well as a psychological aspect. Emotions bridge thought, feeling, and action—they operate in every part of a person, they affect many aspects of a person, and the person affects many aspects of the emotions.'[8]

Bharata discussed this entire phenomenon in *Natyashastra*. He contemplated on the human psyche and mentioned the concept of *rasa* and *bhava* to articulate the functioning of thoughts, emotions, moods, disposition, motivation, and temperaments. *Sattvik abhinaya* is caused by deep penetration into the human psyche, which in turn causes some alterations in the internal body. Therefore, an actor cannot just set the *sattvik abhinaya* in motion the way he or she can activate the *angika* or *vachik abhinaya*s. *Sattvik abhinaya* cannot be enacted without wholly experiencing a particular emotion. Bharata also explicates that a *sattvik* emotion comes into existence in an unruffled mind:

> Going back to Bharata's explanations like 'Sattvam Nama Manah-Prabhavam', Sattva is motivated by mind, and 'Manasah Samadhau Sattvanispattir bhavati', Satva is produced in the 'equipoised' state of mind, one can realise that to reach this state, an actor requires complete identification with the character. This is Sattva, and Bharata correctly regards Sattvik as an important aspect of Abhinaya. It is easy to experience Sattviks in real life but to produce them in the make-believe world of Natya requires tremendous concentration, knowledge of human mind and technical skill on the part of the actor as well as the dramatist...Ultimately, it is Sattvik which heightens the emotional appeal of Angika, Vacika and Aharya. Knowing this, Bharata rightly called Abhinaya resonating with Sattva as the supreme acting. If Angika and Vacika

[8] John D. Mayer, 'Emotions—How To Understand, Identify and Release Your Emotions', The Home of Vibrational Health http://www.mkprojects.com/pf_emotions.html (accessed on 16 April 2018).

are the backbone of the body of the 'Abhinaya Purusa' and Aharya, its limbs, then Sattvik is its soul.'[9]

An actor's emotional involvement with the character is particularly important for *sattvik abhinaya*. The unperturbed mind of an actor or a dancer is important to accomplish complete identification with the character. Many scholars, however, have found these notions of an actor's complete emotional involvement and maintaining a calm mind contradictory, and have questioned how an actor can have a tranquil mind and, at the same time, feel the emotions of the character. Many scholars from earlier times have provided arguments on this concern. According to Bhatta Lollata, the actor creates maya or illusion. They master the art of false identification with their character. Bhatta Lollata gives an example of rope, mistaken for a snake in the dark. The rope is not the snake, but the subject falsely takes it for a snake and feels the emotion of fear. This is how the actor identifies and gets involved with the character. This identification process produces *rasa*. Sri Sankuka debates that the actor does not identify with the character. Sri Sankuka takes the character of Rama, a mythological hero, as an example. According to him, the character playing the role of Rama is not the real Rama. At the same time, while playing the role of Rama, he is not 'non-Rama' either, because of the viewer's perception of him as Rama. He is likewise not similar to Rama, since the viewers do not know the real Rama. Therefore, the character cannot be imitated, but merely suggested or referenced. The audience's identification with the character of Rama is the reason for the aesthetic pleasure attained through watching the character of Rama on stage. Abhinavagupta also opposes the involvement of an actor with the character. Abhinavagupta focuses on Bharata's *sattvik abhinaya* and concludes that the actors internalize the experiences related to the emotions of a character and, without being involved with the character, produce aesthetic experiences.

Kapila Vatsyayan in her book *Bharata: The Natyasastra* mentions *samanya abhinaya*, a concept that Bharata explored in *Natyashastra*. However, this concept is not examined thoroughly by the scholars of *Natyashastra*:

> The chapter on Samanya Abhinaya is a long chapter of some fundamental importance. Here, Bharata is endeavoring to state that the 'inner states' of a

---

[9] 'Indian Dramatic Tradition', uploaded by Anjumvyas on 17 Aug 2014, https://www.scribd.com/document/237009086/Indian-Dramatic-Tradition (accessed on 24 April 2018).

total personality are fundamental. 'Feeling' and its involuntary expression is his concern. Understandably, he emphasizes that the Samanya Abhinaya relates to all parts of body—a totality—and not a single gesture which can reflect some feeling, which is invincible, but can be suggested. Basically, therefore, he is referring to feeling and temperamental (*Sattva*) which is unexpressed, but it can be discerned through physical signs such as tears, horripilation etc...Bharata's purpose is to draw attention to universality and pervasiveness.[10]

Abhinaya, as defined by Bharata, is an exhaustive guideline for actors and dancers to appropriately express the *rasa*s. Even though the *sattvik abhinaya* is considered supreme among all other *abhinaya* techniques, it clearly is augmented by the *angika*, *vachik*, and *aharya abhinaya*s. Bharata emphasizes the importance of all aspects of *abhinaya* in the following verse:

> *Vayonurüpaù prathamastu veño veñänurüpena gatipracäraù*
> *Gatipräcänugatam ca pathyam pathyänurüpo abhinayasca karyaù*
> [Translation: First of all make-up and attire should be worn corresponding to the character's age, temperament and the context and period of the dramatic piece. It should be followed by appropriate movements, gestures, intonation, and speech. Finally, it should evoke the responsive emotional reactions.][11]

Bharata articulates the aforementioned allusion consistently at many places in *Natyashastra*. The following verse is taught to the students of Indian dance:

> *Yato hastastato drishtiryato drishtistato manaha*
> *Yato manahastato bhavo, Yato bhavastato rasah*
> [Translation: Eyes follow where the hands are; mind follows where the eyes move; where the mind is, there is an emotion; and where the emotions are, the *rasa*s are produced.]

---

[10] Vatsyayan, *Bharata: The Natyasastra*, pp. 82–3.

[11] Rajagopalan, 'Aharya Abhinaya—A Study', http://www.jayashreerajagopalan.com/download/Synopsis_of_Thesis_Aharya_Abhinaya.pdf (accessed on 16 April 2018).

VRITTI: FOUR STYLES OF *ABHINAYA*

Bharata also discussed the four styles or *vritti*s of *abhinaya*. In Sanskrit, *vritti* means the literal explanation of each word in a text and deciphering the positioning of a word in a text along with its tone, accentuation, and suggested meaning. The *vritti*s suggested by Bharata take into account the different dimensions of human behaviour that incorporate a person's verbal, physical, mental, and emotional expressions. These expressions and responses are different in each person, depending on such factors as genetics, social norms, culture, conditioning, and attitude, among others. *Vritti*s are important in order to define a character and its situation. This is why *vritti* is defined as *vruttyo natya mataraha* or 'the mother of the theatre'. *Abhinaya* is categorized into four different *vritti*s or styles: *bharati* (verbal), *sattvati* (internal), *kaisiki* (graceful), and *arabhati* (energetic). It is assumed that *bharati vritti* was inspired from the *Rig Veda*, *sattvati* and *arabhati* from the *Yajur Veda*, and *kaisiki* from the *Sama Veda*.

In *bharati vritti*, emphasis is placed on sounds, words, speech, and vocals. *Bharati vritti* is used mostly in *vachik abhinaya*. The word *sattvati* derives from the root word *satva* or mind. In *sattvati vritti*, the internal aspects of a character are emphasized. A character's mental or emotional states are staged. This is where the *rasa*s take birth. *Sattvati vritti* corresponds with the *sattvik abhinaya*. *Kaisiki* is a graceful, delicate, and charming way of expressing. In *arabhati*, vigorous and energetic movements are performed. Both *arabhati* and *kaisiki vritti*s correspond to *angika abhinaya*.

Rachna Ramya   Pandit Rajendra Gangani

Lord Shiva as Nataraja or the Lord of Dance is believed to be a picturesque representation of four types of *abhinaya*. The following verse is called the *dhyan* verse, or the verse for contemplation and meditation:

Angikam Bhuvanam Yasya, Vachikm Sarva Vangmayam Aaharyam Chandra Taradi, TamVande Sattvikm Shivam[12]
[Translation: I bow to the *Sattvik* or pure Shiva, whose body signifies the entire universe, whose speech is the essence of all languages, and whose ornamentations are the moons and the stars.]

VARIETIES OF *BHAVA-ABHIVYAKTI* IN KATHAK

The great masters of Kathak have deliberated on the significance of *bhava-abhivyakti*, directing their attention to the source, development, and expansion of *bhavas*. The *bhavas* of Kathak are organized into seven categories:

1) *Ang bhava*: The *ang bhava* comes under the category of *angika abhinaya*, where the meaning of the song is suggested by a dancer through the body movements and body expressions.
2) *Nritya bhava*: Pure dance combined with bodily and facial expressions.
3) *Shabd bhava* or *bol bhava*: In *shabd* or *bol bhava*, the words of a song are indicated through bodily and facial expressions.
4) *Artha bhava*: A dancer interprets the connotation of a song through bodily and facial expressions. In *artha bhava*, the dancer construes his/her own view of the meaning of the song.
5) *Gat-artha-bhava*: Pure dance, music, song, and facial expressions are combined. Many scholars view the *gat-artha-bhava* as *nritya bhava*.
6) *Nayan bhava*: A dancer expresses through the movements of eyes and eyebrows.
7) *Sabha bhava*: The word *sabha* means a small gathering. *Sabhas* can be compared with earlier chamber music, which was performed in the West in a small house or the room of a palace. Similarly, during the Mughal era, Kathak was performed for small gatherings. *Sabha bhava* is when the dancer expresses in a way that each member of the audience feels that the expression is directed only towards him or her.

---

[12] A traditional prayer performed in Kathak.

Three Facets of *Abhinaya*

ALL ANCIENT INDIAN TREATISES on dramatic arts have adopted a unified approach to dance in which dance is all-inclusive and integrates dance, drama, rhythm, and song in order to provide a wholesome aesthetic and spiritual experience to both the performer and the spectator. Bharata in his *Natyashastra* used the word *natya* expansively to include all theatrical arts and stagecraft. In contrast, Nandikeshvara, the author of *Abhinaya Darpana*, gave dance its own independent identity. In his work, *natya* became a subsection of *abhinaya*. He expounded on three facets of *abhinaya* in dance that clearly characterized dance as a cohesive art form that includes body movements, facial expressions, drama, and music. These three aspects are categorized as *natya*, *nritya*, and *nrtta*.

NATYA

Natya is the dramatic aspect of dance, which utilizes dialogue, characterization, music, representation of emotions and moods, decor, and dancing to interpret a story. The great Indian epics such as *Ramayana* and *Mahabharata* have been the main sources from where most of these stories are drawn and performed using the *natya* aspects of dance. Stories woven around the daily lives of Hindu pantheons portray moral dilemmas and metaphysical viewpoints and, at the same time, raise fundamental questions about life. According to Nandikeshvara, *natya* is a delightful art for incorporating traditional stories.

Dramatic representation is further categorized into two types: *natyadharmi* and *lokadharmi*. *Natyadharmi* is the theatrical presentation of a theme or an idea. It is delicate, sensitive, and sophisticated, and follows the codified dramatic principles of body language, emotions, and expressions. Whereas *natyadharmi* portrayals are highly stylized and exaggerated, *lokadharmi* presentations are realistic and effortlessly simulate the natural way of being. The word *loka* in *lokadharmi* means 'the world'. Therefore, *lokadharmi* is a presentation that is worldly and true to everyday behaviours, actions, and expressions in life. The word *lokadharmi* is not used for materialistic aspects of life; rather, it represents the mundane aspects of life. Although *lokadharmi abhinaya* does not follow the given rules of stagecraft, it has its own manners of expressions, embellishments, improvisations, and accents.

Prerna Shrimali

Natya is not a vital ingredient of a solo Kathak repertoire. However, it is employed in the dance dramas choreographed in Kathak style. Sometimes, *natya* is also used in solo performances when a dancer enacts a narrative. According to Projesh Banerji:

> It cannot be definitely said that there was no *Natya* in traditional Kathak dance. The *Inder Sabha* of Wajid Ali Shah gives us a link to show that *Natya* must have existed in some form or other....Even in earlier times, prior to Muslim rule, *Natya* existed in the Kathak form. The *Raas Leela* dance of today of Vrindavan and the adjoining parts can be said to be *Natya* as it is based on Kathak style.[1]

The *natya* aspect can be witnessed in the *gat-bhaav* repertoire of Kathak. *Gat-bhaav* is a storytelling aspect of Kathak in which the dancer enacts a condensed

<hr />

[1] Kapila Vatsyayan, *Bharata: The Natyasastra* (New Delhi: Sahitya Akademi, 1996), p. 86.

Pandit Rajendra Gangani   Sunayana Hazarilal

version of an episode from traditional literature and interprets it through mime, using appropriate body movements, hand gestures, and facial expressions. The codified gestures and ways of expression to present *natya* are pursued in *gat-bhaav*.

NRITYA

Nritya is the art of expressing poetry or a theme through aesthetically refined and graceful body movements, suggestive hand gestures, and facial expressions. In the *nritya* aspect, the dancer symbolically interprets the meaning of a song through dance. In *natya*, the actors predominantly use speech to deliver dialogues, whereas, in *nritya*, the song and the poetry accompany the dancers. According to Nandikeshvara in his *Abhinaya Darpana*, *nritya* is the dance that correlates sentiments (*rasa*) and psychological states (*bhava*), as he indicates, '*Rasabhaavavyanjanaadiyuktam nruttamitiryate.*'[2]

---

[2] Prem Dave, *Kathak Nritya Parampara* (Jaipur: Panchsheel Prakashan, 2004), p. 10.

Kathak has a rich *nritya* repertoire. Through the presentation of *gat-bhaav, kavitta, dadra, thumri, ghazal*, and *bhajan*, a Kathak dancer expresses many different emotions and poetic interpretations through body movements, hand gestures, and facial expressions. These Kathak arrangements portray short episodes from Hindu mythology with Radha-Krishna episodes as the prevalent theme. In a solo Kathak performance, the dancer pirouettes to change the character, environment, or time. In *gat*, dancers convey different themes and emotions without any vocal support or use of words. *Gat* is a highly refined repertoire of Kathak in which the dancers portray a condensed version of a theme, meaning, or an action through immaculate mime. Sometimes, the syllables of percussion music are used imaginatively on which the dancers convey some meaning and sentiments. Sometimes, an adept Kathak dancer sings these songs himself or herself while expressing the songs.

NRTTA

Nrtta is the interpretation of rhythm through body movements. It is pure dance in which the body movements create various stylized designs and patterns in space and time. According to Nandikeshvara, *nrtta* is a dance that does not relate to any psychological state: '*Bhaavabhinaya heenam tu nrittmityabhidhiyate.*'[3]

Therefore, *nrtta* is mainly an abstract dance that relies heavily on rhythmic patterns and portrays the beauty and virtuosity of a dancer through joyful movements. Acharya Dhananjaya in his scholarly book *Dasharupakam* explains *nrtta* as an aspect of *abhinaya*, which is dependent on time and rhythm: '*Nrttam Tala Layashrayam.*'[4]

Bharata in *Natyashastra* gives an account of detailed possible movements of the major and minor limbs of body, hand gestures, and feet movements. Dr Kapila Vatsyayan expounds upon what Bharata writes about *nrtta* or pure movements:

> Bharata does not forget that the body is capable of moving gracefully, beautifully, without meaning and import, and thus in the case of movements of the hands and the lower limbs he speaks also of pure movements (*Nrtta*). The word he uses for the dimension of applicability is important. He adopts

---

[3] Dave, *Kathak Nritya Parampara*, p. 10.
[4] Ibid.

the term *Viniyoga* (methodology) from Vedic ritual and applies it uniformly in his enumeration of *angikabhinaya* (to express, to communicate, to reach out through the *anga-sarira* [body].[5]

Pandit Rajendra Gangani

Sometimes *nrtta* is mistaken for mundane technicality of dance. But, in *nrtta*, the dancer and the audience experience a deeper state of consciousness that transcends the physical world by the skilful rendition of dance techniques. This is likely why Bharata Muni ascribes the ownership of *nrtta* to the divine plane—the *nrtta* aspect was performed by the ultimate dancer Lord Shiva Himself during His dance of bliss. According to Bharata, the splendour in performance is achieved through the blissful ambiance created by *nrtta*: '*Vinodkaranam cheti Nrttamettpravartitam.*'[6]

Bharata classified musical compositions (sangeet) into two groups: *baddha* and *anibaddha*. *Baddha sangeet* applies to music that is structured and ordered, whereas the *anibaddha sangeet* is unstructured and improvised. Therefore, *nrtta* can either be structured or improvised.

Nrtta aspect is significant in Kathak. The lucid and fluid technique of Kathak takes years to master. The *nrtta* in Kathak is expressed through the various rhythmic ranges of Kathak, where the dancers interpret the rhythm with their feet, hands, and body. Complex and ornate rhythmic structures are arranged into different compositions, where a dancer plays with different time measurements, the silence between the two beats, fractional divisions of beats, stresses, and metres, and various speeds in a time cycle. All these rhythmic intricacies are conveyed through feet and body movements. Dynamic pirouettes and spins of varied beats are dazzling in Kathak. Kathak dancers use different syllables

[5] Vatsyayan, *Bharata: The Natyasastra*, p. 67.
[6] Dave, *Kathak Nritya Parampara*, p. 10.

to articulate these rhythms, many of which are adopted from percussion and vocal music repertoire. The Kathak repertoire such as *aamad, tukda, paran, tihai, parmelu, palta, baant*, and *ladi* deliver the *nrtta* aspect vibrantly. The *nrtta* aspect of Kathak also incorporates *padhant*s, in which a dancer recites the compositions with precise timing, pronunciation, and intonations before presenting the composition through body movements.

Though *natya, nritya*, and *nrtta* are defined as the three distinct aspects of *abhinaya*, often, in a Kathak dance performance, these distinctions get blurred and overlap each other, probably because the creative fusion of these elements provides a more lucid and complete aesthetic and artistic experience in Kathak. The synthesis of these three different aspects also offers a more balanced performance in which rhythm, dance, drama, and music are equalized.

Nayak and Nayika Bhed

NAYAK- AND NAYIKA-BHED are the archetypal male and female characterizations codified in many ancient Indian treatises on dramatic and visual arts, literature, and aesthetics. These characterizations are based on the *nayak* or the *nayika*'s age, temperament, action, a given situation, social class, and inherent dispositions. They are depicted through interpretations, actions, verbal communications, thoughts, feelings, and interactions. In these classifications, the characters became stereotyped. The *nayak*s or heroes and the *nayika*s or heroines were depicted through paintings, music, poetry, and dance. The art of storytelling is an important aspect of Kathak. Kathak dancers portray many mythological and traditional stories in their dances, where the traditional characters correspond to the characters discussed in *nayak-nayika-bhed*.

Natyashastra is considered as the earliest work, referencing the classifications of *nayak*s and *nayika*s. Later, many other ancient and medieval scholars elaborated on this concept and added more categories of characters in their works. Dhananjaya in his *Dasharupakam* (tenth century CE), Vishwanatha Kaviraja in his *Sahitya Darpana* (fourteenth century CE), Damodaragupta in his *Kuttanimata* (late eighth century to early ninth century CE), and many other aestheticians and literary scholars have deliberated on the *nayak-nayika-bhed*. During the Mughal era, eroticism seeped into the arts. Seductive and coquettish sentiments replaced the devotionalism, and the result was the conception of *nayika*s who were more passionate and flirtatious. Many literary works of this time have elaborated on the *nayak-nayika-bhed*, adding more *nayika*s to Bharata's originals. Jayadeva's *Gita Govinda* (twelfth century CE) and Keshavdas's *Rasikpriya* (sixteenth century CE) have beautifully depicted *nayika*s in their poems. The era of Riti Kaal (1700–1850) in Hindi poetry was the period when erotic sentiments became predominant in literature. The poetry of that time was drenched in *shringar rasa*, where the poets took great pleasure in describing the sensual engagements between a *nayak* and a *nayika*. In Bhakti Kaal (1318–1643), the era in Hindi literature that preceded the Riti Kaal, Krishna represented the Supreme Soul and His divine lover Radha symbolized the individual soul. In Riti Kaal, this devotional aspect was reduced to Radha and Krishna's role playing of different *nayak*s and *nayika*s to pacify the taste of royal and aristocratic patrons.

NAYAK BHED

Different qualities of a *nayak* or a male character are described in ancient literature: loving, domineering, vibrant, agreeable, offensive, wicked, untruthful, unruly, boastful, brazen, and malicious.

According to karma or one's deeds, there are three types of *nayak*s: *pati*, *uppati*, and *vaishik*. *Pati*, the first type, is a wedded man, who can further be of five subtypes: *anukula*, who is completely devoted to his wife; *dakshina*, who has many wives and loves them all equally; *dhrishta*, who is insolent towards his wife; *shatha*, who is deceitful towards his wife; and *anabhigna*, who is inexperienced in matters of love. *Uppati*, the second type, is illicitly involved with another woman, and is of two subtypes: *vaak chatur*, who is crafty and uses honeyed words to achieve his desires; and *kriya chatur*, who is cunning and uses actions as a means to his ends. The third type, *vaishik*, is a *nayak* who is unabashed and loves a courtesan. *Vaishik* is of two types: *maani*, a male character who becomes egotistical when his lover behaves incongruously with him; and *proshit*, a character who pines for his lover while away from her.

According to prakriti or inner personality, there are three types of *nayak*s: *uttam*, *madhyam*, and *adham*. *Uttam nayak* has complete control of his senses and possesses virtuous qualities: he is righteous, honourable, honest, kind-hearted, and sincere. *Madhyam nayak* is knowledgeable, insightful, artistic, and well-mannered. *Adham nayak* possesses qualities such as dishonesty, anger, jealousy, and deceitfulness.

Bharata Muni in his *Natyashastra* describes five types of *nayak*s moulded by his passions and how they act towards women: *chatur*, *uttam*, *madhyam*, *adham*, and *sampravriddha*. *Chatur* is expert in the matters of passion and is caring and honest. *Uttam* is dignified, can rise above passion, and is expert in the matters of heart. *Madhyam* is able to discern the emotions of a woman and, at the same time, is appalled by her mistakes. *Adham nayak* is weak and passionately pursues a woman even when she has rejected him. He is unable to leave a woman even after she is dishonest with him. *Sampravriddha* is one who is too old for a woman in either age or behaviour.

There are four classification of *nayak*s based on their temperament and emotional attitudes. *Dhirodatta nayak* is brave, humble, resolute, serene, and is unruffled by any adverse circumstances. He is valiant, compassionate, and confident. The hero of the ancient epic *Ramayana*, Lord Rama, is a great example of *dhirodatta nayak*. *Dhirodhatta nayak* is the opposite of *dhirodatta nayak*. *Dhirodhatta nayak* is brave, wicked, deceptive, egotistical, and jealous. He has *tamasik guna*s or an ominous energy that promotes gloomy attitudes such as destruction, ignorance, death, inactivity, and defiance. The villain of *Ramayana*, Ravana, falls into this category of *nayak*. *Dhiralalita nayak* is brave, charming, amiable, and good-natured. He also engages in arts and music. The lord of Kathak dance, Shri Krishna, as a ruler of Mathura, is the greatest example of *dhiralalita nayak*. *Dhiraprashanta nayak* is spiritual, righteous, gracious, and noble. He possesses *sattvik* qualities such as honour, clarity, serenity and creativity. Gautama Buddha falls under the category of *dhiraprashanta nayak*. Different modern scholars interpret these classifications of *nayak*s in different ways. For example:

> Indirectly Bharata has laid down the four primal positions in the order of social rankings. Bharata lays down that the Gods are *Dhirodhatta*, Kings are *Dhiralalita*, ministers are *Dhirodatta* and Brahmins and men of the business class are *Dhiraprashaanta*. Bharata and Abhinavagupta do not talk about the attributes of these *naayaka*-s. Bharata talks about the nature of the characters in accordance of their status. Thus he lists the qualities of the king, leader of the army, chaplains and ministers, secretaries, judges, wardens of princes and courtiers etc. But the qualities stated have no particular relation with the four types of *Naayaka*. The qualities laid down seem to be in relation to their status and the duties required to be performed for that particular post.[1]

---

[1] Parimal Phadke, 'Concept of Naayaka in Bharata's Natyasastra', http://www.narthaki.com/info/articles/art128.html (accessed on 16 April 2018).

In addition to these classifications, many more categorizations of *nayak*s are expounded upon in ancient literature. The aforementioned *nayak*s are represented and given preference in Kathak traditional repertoire.

NAYIKA BHED

*Nayika*s or female characterizations have received more attention than *nayak*s in ancient and medieval poetic, dramatic, and erotic literature:

> *Nayika*s are described as women, who are capable of producing erotic feelings in someone and who have one or more of following characteristics: *yauvan* (youth), *roop* (beauty), *guna* (qualifications), *sheel* (modesty), *chaturya* (ingenuity), *prem* (love), *kul* (family status), *bhushan* (adornment), *datritva* (responsibility), *panditya* (scholarship), *utsah* (zeal), *and tej* (radiance). [Translation][2]

Male authors who kept the female characterizations limited to the realm of romantic and erotic love categorized *nayika*s. There is definitely a lack of diversity in female characterizations. Bharata in his *Natyashastra* describes many types of *nayika*s, but deliberates primarily on *ashta-nayika*s or the eight different kinds of heroines. Subsequently, more *nayika*s were added and reduced to the descriptions of who they were, based on their social status and functions in a man's life. This especially happened during the post-Vedic and Mughal periods when the status of women in India became inferior to men. During the Mughal Kaal, women were treated as objects of amusement and diversion by the monarchs and royals, who were supporting most of the authors and artists.

Bharata mentions ten different *alankara*s or attributes of *nayika*s that evoke *shringar rasa*. The word *alankara* means 'ornaments'. In the context of *nayika*s, their attributes and qualities are considered their *alankara*s or ornaments. Later on, aesthetes, poets, and artists added many other *alankara*s. Pandit Vishwanath reflected upon twenty-eight *alankara*s in *Sahitya Darpan*, which was written around 1834 CE. These *alankara*s are divided into three categories. The first category of *angaj* is concerned with the physical attributes of a *nayika*. There are three types of *angaj*: *haav*, *bhaav*, and *hela*. *Haav* is when a *nayika*'s face

---

[2] Laxmi Narayan Garg, *Kathak Nritya* (Hathras: Sangeet Karyalaya, 1994), p. 141.

Rachna Ramya

indicates love through the expressions of eyes, eyebrows, lips, and other facial features. *Bhaav* arises in the *nayika*'s mind. In *hela*, the emotion of love is expressed through the entire body. Kathak dancers pay special attention to *haav*, *bhaav*, and *hela* while depicting a *nayika*. *Hela* is referred to as *ang-bhaav* in Kathak.

The second category of *alankara* is *ayatanaj*, which are the inherent attributes of a *nayika* and enhance both her beauty and emotions. *Shobha*, *kanti*, *deepti*, *madhurya*, *pragalbhata*, *audarya*, and *dharya* are the types of *ayatanaj alankara*. *Shobha* is physical beauty, natural poise, and appeal of a *nayika*. After she falls in love, her *shobha* becomes *kanti*, the radiance reflected in her physical body. As the love and passion of a *nayika* intensifies, the *kanti* becomes *deepti* or splendour, reflected in her being. In *madhurya*, the state of mind of a *nayika* is delightful and harmonious. *Pragalbhata* is the collective awe-inspiring qualities in a *nayika*. The *audarya* state of mind makes a *nayika* magnanimous, and, finally, the *dharya* state of mind indicates a resolute *nayika*, who is so sure of her love that she does not care for her own life and is prepared to do anything for love.

The third category of *alankara* is *swabhavaj alankara* in which the qualities in a *nayika* can be inborn, but they can also be acquired from her environment. There are many different types of *swabhavaj alankaras*. *Leela* or play is a *swabhavaj alankara*, wherein the *nayika* emulates her lover in mannerisms. Sometimes, she even dresses up like him. *Vilas* refers to the transformed gestures of a *nayika* when she is with her lover. In the state of *vilas*, her way of standing, sitting, walking, smiling, and all other mannerisms change. *Vichchati* occurs when a *nayika* is enraged with her lover and throws away her jewellery and flower garlands to show her infuriation. However, she adorns herself again, once the *nayak* appeases her. In the state of *bimbbok*, the *nayika* dismisses a desired object and even refuses to agree to a request. In *kilkinchit* state of mind, a *nayika* acts contrary to what the situation requires. For example, she displays fear even when she actually is having a pleasurable time with her lover. *Motayat* is the state of mind of a *nayika* when she feels uneasy when someone refers to the *nayak* in a conversation. In the *vibhram* state of mind, the *nayika* feels bewildered when her lover arrives and, in her confusion, makes simple mistakes such as putting kohl somewhere else on her face instead of applying it to her eyes. *Lalit* is the state when a *nayika* seduces a *nayak* by revealing some of her body parts or adornments. *Viharat* is a state of mind when a *nayika* is not able to convey her feelings to her lover. *Mada* is the pride of a *nayika*, which becomes apparent when she is filled with passion and youthfulness. *Tapan* is the heat of separation that a *nayika* experiences in the absence of her lover. In the state of *mogadhya*, a *nayika* feigns naivety in front of her lover about some matter that she knows very well. In the *vikshep* state, a *nayika* is not able to dress herself properly in front of her lover. In *kutulal*, a *nayika* feels anxious around something beautiful, which reminds her of the *nayak*. *Hasit-chakit* is when a *nayika* is delightful and dazed in her lover's presence. During the state of *keli*, a *nayika* immerses herself in love play.

CLASSIFICATIONS OF NAYIKAS

*Nayika*s are classified on the basis of *dharma-bhed* (social conduct and virtues), and then are further divided into different categories according to *ayu-bhed* (age), *prakriti-bhed* (basic nature), *jati-bhed* (physical appearance), *awastha-bhed* (emotional and mental states), and *swaroop-bhed* (temperament).

Nayikas According to Dharma Bhed

According to *dharma-bhed*, there are three different types of *nayika*s: *swakiya*, *parakiya*, and *samanya*. In *Natyashastra*, these three *nayika*s are mentioned as *vaishya*, *kusaja*, and *preshya*.

Swakiya nayika is morally upright and loves her husband with purity and devotion. She is humble and unassuming and lavishes all her thoughts and attention on her husband. *Swakiya nayika* is divided into three categories based on her age: *mugdha*, *madhya*, and *pragalbha*. *Mugdha nayika* is an adolescent, delicate girl, who is inexperienced in matters of love. She hardly gets enraged and can be pleased very easily when angered, as illustrated in the following verse *Nagananda* by Harshvardhan:

The moment my newly married beloved
Sees me she lowers her eyes,
When I attempt to talk she does not talk,
If embraced by force she starts shivering,
As soon as her friends go out of the room
She also goes out.[3]

Harshvardhan describes the shyness of a young married woman, who is untried and innocent in matters of love. *Mugdha nayika* is subdivided into two main categories: *agyaat yauvana* and *gyaat yauvana*. *Agyaat yauvana* is naïve and, in the natural process of maturing, she does not understand why her body is changing; whereas *gyaat yauvana* understands the changes in her body during puberty and embraces them. *Gyaat yauvana* is of two kinds: *navodha gyaat yauvana nayika* is afraid and shy of being intimate with her husband, and *vishrabdh gyaat yauvana nayika* welcomes the intimacy with her husband with trust and passion. Both Dhananjaya in his *Dasarupa* and Pandit Vishwanatha in his *Sahitya Darpana* classify *mugdha nayika* in different categories. According to Dhananjaya, *mugdha nayika* is of three different kinds, namely *vayomugdha*, *rativama*, and *kaponsvadu*. Pandit Vishwanatha subclassifies *mugdha nayika* as *prathamavatirna yauvana*, *prathamavatirna madana vikara*, *rati vama*, *manmridu*, and *samdhik lajjavati*.

Madhya nayika is skilful in matters of love to a certain extent and is not coy. Pandit Vishwanatha describes *madhya nayika* in a very picturesque manner:

Her eyes are darker and more beautiful than khanjan bird,
Her both hands are vying with the beauty of lotus,
Her rising bosom poses the challenge to karikumbhs' rising
Her glow resembles the golden champa flower,
Nectar drops from her words,
Her side glances are comparable
To a garland of blue lotuses unique in luster.[4]

----

[3] Ved Bhatnagar, *Shringar—The Ras Raj: A Classical Indian View* (New Delhi: Abhinav Publications, 2011), Kindle Edition, location 494

[4] Bhatnagar, *Shringar—The Ras Raj*, Kindle Edition, locations 502–505.

Madhya nayika is subdivided into three categories: *madhya dheera, madhya dheera-dheera*, and *madhya adheera*. *Madhya dheera nayika* is delighted when she is able to make her husband feel regretful after he commits an offense. *Madhya dheera-dheera nayika* uses her tears to make her husband repentant when he commits a misdeed. *Madhya adheera nayika* uses fury and biting words to make her husband remorseful when he wrongs her.

Pragalbha nayika is very proud of her womanhood and is an expert in matters of love. She adorns herself in various ways to look beautiful and sensual. She uses sandal paste for fragrance, and her body bears the love marks instigated by her husband. Pandit Vishwanatha describes a *pragalbha nayika* in the following two verses:

> This beautiful lady by her sweet talk,
> Arching of her eyebrows,
> By the movement of her finger,
> By her natural body movement encouraging love play
> And her unique side glance is
> Urging Kamdev for a victory on Tribhuwan.

> My lord arrange my disheveled hair
> Put in order my bindi on my forehead
> Rejoin the broken garlands hanging on my breasts
> As the lover touched the moon faced lady again
> Being excited she got ready
> For a fresh encounter of love.[5]

Pragalbha nayika is subdivided into three categories: *pragalbha dheera, pragalbha dheera-dheera*, and *pragalbha adheera*. When offended, *pragalbha dheera nayika* hides her anger by smiling sweetly and, at the same time, feels resigned from love play. *Pragalbha dheera-dheera nayika* reprimands her husband with her caustic comments. *Pragalbha adheera nayika* becomes physically offensive and shouts at her husband.

....

[5] Bhatnagar, *Shringar—The Ras Raj*, Kindle Edition, locations 508–13.

Jyeshtha and *kanishtha* are other classifications of *madhya* and *pragalbha* *nayika*s. *Jyeshtha* is one who is very much loved by her husband and attracts all his attention. *Kanishtha nayika* gets less attention from her husband, who does not care much for her.

Parakiya nayika cheats on her husband and secretly loves other men. *Parakiya nayika* is again of two types: *uurha parakiya*, a married woman who falls in love with another man, and *anurha parakiya*, who stays unmarried and falls in love with a man other than her lover. *Parakiya nayika* can be either *udbudhdha* or *udbodhita*. *Udbudhdha parakiya nayika* asks for love from another man and *udbodhita parakiya nayika* is propositioned by another man. *Parakiya nayika* is further divided into six different categories: *surat gupta*, *vidagdha*, *lakshita*, *kulata*, *anushayana*, and *mudita*. *Surat gupta* hides the love marks inflicted by a lover. *Surat gupta nayika* who hides the marks from her last courtship is called a *bhoot-surat sangopana*. A *surat gupta* is called a *vartaman-surat sangopana* when she hides the marks of a recent courtship with her verbal and mental shrewdness. Finally, the one who intends to hide her future love affairs is called a *bhavishyat-surat sangopana*. The *vidagdha parakiya* is very skilful in hiding her love affairs. She is called *vachan vidagdha* when she uses words to hide her secret affairs. She is called a *kriya vidagdha* when she takes an action to hide her secret love affair. The *lakshita parakiya* is a *nayika* whose body shows the smears and marks caused by her secret lover. The *kulata parakiya nayika* is dissatisfied even after having intimate relationships with many men. *Anushayana parakiya* is one who is grief-stricken when she leaves the place where she met her lover. *Mudita parakiya nayika* is delighted just to think of her love plays where her desires will be fulfilled.

The *samanya nayika* is a courtesan and spends her time with any man for materialistic gains. She is highly trained in all kinds of arts, including the art of love. She expresses false love and leaves a man as soon as she achieves her goal. When a courtesan truly falls in love, she is called *samanya nayika*. There are three types of *samanya nayika*: *janani-adheena samanya* is one who works under the guidance of her mother, *swatantra samanya* works independently and makes her own decisions, and *niyama samanya* works regularly.

Nayikas According to *Prakriti Bhed*

There are three different types of *nayika*s according to their *prakriti-bhed* or natural impulse: *uttam*, *madhyam*, and *adham*. *Uttam nayika* is very tolerant and always wishes well for her husband. She has tremendous self-control and forgives her husband's wrongdoings. *Madhyam nayika's* temperament fluctuates. Her behaviour towards her husband is dictated by how he behaves with her. She is agreeable when her husband is caring towards her, and becomes very cross when her husband misbehaves with her. *Adham nayika* has no self-control. She is harsh in her behaviour, uses bitter words, and always negates her husband. Nandikeshvara in his *Abhinaya Darpana* (second century CE) mentions the fourth *nayika*: *anya sambhog dukhit nayika*, who is grief-stricken when her female friend or *sakhi* has an affair with the *nayak*. She becomes angry and abusive.

Nayikas According to *Swaroop Bhed*

Three different types of *nayika*s fall into this category: *divya*, *adivya*, and *divyadivya*. *Divya nayika* has divine qualities and is very spiritual in nature. *Adivya nayika* possesses the qualities of a human being. The *divyadivya nayika* is one who is born endowed with godly qualities.

Nayikas According to *Jati Bhed*

Padmini, *chitrini*, *shankhini*, and *hastini* are four *nayika*s who are segregated according to their *jati-bhed* or physical appearance, which actually reveals their inner personality. Vātsyāyana's *Kama Sutra* (between 400 and 200 BCE) and Kalyanamalla's *Kamaledhiplava* (circa late fifteenth century), which are basically manuals for human sexual behaviour, mention these four *nayika*s in great detail. *Padmini* is a lotus woman who is fair and possesses a face resembling a full moon. Her flesh is soft and her eyes are bright and beautiful. Her gait is swanlike, and her voice is sweet like a *kokila* or cuckoo bird. She dresses finely and adorns herself with beautiful jewels. She is courteous and virtuous and an expert in fine arts. *Chitrini* is middle-statured and has jet-black hair, thin neck, and tender body. Her nose resembles the *til* flower and her eyes are beautiful like a blue lotus. She is fond of music and pleasures, and is modest and amusing. *Shankhini* is a conch-woman, so called because her neck has wrinkles like the spires on a conch shell. *Shankhini* has a lean body and her skin is hot and tawny. Her voice is throaty and her gait is impulsive. She always finds faults in her husband and is impertinent and spiteful. *Hastini* is petite and has a flaccid body. Her flesh is coarse and she has a harsh voice. Her neck is bent and her back is slouchy. She walks very slowly, moving her head up and down like a female *hastini* or an elephant. She is voracious in her desires and can be sadistic and wrathful.

Ashta-Nayikas According to their *Awastha* or Psychological States

*Ashta-nayika*s or the eight *nayika*s who are classified according to their mental, emotional, and psychological states are given prominence in the *abhinaya* of Kathak dance. Bharata Muni placed a lot of emphasis on the behaviour patterns and emotions of *ashta-nayika*s, and later, many poets, dancers, musicians, and visual artists magnificently depicted *ashta nayika*s in their work:

> The *Nayika*s have been discussed in sacred as well as secular texts, which go on to expound the different categories in which these heroines can be delegated. The *Ashta Nayika*s refer to the eight divisions based on the eight stages of the heroines' love life. These categories take into account the different situation she may find herself in, the plethora of emotions she may experience and her response to her various romantic dispositions.[6]

The longings, romantic set-ups, and sensual attitudes of *ashta-nayika*s have attracted artists from time immemorial. They have bedecked the emotions of erotic poems of many famed writers such as Pandit Vishwanatha, Jayadev, Keshavdas, and Bihari Lal. At the same time, they have made their presence on the panels of Chamba Rumal embroidery from Himachal Pradesh, where they are embroidered on fine muslin with silk and gilded silver threads. From the mid-fifteenth century to the late sixteenth century, the Ragmala series painters portrayed *ashta-nayika*s in bright and bold colours with precision. Dancers have used *ashta-nayika*s to convey all different shades of *shringar rasa*. Sculptors have given life to dark caves with brilliant sculptures of *ashta-nayika*s. In Kathak, they have an important place in the renditions of *thumri*s and *bhav batana*. The eight *nayika*s are: *vasaka sajja, swadhinpatika, utkanthita, khandita, vipralabdha, kalahantarita, proshitpatika,* and *abhisarika*.

The *vasaka sajja nayika* adorns herself with fine clothes, flowers, and jewellery and waits for her lover in her enchanting mansion. She beautifies her bed chamber exquisitely for her lover. Her waiting is not smeared with pain

---

[6] Alka Pande, 'Ashtanayika: The Messengers of Love', The Stainless Gallery, Matters of Art, http://mattersofart.blogspot.in/2008/12/ashtanayika-messengers-of-love.html (accessed on 16 April 2018).

Vasaka Sajja Nayika

and agony; she waits with joy and anticipation for the ecstasy that she will be experiencing with her lover. Keshavdas associated the *vasaka sajja nayika* with the Hindu Goddess Rati, who is the consort of Kamadeva, the God of Love, and symbolizes erotic desires and passion.

The *swadhinpatika nayika* is deeply contented because her lover is completely subjugated by her beauty and pleasing behaviours. Many poets and painters have depicted her as a woman who is being pampered by her lover, where he is rearranging her clothes after a love play, painting her feet with *mahawar*, her body with sandalwood paste, and putting a bindi on her forehead.

Independent Heroine (*Swadhinpatika*), *Nayika* Painting Appended to a Ragmala (Garland of Melodies)

The *utkanthita nayika* is tormented by the separation from her lover when he does not arrive at the appointed time. She is distressed by this separation because the *nayak* becomes engaged in other activities and does not come to her even after prearranging a meeting with her. She is usually depicted as waiting on a doorstep for her lover or pining for him in her bed.

The *khandita nayika's* heart is broken into pieces because her lover betrays her. He promised to come to her in the night-time and instead spent his night with another woman. She is depicted as angry, offended, and reprimanding her lover for his infidelity.

The *vipralabdha nayika* is dejected

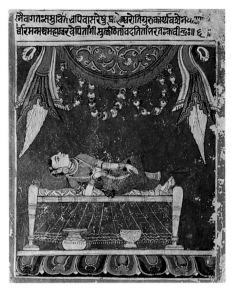

Anxious Heroine (*Utkanthita*), *Nayika* Painting Appended to a Ragmala (Garland of Melodies), Nepal, Bhaktapur, c.1650

because of the unresponsiveness of her lover in matters of love. She sends many messages to her lover, whom she has not seen in many days, but he does not respond, making her feel gloomy and disgraced.

The *kalahantarita nayika* is separated from her lover because of a disagreement that she has with him. She quarrels with him even after he falls on her feet for a pardon. She becomes arrogant and jealous, and when her lover leaves her home, she feels sorrowful and repentant.

The *proshitpatika nayika* is distressed, since her lover is abroad and has not returned. She discards her jewellery, lets her hair loose, and cries in grief. She is often depicted as a woman being negligent of her appearance and consoled by her friends.

Khandita Nayika

Deceived Heroine (*Vipralabdha*),
Nayika Painting Appended to a Ragmala
(Garland of Melodies)

Displeased Heroine (*Kalahantarita*),
Nayika Painting Appended to a Ragmala
(Garland of Melodies)

Forlorn Heroine (*Proshitpatika*),
Nayika Painting Appended to a Ragmala
(Garland of Melodies)

Intoxicated by love and filled with passion, the *abhisarika nayika* secretly goes out to meet her lover for a rendezvous. She is daring and shameless and is often portrayed as dazzlingly dressed and leaving her home in a hurry to reach the appointed meeting place. She confronts many obstacles on her way, such as the beasts of the forest, slithering cobras, and rainstorms. There are three different types of *abhisarika*s. The *shukla-abhisarika nayika*, in her white garments, leaves her home during the night of the full moon to meet her lover. The *krishna-abhisarika nayika*, wearing dark-coloured garments, leaves

Abhisarika Nayika ('The Heroine Going to Meet Her Lover at an Appointed Place')

home at night to meet her lover in the murky forest. The *diva-abhisarika* goes out during the daytime to meet her lover, wearing her usual garments and camouflaging herself among other women.

The female companions of *nayika*s console them during their distressing moments, help them decorate themselves before they meet with their lovers, becoming the observers of their joy and passion, counselling them when needed, and even playing the role of a messenger. These companions often play an important role in the ecstatic union of the *nayak* and the *nayika*. Sometimes, these female companions even pose a threat to the *nayika* when the *nayak* gets fascinated by the *nayika*'s companion, or worse, becomes involved with her. The *nayika*'s companion can be her maidservant, her friend, a neighbour, a bangle seller, the goldsmith's wife, or the like.

Different poets, artists, and scholars also have described the kinds of places and times that are the most fitting and convenient for a *nayak* and *nayika*'s meetings, as well as the psychological states that *nayika*s experience when in passionate love. The meeting places such as scenic meadows, gardens filled with fragrant flowers and enchanting vines, lush forests, enticing, lonely, and dark places, and lovely riversides aid in evoking erotic sentiments in the *nayak* and *nayika*. Similarly, times such as the dark nights, days darkened by rain clouds, dusks when the silvery moon rises, lazy summer afternoons, the season of spring when the fresh breeze is tantalizing intensify the emotions of love.

A *nayika* goes through many emotional and mental states when the arrow of Kamadeva, the God of Love and Desires, strikes her. *Abhilash* is a state when the *nayika* is in love for the first time. Her heart beats faster and she becomes sweaty with desire. She forgets everything else but her intense love for the *nayak. Chinta* is the emotional state when the *nayika* is worried whether her love will be reciprocated, and if the *nayak* feels the same way for her.

> Sagarnandin in his book *Nataklakshanaratnakosh* describes the state of mind of such a *Nayika* who is suggested writing a letter to her lover in a particular style: That slender one should send a letter couched in artistic language written on a *ketaki* leaf, scratched by *kasturi* and wrapped by a silken thread having a symbol of her breasts smeared with sandal paste with his name inscribed on upper *[sic]* portion.[7]

In *anusmaran* state, the *nayika* pines to meet with the *nayak*. She cannot focus on anything and constantly indulges herself in his thoughts. She is unable to live her life normally. During the state of *gunakatha*, she constantly talks about her lover in admiration. *Udveg* is the state where she is completely distraught because she is not able to meet with her lover. In this state, even the beautiful moon feels like vicious fire to her, and the rain clouds feel like venomous cobras. In *vipralap* state, the *nayika* is remorseful for not being able to tell the *nayak* about her feelings. In the state of *aatank*, the *nayika* is fearful of the pangs of love and experiences panic and anxiety. In *unmad*, she has no control over her emotions and spends sleepless nights crying incessantly. *Jadta* is a state where the *nayika* is so traumatized by the absence of her lover that she becomes emotionally numb. And, lastly, in the *maran* stage, she is not able to sustain herself anymore; consumed by the agony of separation, she meets her death.

ATTIRES AND ACCESSORIES OF *NAYIKAS*

Clothing and accessories used by a character either conceal or reveal one's temperament and personality. In his play *King Lear*, Shakespeare conveys the power of clothing in the given lines and describes how they relate to a character's intrinsic qualities: 'Through tattered clothes great vices do appear; Robes and furred gowns hide all. Plate sin with gold and the strong lance of justice hurtless breaks. Arm it in rags, a pigmy's straw does pierce it.'[8]

---

[7] Bhatnagar, *Shringar—The Ras Raj*, Kindle edition, locations 568–76.
[8] *No Fear Shakespeare: King Lear*, act 4, scene 6, p. 7, http://nfs.sparknotes.com/lear/page_244.html (accessed on 16 April 2018).

Vesh-bhusha or the clothing of a character, as well as *saundarya prasadhan* or the beauty aids reflect the mood, social class, age, gender, and personality of a character. Bharata and others have pondered on this subject in minute detail. Creating *rasa* is one of the most critical goals of Indian arts. *The nayak and nayika's vesh-bhusha* and *saundarya prasadhan* are suggested in ancient and medieval treatises on dramatic arts, mainly to evoke the *shringar rasa.* The earliest Sanskrit plays, ancient treatises on dramatic arts, prehistoric rock sculptures and paintings found in caves, and terracotta figurines found in the Indus Valley archaeological excavations suggest that cotton and silk fabrics as well as many different kinds of body accessories and cosmetics were used in ancient India. The ancient and medieval artists and authors have visualized *nayak*s and *nayika*s wearing beautiful garments, ornaments, and make-up. Ved Bhatnagar in his book *Shringar—The Ras Raj: A Classical Indian View* references Kalidas's legendary classical Sanskrit plays *Abhigyan Shakuntalam* and *Meghdootam*, written sometime between the first century BCE and the fourth century CE, to establish the type of clothing that the *nayak*s and the *nayika*s might have worn:

> *Valkal, shaum* and *dukul* were some of the most prevalent and known dresses. *Shaum* was regarded as *mangal vastra* while valkal as *munivastra.* Shakuntala was seen by Dushyant for the first time wearing *valkal* while *shaum* which was of white colour and soft was worn by the affluent. There is reference to wearing of *shaum* by the affluent beautiful ladies of Alka city in verse 5 of *Uttarmegh* of *Meghdootam* by Kalidas. *Dukul* was prepared after crushing the skin of trees in water. After it was crushing *[sic]* fibrous material came out of this process; then spun and fine clothes were prepared. Compared to *shaum* it was smoother and comfortable and figures of birds and animals and various motifs were painted on it.[9]

Cotton apparel was made from cotton buds after they were spun, woven, and dyed. Silk attires were made from a silkworm called Kausheya, using the process of reeling. These clothes were wrapped and tied around the body in various ways. Many new characterizations of *nayika*s were developed during the Mughal period. Miniature paintings of that time portray the *nayak*s and *nayika*s in both Hindu and Mughal costumes made of the finest muslins, velvet, brocades, and silk. The

---

[9] Bhatnagar, *Shringar—The Ras Raj*, Kindle edition, locations 683–91.

*nayak*s portrayed by the Mughal Kaal painters wore *jaama* (a side-fastening frock coat) or a *choga* (a long-sleeved coat with an opening in front), *patka* (a sash tied around the waist), pagri or a turban, and a churidar (tight pants) or a dhoti (a piece of cloth tied around the waist and extended over both legs). The *nayika*s wore *peshwaj* (a loose, high-waisted robe fastened at the front with ties) and *yalek* (long under-tunic) or a lehenga (long skirt), choli (decorated blouse), and churidar (tight-fitting pants) or salwar (loose-fitting pants).

The *nayika*s stole the hearts of their *nayak*s with their striking gold, silver, and copper jewellery, encrusted with precious stones and pearls. Many *nayika*s used their jewellery to attract, distract, charm, and please their *nayak*s. *Nayika*s also thrust aside their jewellery to show their anger and disappointment to a *nayak*. *Nayika*s used *shirobhushan* (head jewellery), *ratnavali* (a decorative small tiara with hanging pearl strands to decorate the hair), *chudamani* (lotus-shaped ornaments for the centre of a bun), *karanbhushan* (earrings), *kanthabhushan* (a short necklace), *lambanam* (a long necklace), *bahu-bhushan* (armlets), *kangan* (wrist bangles), *nasabhushan* (nose rings), *anguthi* (finger rings), *katibandh* (a gold belt for the waist), *mekhla* (multi-stringed beaded hip belt), *kinkini* (anklet with small bells), and *bichiya* (toe rings). *Nayak*s wore ornaments such as *kirita* (a decorative crown), *mauli* (an ornamented turban), *kundal* (ring-shaped ear jewellery), *muktavali* (a necklace of pearls), *keyur* (armlet), *ruchak* (for wrists), and *anguthi* (finger rings). Artists of the Mughal era also portrayed *nayika*s as wearing *meenakari* and *kundan* jewelleries. In *meenakari*, precious stones are set and then enamelled with gold. In *kundan* jewellery, 24-carat exceptionally refined gold is placed between two precious or semi-precious stones. Since flowers stimulate the emotions of love, fragrant flower garlands for the hair or for wearing around the neck are also part of a *nayika*'s *vesh-bhusha*.

Saundarya prasadhan or the natural cosmetics of *nayika*s include fragrant oil for body and hair, *anjan* or kohl for eyes, henna paste and red *mahawar* to decorate hands and feet, red juice of *alaktak* and betel for lips, pollen of red lotus to whiten teeth, vermilion or kumkum powder, sandalwood paste, deer musk, saffron, and camphor to decorate the forehead and other parts of the body.

Nayika-bhed has been one of the most relished elements of ancient and medieval literature and arts. *Ritikaleen* poetry revelled in the beauty and psychology of the *nayika*s. Dancers and artists brought these *nayika*s to life in their arts by portraying them with exuberant imagination. Royal and noble patrons of the arts have enjoyed the erotic depiction of *nayika*s and have rewarded artists and poets with lavish gifts and prizes for creating these arousing *nayika*s. At the same time, those who believe in a woman's strength and her fundamental right to be treated with respect have criticized these depictions. Women have been sexually objectified in *nayika-bhed*, equating their worth with their physical appearance and sexuality. The moral codes set for *nayika*s are harsh, whereas a *nayak*'s frivolity and coquettishness are overlooked. There are many poems written about *nayika*s that are sexually coded representations and semi-pornographic works to stimulate male sexual fantasies. A desirable *nayika* has been depicted as virtuous, chaste, and moral, so that her portrayal does not threaten man's concept of purity and sanctity. The *nayika*s are portrayed as incessantly dependent on their men, passively waiting to be saved, ready to sacrifice their lives, and lamenting the entire night, while the *nayak* is deceiving her with another woman—and all this in the name of love and *shringar rasa*. Her role is limited to becoming a wife, a lover, a mistress, a seductress, or a ruined woman. India has historically been the land of goddesses, where a woman as devi is idealized as a conqueror of time, a tigress roaming fearlessly in the dense and dark forests, an active dimension of the godhead, the bestower of abundance, and a vessel of creative powers and supreme energy. Critics charge that to have *nayika*s in the same land that is rendered so insignificant that they are relegated to mere sexual objects is distressing. However, contemporary literature of India has fiercely avoided the concept of *nayika-bhed*, and many Kathak dancers today are handling the subject of women's roles in society in a very powerful way, edging out the stereotypical, misogynistic image of *nayika*s.

Tala and *Laya*:
Musical Time in Kathak

RHYTHM IS A COMBINATION OF DIFFERENT recurrent elements such as tempo, metre, pulse, or measure. Many different definitions have been offered in the West to characterize the element of time in music. Some music scholars have defined rhythm as the movement of regular or irregular pulses caused in music by the occurrences of strong and weak harmonic and melodic elements. Others have perceived rhythm as the timing of musical events, or as metrical patterns, or as the patterned recurrence of beats. For dancers, rhythm is a measured movement in space. Plato defined rhythm as 'an order of movement'.[1] The order of movement or the patterned recurrence of beats inherently depends on the silence between the beats, which is also referred to as interval or space. The interval between the beats determines the pacing or the rhythm of music and dance. According to the Indian music system, both the regular beats and the interval or space between the beats create rhythm.

INDIAN RHYTHMIC SYSTEM IN ANCIENT TIMES

From ancient times, Indians have understood the complex nature of rhythm and laid emphasis on two distinct characteristics of it: *chhand* and *laya*. *Chhand*, which today is known as *tala*, is the ordered arrangement and measurement of

[1] Peter Crossley-Holland, 'Rhythm', Encyclopaedia Britannica, last updated 31 May 2002, https://www.britannica.com/art/rhythm-music (accessed on 16 April 2018).

time, and *laya* connotes the tempo or the time unit in terms of the rate, duration, and intervals in speed. Both *chhand* and *laya* are intrinsically embedded in music and dance. The human mind is predisposed to organized space-time dimensions; therefore, it looks for the systematized laws of time and space in the musical experience too. With the rhythmic system, *chhand* or *tala* represents the spatial aspect, and *laya* represents the time aspect.

Chhand or Metrical Modes in Vedic Verses

The importance of both rhythm and melody were observed in Vedic literature. The *rik*s (verses) and the *mantra*s (hymns) were given melodies that were very logically organized in different metres. Melody and rhythm were applied to the verses to facilitate the recitation, memorization, and evocation of the effect of philosophically complex verses for the Vedic practitioners. The rhythm was defined as *chhand*, essentially a metrical form, in which the letters and syllables of the verses are measured: '*yad akshara parimaanam tada chhandh*'—That which is measurement of letters is *Chhandh*.[2]

Pingala's *Chandahśāstra* and Kedara's *Vritta Ratnakara* are the two most extensive works on Sanskrit prosody. Bharata in his *Natyashastra* briefly touched upon the subject of Vedic metres. According to Bharata, the words that were created from fourteen vowels and thirty-three consonants, when organized in four lines, were called a metre. These metres were clustered into three groups: *sama* (even metres), *ardha-sama* (semi-even metres), and *vishama* (uneven metres). These three groups have many submetres. Bharata named each type of metre according to its characteristic.

The Vedic metres were mainly determined on the basis of the grouping of padas, which were the metrical units of a verse. The *pada*s were composed of many syllables. Three or four padas together created a stanza and were called a *rik*. The patterns of *guru* or *laghu* syllables in a *pada* determined the length of Vedic metre or *chhand*. Syllables can be light or heavy, characterized by the quality of vowels and their positioning in a verse. The *laghu* syllables were short or light syllables and consisted of one unit. Additionally, the *laghu* syllables were

[2] 'Vedic Recitation, Rhythms and Metrical Forms', Gurubodh: Fragrance of Love and Light, September–October 2005, https://greenopia.in/live/gurujinarayana/wp-content/uploads/2017/06/Vedic-Recitation-Rhythms-and-Metrical-Forms.pdf (accessed on 17 April 2018).

not supposed to be followed by consecutive consonants in a same *pada*. The *guru* syllables were long or heavy syllables and consisted of two units.

Based on the aforementioned elements, three kinds of metres were recognized in Sanskrit poetry: *aksaravrtta*, *varnavrtta*, and *matravrtta*. *Aksaravrtta* metre is found in great epics such as the *Ramayana* and the *Mahabharata*. The number of syllables in a *pada* determined the metres. There was comparatively more liberty in the allocation of light and heavy syllables in *aksaravrtta* metres. *Varnavrtta* metre was also distinguished by the syllable count, but it had fixed numbers of light and heavy syllable patterns. *Matravrtta* metre was decided based upon the duration by looking at the fixed number of syllable units in a verse.

Twenty-one *chhand*s existed in ancient Sanskrit literature. They were grouped into three categories:

> The chhands are metrical forms, the systematic organisation of letters, words and sounds to generate divine spirit. There are 21 metrical forms in three groups, starting with the shortest verse of 24 letters and increasing in steps of 4 letters concluding with the longest verse of 104 letters. This is Arithmetical progression.[3]

Group one consisted of *gayatri* (twenty-four syllables), *ushnik* (twenty-eight syllables), *anushtup* (thirty-two syllables), *brihati* (thirty-six syllables), *pankti* (forty syllables), *trishtup* (forty-four syllables), and *jagati* (forty-eight syllables).

Group two contained *ati jagati* (fifty-two syllables), *shakvari* (fifty-six syllables), *ati shakvari* (six syllables), *ashti* (sixty-four syllables), *atyashti* (sixty-eight syllables), *dhriti* (seventy-two syllables), and *ati dhriti* (seventy-six syllables).

Group three had the following metres: *kruti* (eighty syllables), *prakruti* (eighty-four syllables), *akruti* (eighty-eight syllables), *vikruti* (ninety-two syllables), *sanskruti* (ninety-six syllables), *atikruti* (one hundred syllables), *utkruti* (one hundred and four syllables).

In ancient Gandharva music, *chhand*s were used extensively. Gandharva music was performed during pre-performance rituals, where words were less

---

[3] 'Vedic Recitation, Rhythms and Metrical Forms', Gurubodh: Fragrance of Love and Light, September–October 2005, https://greenopia.in/live/gurujinarayana/wp-content/uploads/2017/06/Vedic-Recitation-Rhythms-and-Metrical-Forms.pdf (accessed on 17 April 2018).

important than the notes and rhythm. Gandharva music was codified and equated to the music of the Gandharvas or celestial musicians. It was regarded as margi or classical music of that time. In Samagana, which existed before Gandharva music, *chhand* was not given much prominence. Gandharva music had different varieties with *gitaka*s as the main arrangement. *Gitaka*s had *tala* structures composed of various segments. The units of these segments, displayed through hand and palm actions, were known as *kaal* or *kriya*. The intervals and duration between two *kriya*s determined the *laya* or the tempo. In an ancient scholarly scripture *Naradiya Shiksha*, presumed to be written prior to the *Natyashastra*, the author uses the word *vritti* for tempo:

> *Abhyasarthe drutam vrittim prayogarthe tu madhyamam*
> *Shishyanamupadesharthe kuryadvittim vilambitam*
> [Translation: The fast *vritti* for practice, medium *vritti* for performance, and slow *vritti* for teaching to disciples should be used.][4]

In his *Natyashastra*, Bharata Muni also mentioned the Dhruva Gana, which was used during a dramatic enactment. The rhythms used in Dhruva Gana were relatively simple. The intervals between the units of *chhand*s were shorter; therefore, the *laya* was usually faster.

In modern North Indian *tala*s, the rules of *chhand*s are not strictly observed, but the integral essence of measuring time in ancient Indian poetry and music has nonetheless inspired the way *tala*s have been formed and applied in present-day Indian music. The way *tala*s are applied in North Indian music today did not become firmly established until the nineteenth century.

THE CONCEPT OF *TALA*

*Tala*s are the fundamental organizing principles in the perception and appreciation of music and Kathak dance. *Tala*s facilitate the classification of rhythmic patterns, so that the audience and the performer can recognize, differentiate, and understand the rhythms with ease. They also provide the rhythmic laws of Indian

---

[4] Thakur Jaideva Singh, *Bharatiya Sangeet ka Itihaas* (Calcutta: Sangeet Research Academy, 1994), p. 68.

music based on stresses, form, regularity, accents, intonation, duration, length, and continuity of the rhythmic patterns.

In music, *tala* is the measurement of time and is cyclical in nature. A *tala* is the canvas of rhythmic cycle upon which music and dance are painted. It is a group of defined beats, repeated over and over in a performance. The system of *tala* in Indian music is very much influenced by the Indian philosophy of the recurring and repetitive nature of the universe, in which the universe undergoes the self-sustaining cycle of creation, preservation, and destruction. Each cycle of a *tala* is divided into subsections that may or may not vary in measurement. The beats of a *tala* can be counted on the fingers and its accents are demonstrated through claps or waves.

Many medieval scriptures have discussed the ten life forces or *dus pran* of *tala*. These ten fundamental limbs of *tala* determine the nature, arrangement, mood, and magnitude of rhythmic cycles. Even though North Indian music today does not precisely follow these elements in a precise, they have relevance in the sense that they have profoundly influenced the characteristics of the modern-day *tala* system. Some of these elements are still used. However, they are termed differently.

TALA KE DUS PRAN

The ten elements of *tala* are: *kaal, marg, kriya, anga, graha, jati, kala, laya, yati,* and *prastara*. Precisely how and when the *tala's dus pran* came into practice is difficult to determine, but they have had a definite influence on the modern-day rhythmic system of North Indian classical music and dance.

These ten elements of *tala* are based on the two basic aspects of action and the interval between two actions. *Kaal, marga, anga, jati,* and *laya* convey the interval aspect of *tala* where the nature of the rest between the two beats is explored. The word *kriya* means 'action'. *Kriya* denotes the concept of action in rhythm. The element *graha* conveys the link between the *tala* and music. *Prastara* indicates the elaborative aspect of a *tala* and how the *tala* is expanded.

1) *Kaal* The word *kaal* means 'time'. *Kaal* is the basic structure of *tala* and stands for the time units used in music. *Kaal* determines the beats (*matras*), the parts (*angas*), and the cycles (*avartans*) of a particular *tala*, and helps in resolving the duration or time of a *tala*. This can be explained through an example of a day, where a day consists of hours, minutes, and seconds. An *avartan* is a like a day; the hours in a particular day are *angas*; and the seconds of an hour are *matras*. There are two types of *kaal*: *sukshma kaal* and *sthula kaal*. *Sukshma* and *sthula kaal* have six varieties each.

Sukshma kaal is barely perceptible. The six varieties of *sukshma kaal* are:

a) *Kshana*: Understanding *kshana* makes the comprehension of other *kaals* simple. To describe *kshana*, the example of 'piercing a pile of one hundred lotus petals with a needle' is used. The time utilized in passing a needle from one petal to another is *kshana*. This concept is comparable to the concept of milliseconds.

b) *Lavana*: Eight *kshanas* equal one *lavana*.

c) *Kashtha*: Eight *lavanas* equal one *kashtha*.

d) *Nimisha*: Eight *kashthas* equal one *nimisha*.

e) *Kaala*: Eight *nimishas* equal one *kaala*. *Kaala* is described as the time it takes to blink an eye.

f) *Chaturbhaga*: Two *kaalas* equal one *chaturbhaga*.

Sthula kaal can be deciphered more easily than *sukshma kaal*. It also has six varieties.

a) *Anudruta*: Two *chaturbhagas* equal 1 *anudruta*.

b) *Druta*: Two *anudrutas* equal one *druta*.

c) *Laghu*: Two *drutas* equal one *laghu*.

d) *Guru*: Two *laghus* equal one *guru*.

e) *Pluta*: Three *laghus* equal one *pluta*.

f) *Kakpada*: Four *laghus* equal one *kakpada*.

Kaal is basically a method of standardizing the *tala* units. This standardization process is not observed in contemporary music. The compositions of North Indian music are not rigidly standardized. The musicians and dancers determine the tempo they want for their compositions. These tempos are approximated, but not rigidly restricted to standardized *tala* units.

2) Marga The word *marga* means 'a path'. *Marga* prescribes the way to apply the durations of *kaal* (time units) by using *akhsharas* (sub units) in a *matra* (main unit). There are six ways to determine the tempo or the pace of the music. These six ways are called *shadmargas*.

a)   *Dakshina*: Eight *akshara*s equal one *matra*.

b)   *Vardhika*: Four *akshara*s equal one *matra*.

c)   *Chitra*: Two *akshara*s equal one *matra*.

d)   *Chitratara*: One *akshara* equals one *matra*.

e)   *Chitratama*: Half *akshara* equals one *matra*.

f)   *Atichitratama*: One-fourth *akshara* equals one *matra*.

3) *Kriya* *Kriya* is characterized by the use of hand movements to demonstrate a *tala*. There are two types of *kriya*s or hand movements: *marga* and *desi*. Both *marga* and *desi* are further of two types: *sashabd* and *nishabd*. *Sashabd* means 'with sound' and *nishabd* means 'absence of sound'. Bharata Muni has used the word *pata* for *sashabd kriya*s and *kaal* for *nishabd kriya*s. However, he never used any general term for *kriya*.

***Marga Sashabd and Nishabd Kriya*s:** There are of four kinds of *marga sashabd kriya*s:

a)   *Dhruva*: Snapping the thumb and middle finger to suggest a beat.

b)   *Samya*: Clapping the right palm onto the left palm.

c)   *Tali*: Clapping the left palm onto the right palm.

d)   *Sannipata*: Striking both palms together.

*Marga nishabd kriya*s are also of four kinds. *Nishabd kriya*s are performed after the *sashabd kriya*s. All the hand actions of *nishabd kriya*s are silent. The four kinds of *marga nishabd kriya*s are:

a)   *Avapa*: Raising the hand while closing the fingers.

b)   *Nishkarma*: Lowering the hands from *avapa* position while unfolding the fingers.

c)   *Vikshepa*: From *nishkarma* position, moving the hand to the right side.

d)   *Pravesha*: Bringing the hand back in from *vikshepa* position.

***Desi Sashabd and Nishabd Kriya*s:** *Desi kriya*s were used commonly in popular music. There are eight varieties of *desi kriya*s.

a)   *Dhruvaka*: *Dhruvaka* is the only *desi sashabd kriya*. In this *kriya*, the beat is kept by striking the palms together.
     All other following *kriya*s are *desi nishabd kriya*s.

b)   *Sarpini*: Waving of right palm to the right side.

c)   *Krishya*: Stretching the right palm up and waving it from left to right.

d)   *Padmini*: Turning the palm down and bringing the hand downward.

e)   *Visarjita*: Raising the right hand up with palm facing downward.

f)   *Vikshipta*: Making a fist and bringing the hand towards the self.

g)   *Pataka*: Raising the hand up with palm facing upward.

h)   *Patitta*: Bringing the hand downward from Pataka position.

Today, in North Indian music, four different types of *kriya*s are used: *tali* or clap, *khali* or wave of the hand, counting on one palm with the fingertips of the other hand, and counting on finger ridges with the same hand.

4) Anga *Anga* is the limb of a *tala*. If *tala* is the measurement of time, the *anga*s are the components by which the *tala* is measured. The names of *anga*s and *kaal*s are the same because *anga*s are basically the practical applications of the *sthula kaal*s that are perceptible to the human ear. There are six *anga*s, referred to as the *shadanga*.

a)   *Anudruta*: One *matra* or beat expressed through the *dhruvaka kriya*. The symbol for *anudruta* is U.

b)   *Druta*: Two beats expressed through the *dhruvaka* and *visarjita kriya*s. The symbol for *druta* is 0.

c)   *Laghu*: *Laghu* depends on the *jati*s of a *tala*. Each *jati* consists of different numbers of beats. *Laghu* is a beat followed by counting the ridges of the fingers for the rest of the beats of a *jati*. *Laghu* is expressed through the *dhruvaka* and *vikshipta kriya*s. The symbol for *laghu* is a vertical line.

d)   *Guru*: Eight beats expressed through *dhruvaka*, *vikshipta*, and *patitta kriya*s. The symbol for *guru* is S.

e)   *Pluta*: Twelve beats expressed through the *dhruvaka*, *vikshipta*, *sarpini*, and *patitta kriya*s. The symbol for *pluta* is a vertical line above the symbol of *guru anga*.

f)   *Kakpada*: Sixteen beats expressed through *sarpini*, *krishya*, *pataka*, and *patitta kriya*s. The symbol for *kakpada* is +.

Many varieties of *tala*s in ancient and medieval music are now obsolete. In old times, which type of *anga* had to be used in which *tala* was meticulously prescribed. Today, the rules of *anga*s are not followed in North Indian music.

5) Graha The word *graha* means 'to seize' or 'to get hold of'. *Graha* is the starting point of a song in a *tala*. This starting point grounds the entire composition. There are two types of *graha*: *sama* and *vishama*. In *sama graha*, the music starts with the first beat or the beginning of the *tala*—the *tala* and music start simultaneously. In *vishama graha*, the music does not start with the commencement of the *tala*. There are two types of *vishama graha*: *ateet vishama graha* and *anaghaat graha*. In *ateet vishama graha*, the music starts before the *tala* begins. In *anaghaat graha*, the music begins after the *tala* has started.

6) Jati *Jati*s refer to the number of beats in a *laghu anga*. The *laghu anga* depends on *jati*. The variability in time units of *laghu* determines the *jati*. *Laghu* can diverge by taking up the time units of three, four, five, seven, and nine beats. Therefore, *jati* also establishes the value of the *laghu*. There are five *jati*s:

a) *Tishra*: Three *matra*s or a multiple of three *matra*s with the exception of nine. Although nine is a multiple of three, a *jati* of nine matras is not considered a *tishra jati*. *Tishra* is indicated by one *dhruvaka* and two *vikshipta kriya*s.

b) *Chatushra*: Four *matra*s or a multiple of four *matra*s. It is indicated by one *dhruvaka* and three *vikshipta kriya*s.

c) *Khanda*: Five *matra*s or a multiple of five *matra*s. It is indicated by one *dhruvaka* and four *vikshipta kriya*s.

d) *Mishra*: Seven *matra*s or a multiple of seven *matra*s. It is indicated by one *dhruvaka* and six *vikshipta kriya*s.

e) *Sankirna*: Nine *matra*s. It is indicated by one *dhruvaka* and nine *vikshipta kriya*s.

7) Kala The micro beat of a beat is called *kala*. For example, *teental* consists of sixteen beats, and if each beat is divided into four micro beats, then *teental* has a total of sixty-four micro beats. There are two types of *kala*s:

a) *Vardhamaana Kala*: In this type of *kala*, the number of micro beats increase in the succeeding cycles of a *tala*.

b) *Nashta Kala*: In *nashta kala*, the micro beats gradually decrease in the succeeding cycles of a *tala*.

8) Laya The word *laya* means 'tempo'. *Laya* is the inherent rhythm of music. In music, sometimes *laya* is not demonstrated by a percussive instrument. However, even musical parts without rhythm have an inherent *laya* that is aesthetically regulated. *Laya* is the interval between two successive beats—the pacing or the speed of the music. There are three types of *laya*: *vilambit laya* (slow tempo), *madhya laya* (medium tempo), and the *drut laya* (fast tempo).

9) Yati Variability in the arrangements of the *laya* or tempo is called *yati*. The various ways of presenting *laya* and modifications of the basic *laya* is *yati*. *Yati* is the system that determines the patterns of the tempo in a composition by arranging the *anga*s or units in various ways. In their written form, *yati*s take the shape of geometrical designs. Therefore, it is easier to understand the *yati*s if the *anga*s of each *yati* are demonstrated by alphabetical letters.

Following are the different kinds of *yati*s:

a) *Sama Yati*: The *anga*s or units used in the beginning, middle, and the ending parts of the composition are the same. All the *anga*s of a composition carry the equal value in *sama yati*.

A B C D

A B C D

A B C D

A B C D

b) *Strotvaha Yati*: The word *strotvaha* means 'the transformation of a stream into a river'. In this type of *yati*, the *anga*s progressively get longer in the same way a stream flows forward to meet with the river and starts to take a wider shape.

A

A B

A B C

A B C D

A B C D E

c) *Mridanga Yati*: The mridangam, an Indian percussive instrument, is shaped like a cylinder with narrow ends and broad body. In *mridanga yati*, *anga*s are arranged in a composition in an increasing and then decreasing manner.

A

A B

A B C

A B

A

d) *Gopuccha Yati*: The word *gopuccha* means 'cow's tail'. In *gopuccha yati*, the *anga*s decrease as the composition progresses. In the beginning, there are longer *anga*s followed by shorter *anga*s, giving an impression of a narrowing cow's tail.

A B C D E

A B C D

A B C

A B

A

e) *Pipilika Yati*: The word *pipilika* means 'ant'. The *laya* in *pipilika yati* has an unsteady and weaving pattern like an ant's gait. In *pipilika yati*, the *anga*s are arranged in both increasing and decreasing manners.

A B C

A B

A

A B

A B C

A B

A

f) *Damaru Yati*: *Damaru* is an hourglass-shaped drum. In this *yati*, the *anga*s are arranged in a composition in a decreasing and then again in an increasing manner. *Damaru yati* always expands back to its original length after decreasing.

A B C

A B

A

A B

A B C

g) *Vishama Yati*: In *vishama yati*, the *anga*s are not arranged in any specific manner. It uses random patterns.

10) *Prastara* Expansion of different *anga*s of the *tala* by combining and transforming them. *Prastara* is improvising and elaborating the *anga*s of a *tala* by bringing different variations and permutations into play.

The *tala*'s *dus pran* is not practised in its entirety in modern North Indian music. Yet, it has contributed in shaping the present-day *tala* system. The *tala*'s *dus pran* provides the rationale and methodology upon which the present-day *tala* system has been constructed. Many aspects of this theory are still in practice and lend both regulation and beauty to the North Indian rhythm system.

LAYA AND TALA IN NORTH INDIAN MUSIC AND DANCE

The Hindustani classical music and dance repertoires contain a wealth of both fixed and improvised rhythmic patterns. These rhythms are inspired by many cultural, musical, and artistic traditions that North India has witnessed over the past two millennia. The *tala* system in today's North Indian music and dance has its roots in ancient Indian *tala* theory. The development of the Hindustani classical rhythmic system is the result of continual political, artistic, and cultural changes that India experienced during the Mughal period. Since then, it has evolved, progressed, and has reached the pinnacle of refinement.

Components of North Indian *Tala*

There are over three hundred *tala*s in Hindustani music. *Tala*'s function is to measure the time in music. *Tala* is the time cycle which establishes the rhythmic structure of a composition. Each *tala* consists of a certain number of beats in a cycle. The percussionist, as an accompanying artist, plays the basic pattern of *tala* repeatedly to mark the time in a performance. *Tala* is played not only to indicate and regulate time, but also to add aesthetic appeal to a performance. *Tala*'s function is also to organize and coordinate the different musical activities in a performance. For example, in Kathak and percussion musical performances, the *tala* is maintained through *lehra*, also known as *nagma*. *Lehra* is a melodious grouping of notes, prearranged to account for the beats of a *tala*. The same notes are played repeatedly throughout the performance and mark the first beat and the stressed beats of a *tala*. The ascending and descending notes of *lehra* form the basis of *tala* in Kathak. *Lehra* maintains the *tala* so that the dancers and drummers can execute the compositions in the correct time specified by the *tala* in which they are performing. *Lehra* also serves as a moderator to evaluate whether a dancer or drummer is performing accurately in a *tala*. The *tala* that is kept by *lehra* serves as a coordinator between the singers, instrumentalists, drummers, and dancers in a performance.

The *matras*, *vibhag*, *avartan*, *theka*, *tali*, *khali*, and *sum* are the main components of the Hindustani *tala* system. They provide the basic structure and shape to a *tala*. Beats of a *tala* are referred to as *matras*. Each *tala* is a grouping of a certain number of *matras*. *Matras* are the basic units and divisions in time. The intervals between the *matras* in a *tala* have equal duration. The *matras* in a *tala* are further grouped and divided in smaller sections. These subdivisions of a *tala* within a grouping of *matras* are referred to as *vibhags* or *khandas*. *Vibhag* is notated with a vertical line. Each subdivision is specified by a clap or a wave, and consists of a certain number of beats. The *vibhags* of a *tala* need not be of equal length. Some sections can be short with fewer *matras*, and the others can be long with more *matras*.

The first *matra* of each *vibhag* is indicated by a hand gesture of *tali* or *khali* to demonstrate the emphasis and prominence of certain beats in a *tala*. The word *tali* literally means 'clap'. When a *vibhag* is demonstrated by a clap, it is called the *tali* section of a *tala*. In the *tali* section of *tala*, the tabla player plays both right- and left-hand drums. In the notation of a *tala*, the clap sections are specified by numbers such as 2, 3, and so forth. *Sum*, the first beat of a *tala*, is stressed in order to show the beginning of a new cycle. *Sum* is the most emphatic beat, which is clapped and is notated by X or sometimes +. As opposed to *tali*, *khali* is an empty or moderately stressed beat, which is demonstrated by the wave of the hand. *Khali* is notated as 0. During the *khali* section of a *tala*, the tabla player plays only the *dayan* or the right-hand, high-pitched drum. Usually, the *khali* section in a *tala* comes at halfway through the *tala* or somewhere between the two stressed points. However, there are some exceptions where the generic rule of *khali* is not followed in a *tala*. There are also *talas* that do not have a *khali* section at all. Usually, the *khali* section allows dancers and musicians to have a silent communication regarding where in the cycle of a *tala* they all are, without interrupting the flow of music. An *avartan* or *aavriti* is a cycle of a *tala*. *Vibhags* of a *tala*, each containing several beats, form an *avartan* of a *tala*. The concept of *avartan* provides the sense of finality and conclusion to a *tala*.

Sum is a unique aspect of the *tala* system. All structured and improvised music and dance compositions ultimately return on *sum*. In Sanskrit, the word *sum* means 'collective' or 'shared'. *Sum* in music is, in fact, the summing up or concluding point of the musical arrangements in a piece, where the dancers and musicians find the shared meeting point. Most of the compositions in Indian music and dance start on *sum* and resolve on *sum*. Even in compositions that start at different points in a cycle, they always conclude on *sum*. *Sum* provides the circular and cyclical nature to a *tala*. Indian music and dance are strongly influenced by ancient Indian philosophy. The concept of cyclical patterns forms the basis for Indian philosophy. Indians have always believed in the eternal recurrence of life and the universe, and that all natural courses are cyclical. *Kaal* or time in Vedic philosophy is viewed as non-linear; therefore, the rhythmic motion of the universe is also believed to be non-linear. The concept of *sum* in Indian music is inspired by the Vedic philosophy of the cyclical aspect of nature. The main aspect of *sum* is to display the beginning of the cycle; the cycle then concludes on a *sum*, which is also the beginning point for the next cycle. *Sum* is accented more than any other beat in a *tala*.

The concepts of *sum*, *tali*, and *khali* attest to the structural importance of the number of beats or *matra*s, but the configuration of a *tala* is mainly established through the beats that carry motion. The *sum*, *tali*, and *khali* weave the design of a *tala* on the surface of beats. Therefore, *tala* has two-fold characteristics of measuring the time as well as establishing the stressed beat model within a *tala*. In the *tala* system, time is structured through hand and palm actions, stressed beats, and sometimes even pauses.

Bol is the mnemonic device in Indian music that aids in memorizing the patterns of a *tala*. Each drum stroke is allied with a syllable, and these syllables are called *bol*s. Therefore, *bol*s are the onomatopoeic syllables that correspond to the sounds of the drum. These drum strokes, along with *vibhag* and the *matra*s of a *tala*, create the *theka* of a *tala*. The word *theka* means to 'sustain' or 'uphold'. *Theka* establishes the blueprint of a *tala* and helps in identifying a particular *tala*. It is essentially the phonetic depiction of a *tala*, which is used as an accompaniment arrangement during a music or dance performance. *Tali*s and *khali*s, along with *theka*, help the dancer or musician to infer which beat of *tala* is being played. According to many scholars, the use of *theka* in a *tala* is associated with the creation of tabla during the Mughal era. During the pre-Mughal era, the cylindrical drum pakhawaj was used for the Dhrupad style of singing. In Dhrupad performances, the singers kept the time with their hands and palms, which gave freedom to the percussionist to play more elaborate and ornamental rhythmic patterns. During the Mughal era, with the creation of the percussion instrument tabla and vocal styles such as *khyal* and *thumri*, the use of *theka* became more prominent. Keeping the *theka* to show the time structure became the responsibility of the tabla player, which in turn gave scope to singers and dancers to elaborate their performances with intricacy. This notion of the birth of tabla is speculative, as there is not enough evidence to support it. However, in light of the nature of Mughal arts, this view seems quite probable. The main characteristic of Mughal art was to fill a fixed space with intricate designs and patterns, with more delicate designs and patterns nested inside. Similarly, the tabla player gives a fixed space of a *tala* to a musician or a dancer as a blank canvas on which the performers create intricate designs of rhythmic patterns.

Another fascinating aspect of *tala* is that the patterns within a *tala* can be non-uniform. That is, the measures of *tala* can be broken into different beat patterns. For example, the *tala jhaptal* has ten beats, and the divisions are arranged in a 2+3+2+3 pattern, making the syllable patterns within a *tala* of inconsistent duration. Some *tala*s use half beats; some have fewer *bol*s and more *matra*s; and some have *matra*s that are silent. Almost every *tala* starts with a *tali* section. However, there are a few exceptions. For example, *tala rupak* starts with a *khali*.

An example of symmetrical and uniform *tala teental*:

Teental is the most employed *tala* in North Indian classical music and dance. The structure of *teental* is symmetrical and uniform. *Teental* has sixteen *matra*s, four *vibhag*s, three *tali*s, and one *khali*. The arrangement of *teental* is so uniform that it allows a musician, dancer, or a singer to decorate it with their dance or music comfortably (*see Table 1, p. 304*).

An example of non-uniform *tala jhaptal*:

The structure of *jhaptal* is asymmetrical. *Jhaptal* has ten *matra*s, four *vibhag*s, three *tali*s, and one *khali* (*see Table 2, p. 304*).

An example of *tala* with fewer *bol*s and more *matra*s:

Tala deepchandi is another very popular *tala*. A fascinating characteristic of this *tala* is that it has fewer *bol*s and more *matra*s. A few *matra*s in this *tala* are silent. The silence is indicated by the sign (-) dash. This *tala* is also arranged asymmetrically in groupings of 3+4+3+4. *Tala deepchandi* has fourteen *matras*, four *vibhags*, three *talis*, and one *khali* (*see Table 3, p. 304*).

An example of *tala* that starts with *khali*:

Rupak tala falls under the category of unique *talas* that start with a *khali* or a wave of the hand. *Rupak* is a very common *tala* and is used in different genres of North Indian classical, semi-classical, and non-classical music. This *tala* is arranged asymmetrically in the groupings of 3+2+2. It has seven *matras*, three *vibhags*, and one *khali* on the first beat, and two *talis* (*see Table 4, p. 304*).

An example of a *tala* with no *khali*:

Just like *rupak tala*, the asymmetrical *tevra tala* has seven beats in the groupings of 3+2+2. However, it has all *tali* sections (*see Table 5, p. 304*).

The Concept and Performance of *Laya*

The word *laya* has many different connotations in Sanskrit, depending upon the context. When associated with Lord Shiva, the word *laya* means dissolution, and in yoga, it refers to the state of mental stillness through the regulation of breath. In other contexts, it can mean integration, observance, absorption, repose, and deep concentration. In music and dance, the word *laya* refers to the pacing of time.

Tala is the measurement of time that is aesthetically standardized. *Nibaddha* music, or rhythm-bound music, employs both *tala* and *laya*. The tempo or the pacing of time is referred to as *laya* in Indian music. *Laya* is the interval between two beats. In Western music, the term for the measurement of tempo is same as the measurement of the heart pulse beats per minute (BPM). In the North Indian music system, the pace or the tempo of music is generally measured by the number of beats that are played in an *avartan* of a *tala*. At the same time, the significance of *laya* in Indian music is much broader than the pacing of beats in a *tala*. *Laya* is the inherent disposition of music. It is a combination of the primary pulse rate of a *tala* as well as the frequency, quality, and texture of the tempo. This is why the application of *laya* is keenly observed and practised in *anibaddha sangeet* or music that is not rhythm-bound. The pauses, silences, and timing of the notes and phrases create the *laya* in *anibaddha sangeet*.

The three fundamental *laya*s are *vilambit*, *madhya*, and *drut*. The *vilambit laya* refers to slow tempo. In this tempo, the dance and music use the beats in deliberated, extended, and slow manner. When the *vilambit laya* is very slow, it is called *ati-vilambit*. When the *vilambit laya* is moderately slow, it is called the *madhya-vilambit*. In *vilambit laya*, the interval between two beats is long and divided into sub-beats. Some dancers and musicians refer to these sub-beats as *khanapuri*. Often, the accompanying tabla player plays these sub-beats in a very subtle way. In a way, these sub-beats become the beats in themselves. For example, *tala teental* has sixteen beats. In a very slow tempo, due to the long interval between two beats, four sub-beats are used for each *matra*. In this case, each sub-beat is one-fourth beat long and four one-fourth beats make one whole beat. *Teental*, in a very slow tempo, has sixty-four sub-beats in total. Since the interval between two beats is very long, these sub-beats almost seem like whole beats. It is also referred to as *chaunsat ki laya*, where *chaunsat* means sixty-four. A substantial repertoire of Kathak is danced in *vilambit laya*, which makes the repertoire quite complex. The *madhya laya* refers to a medium tempo. The *drut laya* refers to a fast tempo. When the *drut laya* becomes very fast, it is called *ati-drut*. The footwork of Kathak in *ati-drut* speed is absolutely spectacular and is performed at a lightning speed.

Some musicians and dancers also work with *ati-ati vilambit* and *ati-ati drut laya*s, which are extremely slow and fast speeds respectively. There is no set mathematical time rate in Indian music to indicate whether the *laya* is *vilambit*, *madhya*, or *drut*. It is been observed that singers use a slower tempo for *vilambit* than dancers and instrumentalists. Still, there is an approximate gauge that dancers and musicians use to decide upon the *vilambit laya*, and usually *madhya* and *drut laya*s are set in reference to that estimated *vilambit laya*. For example:

> In ancient musicological treatises, musical time was measured with reference to certain non-musical standards such as the average speed of the normal blinking of the eye or the average speed of the normal cawing of the crow. The late Dr Bimal Roy (the foremost musicologist of 20th century India and with whom both the resource persons of this site Dr Chintamani Rath and Prof. Basavi Mukerji have studied) empirically measured this last standard of time used as a constant measure (the call of the crow) and found it to correspond to ninety beats per minute. To

simplify counting, Dr Roy worked by taking this standard to be to be the more familiar ninty-six beats per minute.[5]

Generally, the *vilambit laya* is approximately set between thirty and sixty beats per minute, the *madhya laya* is set between eighty and one hundred and thirty beats per minute, and the *drut laya* is set at one hundred and sixty beats or more per minute. The *ati-ati vilambit laya* is usually as slow as ten beats per minute, and *ati-ati drut laya* is as fast as six hundred and forty beats per minute. Sometimes, *ati-ati vilambit laya* is so prolonged and *ati-ati drut laya* is so hasty that they not only become cumbersome for the practitioners, but are also not very aesthetically appealing for viewers. The *laya* between *vilambit* and *madhya* is referred to as *vilambit-madhya*. Similarly, the *laya* between *madhya* and *drut* is suggested as *madhya-drut*.

Martin Clayton in his scholarly paper 'Metre and Tala in North Indian Music' notes:

> Changes in the practice of Hindustani music over the last 150–200 years have resulted in the use of a very wide range of *matra* rates in performance: measured in *matra*s per minute, the range would be from around 10MM to well over 700MM. Not only may we speculate that this is too wide a range for tempo, but it also implies a range of cycle lengths from around 1.5 secs to more than a minute. Thus the tempo range is too extreme at both ends for *Tala* to function in practice as the model outlined above suggests it should— when very fast, the *matra* rate is too high to function metrically, when very slow the cycle is too long to be retained by the perceptual present.[6]

The most appropriate *laya* for a composition is the primary criterion for setting a tempo. The kind of *laya* suitable for a composition is determined by examining the nature and temperament of the composition. The artistic maturity of a dancer and musician becomes noticeable in their practice when they choose an appropriate *laya*

[5] 'Laya and Tala', https://www.ragaculture.com/laya_and_tala.html (accessed on 2 May 2018).
[6] Martin Clayton, 'Metre and Tal in North Indian Music', https://www.researchgate.net/profile/Martin_Clayton/publication/265654904_METRE_AND_TAL_IN_NORTH_INDIAN_MUSIC/links/54b91ba00cf28faced626e41/METRE-AND-TAL-IN-NORTH-INDIAN-MUSIC.pdf (accessed on 16 April 2018).

for the compositions, so that the beauty of the composition is not clouded by an inapt choice of tempo. During training sessions, the masters of Indian music and dance always iterate this point by giving examples of elements of the nature. Making the choice of a tempo for a composition is compared with the gait of different animals. The masters of Indian music and dance always say that if a rabbit walks like an elephant, it will not suit its personality. Similarly, if an elephant hops like a rabbit, it will tarnish its character. This is why choosing the appropriate *laya* for different compositions is considered to be one of the most important artistic discretions.

TALA, LAYA, AND RASA

While *tala* is the rhythmic structure to measure time, it also assists in evoking *rasa* during a performance. There are hundreds of *tala*s in Indian music, and they are comprised of anywhere from three to one hundred and eight beats. Some of these *tala*s are thousands of years old. Selecting the proper *tala* and *laya* for a composition facilitates in bringing out the emotional aspect of a performance. In written and spoken forms, *tala*s seem a merely organized time structure. However, the performance of *tala* creates a certain mood, depending on the nature of the composition being performed. This is why the performers are very discriminating in choosing the *tala*, *laya*, and the percussion instrument on which the *tala* is executed. An aesthetically regulated time structure of *tala* is essentially exercised for music and dance to flow.

Each *tala* has its own personality that influences the compositions. Conversely, the compositions that are created to fit in a *tala* are crafted carefully so that they seem integrated with the *tala*. Understanding the personality of a *tala* and harmonizing it with the temperament of a composition helps in evoking *rasa*. Similarly, *laya*s are determined by the nature of compositions. This is why there are many *tala*s of the same number of beats in Hindustani music. These different *tala*s of a similar number of beats induce different *rasa*s.

Theka of a *tala* is extremely important in creating *rasa*. For example, the *theka* of *tala chautal* is masculine in nature, and it takes its *bol*s from the pakhawaj repertoire; therefore, many Kathak dancers use pakhawaj while performing their compositions that are bound in *tala chautal*. The sound of the pakhawaj is more masculine than the sounds of the tabla. This does not imply that the tabla cannot be used as an accompaniment drum while dancing in *tala chautal*. But the forceful compositions of *tala chautal* become more majestic when accompanied by pakhawaj. Even if the tabla players accompany *chautal* compositions, they will use more forceful strokes to express the mood of *chautal*. *Ektal*, which, like *chautal*, has twelve *matra*s, four *tali*s, two *khali*s, and six *vibhag*s, is more striking and charming when played on a tabla, since the *bol*s of *theka* of *ektal* are taken from the tabla repertoire. Looking at the nature of *tala chautal* and *ektal*, it is evident that *tala chautal* is used mostly for the emotions that are represented by the *veera* or *raudra rasa*s. *Ektal* is apparently more suitable for the *shringar rasa* (*see Table 6, p. 304; Table 7, p. 305*).

The compositions are also very carefully crafted looking at the nature of a *tala*. In vocal music, *khyal* is not sung in *dhamar tala*, since the *khyal* repertoire is more imaginative, stylistic, flexible, and romantic in nature, and is not complemented very effectively with the robust nature of *dhamar tala*. Similarly, Kathak dancers use more of *paran*s than *tukda*s and *toda*s in *dhamar tala*. The temperament of *paran*s becomes more compelling in *dhamar tala*.

This is why speaking the *tala*s in a fitting way is given so much importance. While speaking the *tala*s, musicians and dancers use voice modulations not only to show the stressed beats, but also to create emotions. For example, *tala teental* has sixteen beats and the *khali* section of this *tala* is halfway between the *tala* on the ninth beat. Usually, while speaking this *tala*, the pitch is raised on the *khali* section and then the voice is lowered on the last four beats to show the anticipation of coming back to *sum*. A similar technique is used in *lehra* playing and percussion accompaniment, which creates the emotional urgency of coming back home, or, in this case, the *sum*. It undoubtedly helps the dancers and musicians to know where in a cycle of *tala* they are while executing the fixed compositions, as well as performing improvisations. At the same time, it also helps in generating emotions.

Theka Ke Prakar *Theka ke prakar* is another concept that helps in creating *rasa*. Each *tala* has a fixed *theka*, but to suit the mood of the compositions or to aesthetically decorate the empty spaces in a performance, different variations of *theka* are used. These variations of a *theka* are called *theka ke prakar*. *Theka ke prakar* refers to both the modifications in original *bol*s of *theka* and the ornamentation of the *theka*. However, both techniques faithfully abide by the rules and structure of a particular *tala*. Just like *theka*, *prakar*s are cyclical in nature.

Keeping simple *theka* during a performance can be uninspiring and tedious for both the performer and the audience. *Theka ke prakar* adds lustre and imagination in a performance, imparting an emotional appeal. Both *dadra* and *keharwa talas*, which are widely used *talas* in folk and light classical music genres, have numerous *theka ke prakars*. To bring out the emotional content and essence of both a particular genre and its compositions, different variations of these *talas* have been created. This is why playing even the *theka* of a *tala* is a challenge. An accompanying artist has to make a sensible decision regarding which *prakar* to play in order to enhance the mood of a composition. Percussionists also continually change the *prakars* during a performance to suit the sections of a composition.

Keharwa tala is a rhythmic cycle of eight beats. It has two evenly spaced *vibhags*, one *tali*, and one *khali*. In Kathak, many *prakars* of *keharwa* are used during the performance of *ghazal*, *bhajan*, and so forth. Sometimes, *teental* is played in *keharwa ang* for the *gat* repertoire, which means that the sixteen-beat-cycle *teental* has the feel of *keharwa tala*. This is done both for stylistic reasons and to create mood (*see Table 8 and Table 9, p. 305*).

The most important way of creating *rasa* through *tala* and *laya* is through *laykari*, or the various types of rhythmic patterns and designs in a given space. *Chanda, grahas, gunas, jatis,* and many other types of *laykaris* make a performance exquisite and vivacious.

Laykari

LAYKARI IS THE PERFORMANCE of dramatic and fascinating variations and patterns in tempo that enables performers to express themselves through various types of rhythms. *Laykari* is executed on the solid foundation of *tala*. *Tala* is cyclical; therefore, all *laykari*s conclude on *sum*, the first beat of *tala*. *Laykari* is also the elaborative pattern of an established *tala* and *laya*. It is an integral aspect of the rhythm-oriented Kathak dance.

Barabar ki laya is used as a reference point for many types of *laykari*. The performance of one *matra* or one beat of a *tala* is called *barabar ki laya* (ratio of 1:1). *Barabar ki laya* is also referred to as *ekguna*. It is the foundation upon which musicians and dancers build their enthralling rhythmic structures with ease.

The main techniques of *laykari* are the changes in the ratio of actions per *matra*, dividing the original composition into different combinations and grouping beats in various ways. The concept of ratio in terms of *laykari* suggests how many sub-beats are utilized in a single beat, and how many total sub-beats are used in a cycle of a *tala*. The evenly spaced subdivisions of a beat create the ratio of beats to *tala*. The divisions of the theme phrase of a rhythmic composition suggest that the components of phrases are nestled within the theme itself, and they can be rearranged and reorganized. Grouping of beats in a variety of ways within a *tala* changes the scheme of accents on the regularly recurring beat pattern of a *tala*, making it more exciting. Most of the *laykari*s operate within these principles.

GUNAS OF LAYA

*Guna*s of *laya* specifically deal with the categorization of the ratio of sub-beats to a beat or the ratio of total sub-beats to the total beats of a *tala*. Simple *guna*s are the result of performing different speeds of *barabar ki laya*. More complicated *guna*s are derived from ratios involving complex fractions. For simplicity, the following *guna*s are examined in relation to four *matra*s or beats.

a) **Pawguna:** One *matra* placed on four *matra*s (ratio of 1:4)

b) **Adh-guna:** Two *matra*s placed on four *matra*s (ratio of 2:4)

c) **Paun-guna:** Three *matra*s evenly placed on four *matra*s (ratio of 3:4)

d) **Ekguna:** Also referred to as *barabar ki laya* or *thah laya*. One *matra* for every *matra* is called *ekguna* (ratio of 1:1)

e) **Sawaguna:** Also referred as *kuwar laya*. Five *matra*s evenly placed on four *matra*s (ratio of 5:4)

f) **Dedh-guna:** Also called the *aar laya*. Six *matra*s are evenly distributed on four *matra*s (ratio of 6:4)

g) **Paune-do-guna:** Also known as *biad laya*. Seven equally spaced *matra*s are placed on four *matra*s (ratio of 7:4)

h) **Duguna:** Eight evenly spaced *matra*s on four *matra*s (ratio of 8:4)

i) **Sawa-do-guna:** Nine *matra*s are evenly placed on four *matra*s (ratio of 9:4)

j) **Dhai-guna:** Ten *matra*s are evenly placed on four *matra*s (ratio of 10:4 or 5:2)

k) **Paune-teen-guna:** Eleven evenly placed *matra*s on four *matra*s (ratio of 11:4)

l) **Tiguna:** Twelve evenly spaced *matra*s on four *matra*s (ratio of 12:4)

m) **Chauguna:** Sixteen evenly spaced *matra*s on four *matra*s (ratio of 16:4)

In Table 10, the dash indicates the rest between two beats (*p. 306*).

All the aforementioned *guna*s are also performed in double, triple, and quadruple speeds. When *kuwar*, *aar*, and *biad laya*s are presented in double speed, they are called *maha-kuwar*, *maha-aar*, and *maha-biad laya*s. *Duguna* is the double speed of *ekguna* and *chauguna* is the double speed of *duguna*. Similarly, *tiguna* is the double speed of *dedh-guna*. *Dedh-guna* also corresponds to triple time and the multiples of triple time. *Sawaguna* corresponds to the multiples of five beats, and *paune-do-guna laya* to the multiples of seven beats. Complicated *guna*s require a lot of mental concentration. Only a very few masters of classical Indian music and dance are able to perform the complicated *guna*s. The most challenging aspect of practising the *guna*s is to accent not the numbers, but the *matra*s. For instance, in the example of *paun-guna*, the accents are not on the numbers 2 and 3, but on 1; the third space after 1; the second space after 2; and the first space after 3, since the main *matra*s fall on those spaces (*see Table 11, p. 306*).

In written form, the *gunas* look very mathematical in nature. However, the masters acquire the feel for these *gunas* by practising them over and over. Their minds are not engaged in deciphering the mathematics of it. The complex *gunas* in *ati vilambit laya* are even more difficult to perform. In *ati vilambit laya*, the time gap between two *matras* is so large that keeping the track of sub-beats that have many spaces in between becomes very hard. Still, the idea of complex *gunas* is not just theoretical. These complicated *gunas* have been practically applied in the art of Hindustani music and dance.

CHHAND

Chhand is basically the rhythmic characteristics of a *tala* that are played or danced in the scheme of another *tala*. Many times, the musicians and dancers bring into play the *theka* of one *tala* within another *tala* in order to create the feeling of *chhand*. Rhythmic characteristics of any *tala* are its *sum*, *vibhag*, *tali*, *khali*, and *theka* that determine both a *tala*'s syllabic design and its accentual patterns. Sometimes, while performing a *chhand*, the syllables of one *tala* in another *tala* are not used diametrically, but more importance is given to the accentual patterns of the intended *tala*, which is being laid over the original *tala*. In other words, more than the syllables, the feel of one *tala* in another *tala* is used as *chhand*. *Chhand* is performed by stressing the important beats of a *tala* and lengthening or shortening the beats a little. Sometimes, *chhands* also are achieved by applying the rules of *guna*.

JATI

The word *jati* literally means 'classification'. *Jati* refers to the variability in *matras*. The way the term *jati* is used in the North Indian *tala* system is quite different from the way it is used in the South Indian *tala* system.

In the South Indian *tala* system, there are seven main *talas*. Each of these seven *talas* creates five other *talas*. When they are combined with five *jatis*, they produce a total of thirty-five *talas*. In the North Indian system, *jati* is treated more as a rate of action per *matra*.

Jati determines the basic lengths of *matra*s and segregates the rhythm into five different classes: *tishra, chatushra, khanda, mishra,* and *sankirna jati*s (*see Table 12, p. 306*).

Both *jati*s and *guna*s are subdivisions of beats, but they are different in that *jati*s have a continuous pulse, whereas the *guna*s can have gaps of silence. This is because *jati*s are in reference to each *matra*, whereas the *guna*s are executed in relation to the entire cycle of a *tala*.

In *jati*s, the sub-beats are more concrete and distinct. For example, *tishra jati* has three sub-beats in each *matra*, and these sub-beats can be comprised of any rhythmic syllables, independent of the *theka* of a *tala*. In *tiguna*, each *matra* also contains three beats, but the *theka* of a *tala* is performed three times only.

*Guna*s, *jati*s, and *chhand*s constitute the basis for *laykari* in Hindustani music and dance. The rhythmic compositions use *laykari* both in simple and complex ways to electrify a performance. Mastering *laykari* is one of the most important aspects of training and requires great dedication, discipline, and intense practice so that it can be applied and executed with total command. The command on *laykari* involves not only performing the complex rhythms with mastery, but also using the rhythmic variations in a way that it aids in creating the proper *rasa*. *Laykari* is carried out through various compositions in different *tala*s and *laya*s. It is also reflected in the ways in which a composition arrives at the *sum*.

Ways of Resolving
a Composition on *Sum*

SUM IS THE MOST CRUCIAL BEAT of Kathak. All compositions resolve on *sum*. The way in which the compositions return on *sum* also facilitates the dynamic *laykari* of a composition. *Graha*s of *laya*, *tihai*, and so forth enable dancers to create rhythmic compositions that make the arrival on *sum* incredibly appealing.

GRAHAS OF LAYA

The *graha*s are one of the determinants of the conclusion of the variations in *laya*. In ancient texts, *graha* is considered as a starting point of a *tala*. Today, *graha*s are viewed as a way of expressing and conveying *sum* through a specific composition. There are three *graha*s of *laya*: *sama*, *ateet*, and *anaghat*. In a *sama graha*, the composition ends on *sum*. In *ateet graha*, the composition ends just before *sum*. In *anaghat graha*, the composition ends just after *sum*. Dancers and musicians look at these *graha*s from a different approach. In *ateet graha*, the composition starts before *sum*, and in *anaghat graha*, the composition starts after *sum*.

Ateet and *anaghat graha*s have an effect on the development and expansion of the composition. Usually, the compositions that conclude as *ateet* or *anaghat* deal with the concept of fractions of a *matra* or beat, which is more evident in *vilambit laya*, since the duration between two beats in *vilambit laya* is long. If the *ateet* and *anaghat* are played or danced before or after a full beat, the intensity is not the same. Since these *graha*s deal with a fraction of a *matra*, they impact the overall composition substantially. These kinds of compositions have a certain tension, which is released only on *sum*.

TIHAI: TRIADIC STRUCTURES

The word *tihai* means 'one third of the total'. Therefore, in *tihai*s, the same phrase is repeated three times successively to conclude a composition on *sum*. The three sections of a *tihai* are referred as the three *palla*s. Syllabically, the three *palla*s are often not exactly the same, but the rhythmic or melodic arrangement of all three *palla*s of a *tihai* are equal and matching. *Tihai*s may start on any beat of a *tala*, but they always conclude on *sum* after creating much rhythmic tension and then releasing that tension on *sum*. In vocal and instrumental music, the *tihai* can also end at the *mukhda* or where the song starts.

The Aesthetical Functions of *Tihai*

Tihai or *tiya* is a triadic cadential configuration that creates a sense of conclusion. It provides the feeling of finality, indicating that the phrase has concluded. Hindustani music and dance always end with a *tihai*. The *tihai*s executed during a performance offers some respite from the excitement and build-up of energy. *Tihai*s are also used to end a particular composition. In this case, *tihai* provides the composition a sense of conclusion and also anticipation that soon a new composition will start. Therefore, *tihai* has diverse functions: providing resolution for an entire performance, giving a temporary rest or 'breather' between sections of a performance, transitioning from one composition to another, creating the experience of tension and release, and finally demonstrating the exhilarating rhythmic virtuosity of a performer.

Tihai reveals a performer's rhythmic genius and command on *laya* and *tala*. Great musicians and dancers are able to create *tihai*s extemporaneously and can perform them with spontaneity. Proper execution of *tihai*s requires rigorous training in *laya* and *tala* with intense concentration. The artist's understanding and appreciation of the compositions being rendered will affect the accurate execution of *tihai*s. Each composition has its own temperament, and the *tihai*, to end a particular composition, must suit the mood of the composition. For example, if a composition is of serious mood, a playful and bouncy *tihai* would not be appropriate. Competent performers not only have expertise in the area of *laya* and *tala*, but also a remarkable insight into the mood of the compositions. This is how they are able to create and perform *tihai*s that immensely help in producing the intended *rasa*.

*Tihai*s affect the audience on a psychological level in the sense that the successive repetition of a phrase three times is psychologically persuasive. In the first *palla* of a *tihai*, the audience watches or hears the phrase; in second *palla*, the audience recognizes and identifies the phrase; and during the third *palla* of a *tihai*, the audience relates to the phrase. Relating to or involving the audience in a performance is considered one of the most important aspirations of Indian music and dance.

In *tihai*, the total number of beats in a *tala* is divided into three equal sections. The second *palla* of the *tihai* usually has the feel of an offbeat rhythm, since the weak beats are accented. The first beat is always the strongest beat. Other strong beats are the ones in which the *tali* or *khali* sections start. Often, the second section of *tihai* falls on the weaker beats of a *tala*, giving the second *palla* of *tihai* the offbeat feel. This creates substantial rhythmic tension that seeks release at the end of the *tihai*. The normal accent beats of a *tala* are restored in the third *palla* of the *tihai* and the phrase moves to the *sum*, the point of resolve.

In Table 13, the strong beats of *teental* are in bold letters. It can be clearly seen that the first and the third *palla*s of the *tihai* start on the strong beats—the first and the thirteenth beat. Starting on the strong beats gives the feeling of straightforward motion. But the second *palla* of the *tihai* starts on the seventh beat. Even though the second *palla* has a straightforward motion, it gives the feeling of indirect motion or the offbeat feel, which creates rhythmic divergence in the *tihai*. The final release comes on the last *palla*, which concludes on *sum* (*see p. 307*).

The above-mentioned *tihai* is a very simple one which takes the time span of one *avartan* (one cycle) of a *tala*. There are many different types of *tihai*, spanning to two or more *avartan*s of a *tala*. All *tihai*s have various mathematical formulas associated with them.

The Components of *Tihai*

Dr Chintamani Rath in his essay 'A Grammar of the *Tihai*' articulates that every *tihai* has three main components: *shareera*, *aghat*, and *virama*. The word *shareera* means the 'body', which is the main phrase of a *tihai*. The word *aghat* means the 'stroke', which is the accent at the last beat of each *palla*. The *virama* or the 'rest' is the space or time interval between the *palla*s of a *tihai*. As Dr Rath states:

> The 'stroke' of a Tihai is the accent at the end of each of the first two phrases of the Tihai. The accent or stroke at the end of the third phrase, coinciding with the Sum or other predetermined point, is outside the Matra count of

the Tihai and so is not relevant for the present. The 'body' of a Tihai is the musical event (melodic/rhythmic figure or phrase) occurring from the start of the Tihai to the first stroke. The body occurs thrice in the course of a Tihai. The 'gap' in a Tihai is the rest, silence or pause occurring after a stroke and before the commencement of the subsequent body. A Tihai may or may not have a gap (i.e., the value of a gap may be zero); however, if there are gaps, the duration of the gaps must be identical.[1]

Sum Position—Pandit Rajendra Gangani

In the previous example of *tihai*, the syllables *Tig dha dig dig* are the *shareera* or body of the *tihai*. The syllable *Thai* on the first, fifth, and eleventh beats are the *aghat* or the stroke. The gaps on sixth and twelfth beats are the *virama* or the gap in the *tihai*.

The *shareera* of a *tihai* can also be divided into two parts: *bol and mukhda*. The *bol* is the syllabic arrangement, which functions as the body of the composition. The word *mukhda* means 'face'. *Mukhda*s are short rhythmic flourishes and additions that conclude on *sum*. Together, the *bol* and *mukhda* make the *shareera* of a *tihai*.

The Rules of *Tihai*

*Tihai*s are logic-based in nature; therefore, there are rules and formulas for creating *tihai*s that help the musicians and dancers to work out the order in which they can divide the cycles of a *tala* into three equal parts and create phrases for different types of *tihai*s.

The most important rule for *tihai* is that all three *palla*s of a *tihai*, their gaps, and their strokes need to be of equal length and equal duration. The *tihai*s that

---

[1] Chintamani Rath, 'A Grammar of the *Tihai*' (Essay written in August 1989, Appendices in March 2008), http://www.ragaculture.com/tihai.html (accessed on 16 April 2018).

have spaces between *palla*s must have two gaps overall. These gaps are between the first and second *palla*s, and then again between the second and third *palla*s. In the earlier example, all three *palla*s of the *tihai* have the same duration and gaps. Each *palla* has a *shareera* or body of four syllables—*Tig dha dig dig*. Each *palla* has three strokes, which is articulated as *thai*. And the gaps between the *palla*s are of one *matra*.

In Kathak, the gaps between the *tihai*s are often filled by body movements or claps. The body movements for each *palla* in Kathak can be different; however, the footwork for each *palla* is the same in order to produce a similar rhythmic phrase. Sometimes, the *bol*s in *palla*s can be ornamented; still, each *palla* is of the same length.

Most *tihai*s conclude on *sum*. However, there are some exceptions in raga music in which the *tihai*s can also end at the beginning of a song or a melodic composition. The *tihai*s that end at the commencement of a song are used in Kathak repertoire based on raga music compositions, such as *khyal ang* songs, *trivat*, and *chaturang*.

TYPES AND MATHEMATICS OF *TIHAI*

There are different types of *tihai*s based on the application of gaps and pauses, the time span of *bol*s, number of strokes in a *palla*, way of arriving at *sum*, and the *laykari* and compositional qualities. All forthcoming examples of different types of *tihai*s are in *tala teental*, which has sixteen beats. Similar formulas are applied to different *tala*s; only the *matra* counts of phrases change.

Dumdar Tihai

The word *dum* means 'breath'. A *tihai* with pauses between the three *palla*s is a *dumdar tihai*. The previous example of *tihai* is also an example of *dumdar tihai*, since it has time intervals or *virama*s between the *palla*s that give performers a chance to catch their breath. The simple mathematical formula for a *dumdar tihai* in *teental* in one *avartan* of *barabar ki laya* is to take a *bol* of four *matra*s and end it with an *aghat* or a stroke, which will become the fifth *matra*, and then give a rest of one *matra* (*see Table 14, p. 307*).

Another very simple formula for *dumdar tihai* is to create a *bol* of fourteen *matra*s, end it with the *aghat*, which will become the fifteenth *matra*, and then give a rest of two *matra*s (*see Table 15, p. 307*).

Bedumdar Tihai

A *tihai* with no time interval between the three *palla*s is a *bedumdar tihai*. Given is an example of a simple *bedumdar tihai*:

Ta thai	thai TaT	Aa thai	thai TaT
X			
thai Ta	thai Ta	thai thai	TaT Aa
2			
thai thai	TaT thai	Ta thai	Ta thai
0			
thai TaT	Aa thai	thai TaT	thai Ta
3			
Thai			
X			

A simple way to create a *bedumdar tihai* is to take the total *matra*s of a *tala* in one *avartan* and divide them by three. For most of the *tala*s, the quotient will be in decimals. When the half *matra* is added to the place value of this decimal and is played three times without any gap, it becomes the *bedumdar tihai*. For example, in the example of *tihai* of *teental*, the total *matra*s of *teental* (sixteen beats) are divided by three. The quotient is 5.3. The place value of the number is five and the half *matra* is added to it. Therefore, any *bol* which takes five and a half *matra*s, if played three times, will become the *bedumdar tihai* of *tala teental*: 5 ½ x 3 = 16 ½. In the earlier equation, sixteen *matra*s are for *teental*, and the last half *matra* is to arrive on *sum*. The concept of *bedumdar tihai* depends on *laya*. In *vilambit laya*, even a very short gap is more noticeable. Therefore, even if a *tihai* is *bedumdar*, the smallest gap will give the impression of a *dumdar tihai*. In faster speeds, the *bedumdar tihai*s becomes more effective.

Chakkardar Tihai

Chakkardar tihai is simply a *tihai* within a *tihai*. A *chakkardar tihiai* is created when a *tihai* is repeated three times before concluding on *sum*. *Chakkardar tihai*s are usually concluded after several *avartan*s.

An example of a *chakkardar tihai* in *teental*:

Ta thai thai TaT	Aa thai thai TaT	thai - Ta -	thai - Ta thai
X			
thai TaT Aa thai	thai TaT thai -	Ta - thai -	Ta thai thai TaT
2			
Aa thai thai TaT	thai - Ta -	thai - - -	Ta thai thai TaT
0			
Aa thai thai TaT	thai - Ta -	thai - Ta thai	thai TaT Aa thai
3			
thai TaT thai -	Ta - thai -	Ta thai thai TaT	Aa thai thai TaT
X			
thai - Ta -	thai - - -	Ta thai thai TaT	Aa thai thai TaT
2			
thai - Ta -	thai - Ta thai	thai TaT Aa thai	thai TaT thai -
0			
Ta - thai -	Ta thai thai TaT	Aa thai thai TaT	thai - Ta -
3			
Thai			
X			

In the given *tihai*, all the *palla*s have the format of *tihai* itself, which is the characteristic of a *chakkardar tihai*. The mathematical formula for this structure can be decoded as:

Tihai of eleven *matra*s with the eleventh *matra* as a stroke (11 x 3 = 33). A phrase of thirty-three beats is needed to finish a *chakkardar tihai* in two *avartan*s of *teental* (thirty-two beats for two *avartan*s + one beat to conclude on *sum*). The *laya* for this *tihai* is *chauguna*, or the fourth speed, since there are four *bol*s in each *matra*. In *athguna laya* (eight *matra*s per beat), this *tihai* will fit into one *avartan*. When observed in a written format, it seems like there are many pauses between other than the main pause after the first *palla* of the *tihai*. However, these pauses are so short that their duration in a performance is insignificant. In contrast, the gaps between the *palla*s (*Thai* - - -) are substantial enough to be heard properly.

There are many ways to create *chakkardar tihai*s. Following is another formula: *tihai* of twenty-seven *matra*s with the twenty-seventh *matra* as a stroke

(27 x 3 = 81) will create a *chakkardar tihai* that will fit in the five *avartan*s of *teental* (16 x 5 = 80), with the eighty-first *matra* as *sum*.

Most of the *chakkardar tihai*s have nine *Dha*s or nine *aghat*s. Therefore, they are also deemed *navdha* or *nauhakka tihai*s.

Farmaishi chakkardar and *kamali chakkardar* are two rare categories of *chakkardar tihai*. These unique *tihai*s are performed by very few musicians and dancers, since they involve complex mathematics. These *tihai*s are taught surreptitiously only to dedicated students. Even though the formulas of these *tihai*s are precise, practising and performing them is a difficult task indeed.

Farmaishi Chakkardar Tihai

The word *farmaishi* means 'by request'. The *farmaishi chakkardar*s are exclusive *tihai*s that very few dancers and musicians can perform with ease. In this kind of *tihai*, each *palla* is composed of *bol*, *mukhda*, and *aghat*. Since it is a type of a *chakkardar tihai*, each *palla* of *tihai* follows the triadic structure of a *tihai*. The first stroke or *aghat* of the first *palla*, the second stroke of the second *palla*, and the third stroke of the third *palla* coincide with *sum*. Following is the arrangement of a *farmaishi tihai* in which the highlighted *Dha*s are on *sum*:

1st *Palla* of *Tihai*: *Bol* + *Mukhda* + **Dha** + *Mukhda* + *Dha* + *Mukhda* + *Dha*
2nd *Palla* of *Tihai*: *Bol* + *Mukhda* + *Dha* + *Mukhda* + **Dha** + *Mukhda* + *Dha*
3rd *Palla* of *Tihai*: *Bol* + *Mukhda* + *Dha* + *Mukhda* + *Dha* + *Mukhda* + **Dha**[2]

In the given table of a traditional *farmaishi chakkardar tihai*, the *bol*s are: *Taka Taka Takita, Taka Taka Takita, Taka Taka Takita, Taka Taka Takita, Taka Takita, Taka Takita, Taka Takita, Taka Takita.*

The *mukhda* is: *Takita dhikita, Takita dhikita, Takita dhikita, Takita dhikita.* And the *aghat* is *Dha*. Each *palla* of a *farmaishi chakkardar* will look like the following with two *virama*s or gaps in between the *palla*s:

Bol of twelve *matra*s + *mukhda* of four *matra*s + one *Dha* + *bol* of twelve *matra*s + *mukhda* of four *matra*s + one *Dha* + *bol* of twelve *matra*s + *mukhda* of four *matra*s + one *Dha* (*see Table 16, pp. 308–309*).

---

[2] Sri Bhagwatsharan Sharma, *Tala Ank* (Hathras: Sangeet Karyalaya, year: n.a.).

Kamali Chakkardar Tihai

The word *kamali* means 'wondrous' or 'phenomenal'. Like the *farmaishi chakkardar*s, the *kamali chakkardar*s are also rare types of *tihai*. *Kamali chakkardar* is a variety of *chakkardar*, and has the characteristics of *tihai* within a *tihai*. Therefore, it has three *palla*s, which in turn are composed of three sub-*palla*s. Each sub-*palla* of *kamali chakkardar* ends with three *aghat*s or strokes. The beauty of this type of *tihai* is that the first stroke of first sub-*palla* of the first *palla*, the second stroke of second sub-*palla* of the second *palla*, and the third stroke of the third sub-*palla* of the third *palla* correspond to the *sum*.

Following is the arrangement of a *kamali chakkardar tihai* in which the highlighted *Dha*s are on *sum*.

1st *Palla* of *Tihai*: *Bol* + *Mukhda* + **Dha** Dha Dha + *Mukhda* + Dha Dha Dha + *Mukhda* + Dha Dha Dha

2nd *Palla* of *Tihai*: *Bol* + *Mukhda* + Dha Dha Dha + *Mukhda* + Dha **Dha** Dha + *Mukhda* + Dha Dha Dha

3rd *Palla* of *Tihai*: *Bol* + *Mukhda* + Dha Dha Dha + *Mukhda* + Dha Dha Dha + *Mukhda* + Dha Dha **Dha**[3]

The *kamali chakkardar* generally takes up seven *avartan*s. Seven *avartan*s of *teental* has one hundred and twelve beats (16 x 7). To create this *tihai*, one hundred and thirteen beats are needed for the hundred and thirteenth beat to conclude on *sum*. After dividing one hundred and thirteen by three, the quotient is thirty-seven with a remainder of two. Each *palla* of this *tihai* will be thirty-seven *matra*s long. The remainder of two can be used as *virama* between the three *palla*s of a *tihai*. The *bol* of ten *matra*s can be taken with the *mukhda* of six *matra*s and three *Dha*s. Each *palla* of a *kamali chakkardar* will look like the following with two *virama*s or gaps in between the *palla*s:

Bol of ten *matra*s + *mukhda* of six *matra*s + three *Dha*s + *mukhda* of six *matra*s + three *Dha*s + *mukhda* of six *matra*s + three *Dha*s = thirty-seven *matra*s (*see Table 17, p. 310*).[4]

....

[3] Ibid.

[4] Ibid.

There are many different variations of *kamali chakkardar tihai*, such as *kamali chakkardar* with four *Dha*s and *kamali chakkardar* with five *Dha*s. *Kamali chakkardar* of four *Dha*s have the same characteristics as *kamali chakkardar* of three *Dha*s. In this type of *tihai*, the first stroke of the first sub-*palla* of the first *palla*, the second stroke of the second sub-*palla* of the second *palla*, the third stroke of the third sub-*palla* of the third *palla*, and the fourth stroke of the fourth sub-*palla* of the fourth *palla* correspond to *sum*. Similarly, *kamali chakkardar* of five *Dha*s have five main *palla*s and the *sum* corresponds to the first stroke of the first sub-*palla* of the first *palla*, the second stroke of the second sub-*palla* of the second *palla*, the third stroke of the third sub-*palla* of the third *palla*, the fourth stroke of the fourth sub-*palla* of the fourth *palla*, and the fifth stroke of the fifth sub-*palla* of the fifth *palla*.

Kamali chakkardar of four *Dha*s has four *palla*s and uses the following formula:

Bol of fourteen *matras* + *mukhda* of two *matras* + *Dha Dha Dha Dha* + *mukhda* of two *matras* + *Dha Dha Dha Dha* + *mukhda* of two *matras* + *Dha Dha Dha Dha* + *mukhda* of two *matras* + *Dha Dha Dha Dha* + gap of three *matras*. This entire arrangement is performed four times. *Kamali chakkardar* of four *Dha*s takes up to one hundred and sixty-one *matras* [Translation].[5]

Kamali chakkardar of five *Dha*s has five *palla*s and uses the following equation:

Bol of thirteen *matras* + *mukhda* of three *matras* + *Dha Dha Dha Dha Dha* + *mukhda* of three *matras* + *Dha Dha Dha Dha Dha* + *mukhda* of three *matras* + *Dha Dha Dha Dha Dha* + *mukhda* of two *matras* + *Dha Dha Dha Dha Dha* + *mukhda* of three *matras* + *Dha Dha Dha Dha Dha* + *gap* of two *matras* (this entire arrangement is performed five times). *Kamali chakkardar* of five *Dha*s takes up to two hundred and seventy-eight beats.

Kamali chakkardar of four and five *Dha*s have immaculate mathematical qualities and are extremely difficult to perform. However, these types of *tihai*s are more to show the genius of a performer. Many artists do not include *kamali chakkardar* of four and five *Dha*s under the field of *tihai*, since the exclusivity of a *tihai* is that it is comprised of three *palla*s.

Sama and Vishama Tihais

*Tihai*s can be either *sama* or *vishama* and use the notion of *grahas* of *laya*. *Sama tihai*s end on *sum*, and *vishama tihai*s have either *ateet* or *anaghat*

----

[5] Ibid.

conclusion. Most *tihai*s are *sama tihai*s and end on *sum*. *Vishama tihai*s are used sparingly to add more appeal to a performance. The *tihai*s that end just before the *sum* are called *ateet*, and the *tihai*s that end after the *sum* are called *anaghat tihai*.

Ginati Ki Tihai

The word *ginati* means 'numerals'. *Ginati ki tihai*s are exercised very liberally by Kathak dancers, in which the numbers are used to create *tihai*s. Different geometrical shapes are created by *ginati ki tihai*s, which are more apparent when they are written. Given are some examples of the shape and rhythmic notation of a traditional *ginati ki tihai* in *teental* (*see Table 18, p. 311*).

12

123

1234

12345

12345

12345678

12345678

1

*Ginati ki tihai*s are amusing not only because of their shapes, but also because of their numerical diversions and playful gaps, which become very entertaining when a performer recites and performs them. Table 19 is another example of a *ginati ki tihai* with gaps, which makes this *tihai* seem like a puzzle (*see p. 311*).

12 - 34 - 56 - 78 -

123 - 456 - 78

1234 - 5678 -

12345678

1

Gopuchcha Tihai

The word *gopuchcha* means 'cow's tail'. In *gopuchcha tihai*, the *bols* decrease in length in a sequential manner. Initially, there are *bols* that take up more *matras*, followed by shorter *bol*s that successively take fewer and fewer *matra*s, giving the impression of a narrowing cow's tail. Table 20 is an example of the *bol*s of a *gopuchcha tihai* (*see p. 311*).

Tig dha dig dig thai
dha dig dig thai
dig dig thai
dig thai
Ta thai
Ta thai
dig thai
Ta thai
Ta thai
dig thai
Ta thai
Ta thai

There are many more organizations and variations of *tihai*s. More difficult *tihai*s such as *kamali chakkardar*s and *farmaishi chakkardar*s can be presented from different *matra*s. Different equations are used for the *tihai*s that start from different *matra*s. Creating, interpreting, and performing different types of *tihai*s takes great artistic skill, which is mastered by all great Indian musicians and dancers.

Every artist endeavours to present extraordinary rhythmic puzzles through *laykari* and *tihai*s. There are many different equations that the practitioners master in order to execute the *tihai*s in an exact manner. There are also equations for using the same *tihai* in different *tala*s.

EQUATIONS FOR NINE-*MATRA TIHAI* TO BE USED IN DIFFERENT TALAS

A specific equation based on the subtraction technique is used to figure out how a *tihai* that is nine *matra*s long can be used in different *tala*s. In this method, the total *matra*s of a *tala* is counted from *sum* to *sum* and the total number of *bol*s of a *tihai* is subtracted from that number. The remainder is the number of *matra*s that needs to be left before starting that particular *tihai*. For example, the following nine-*matra tihai* can be used in any *tala*:

Tigdha   Digdig   Thai,   Tigdha   Digdig   Thai,   Tigdha   Digdig   Thai

In this *tihai*, there is a *bol* of three *matra*s, which is repeated three times for a total of a *tihai* of nine *matra*s where the ninth *matra* culminates in *sum*. There are seventeen *matra*s in *teental*, if counted from *sum* to *sum* (sixteen *matra*s of *teental* + one *matra* for *sum*). The equation is:

17 (total *matra*s of *tala* including *sum*) - 9 (total *matra*s of *tihai*) = 8 *matra*s. Therefore, eight *matra*s will be left in the cycle of *teental* and the *tihai* will start from the ninth beat. In Tables 21–24, the line in bold is the actual *theka* of the *tala* (*see Table 21, p. 311*).

The same *tihai* can be used in other *tala*s by using this equation:

11 (total *matra*s of *jhaptal* including *sum*) - 9 (total *matra*s of *tihai*) = 2 *matra*s. In *jhaptal*, the same *tihai* will start on the third beat (*see Table 22, p. 312*).

13 (total *matra*s of *ektal* including *sum*) - 9 (total *matra*s of *tihai*) = 4 *matra*s. In *ektal*, the same *tihai* will start on the fifth beat (*see Table 23, p. 312*).

15 (total *matra*s of *dhamar* including *sum*) - 9 (total *matra*s of *tihai*) = 6 *matra*s. In *tala dhamar*, this *tihai* will start on the seventh beat (*see Table 24, p. 312*).

SIMPLE *TIHAIS* FOR FOUR *MATRA*- TO FIFTEEN-MATRA-LONG *TALAS*

The *tihai*s given here are of different lengths. These *tihai*s can be used in different *tala*s, depending on the number of *matra*s in a *tala*. For example, the seven-*matra* *tihai* can be used for a *tala* which is six *matra*s long. Likewise, when repeated three times, it can be used in *jhaptal* as a *chakkardar tihai*. *Jhaptal* has ten *matra*s. A seven-*matra* *tihai*, when repeated three times, will have twenty-one *matra*s. It will fit in two *avartan*s of *teental* with the twenty-first beat as its *sum* (*See Table 25, p. 312*).

The previous *tihai* can be used for a *tala* which is four *matra*s long. It will also fit into a fourteen-*matra* *tala* as a *chakkardar tihai*. In *teental*, it will fit with a gap of one *matra* after each *palla* (*see Table 26, p. 312; Tables 27–32, pp. 314–15; Tables 33–36, pp. 316–17*).

ANOTHER WAY OF CREATING *TIHAIS* IN DIFFERENT *TALAS*

There are many ways to create *tihais* in different *talas*, which can be explored by using the formulas that will allow the numbers to be divided into three equal parts. For example, another way to create a *tihai* in different *talas* is to take the *bol* of one *matra* less than the total number of *matras* of any *tala* and place the gaps of two *matras* between the *pallas*. For example, for the seven-*matra rupak tala*, a *tihai* can be created by taking a *bol* of six *matras* (one *matra* less than the total number of *matras* of *rupak tala*) and by placing the gaps of two beats between the three *pallas* (*see Table 37, pp. 316–17*).

This formula can be applied to any *tala*. In the same way, different types of simple *tihais*, *chakkardar tihais*, and other kinds of *tihais* can be formulated in any *tala*. However, the *bols* of a *tihai* need to be chosen according to the characteristics of the *tala*.

TIHAIS FROM DIFFERENT *MATRAS* OF *TEENTAL*

It is important for a dancer and a musician to be able to start *tihais* from different *matras* of a *tala*. In Kathak dance, *tihais* are performed from different *matras*, mainly in *vilambit laya*. In *vilambit laya*, one *avartan* of a *tala* is long. Competent dancers employ their autonomy to improvise and decorate the *avartans* with movements or *tihais*. Sometimes, the *avartans* are ornamented with both movements and a *tihai*, starting from any *matra* to return back on *sum*. The given *tihais* in *vilambit laya* are simple *tihais* in *teental* from different *matras*. The *tihais* that are shorter than four *matras* usually start at the sub-beats of a *matra*. In this case, each beat is divided into four sub-beats. Many *tihais* use the same *bols* or counts, but the gaps between the *pallas* change. Wise use of the gaps is crucial, so that a *tihai* concludes on *sum* (*see Tables 38–44, p. 318; Tables 45–51, p. 319; Tables 52–53, p. 319*).

In the aforementioned *tihais*, the counts can be substituted with appropriate *bols*. For example, the following *bols* can be used for the earlier set of counts:

1 2 = Ta dha
1 2 3 = TaT TaT thai
1 2 3 4 5 = Tig dha dig dig thai

1 2 3 4 5 6 7 8 = Ta thai thai TaT, Aa thai thai TaT

Depending on the *bols*, the footwork in Kathak and the strokes in tabla will change. Using a different set of *bols* will give these *tihais* an entirely different feel. There are numerous ways of creating *tihais* from different *matras*.

The subject of the *tihai* in Indian music and dance is enormous and can get very complicated. This is why the use of *tihais* in a performance undoubtedly shows the virtuosity and artistry of a performer. A remarkable performer creates *tihais* at the spur of the moment. Therefore, spontaneity and the ability to improvise are at once rare and excellent qualities in a performer.

Nrtta:
Rhythmic Interpretation

THE CAPTIVATING EXECUTION of the complex rhythms of Kathak is carried out through a vast repertoire of compositions, which can be either pre-structured or improvised. The rhythmic repertoire of Kathak falls under the category of *nrtta* or the art of pure dance, which is abstract in nature and stimulates the audience's deeper state of consciousness. In Kathak, the *nrtta* aspect is the interpretation of rhythm through intricate footwork, rigorous body movements, and spectacular spins. The ornate rhythms and *laykari* make the *nrtta* of Kathak dazzling and elegant. The astounding *laykari* and complex rhythmic permutations are conveyed through the Kathak repertoire such as *that*, *aamad*, *tukda*, *paran*, *tihai*, and *baant*, among others. The *tala* or the metrical cycle provides the basis upon which these rhythmic structures are built.

PADHANT

All rhythmic patterns of Kathak are articulated through *padhant*, a recitation of the *bol*s of the rhythmic repertoire of Kathak set in a particular *laya* and *tala*. The *bol*s of Kathak are derived from many sound sources, such as the sounds of *ghungru*s (bells), ancient mantras, different musical instruments, and the elements and forces of nature. A lot of emphasis is placed on *padhant*. The dancer recites the *padhant* of each composition with exact timing, voice modulation, stresses, silences, and pronunciation before performing them through body movements. *Padhant* is accompanied by *kriya*s or hand actions to demonstrate the *tali*s, *khali*s, and *matra*s of a *tala*. *Padhant* not only helps a dancer in memorizing a composition; it also enables a dancer to perform complex compositions in *laya* and *tala*. Additionally, the voice modulation and musicality of *padhant* helps dancers to create, categorize, and perform the movements in a more expressive manner. *Padhant* also helps develop the powers of perception and imagination in a dancer. The multifaceted repertoires of Kathak become more comprehensible and enjoyable for the audience when they are expressed through *padhant* before performing them. The *padhant*s are articulated with controlled yet effortless verbal and bodily expressions. Following are a few *bol*s from the enormous assortment of the *bol*s of *padhant* that are practised in various *laya*s for clarity and fluidity:

a) *Dig dig dig dig, dig dig dig dig*
b) *Dig dig Ta, -, dig dig Ta-, dig dig dig dig dig dig Ta-*
c) *Tho dig dig, tho dig dig, dig dig*
d) *TaT TaT thai - Tig dha dig dig thai -*
e) *Dha Tira kita Taka, Ta Tira kita Taka*
f) *Dhir dhir kita Taka, dhir dhir kita Taka*
g) *Takita dhikita Taka*
h) *Chum chum chananana, Chum chum chananana*
i) *Tram thai, Tram thai, Tram thai*
j) *Dha Traka dhikita, dha Traka dhikita, dha dha kirdha Tita*
k) *Dha ge Te te, dha ge Te te, kirdha Te te, dha ge Te te*
l) *KaTita Taghanna dhage Titaka Ta gadi gina*
m) *Kina tharri, kukku tharri, tharri kukku jhanga jhanga*
n) *Taka dhlanga dhalanga dhalanga*
o) *Ghe Tirakita Taka ghittan ghinna Tada-na*
p) *Naga dig, naga dig, tharri tharri naga dig*

The *nrtta ang* of Kathak and its syllabic repertoire also depends on the gharanas or the schools of Kathak. All gharanas share certain *nrtta ang* selections, and some are the discernible characteristics of a particular gharana.

PAD-KRIYA OR THE RHYTHMIC FOOTWORK IN KATHAK

A great deal of *laykari* in Kathak is performed through footwork. Kathak dancers wear bells around their ankles (*ghungrus*) and produce various sounds using their feet. Characteristic sounds are produced by two different methods. The first approach is the manipulation of volume, in which the dancers control the intensity of a sound by striking their feet on the floor forcefully or gently. To emphasize a particular *bol*, the dancer's feet strike the floor forcefully in what is called the *vajan* or dynamic accent. The practice of *vajan* is done in order to have more control over the foot movements. At the same time, the concept of *vajan* is also used to create *laykari*. The second approach to producing sound is to use different parts of the foot, each of which creates a noticeably different and unique sound. This wide range of sound is produced from the sole, heel, toe, and sides of the feet. All footwork-related compositions end with a *tihai*.

The basic footwork in any *tala* is called *tatkar*, which is produced by striking the foot on floor. The word *tatkar* is purportedly over 700 years old, and is found in different scriptures in conjunction with dance. According to many Kathak maestros, the *tatkar* mainly incorporates three *bols*: *Ta*, *thai*, and *Tat*. The syllable *Ta* changes to syllable *Aa* for the *khali* section of the *tala* in which the *tatkar* is being performed. The *tatkar* always starts with the right foot and corresponds to the *theka* of the *tala*. In *vilambit* and *madhya laya*s, *tatkar* is usually produced through a flat foot stroke, striking the floor with the entire sole of the foot. In *drut laya*, different parts of the feet are used; however, the syllables *Ta* and *Aa*, which represent *tali* and *khali* of a *tala*, are always done with the flat-foot technique. The upper body of a dancer is isolated from the lower body and is kept still while performing *tatkar*. During practice sessions, dancers keep their bodies in a neutral standing position with feet open in a reverse 'V' shape, and the hands are locked together in front of the chest in order to have more control over the body. However, during performances, dancers have the freedom to use hand movements during *tatkar*.

Tala teental has sixteen *matras*, but the *tatkar* of *teental* in Kathak is made up of eight *matras*: *Ta thai thai Tat, Aa thai thai Tat* (*see Table 54, p. 320*).

The *tatkar* is practised in different *gunas*, such as *duguna, tiguna, chauguna, athguna, aar, paun-guna,* and *sawa-guna*. The table cited here demonstrates the *tatkar* in *teental* in a *barabar ki laya, duguna, tiguna,* and *chauguna* to illustrate the inherent aspect of *laykari* in Kathak (*see Table 55, p. 320*).

Tatkar Ke Prakar

Tatkar can be compared with the *theka* of the percussive instruments. Tabla players create variations of the basic *theka* of a *tala* for the purpose of creating *rasa*. Similarly, Kathak dancers also modify the original *bol*s of *tatkar* without distorting the basic nature of the *tala*. This mode of variation is called *tatkar ke prakar*. *Tatkar ke prakar* is practised and performed in different *laya*s and uses many different kinds of *laykari* against the backdrop of *lehra* or *nagma*. The nature of the *tala* is preserved while performing *tatkar ke prakar*. *Tatkar ke prakar* can be performed between the Kathak compositions to ornament the *avartan*s or cycles. Alternatively, they can be categorized and set in rhythmic compositional forms called *chala*, *palta*s, or *ladi*s. Essentially, *tatkar ke prakar* are the groupings of *bol*s in Kathak, which are expanded in rhythmically oriented compositions for footwork. The most competent Kathak dancers take a *tatkar ke prakar* as a theme and spontaneously improvise on it (*see Table 56, p. 321*).

Paltas of Tatkar or Baant

When the *bol*s of *tatkar ke prakar* are arranged in a way that they construct a concrete structure in a framework of *tala*, it is called *palta*s of *tatkar*. *Palta*s of *tatkar* always conclude with a corresponding *tihai*. These *palta*s are also called *baant*. *Baant* means 'to divide in equal parts'. In *palta*s, the fundamental *bol*s of *tatkar*, other phrases, and patterns are grouped together and then equally divided in the structure of the *avartan*s of a *tala*. It is further developed and creates a larger structure by combining all shorter arrangements in the *avartan*s, resulting in an appealing footwork piece. Essentially, *palta*s or *baant*s are the permutation and expansion of the *bol*s and of the *tatkar* (the basic footwork) of a given *tala*. The important phrases of the theme are broken into their proper components. Table 57 is an example of *palta*s of *tatkar* in *teental* (*see p. 322*).

This example is in *duguna laya*. In this *laya*, the *palta*s from two to seven will finish on the left foot and the entire *palta* will be performed again from the left foot so that it ends on the right foot. All footwork in Kathak starts and ends on the right foot. When supplemented with *laykari*, the *baant* or the *palta*s can become very complex and involved. The entire *palta* or a section of the *palta* can be executed in different *jati*s and *guna*s.

Practice of *palta*s not only grants unprecedented command on footwork, but also makes the categorization and structural grouping processes of *bol*s more comprehensible for dancers. *Palta*s also help in learning the *laykari* as well as improvisational techniques. While practising *palta*s, students learn ways to improvise in a sequential, consistent, and stylistically proper manner. Divisions and subdivisions of the *bol* structures and *laykari* of these groupings create very complex rhythmic patterns, making *palta*s very stimulating both for the dancer and the audience.

Ladi and Rela

A *ladi* is a garland and a *rela* is a rivulet. The terms *rela* and *ladi* are used interchangeably for a very swift and rapid manipulation of short phrases, giving the structure the feel of a garland of separate pearls or a torrent moving forward. *Rela* and *ladi* are usually performed in *drut laya* and are concluded with a *tihai*. *Rela*s principally use the *bol*s of tabla, since this term is borrowed from the tabla repertoire, whereas the *bol*s of *ladi* are comprised of the syllables from both dance and tabla repertoires. In both *rela* and *ladi*, the *bol*s designed for high speed are sequentially developed and improvised with quick flourishes. Short and fewer phrases are used for *rela*s and *ladi*s to make structures less complicated. Beauty and strength are derived from the sounds of feet and *ghungru*s, as the feet move with astounding speed. A greater sense of freedom is embedded in these rhythmic compositions. Dancers have freedom to add many different shades and tones to the thematic structure of *rela* and *ladi* (*see Table 58, p. 323*).

The entire *ladi* will be performed in *drut laya*, wherein the *bol*s in two *matra*s in the previous example will fit in one *matra*. A competent dancer sometimes takes the theme line, which is the first line of a *ladi*, and improvises on it for a few minutes. The characteristic *bol*s of *ladi* and *rela* are very short and are repeated in a very organized manner. The main *bol*s of *ladi* are highlighted and more *bol*s are added to it. For example, the short *bol*s such as *Ta*, *kirdhin*, and *tirkita* can be added to the aforementioned *ladi*, depending on the mood of the performer.

Chala

The meaning of *chala* is 'pace' or 'to carry'. *Chala* is the specialty of the Jaipur Gharana of Kathak, where a rhythmic composition through footwork in *vilambit laya* in the beginning of a performance creates an ambience for the entire presentation of a certain *tala*. A rhythmic theme in slow reflective tempo is selected and is structurally and rhythmically improvised slowly, using myriad *laykari*s, in order to set the mood for the performance. *Chala* provides a lot of freedom to a dancer's imagination. A multitude of *bol*s can be added to the theme while improvising a *chala*. The *chala*s are both sophisticated and complicated in nature. They include many different kinds of *laykari*s and *bol*s and are developed to impeccable refinement. *Chala*s conclude with a complex *tihai*. The most appealing part of the *chala* is that initially small sections of the theme are modified, and then slowly all the sections are altered, all the while keeping the mood of the theme, yet changing the *laya* and texture of the composition in a gradual manner within the framework of the originally established *laya*. The table cited here is an example of a simple *chala* in *teental* from Jaipur Gharana (*see Table 59, pp. 324–25*).

SOME OTHER *KRIYAS* OF FOOTWORK

In Kathak, the compositions set for footwork are often rhythmically so intricate and striking that special practices are done to have a better hold on *laya* and to have better control of the foot movements. Practice of *laykari*, especially the *laya* ratios or *guna*s and *jati*s, are done devotedly in the framework of different *tala*s. The practice of *laykari* prepares a dancer to have a command on *laya*. Nevertheless, the practices for the command of foot movements are equally important. Different *kriya*s or actions are practised to acquire control and strength over footwork. Following are the practices for accents, silences, and weight on certain beats in order to have a firm grasp of the *matra*s and foot movements. These compositions can also be presented as a performance piece with a *tihai*.

Vajan Kriya or Accenting

The word *vajan* means 'weight'. In *vajan*, accenting a particular beat is emphasized or given extra weight by making it louder. Merely striking the foot hard on the floor does not produce a loud sound in Kathak. The accenting is qualitative in nature and is accomplished by using the exact technique of striking the right parts of the bottom of the feet. Each *tala* has its characteristically accented beats. During the presentation of footwork of *vajan*, the *tala's* accentuated beats are not compromised. The integral accented beats of *tala* are kept intact and, at the same time, intended beats are emphasized even more. The table given here is a practice of *vajan* in *teental* in *barabar ki laya*, in which the highlighted *bol*s are dynamically accented. The slight accents will also be on the first, fifth, ninth, and thirteenth beats, since they are the characteristically accented beats of *teental* (*see Table 60, p. 326*).

This practice can be improvised in many different ways: by starting the accent on the first beat and moving forward by accenting the successive beats, by accenting more than one beat in each *avartan*, or by performing it in different *laya*s, such as *duguna*, *tiguna*, or *chauguna*. Performers present the idea of *vajan* in a compositional form called the *vajan ki baant*.

Table 61 is on the traditional *vajan ki baant* in *teental*, concluding with a *chakkardar tihai* (*see p. 327*).

Dum and Aujhad Kriyas

Dum and *aujhad kriya*s are diametrically opposite the *vajan kriya*. The word *dum* means 'a breath'. The silences created between the footwork through well-defined and competently placed rests and pauses make the footwork with *dum* dynamic and interesting. The empty beats become primary, and simultaneously they disperse the other beats forcefully. In *aujhad kriya*, the rests are longer than they are in *dum kriya*. *Aujhad* is a *kriya* performed in *tala*s with many *matra*s, so that the rests can be longer. They are also performed in usually one *avartan*. Both *dum* and *aujhad kriya*s end with a short rhythmic piece in faster *laya* called *uran*. *Uran* means 'to soar'. *Aujhad* gives the *avartan* a contrasting feel of both solidity and fluidity. The rest part of *aujhad* gives the *avartan* a feel of suspension, and the *uran* in fast speed makes it vibrant to complete the *avartan*. Short *tihai*s consisting of a very few *matra*s can also be used as the *uran*.

This footwork with the *kriya* of *dum* will stand out in medium tempo, since the gaps will be small but will appear magnified. Many improvisations can be worked into this footwork. *Dum* and *aujhad kriya*s can be done with varied *bol*s and in different *laya*s (*see Table 62 and Table 63, pp. 328–29*).

In Table 63, the compilation of *bol*s—*Ta dha - -, dha Tita dha - , dha TirkitaTaka, TatirkitTaka*—is an *uran*. *Aujhad*s are performed between two sizeable compositions to lighten the mood of the performance and provide respite both to the performer and to the audience.

Khade Per ki Tatkar

Most of the *tatkar*s fall under the non-locomotor movements—dancers perform them in one spot in a stationary position. *Khade per ki tatkar* not only has a sound quality that is very enticing, but it also allows a dancer to travel from one place to another while doing footwork. In this *tatkar*, one foot is balanced on the toes and helps a dancer to move. The motion of the foot on the toes has a pulling and shifting quality, wherein it drags the other foot with it. The *bol*s *dha dhin dhin dha* change into *na dhin dhin na*, since the sounds produced in *khade* *per ki tatkar* have a softness to them. Table 64 is an example of *khade per ki tatkar* (*see pp. 330–31*).

Ghungru ki Tatkar

*Ghungru*s are the bells worn around the ankles by a Kathak dancer. The meticulous footwork of Kathak uses all parts of the feet, making many different sounds. In *ghungru ki tatkar*, the sounds of *ghungru*s are predominant, giving a delicate ethereal quality to footwork. Sometimes, dancers create sound from one *ghungru* out of hundreds of *ghungru*s worn around their ankle. Sounds such as *dig dig* are created from the heels, which amplifies the sounds of *ghungru*s. *Ta*, as an example in Table 65, is a flat foot sound, which actually highlights the clarity and glimmer of *dig dig* sound even more (*see pp. 330–31*).

Both *khade per ki tatkar* and *ghungru ki tatkar* seem easy in a written form, but both repertoires require tremendous balance and control over the feet.

Footwork—Pandit Rajendra Gangani

All Kathak footwork uses many different *laykari*s, and a proficient dancer will improvise all these footwork varieties. The ability to improvise footwork shows the true genius of a Kathak artist and requires dedicated and arduous training. Every dancer's technique and personality differs, and the spontaneous improvisation allows one to put one's own stamp on a performance. Creating sound imagery through footwork is one of the most dazzling aspects of Kathak, when the feelings of joy, passion, and marvel besiege both the dancer and the audience.

Rhythmic Interpretation through Body Movements

LAYKARI AND NRTTA TECHNICALITIES are strewn brilliantly throughout a Kathak performance. In addition to footwork, there are many other repertoires in Kathak that entail *laykari* through engaging body movements. A Kathak performance always starts with the compositions in *vilambit laya*, which gives an opportunity to a performer to delve deeply into both the movements and the rhythm. The pieces performed in *vilambit laya* are intense, multilayered, and concentrated. In *vilambit laya*, the space and silence between two beats are substantial during which a great deal of action can be performed. A Kathak dancer fills this space with facial expressions, body movements, or rhythmic feats. In *vilambit laya*, each beat is equally divided into sub-beats of two or four in order to start compositions and actions on the fraction of a beat. *Salami, that, aamad, chala, uthan,* and *paran-aamad* are some selections that are performed in *vilambit laya*. Some of these pieces are an identifiable repertoire of a specific gharana or school of Kathak.

Salaam, or greeting, is an Arabic word which means 'peace'. In Kathak, *salami* is a courteous greeting to the musicians, gurus, and audience. *Salami* was introduced in Kathak during the Mughal era. In modern Kathak, dancers sometimes use namaskar instead of *salami*. Namaskar is a Hindu greeting performed with both hands folded in *anjali mudra*. It is a reverential and a cordial bow. Some dancers perform both *salami* and namaskar in the same composition, while others omit *salami* and replace it with *stuti* or *vandana*—an invocation. In *salami* or namaskar, a brief movement phrase is performed. During this movement phrase, the gestures of *salami* and namaskar are carried out. These movement phrases take one or more *avartan*.

Uthan is an introductory rhythmic composition. The word *uthan* means 'to elevate' and is taken from the tabla repertoire. With these rhythmic compositions, the mood for *nrtta* is elevated in the beginning of a performance and the stage is set for the next repertoire called *that*. The dancer starts an *uthan* on different beats of a *tala* and arrives on *sum*. Sometimes, brief footwork is introduced in an *uthan*. On many occasions, *tihai*s are used to end an *uthan*.

That means 'a graceful stance'. However, *that* is much more than merely a standing posture in Kathak. In *that*, after a brief movement phrase, which starts at different *matra*s or sub-*matra*s of a *tala*, the dancer stands in an angular posture of Kathak. The first posture of a *that* creates the mood for the performance, wherein the dancer expresses the underlying rhythm through the movements of wrist, eyes, eyebrows, neck, and other *ang*, *pratyang*, and *upang*. The great dancers of Kathak show their mastery over this dance form through the effective presentation of *that*, where the proper execution of *laya* is presented in a very subtle way. One *that* after another is framed in a way such that the presentation of *that*s becomes circular in nature, giving the feeling that the movements are melting into each other and creating wave cycles. The final stance after each *that* demarcates the first beat of a *tala*. The brief movement phrases before the final pose on *sum* employ concentrated *laykari*. Even the *theka* played before the movement phrase is ornamented to create an atmosphere of delicate expressions and tantalizing mood.

The final stance centres on both the dancer and the audience, as the accumulated energy flows through different parts of the body, manifested in subtle movements of the major and the minor limbs. This creates tranquility, intensity, and beauty. The final poses of *that* are picturesque and captivating. Once the dancer is in a specific position, the *laykari*, including *tihai* to culminate a *that*, is shown through alluring and provoking movements of the eyes, wrists, and other minor limbs. The dancer's eyes seem to be fixed at one place and, at the same time, they mysteriously express many inner feelings and subtle expressions of *shringar rasa*. In Jaipur Gharana, dancers sometimes glide on a stage after striking a pose, which makes them look as if they are floating in space.

The main syllables used in *that* are the soft-sounding dance syllables such as *Ta, thai, Aa, dig*, and *Taka Ta*. *That*s can start from any beat of a *tala*, including the *sum*. The gradual increase of the dimension of *that* movement phrases stirs both the dancer and the audience. The ornamented *theka* of *teental* between two *that*s is magical and is translated in the movements of a dancer. Sometimes, a *that* can consist of more than one *avartan* and employ many different kinds of *laykari*.

Aamad is an Urdu word, which means 'entrance'. The word *aamad* was introduced in Kathak during the Mughal period. Even though *aamad*s are performed after *salami*, *uthan*, and *that*, they are considered to be a dancer's formal entry into a performance. An *aamad* is more like a preface to a performance. Most dancers conclude the performance of *vilambit laya* with a variety of *aamad*s, where *aamad*s serve the purpose of entrance into the *madhya laya* repertoire. Therefore, the *laya* of *aamad* is a little faster than the *laya* of *that*. *Aamad*s are the compositions that start and end on *sum*. *Aamad*s have flowing and graceful movements that are symmetrical in nature. Generally, whatever is performed on the right side is also projected through the left side of the body. Sometimes, the rule of symmetry is ignored in order to perform a variety of movements. Usually, the *bol*s of *tatkar* are used in *aamad*. However, dancers from every gharana take the liberty of using an assortment of *bol*s of Kathak. Sometimes, *tukda*s, *paran*s, and *primalu*s are added at the beginning or at the end of the *aamad* to make it more versatile. These kinds of *aamad*s are called *paran-aamad*, and they have a feel of a *paran* or a *tukda* in *vilambit laya*. *Aamad*s are created in such a way as to emulate the nature of a *tala*.

Natwari tukda uses the melodious and delicate *bol*s of *tatkar*, such as *Ta thai tat*, *Tigdha*. These are the pure dance *bol*s that do not derive from either tabla or pakhawaj. *Natwari bol*s are believed to have been received from the dance of Lord Krishna. When Shri Krishna danced on the hood of the great cobra Kaliya, the *bol*s that emanated from His dance were the *natwari bol*s. Many Kathak dancers perform *natwari tukda* in *vilambit laya*, which has a slightly faster tempo than the initially established *vilambit laya*. Some dancers combine *aamad* or other *vilambit laya* repertoires of Kathak with *natwari tukda*s. *Natwari tukda*s use graceful movements of Kathak, and employ many different varieties of the movement vocabulary. The exquisite body movements make these types of compositions quite vibrant. The underlying mood of *natwari tukda*s is *shringar rasa*, and it is mostly performed by the dancers of Lucknow Gharana.

The Kathak compositions in *madhya laya* are varied in nature and are performed with great vigour and splendour. The tempo of the initially established *madhya laya* can be increased gradually to suit the repertoires. Following are the Kathak repertoires that are performed mainly in *madhya laya*.

The word *tukda* and *tora* are usually used interchangeably in Kathak. The word *tukda* means a piece or a section. The *tukda* compositions employ the *bols* of tabla and dance and are comprised of short rhythmic phrases. These rhythmic phrases usually start on *sum* and always end on *sum* after a few *avartans*. Many dancers do not distinguish between *tukdas* and *todas*, while others identify a long *tukda* as *toda*. Some dancers also believe that the *tukda* is a section of a *toda*. *Tukdas* are simple, yet dense and concrete in nature, and are performed with energetic, dazzling body movements. *Tukdas* use a wide range of *bols* of tabla and dance. Sometimes, *tihais* are used at the end of a *tukda* or a *toda*. The expressive aspects along with *nrtta* are also sometimes performed through these compositions. There are many different types of *tukda* such as *sada tukda*, *chakkardar tukda*, *sangeet ka tukda*, and *kavitta ka tukda*. They are distinguished by many different factors such as complexity, execution of different *chhands*, use of various layers of rhythms, and application of different kinds of *bols*. *Chakkardar tukdas* are very attractive and appealing in nature. An entire *tukda* is performed three times in a *chakkardar tukda*, and these types of *tukdas* also use different kinds of turns and pirouettes. It is breathtaking when, after many *chakkars* or turns, a dancer comes back on *sum* in a striking pose.

The word *primalu* is pronounced in many different ways, such as *primalu*, *pramelu*, and *parimal*. *Primalu* is a compound word made up of two Sanskrit words: *par* and *malu*. The word *par* means 'other' or 'additional', and the word *malu* means 'to blend'. In *primalu*, the *bols* of nature, literature, vocal, and instrumental music are blended with the *bols* of dance. *Primalu* compositions supplement the *bols* with graceful body movements and expressions to bring out the mood and intention of the *bols*. These delicate body movements are referred to as the *primalu ang*. The *bols* of *primalu* are sweet-sounding and appealing. Some of the *bols* used in *primalu* compositions are *tharri*, *kuku*, *drag*, *jhananananana*, *nagannagannaga*, *ta traka*, *digdigdigdig thai*, *tak tho*, *kukkujhana*, and *jhenkukku*.

According to some scholars, the word *paran* is derived from *pran*, the Sanskrit word for an agreement, pledge, or promise. In earlier times, disciples were taught *parans* with an agreement of keeping the sanctity of the *bols*. In today's world, this meaning does not apply. Yet, *paran* is one of the most important repertoires of Kathak in which the heavy and vigorous *bols* of pakhawaj are used. The pakhawaj is a deep-sounding percussion instrument, and the weighty *bols* of the pakhawaj reflect the heavy and profound tone. *Paran* compositions, unlike *tukdas*, use many *avartans*, are more sombre in nature, and use strong, powerful movements of Kathak. Sometimes, the *bols* of tabla are combined with the *bols* of pakhawaj in *parans*. Even though the *bols* of *parans* are taken from pakhawaj, they are played widely by tabla players and performed by Kathak dancers. *Parans* are longer than *tukdas*. Some categories of *paran* in Kathak are the same as the *paran* repertoire in tabla. Many different *laykaris* are employed in these compositions. *Parans* can be concluded with or without a *tihai*. However, most of the dancers prefer to use a *tihai* at the end of a *paran* to give it a concrete completion. There are many different types of *paran*. *Daupalli*, *tripalli*, *chaupalli*, and *panchpalli parans* use progression and layering of different tempos in one composition. A composition is performed in two tempos in *daupalli*, in three tempos in *tripalli*, in four tempos in *chaupalli*, and in five tempos in *panchpalli*. The beauty of these *parans* is that the same set of *bols*, established in first tempo, are utilized and manipulated in different *gunas* in a composition. Because of the use of different tempos, these *parans* tend to be extended. *Tripallis*, *chaupallis*, and *panchpallis* are mostly performed in *vilambit laya*, since the last layering of tempo in these *parans* become quite fast, and in dance, the clarity and beauty of body movements must not be compromised. *Sada paran* is a simple composition consisting of heavy *bols* of the pakhawaj.

Chakkardar paran is a type of *paran* which is performed three times. *Chakkardar parans* are very demanding on a dancer's stamina and are highly energetic. Most of the *chakkardar parans* also use many *chakkars* or turns, and are often many *avartans* long. Often, *tihais* are embedded in a *chakkardar paran*. *Farmaishi* and *kamali chakkardar parans* are performed as encore pieces. In *mehfils* or small gatherings, these types of *parans* are performed at the request of the audience. Contemporary dancers include them even in their performances for a larger audience to show their expertise in *laykari*. *Farmaishi* and *kamali chakkardar parans* use the same mathematical formulas as the *farmaishi* and *kamali chakkardar tihais*.

In *pakshi paran*, *bols* resembling birdsong are used, such as *tehu tehu* or *kukkuo kukkuo*. *Jati parans* are composed in different *jatis*. There are five *jatis*: *tishra* (multiples of three beats), *chatushra* (multiples of four beats), *khand* (multiples of five beats), *mishra* (multiples of seven beats), and *sankirna* (multiples of nine beats). *Raas paran* is descriptive in nature. It has the *bols* taken from Raas Leela performed by Krishna and His consorts. There are also *parans* which describe the attributes of different gods and deities. In these types of *parans*, the poetry is beautifully inlaid in the dance and the *bols* of the pakhawaj. Even though these *paran*s are highly rhythmic and considered as a part of *nrtta*, in a way, they do make reference to the *nritya* aspect of dance.

The vibrant *nrtta* aspect of Kathak is a blend of rhythm and movements. The movements are beautifully woven with rhythm without excluding or compromising graceful body movements. Kathak dancers treat each composition as having their own character. The way these *nrtta* compositions progress, the way they possess inherent moods, the way they react to the

Madhu Nataraj

body movements or music, and the way they touch a dancer's heart give them specific personalities, as if they are living beings. Although these compositions do not illustrate any specific *bhava*, they are not devoid of emotions. The *laykari* in Kathak compositions is complicated, but this complexity also makes it exhilarating and highly spirited. The key to performing these compositions masterfully is to strike a balance between complexity and beauty.

Nritya Aspect in Kathak

NRITYA, A COMBINATION OF RHYTHMIC body movements and facial expressions to interpret *rasa*s, is a remarkably rich aspect of Kathak. It originated as a storytelling art form; therefore, the refined *nritya* portion of Kathak portrays graceful body movements along with delicate sentiments and emotions. Different *nritya* repertoires are presented during a Kathak performance, where *bhav-batana* or *abhinaya* is subtle and sophisticated.

This *nritya* aspect of Kathak broadly falls into two categories: *gat-bhava* and *artha-bhava*. *Gat-bhava* presentations are very rhythmic in nature and apply *abhinaya* against the backdrop of rhythm to tell a story. Words and poetry are not used in *gat-bhava*. *Artha-bhava* is the interpretation of rhythmic poetry and is the forte of the Jaipur Gharana of Kathak. These poems are a wonderful combination of poetry, the *bol*s of Kathak, percussion music, and lyrics of vocal music. A wide variety of repertoire includes vocal support and is inspired by the different genres of Hindustani vocal music.

Angika, vachika, and *sattvik abhinaya*s are used abundantly in Kathak. *Aharya abhinaya* is used mostly in Kathak presentations that are set in dance-drama style. *Angika* and *vachika abhinaya* are the means to achieve the *sattvik abhinaya*. The *nritya* aspect of Kathak is a glorious amalgamation of ancient Mugulkaleen and contemporary Kathak. The most frequently interpreted episodes are taken from ancient Hindu mythology, among which the charming love story of Radha and Krishna is the most favourite of Kathak dancers. From the earliest history of Kathak, *kathakar*s (storytellers) were devotees of Krishna and they recited the Krishna legends through movement, music, and drama. The *Mahabharata*, one of the greatest epic poems of India, is the story of Lord Krishna. In this epic poem, the word 'Kathak' is mentioned as a dance form. By the fifth century, this dance form took a great leap and emerged as a theatrical dance performance in the region of Mathura, where the vivid, soul-stirring episodes of Lord Krishna's life were presented splendidly. The poems of the great saint-poets and devotees of Krishna became the central repertoire of a Kathak performance. Nevertheless, episodes from the lives of different gods and goddesses, mythological and historical personalities, portrayal of elements of nature, and the characters from Indian literature made their way into Kathak performances, making the dance form even more abundant and inclusive. Furthermore, in today's Kathak, the subject matters of *abhinaya* are not limited to traditional characters and objects. Many contemporary Kathak dancers have used modern and contemporary poems to express a myriad of sentiments that dominate our world today.

The following repertoire of Kathak represents the *nritya* characteristics through dramatic interpretation and tantalizing *abhinaya*.

GATKARI

The word *gat* has been derived from the Sanskrit word *gati*, which has different meanings in different contexts, such as gait, pace, stride, momentum, velocity, movement, and progression. The *gats* in Kathak signify all of these. *Gatkari* is the presentation of a *gat* through *gat-nikas*, *gat-bhaav*, *gat-prasang*, and *gat-leela*. *Gats* are mimetic presentations of stories and events without the support of words. The *abhinaya* is beautifully expressed in *gats* with stylized body movements, hand gestures, and facial expressions, synchronized with rhythm. A single dancer portrays many characters. Change of character, time, or environment is portrayed through different types of turns.

The *chaal* and *palta* are two integral aspects of *gat*. *Chaal* is a formalized rhythmic walk in Kathak style. There are many different *chaals* to portray different characters or moods. *Palta* is a specific part of *gat*, when a dancer performs a rhythmic movement with half turns from both right and left sides. *Paltas* are also used to change character, time, and the environment. All *gatkaris* end with a basic, short *tihai*.

Gat-nikas is a type of *gat* where a sentiment is portrayed through decorative *chaals*. The word *nikas* translates to the source from which something materializes, a door through which someone passes, or simply the action of leaving in order to arrive somewhere. *Gat-nikas* is the source movement through which a dancer arrives at a final sentiment. Through these sentiments, the characters and their moods are conveyed. *Gat-nikas* combines staple upper-body poses of Kathak with *chaal*s to depict a certain emotion or feeling. The portrayal of Krishna through *gat-nikas* can be depicted as Krishna holding His celestial flute. The facial expression during this pose will show the precise mood of Krishna being portrayed. Sometimes, the elements of nature are mimicked through *chaal*s. During the Mughal era, many *gat-nikas* were added, such as *ada ki gat*, *husn ki gat*, and *pari ki gat*.

Gat-bhaav is a slightly extended component of *gat* in which a particular sentiment is emphasized in a greater detail in order to create a story. The mime aspect of drama is highlighted in *gat-bhaav*, where a theme is presented in detail through mime and is embellished with *nikas*, *palta*s, and *chaal*s. The example of Krishna holding a flute would take the shape of a short episode in *gat-bhaav*. More characters are introduced in a *gat-bhaav* than in *gat-nikas*. For example, the character of Radha can be introduced when Krishna plays a prank on Her or meets Her in the dense forest. The consequences of Krishna's actions can be developed further. *Gat-bhaav* is more interpretative than *gat-nikas*.

Gat-prasang is a shorter version of *gat-leela* and a longer version of *gat-bhaav*. Informally, *gat-prasang* is also referred to as *choti gat*, meaning a condensed *gat*. *Gat-prasang* is often composed of many *gat-bhaav*s and *gat-nikas*. The story in this section is artfully developed further with vivid imagination. The dancers usually need time to improvise the story to a point where it finds completion by means of introducing many subsequences. In the example of Krishna, *gat-prasang* will deal more elaborately with the feelings, emotions, conflicts, and resolutions of the characters. A dancer might choose to initiate the episode with Radha, who is desperate to meet Krishna. She leaves home by making an excuse to fetch water from the Yamuna River and meets Krishna when He breaks Her water-pot. Radha's different emotions can be depicted to create Her fully developed character: Her desperation, looking for Krishna, waiting for Him, identifying Herself with the flowing waves of the river, despair when She is unable to find Krishna, annoyance when He breaks Her pot, complaining, and concealing Her joy of seeing Krishna. More characters can be introduced, such as *sakhi*s, Radha's friends, who tease Her when Her water-pot is broken. The same theme can be interpreted and improvised in many ways, depending on a dancer's frame of mind at the time of the performance.

Gat-leela is the longest element of *gatkari*. The word *leela* is a Sanskrit word which can be translated as 'a divine play'. *Gat-leela* is also called a *badi gat*, meaning an expanded *gat*. The story in this section is fully developed to convey a meaning, a philosophy. *Gat-leela* is presented in such a way as to create an entire atmosphere of the story being presented, where the audience can be transported back in time. If *gat-prasang* is a chapter of a story, then *gat-leela* is the entire story. The dancer first sets the scene and then introduces a conflict to suggest some tension, which eventually reaches to a climax. Depending on the story, sometimes the episodes end with a resolution. However, finding a resolution is not always the goal for a Kathak dancer. More than finding a resolution, emphasis is given on creating the *rasa*. *Gat-leela* combines *natya*, *nritya*, and *nrtta* to depict an episode. The earlier example of Krishna can go to the extent that Krishna leaves Braj to fight with Kansa in Mathura, leaving Radha and all the *sakhi*s grief-stricken. The philosophical implication of leaving the story at such a juncture is to suggest that Krishna represents the Divine Absolute and Radha and other *sakhi*s are individual souls. At the end, the soul is desperately seeking for the Divine Absolute. The same episode can be interpreted in different ways by different dancers, which makes each *gatkari* performance unique.

Gat-nikas represents sentiments, emotions, and feelings; *gat-prasang* is portrayed in a style of a vignette; *gat-bhaav* is a chapter of a story; and *gat-leela* is a fully developed story. *Gatkari* is usually performed towards the end of a traditional solo performance after the performance of *nrtta* or the technique of Kathak, which always leaves the audience with the experience of a *rasa*, the ultimate goal of Indian arts.

KAVITTA

Kavitta derives from the Hindi word *kavita*, meaning 'poetry'. The Bhakti Kaal (1375 CE–1700 CE) and Riti Kaal (1700 CE–1900 CE) in Indian literature have influenced Kathak. Bhakti Kaal is considered to be the golden age of Indian poetry. The saint-poets of that time wrote splendid, devotional poems that marked the theoretical development in poetic theory. Riti Kaal poets took poetry to a different level, where the sensuality and erotic aspects of Krishna's life were emphasized through poetry, while, at the same time, the art of poetry was more formalized and theorized. Many of the Bhakti and Riti Kaal poets received patronage from the royal courts. Many Kathak dancers at that time already had become an important part of the royal courts of India. The exchange of ideas and emotions must have taken place between the poets and the dancers. Kathak dancers were inspired by these great poets, and this is when poetry made its way into Kathak.

A forte of the Jaipur Gharana, *kavitta*s are rhythmic poems interwoven with the *bol*s of dance and music. These poems are meticulously set in a particular *tala*. The metre of these poems in Kathak depends on long and short patterns and the groupings of light and heavy syllables. The dancers interpret the words and the meanings of these *kavitta*s through hand gestures, facial expressions, and body movements. *Kavitta*s are arranged in various ways, such as poems composed in rhyming patterns or piled over one another, and each last word rhyming with the last word of the previous line or set in different rhythmic patterns.

Even though Lord Krishna and legends associated with Him are the most favourite subject matter for the *kavitta*s, there are also *kavitta*s that depict the attributes and stories of other Hindu gods and goddesses. The wide-ranging characters of *kavitta* repertoire open up the possibilities of the portrayal of various *rasa*s. Sometimes, appropriate *tukda*s, *paran*s, and *tihai*s are added at the end of a *kavitta*. This makes *kavitta*s both aesthetically and spiritually uplifting. Sometimes, an entire episode is composed as a poem and is performed in a *kavitta* form. In these kinds of poetic compositions, *kavitta* also becomes a form of storytelling. The rhythms of a *kavitta* are executed through foot and body movements, whereas the emotions of the poem are depicted through hand gestures, body movements, and facial expressions. The *kavitta*s are usually performed in *madhya laya*, where the words of a poem become more lively and dynamic. Dancers first recite the *kavitta*s, during which the right pronunciation, facial expressions, emotions, projection, and enunciation are imperative.

An Example of a Krishna *Kavitta*

This particular *kavitta* describes the enchanting, magnificent dance of Lord Krishna, accompanied by the rhythm played on mridangam and the lush tune of the flute. In this *kavitta*, a *tihai* is created with the word 'Krishna' (*see Table 66, pp. 332–33*).

> *Bajat tala mridang murali dhun*
> *Ta dhalang dhumakita Taka dadigina*
> *Ta na na na sugandh, man bhaye umang*
> *nirat karat krishna krishna krishna*

An Example of a Ganesh *Kavitta*

This particular *kavitta* is an invocation to the elephant head Lord Ganesha, who is the remover of all obstacles and brings prosperity and luck into His devotees' lives. The *bol*s of the pakhawaj, supposedly a derivative of the ancient percussion instrument mridangam, are used towards the end of the *kavitta*. According to mythology, Lord Brahma created the mridangam and initiated Lord Ganesha to it (*see Table 67, pp. 332–33*).

Gan gan ganpati gajmukh mandal
Ghitghir ghitghir ghitghir thun thun tat tat thai
Jai jag vandan, vakra tund dhani dhata
Vighna harán, shubh karan
Dha ge na dha ge dhumkita dhumkita
Tharung Tharung dadigina thai

Kavitta—Kaliya Daman

The story of Krishna's fight with the deadly, dark serpent Kaliya is depicted in the following *kavitta*. Kaliya, who resided in the deep waters of the Yamuna River and had caused the river to become poisonous, was terrorizing the villagers and other beings. Once, Krishna, as a child, was playing with His friends when His ball fell in the river. Krishna jumped into the river to fetch the ball, and His ensuing ferocious fight with Kaliya is depicted in this poem. Krishna freed Himself from the fatal coil of Kaliya and won the battle. After Kaliya's fearful wives begged Krishna to spare their husband's life, Krishna tamed Kaliya and danced on his hood. His triumph overjoyed the villagers. Krishna's mother and father welcomed Him back with joy and affection.

Even though the main theme is the lethal combat between Krishna and Kaliya, portraying the *veer rasa*, this *kavitta* also depicts other *rasa*s, such as *bhayanak* (fear) and *vatsalya* (fondness between parents and child) *rasa*s (*see Table 68, pp. 332–33*).

Gend khelat hirat firat, karat chal-bal karideh me kood gaye
Maar gota naag ji ke paas, jab tab pahunch gaye
Naginyon se kahan laage, uthao naag dev ko
Naginyan tab chamak uththi, tum ho baal gopal lala
Hamko aavatah taras tumpe, hanste hanste krishna bole

Naag nathan aayo main, naag ji ne uth ke dekha
Krodh se maari phunkar, sananana phunkaaar ke jab
Gunj dhwani cha gayee, krishna ji tab neel baranan
Bhaye lage do yuddha karne, jahatak jhat jhat, patak pat pat
Naag ji ko naath liyo, naath se tab kheench karle aaye jamuna dhaar me
Fananana upar charanana dhar, na digdig nadigdig dig dig,
tho digdig tho digdig dig dig,
Tram TaTa Thai, Tram TaTa Thai, nirat tattat karan lage saanwre gopal lala
Tharara rararara naginyan kaanp uththi, charanana par prabhu ke vinati kar
kahne lagin
Abhun janu tumho krishna avatar, prabhu ji hamko deo suhaag lala
Naginion ki ter sun kar nagji ko de diyo
Bhumi braj me dhum mach gayee, krishna jaijaikar mach gayee
Nand baba magan bhaye jab, ma yashoda karat aarti
Motiyan ke thaal bhar bhar det narayan ko
Guna prabhu ke gai gai ke, nach nach ke
Magan bhaye bhaye, magan bhaye bhaye, magan bhaye bhaye narayan dha.

Kavitta, a beautiful blend of poetry, dance, and rhythm, is one of the most expressive aspects of Kathak, endorsing the fact that in Indian aesthetics, all art forms are inclusive of each other. The separation of art forms is not the intention of Indian aesthetics, which is based on the idea of natural harmony. Therefore, fusing literature with dance makes Kathak an inclusive art form.

Nrtta–Nritya Repertoire
Based on Vocal Music Genres

THROUGHOUT THE CENTURIES, Hindustani vocalists and Kathak dancers have influenced and inspired each other. The light classical vocal genres such as *thumri, dadra, bhajan, chaiti, tarana, ghazal, vandana, chaturang*, and *trivat* have acquired a very important place in the performance of Kathak because they incorporate the elements of both poetry and dance. A Kathak dancer's sensibilities become apparent in the performance of these vocal repertoires through bodily movements, hand gestures, and facial expressions. Certain *cheshta*s or gesticulations are practised to gain a better grasp of the art of expressing poetry and the lyrics of a song.

CHESHTAS OR GESTICULATIONS

*Cheshta*s are gestures combined with facial expressions to convey nuances of emotions and sentiments. *Cheshta*s are also commonly referred to as *haav-bhaav, bol-batana, bhav-bhangima, pradarshan*, or *adayagi*. A *cheshta* is a response to deep feelings.

Gestures associated with certain emotions, sentiments, and feelings are highly social. They reveal our involuntary responses as well as learned social and cultural behaviours. Some of these responses are universal and others are culture-specific. For example, a woman wiping her tears is a universal response of a deep feeling of grief, whereas her response of hiding her face in her veil is a cultural response to the same feeling. A strong arousal of the same feeling is an emotion that is more instinctive and physiological in nature, and can be shown by the woman beating her chest to show the emotional response of her grieving. Emotions also depend on other factors, such as different personality traits, sexual and cultural orientation of a person, or age.

*Cheshta*s in Kathak dance deal with these cultural, subtle, and instinctive responses that manifest in bodily and facial expressions. Following are some *cheshta*s that have special hand gestures and facial expressions practised thoroughly by a dancer in order to unfold the meaning of the lyrics in a song: observing one's lover in certain circumstances, being sidetracked, a fluttering heart, gazing, seducing, sighing, aching, yearning, longing, craving, tantalizing, desiring, feeling shy, falling in love, crying, hinting, insinuating, modesty, blushing, aggravation, madness, agony, separation, clinging, securing, sulking, wobbliness, scandalizing, startling, embracing, romancing, loving, passion, nostalgia, lust, and distancing. The personality traits of a character can be accessible, adventurous, amiable, captivating, charismatic, charming, cheerful, playful, perceptive, persuasive, romantic, sensitive, sporting, steadfast, suave, sweet, vivacious, faithful, youthful, amusing, or vindictive.

The pure *nritya* aspect of compositions based on vocal genres also depends on whether an idea is established as a subject or an object, which determines the structure of a characterization. For example, in a scene where a dancer is dancing as Krishna with the maidens of Braj, the dancer can act like Krishna, in which case Krishna becomes the subject modified by the predicate, the maidens of the Braj. However, if someone else is describing the scene of Krishna dancing with the maidens, then Krishna is portrayed as an object. The portrayal of Krishna as a subject or an object changes not only the characterization, but also the mood and temperament of the piece.

THUMRI

One of the most sensuous and passionate genres of vocal music, *thumri* is a semi-classical vocal style that came into practice around the fifteenth century. A few books written by great music scholars of that time mention the word *thumri* in the context of the lighter aspect of music filled with romantic devotion and eroticism. The word *thumri* is believed to have originated from the word *thumak*, meaning 'graceful swaying' or 'charming dance-like movements'. *Thumri* singers, at expressive and content levels, maintain the emotional, sensitive, and delightful aspects of dance. The romantic and mystical love of Radha-Krishna expressed by Madhura Bhakti poets is the predominant theme of *thumri*. The imaginative poetry and enchanting performance of *thumri* are highly sentimental and sophisticated in nature.

The origin of the *thumri* style of singing is difficult to pinpoint. Most scholars believe that this style originated and developed during medieval times and took its inspiration from the romantic devotional literature of the Bhakti Movement and the folk music traditions of North India. The mesmerizing folk music traditions of North India such as *chaiti*, *kajri*, and *biraha* influenced the expressional aspects of *thumri* considerably. Similarly, the *saguna* and *nirguna* poets of Bhakti Kaal had a marked influence on the content and lyrics of *thumri*s. However, according to some other scholars, many characteristics of *thumri* can be traced to the ancient music of India. These scholars believe that *thumri* probably took its inspiration from ancient singing styles, such as *charchari prabandh* and *hallisak geeti*:

> …The main characteristics of Thumari, viz., latitude in elaboration of Ragas, predominance of amorous sentiments in songs, greater emphasis on verbal-tonal embellishments rather than on purely tonal ones, preference for the feminine voice etc., are all features of light musical patterns recognized by the traditional Sangitshastra. Which means that styles resembling Thumari have been in vogue from times immemorial, and Thumari must have had parent styles of which in the absence of notated records no definite information is available.[1]

According to other scholars, *thumri* was instigated in the court of Nawab Asaf-ud-Daula of Awadh (1748–1797). Shori Mian, a famed musician from his court, started a new style of light classical music called *tappa*. With *tappa* style, the seed of *thumri* started to take shape. *Thumri* gained tremendous popularity in the nineteenth century. It is believed that the nawab of Awadh Wajid Ali Shah (1822–1887) and his court musician Sadiq Ali Khan, along with many other court musicians and dancers, played major roles in the advancement of *thumri* creations and performances. Generally, it is believed that Sadiq Ali Khan invented

[1] Prem Lata Sharma, 'The Origin of Thumari', *Aspects of Indian Music* (Delhi: Publications Division, Ministry of Information and Broadcasting, Government of India, 2006), pp. 81–2.

thumri, and that Wajid Ali Shah popularized it. Wajid Ali Shah was one of the most artistic rulers who was more concerned with the arts, music, dance, and poetry than political affairs. He himself was a distinguished performer. Wajid Ali Shah wrote and performed many *thumri*s under his pen name, Akhtar Piya. Following is a famous *thumri* written by Wajid Ali Shah:

Babul mora naihar chuto hi jaye
Char Kahar mil doliya mangavo, mora apna begana chuto jaye.
Angna to parbat bhayo, aur dehri bhayee bidesh
Jaye babul ghar aapno, main chali piya ke desh

[Translation: Father, my maternal home is slipping away from me. Four bearers are carrying my palanquin. People who were my own are being separated from me. Your courtyard is like a mountain now and your doorsill has become foreign. I am leaving your house and going to my beloved's.]

The aforementioned *thumri* has multilayered meanings. It depicts the bride leaving her maternal home to join her husband. At the same time, it represents the Indian funeral procession when the corpse is taken to the cremation ground on a palanquin, symbolizing the soul's meeting with God. Finally, it signifies Wajid Ali Shah's agony when he was exiled from Lucknow.

The *thumri*, as we experience it today, acquired discernible characteristics during the time of Wajid Ali Shah. Other nawabs during this time also contributed to *thumri* to give it a concrete shape. During Wajid Ali Shah's time, *thumri* performers were mostly court musicians, dancers, and *twaif*s, who sang and danced the *thumri*s simultaneously under the patronage of royal courts. Most of the early *thumri* performers were well trained in both vocal music and dance. The great Kathak dancer Pandit Bindadin Maharaj (1830–1918), founder of the Lucknow Gharana of Kathak, is known for creating over 1,500 *thumri*s. He was not only a Kathak performer, but also a great *thumri* singer who trained many celebrated *thumri* singers of that time.

Most *thumri*s are created in vernacular languages of Hindi, such as Braj Bhasha, Awadhi, or Bhojpuri, and are composed in Hindustani ragas that are light and delightful in mood, and suitable for the expressions of love and romance specific to *shringar rasa*. *Thumri* is viewed under the genre of light classical music and gives singers the liberty to deviate from the original raga. *Khyal* singing in Hindustani classical music strictly follows the rules of a raga and develops a raga

Guru Dr Maya Rao

in a conventional way. Even though *thumri*s are set in particular ragas, the primary goal is not to unfold a raga, but mainly to expand and express the emotions of lyrics. The appropriate *tala*s for *thumri* are *addha* (sixteen beats), *deepchandi* (fourteen beats), *keharwa* (eight beats), and the *tala*s that support the emotional aspects of the lyrics.

The sumptuous devotional-romantic poems of Madhura Bhakti are not the only inspiration for *thumri*s. The passionate, mystic Sufi poems and appealing folk love-song lyrics and tales of North India also had profound effects on the development of this genre. *Thumri*s are romantic in nature. Even the devotional aspects of *thumri* are delicately coloured by different facets of romance such as *virah* (separation) and *milan* (union). *Shringar rasa* is woven into every strand of the dramatic fabric of *thumri*, where the spectacular threads of passion and romance create assorted hues of sentiments. *Thumri* lyrics portray beautiful image scapes, such as lovers longing for each other while watching peacocks dance under a dark cloudy sky, their meeting in lush forests illuminated with fireflies, or the songs of lovebirds' flaming passion in their hearts. *Shringar rasa* depicted in *thumri*s may sometimes seem mundane and worldly; however, their expressions in dance and music transcend into more spiritual realms. The two lovers become the manifestation of soul and its higher dimension. Lyrics are very important in *thumri*, and the words and lines are repeated over and over, each time mysteriously revealing another hidden layer of the same emotion, and sometimes creating myriad emotions. Improvisations, wordplay, and persuasive interpretations through metaphors, similes, and personifications make the lyrics of *thumri*s highly alluring.

*Thumri*s are feminine in nature, avoiding the vigour and power of *khyal* singing in this style. A *thumri* singer's voice must be supple and melodious. Just

Guru Dr Maya Rao

like *thumri* singers train their voices to become more pliant and delicate in order to bring out the heart-rending emotions in the lyrics, Kathak dancers also learn and practice different *cheshta*s to express the soulful aspects of *thumri*. A comprehensive understanding of *nayak-nayika-bhed* is essential for the suitable characterization and portrayal of personality traits depicted in the lyrics. Tabla players play *laggi* or very fast and resonant strokes between the *sthayi* (the first half of the song) and the *antara* (the second half of the song) of a *thumri*. This gives an opportunity to Kathak dancers to perform fast footwork while performing a *thumri*. This footwork is fast, but musical; not aggressive.

*Thumri*s are usually performed after all the technical and rigorous aspects of Kathak have been performed. This suggests the ultimate goal of Indian dances: to leave the audience with some deep emotional experience in order to touch their hearts rather than to excite their minds.

Kathak dancers also perform in other semi-classical singing styles in folk dialects such as *dadra, chaiti, holi, kajri,* or *birha,* in which *shringar rasa* reigns. *Dadra* is considered a faster and more compact version of *thumri*. *Dadra*s have more lines in their lyrics and are usually sung in *tal dadra,* which is a six-beat rhythmic cycle. *Hori, kajri,* and *jhoola* depict the effect of seasons on human feelings and emotions. The word *kajri* means 'dark like kohl'. In *kajri*s, the effect of dark clouds of the rainy season on lovers is portrayed. In the lovers' separation, these dark clouds become pathos, and in togetherness, the same clouds rain love and joy. *Chaiti* style corresponds to Chaitra, a month in the Hindu calendar which marks the beginning of spring. *Chaiti* lyrics are hopeful and joyous. Holi corresponds to the cheerful festival of colours, where love and romance colour lovers' hearts. *Jhoola*s are songs sung by young girls during the early rainy season while swinging on swing sets.

The content of lyrics is not the only indicator of a particular style. The approach and technique of singing and presentation also determine the style. *Thumri* can have similar lyrics to any subgenre of light classical music, but the technical scheme applied while singing a *thumri* is different. All these light classical genres fit in the broad spectrum of *abhinaya* or *bhav batana* and closely follow similar conventions that are employed in *thumri*. However, *thumri* consists of the most poignant *abhinaya* and improvisational aspects of Kathak and dominates the world of *nritya* in Kathak.

GHAZAL

Unrequited love perfumed with passion creates the canvas for the poetic form *ghazal*, where the longing, ecstasy, agony, seduction, flirtation, separation, and a multitude of other emotions along with mysticism are painted in vivid colours. The Urdu *ghazals*, which derived from the ancient Arabic and Persian *ghazals*, are regarded as one of the most poignant *nritya* repertoires of Kathak. In Arabic, the word *ghazal* means 'the words of love'. A new spin is given by some scholars as to the etymology of the word *ghazal* in order to draw a parallel to its stirring content. According to them, *ghazal* means 'the melancholic cry of a gazelle' or the musk deer. Persian *ghazals* are considered equivalent to the Persian *ghoul*, which means 'melodic poetry'. The Urdu *ghazals* have developed from the Arabic and Persian *ghazals*.

The structure of *ghazal* is unique. Traditionally, the essential poetic features of *ghazals* are its couplets and a refrain. *Shers* or couplets are composed of two rhyming lines of the same metre that establish an idea or a mood. Rhythm and rhyme are two crucial aspects of couplets. *Beher* is the rhythmic structure which determines the metre or length of a line. All the *shers* in *ghazal* have the same *beher*, or length of lines, that share the same syllabic weight or stress. *Quafiya* is the rhythmic pattern of a *ghazal*, which is created with rhyming words and is followed by a *radif*. *Radif*, often used as a refrain, is the last phrase of the couplets. It is the same in all couplets. The ending phrase of the first couplet of a *ghazal* functions as a refrain. Many modern *ghazals* do not use the concept of *radif*. The first couplet of a *ghazal* is called *matla*. *Matla* creates the central mood for the *ghazal*, and the couplets are variations or slight deviations of that mood. The *matla* has *radif* and *quafiya* in both lines, accenting both the rhythmic pattern and the last phrase of the couplet. Seldom does a *ghazal* have two *matlas*, but if it does, the second *matla* is called the *matla-e-saani* or the second *matla*. The second *matla* is used to strengthen the theme of a *ghazal* in an alluring way. Perhaps, this is why it is also referred to as a *husn-e-matla* or 'the exquisite beauty' of *matla*. Sometimes, the *ghazal* writers or *shayars* use the technique of closed couplets, meaning each couplet is independent and can complete an idea on its own, contrary to the open couplets which depend on a *matla* or other couplets of a poem to complete a thought. Many *shayars* use a pen name or a *takhallus*, which is used in the final couplet of a *ghazal*, making the last couplet their signature couplet. This signature couplet is called a *maqta*. The *takhallus* can be used in first, second, or third person voice. It is very interesting to observe how a *shayar* uses his *takhallus*. In modern-day *ghazals*, many *shayars* choose not to use their pseudonym in *maqta*. The general rule of a *ghazal* is that it consists of a minimum of five couplets.

The Urdu language started to evolve in India around the eleventh century after India was invaded by the Muslim conquerors from the Middle East. Khariboli, the Indo-Aryan language of that time, was mixed with Persian and Arabic words that formed a whole new language known as Urdu. It became one of the major languages of India in the Mughal period. Urdu poetry, heavily influenced by the Sufi poets, started to carve its way into royal courts as well as among the common people. Sufism is a mystical dimension of Islam, and is considered a philosophy for the living and the loving. Ecstatic divine love marked by irrepressible madness, eroticism, higher consciousness in human beings, and mystical pain in search of meaning are the powerful premises that became the prevalent theme of Sufi poetry, music, and dancing. Persian poets influenced the Urdu *ghazals*, which were evolving and taking shape as an exquisite art form in the Mughal courts of India. Two great Persian Sufis, Rumi (1207–1273 CE) and Hafiz (1325–1389 CE), wrote beautiful *ghazals*, which were the product of their spiritual expressions. The agonizing separation or the rapturous union with the beloved, who was the symbol for the Divine, brought out shades of melancholy and ecstasy in their *ghazals* and, at the same time, posed many metaphysical inquiries. The ultimate lover, who was treasured in the deep chambers of the heart, was expressed as the greatest friend, radiant soul, idol, moon-faced lover, and sometimes even as a betrayer who is heartless and brutal, but nonetheless capturer of the heart. Rumi's longing for his lover comes across as madness of complete surrender in his poems:

> You cannot see yourself without a mirror;
> Look at the beloved, He is the brightest mirror.

[From 'Thief of Sleep' by Shahram Shiva][2]

Hafiz's *ghazal*s have multilayered meanings with intellectual stamina, balance of materialist and spiritual feelings, and sometimes even mystifying satire:

> I said because of your infliction I shall leave my house
> Smilingly said go ahead Hafiz, with chained hooves and paws.

[Translated by Shahriar Shahriari] [3]

The lyrical and imagery-rich *ghazal*s of the Persian poets greatly inspired the Urdu *ghazal*s. Ab'ul Hasan Yamin al-Din Khusrow (1253–1325 CE), who is popularly acknowledged by his pseudonym Amir Khusrow, was a great classical poet, mystic, scholar, and musician. Amir Khusrow was associated with more than seven rulers of the Delhi Sultanate. The iconic Khusrow's contribution is enormous in the multicultural endeavours of the fusion of Persian and Indian culture, music, poetry, and arts. The resulting amalgamation strengthened the ties between the Indian and Middle-Eastern rulers. Amir Khusrow wrote poems in many languages. He wrote many *ghazal*s in Hindavi, the language considered the main foundation of Urdu. Hindavi, also known as Dehlavi, was a mixture of Arabic, Persian, and Indian languages.

Ghazal developed rapidly as a literary form during the sixteenth and seventeenth centuries in South India, especially in the courts of Golkonda and Bijapur. It was popularized by the great poets of the era. Nusrati, Muhammad Quli Qutub Shah, Wajhi, Wali, and Hashmi were the distinguished *ghazal* writers of that time. Wali is credited with popularizing the richness of the Urdu language and the magnificence of *ghazal*s in North India. By the nineteenth century, *ghazal* became a major poetic form in North India.

It is difficult to speculate when the *ghazal* made its way into the musical sphere. Historians estimate that by the eighteenth and nineteenth centuries, this poetic form was embraced by court musicians and dancers. Rich dramatic, erotic,

....

[2] 'Rumi Love and Ecstasy Poems', http://peacefulrivers.homestead.com/rumilove.html (accessed on 16 April 2018).

[3] Shahriar Shahriari, 'Hafiz-e-Shirazi', 2012, http://www.hafizonlove.com/divan/01/032.htm (accessed on 16 April 2018).

and spiritual aspects of *ghazal*, along with its rhythmic form, attracted courtesans and the musicians so profoundly that *ghazals* became an important genre of dance and music by the twentieth century. Many royal dancers wrote their own *ghazals* and sang them while performing the *nritya* aspect of Kathak to express poetry. The mystical, soulful romance of *ghazal* was expressed through hand gestures and facial expressions, minimizing body movements. Body movements were used only to the point of accenting the theme and keeping the soul of the *ghazal* alive.

Today, *ghazal* presentation in Kathak is mostly performed by the dancers of the Lucknow Gharana. The delicate and malleable movements of that gharana complement the mood of *ghazals*. Dancers select the poetry of great poets from the past and the present and express it through the *nritya* aspect of dance. Sometimes, appropriate footwork and other Kathak techniques are used between the couplets to make the *ghazal* performance more appealing. The beauty of *ghazals* in Kathak is more evident in an intimate performing environment, in which the audience becomes an integral part of the *ghazal* performance, and the mood of the poetry can be shared between the dancer, singer, and audience.

BHAJAN

Bhajans are devotional poems adorned with musical notes and spiritual expressions. The word *bhajan* originated from the word *bhaj*, meaning 'to pray'. Expressing the attributes and praises of different gods and deities has always been an integral part of the daily rituals of Indian life. This veneration for the Divine very naturally seeped into the realm of dance, music, and poetry.

The widespread popularity of the Bhakti Movement in India from the fourteenth to the seventeenth centuries brought many saint-poets to light, who wrote soulful lyrical *bhajans* to express their committed love and adoration for their chosen deities. The Bhakti Movement started in the seventh century in South India. Because of its simplicity, sensitivity, and accessibility, its philosophy spread throughout India by the fourteenth century. The word *bhakti* means 'devotion'. The followers of the Bhakti Movement believed that the Divine Being was reachable by everyone, and each had the capacity to attain moksha or spiritual liberation. They believed that pure love and selfless devotion was the only way to find and become one with God, who had a personal relationship with each being. The saint-poets produced a magnificent collection of devotional writings. This body of literature was so lyrical in nature that it became an integral part of the music and dance repertoire. These saint-poets were not bound by the orthodox mentality of the Brahmins and priests, who belonged to the well-educated elite class and had encumbered religion with many strict traditions and rigid rituals. Their devotional poetry in local dialects was filled with genuine emotion, which touched devotees from every class and creed. Some of the *bhajan*s written during this time were literal, and some were mystical and abstract. Great philosophical and spiritual ideas were written in the form of poetry with such simplicity that even a commoner was able to understand them. The poetry of the Bhakti Movement was also a synthesis of Muslim and Hindu cultures and philosophies. Many Muslim poets wrote about Hindu gods, which promoted cultural harmony in India. Different views from different branches of Hinduism such as Shaivism, Vaishnavism, and Shaktism received equal recognition during the Bhakti Movement. Many great poets of this time were also musicians. They wrote *bhajan*s in specific ragas to suit the mood of their poetry. In turn, classical musicians of India became very fascinated by *bhajan*s. Around the same time, highly sophisticated *dhrupad* singing was acquiring great fame in the Mughal courts of India. The lyrics of *dhrupad*s were devotional and were influenced by the Bhakti Movement and the *bhajan*. Later, the famed musicians Pandit D V Paluskar and Pandit Vishnu Narayan Bhatkhande popularized *bhajan*s in the classical music field in the nineteenth and twentieth centuries. Dance was also influenced by the beautiful sentiments of *bhajan*s, and magnificent devotional and passionate poems found their place in Kathak. The mystic poet Meera Bai (1498–1546 CE) was a great devotee of Lord Krishna. In moments of devotional trance, she composed many *bhajan*s in different ragas. Meera Bai was also known as a dancer, who danced passionately while singing her *bhajan*s. Many Meera *bhajan*s are performed in Kathak even today. Following is a beautiful *bhajan* by Meera Bai, in which the devotion, romance, love, adoration, reverence, and exaltation create a colourful tapestry of emotions:

Rang de chunariya
Shyam piya mori rang de chunariya
Aisi rang de ki rang nahi chhute
Dhobiya dhove chahe ye saari umariya
Laal na rangau main to hari na rangau

Apne hi rang mein rang de chunariya
Bina rangaye main to ghar nahi jaungi
Beet hi jaaye chahe ye saari umariya
Meera ke prabhu giridhar naagar
Hari charnan mein Jaoon balihariya
[Translation: My beloved Shyam (another name for Lord Krishna), colour my *chunariya* (a long scarf to adorn the upper body) in a way that the colour is steadfast and never fades, even if the washerman washes it for his entire life. I don't ask you to dye it in red or green colours, just dye it in your own colour. Even if it takes my whole life—without you colouring my *chunariya*, I won't go back home. Meera's (the poet) idol is Giridhar (Lord Krishna's other name), on whose lotus I delight.]

The image of the shawl in this verse is used as a symbol for life. The later verses imply that only the colour of Krishna's love will never grow faint. Chaitanya Mahaprabhu, Tulsidas, Vallabhacharya, Surdas, Kabir Das, and Namdev are some other important saint-poets whose names have become synonymous with *bhajan*. Their poetry is still sung in classical music and performed by Kathak dancers. Many maestros of Kathak have written their own *bhajan*s, which have become a part of the *nritya* aspect of Kathak repertoire.

VANDANA AND SHLOKA

*Vandana*s and *shloka*s are performed in Kathak at the commencement of a performance as an invocation. Both devotional poetic forms derive from Sanskrit literature. *Shloka*s usually have two lines with a specific metre and pattern. Most of the Sanskrit *shloka*s have sixteen syllables in each line. These sixteen syllables are divided into two sets of eight syllables and are called *pada*s. Sometimes, a group of *shloka*s creates a complete *vandana*. However, there are also *vandana*s that are independent of the literary rules of *shloka*s. Later, many *vandana*s were written in other languages of India. Both *shloka*s and *vandana*s were created as prayers. They describe the divine attributes and praises of a specific deity.

*Vandana*s and *shloka*s are integral to Kathak. A traditional Kathak performance starts with a *vandana* or a *shloka*. Bharata in his *Natyashastra* mentions the act of *purvarang* in great detail. *Purvarang* was an elaborate and auspicious ritual that was performed before any theatrical production in order to please the gods and to receive favourable results. *Vandana*s and *shloka*s in Kathak take inspiration from Bharata's *purvarang* for an auspicious beginning of a performance.

Vandana—Pandit Rajendra Gangani

TARANA

Tarana is one of the most exciting repertoires of Kathak because of its swift, expressive, and electrifying characteristics. It is believed that the word *tarana* originated from the Persian word *tarannum*, which means 'melody'. The great court musician, poet, and scholar of the fourteenth century Amir Khusrow (1253–1325 CE) is credited for adding *tarana* to the gamut of Hindustani vocal music. Instead of poetic lyrics, meaningless syllables are used in *tarana*s. Many scholars believe that Amir Khusrow was inspired by the ancient Indian music termed *nirgeet* or *shushka-akshara*s. *Nirgeet* was a melodious composition comprised of a song with no literal meaning. Bharata Muni has also mentioned the *nirgeet* variety of songs. *Nirgeet* music used hard consonants. However, Amir Khusrow introduced Persian and Arabic words with soft consonants in *tarana*, such as *odani dani*, *yalali*, *derena*, *tadare*, and *tana*. He also added mnemonic syllables of Indian percussive instruments in *tarana*, which made renditions of *tarana*s not only complex but also fast-paced, appealing, and exhilarating. Some scholars also believe that *tarana* has some resemblance to *kaivad prabandh*, another variety of Indian ancient musical composition:

> If we peek into the history of Indian musical forms, one can find a similar musical form named Kaivad Prabandh in 'Sangeet Ratnakar,' a book written by Sharangdeo in [the] 12th century. Prabandh' the musical form sung in that period were composed by combining two parts, Dhatu and Ang. Kaivad Prabandh was composed by selecting three Angs namely, Tenak, Paat, and

Swar out of six. Tenak refers to auspicious words, Paat or Paatakshara are the bols of Mridang, and Swar are the notes.[4]

Later on, many composers started to use dance *bols* and the syllables of Indian string instruments in *tarana* compositions. *Tarana*s are usually short with a few lines that are repeated over and over. Because of its rapid pace, mystical characteristics, and rhythmic qualities, *tarana* has such magnetism that it has also made its way into South Indian vocal music and dance. In South Indian music, it is known as *thillana*. The purity of ragas is maintained even in the fast speed of *tarana*. *Tarana*s are composed in various classical *tala*s, such as *teental*, *ektal*, and *ada-chaartal*. Most of the *tarana*s are performed in *drut laya*, but they can also be performed in *madhya laya*, which slowly progresses to a faster tempo. Since *tarana*s do not have the restraints of meaningful words, they evoke shades of many emotions from excitement to a meditative mood.

*Tarana*s are very popular in Kathak performances and they show the rhythmic virtuosity of a dancer. Kathak dancers create graceful geometrical designs with their bodies while performing *tarana*s. *Tukda*s, *tihai*s, and *paran*s are also performed in a *tarana* repertoire. *Tarana*s are always concluded with very fast-paced footwork in *drut laya*. A good sense of *laykari* is extremely important for the performance of *tarana*, where the dancers create an intricate motif of complex *laykari*.

DHRUPAD AND DHAMAR

Dhrupad is a compound word, made up of two words: *dhruva* and *pada*. The word *dhruva* means 'preset' or 'permanent', and the word *pada* means 'literary composition'. *Dhrupad* is one of the oldest styles of singing. Its origin is related to the ancient spiritual Sanskrit texts. Therefore, the mood of *dhrupad* singing is devotional and meditative. *Dhrupad*s are believed to have been part of the daily prayers in the temples of ancient India. Later, *dhrupad* evolved as a complex style of singing. Sometime after the twelfth century, the language of *dhrupad* changed from Sanskrit to the dialects of India, and this genre became a significant singing style in the Mughal courts of India:

---

[4] Anjali Malkar, 'Tarana—An Aesthetic Musical Thought Beyond Words', http://www.shadjamadhyam.com/tarana (accessed on 16 April 2018).

Abul Fazl, courtier and chronicler at the court of the Emperor Akbar, defines the dhrupad verse form in his Ain-e-Akbari as 'four rhyming lines, each of indefinite prosodic length'. Thematic matter ranges from the religious and spiritual (mostly in praise of Hindu deities) to royal panegyrics, musicology and romance. However, the musical background of dhrupad is commonly through to have a long history, traceable back to the Vedas. The Yugala Shataka of Shri Shribhatta in the Nimbarka Sampradaya, written in 1294 CE, contains lyrics of similar fashion, Swami Haridas (also in the Nimbarka Sampradaya), the guru of Miyan Tansen, was a well known dhrupad singer.[5]

From ancient times to today, *dhrupad* has followed strict rules where the purity of *tala* and *raga* are given an enormous prominence. Its approach and technique of using musical notes are unique and have even been adopted by classical instrumentalists. *Tala*s such as *chartal* (twelve beats), *tivra* (seven beats), and *sulfakta* (ten beats) are commonly used in *dhrupad* compositions. Sometimes, nine-beat and fourteen-beat *tala*s such as *matta* and *farodast* are also used.

Although *dhrupad* is not performed commonly in Kathak, it has made its way into Kathak performances because of its meditative and contemplative moods, which allow Kathak dancers to beautifully execute deliberate and elegant movements.

The lighter style of *dhrupad* called *tala dhamar* is set in a fourteen-beat rhythmic cycle. It is recognized as the *dhamar* genre of Hindustani classical music. *Dhamar* is sometimes called *pakki-hori*, since the lyrics of *dhamar* exemplify the romantic themes of Radha and Krishna during the spring festival of colours, Holi. *Dhamar* differs with the light classical style of *hori* in that it is sung in *dhrupad* style and the *tala* used in this form is masculine in nature. *Hori*s are sung more in *thumri* style and incorporate free-flowing elements. *Dhrupad* is devotional in nature, whereas *dhamar* leans towards the *shringar rasa*.

---

[5] Ritwik Sanyal and Richard Widdness, 'Dhrupad: Tradition and Performance in Indian Music', SOAS Musicology Series (Hampshire, England, and Burlington, VT: Ashgate, 2004), https://ipfs.io/ipfs/QmXoypizjW3WknFiJnKLwHCnL72vedxjQkDDP1mXWo6uco/wiki/Dhrupad.html (accessed on 16 April 2018).

CHATURANG AND *TRIVAT*

Chaturang and *trivat* are blends of *tarana*, literature, *bols* of tabla, and musical notes. The word *chaturang* means 'four colours'; therefore, it is a combination of all of the given musical arrangements, whereas *trivat* uses only three.

All of these Kathak repertoire based on vocal music genres have the elements of both *nrtta* and *nritya*. With the exception of *taranas*, all of these genres have literature embedded in them, which gives a great scope for presenting the *nritya* aspect. *Thumris* and *ghazals* that lean more towards the *nritya* aspect can also sometimes feature *laykari*, depending on the prerogative of a dancer. Most of the great gurus of Kathak delved into the art of vocal music. They were so inspired by the unique characteristics of different vocal genres that they could not help but weave them into the repertoire of Kathak. *Dhrupad, dhamar, chaturang,* and *trivat* are not performed frequently, yet they have a place in the art of Kathak. *Tarana, bhajan, ghazal,* and *thumri* have become inseparable from Kathak. Herein lies the magnitude of Kathak in that it has integrated dance with many exquisite genres of Hindustani classical music, which makes this dance form so musical and complete.

*Chakkar*s or Pirouettes

THE BRAHMA SUTRA, or the thread of Brahma, is the vertical median plane, an imaginary perfect line in the centre of the body that represents the earth-sky precept. The vertical median plane is defined as the plane passing longitudinally through the body, dividing it into right and left halves, and is perpendicular to the horizontal plane. In Kathak, very few deflections take place from the Brahma Sutra, giving the dance form a two-dimensional look. The body of a Kathak dancer remains straight with a neutral pelvic position. The vertebrae in the back are aligned, and the weight is equally distributed between both sides of body. The feet are kept together, facing forward, and the body stays erect. In most of the Kathak movements, the legs do not extend, the upper body does not bend, and the feet are not flexed. Even though the bending of legs and torso have been incorporated in modern Kathak movement vocabulary, they are used sparsely, since the power in Kathak comes from keeping the body straight. A straight body makes it easier to extract energy from the navel area, which is imperative for fast footwork and the dynamic movements of Kathak.

*Chakkar*s or pirouettes are one of the most exciting features of Kathak, making Kathak seem fluid and ethereal. Even though *chakkar*s are performed along the vertical median plane, they give the illusion of a third dimension to this dance form. The spins and turns in Kathak are the amalgamation of balance, rhythm, finesse, and strength. Steadiness of body and mind is an absolute requirement to execute convoluted spins. Building endurance is another important aspect, since the Kathak dancers perform many combinations and numbers of spins at once.

In old schools of Kathak, *chakkar*s were also called *bhramari*s. Nandikeshvara in his *Abhinaya Darpana* refers to the *chakkar*s as *ghumariya*. In Kathak, many different varieties of *chakkar*s are used.

In most of the *chakkars*, both hands extend horizontally and come back to the basic hand position of Kathak when the turn is completed. Also, all *chakkars* start on the right foot. *Chakkar* of eight beats (*Tig dha dig dig, tig dha dig dig*) uses the *bols* of *tatkar*. The dancer completes one turn while doing the basic eight beats with the feet. In *chakkars* of five beats (*Tig dha dig dig thai*), the feet strike five times to complete one turn. Similarly, in *chakkars* of four beats (*Tig dha tig dha*) and *chakkars* of three beats (*Tat Tat thai*), the feet strike four and three times, respectively, to complete a turn. All the specified *chakkars* are presented at one spot, and the *bols* of the previous *chakkars* can change according to the *bols* of compositions. *Chakkar* of five beats is also practised with seven strokes of the feet, where the *bol Tig dha dig dig thai* is divided into seven beats: *Tig dha di ga di ga thai*. Different gharanas use different *bols* for these *chakkars*. The *chakkar* of two beats is used to move in space from one place to another.

Along with all other *chakkars*, the pirouette is also used very effectively in Kathak. In pirouette, a complete turnaround is performed while balancing on one foot. This is also known as the *chakkar* of one beat. In Kathak, pirouettes are done on the heel. In earlier times, pirouettes were also taken on the ball of the foot. Many *tukdas* and *parans* in Kathak end with *chakkars*. Most of the compositions have a number of *chakkars* that are odd, such as eleven, twenty-one, or fifty-one.

Chakkars can be performed in variety of ways. *Seedha chakkar* is performed counterclockwise and the dancer turns towards the supporting left leg. *Ulta chakkar* is the opposite of *seedha chakkar*, and the dancer turns towards the supporting right leg in clockwise direction. In some gharanas, dancers perform *akash chari chakkars*, in which they take a jump while turning. Pandit Gopi Krishna also experimented with turning on his knees, which he performed all around the stage. Many compositions of Kathak utilize half turns from both the right and left side. In *band haath ka chakkar*, the hands are not extended horizontally, but are kept in front of the chest. In some *chakkars*, one hand is extended horizontally and the other hand is extended vertically. In other types of *chakkars*, both hands are extended vertically in an alternative pattern. One hand can also be kept near the chest and the other hand can be extended. In Jaipur Gharana, many dancers keep their hands in a semicircular position to perform the *chakkars*. Dancers also choose whether to keep the palms of the extended hands up or down while performing a *chakkar*.

All *chakkars* are initiated from the neck area and the body follows the momentum created from a snap of the head. Maintaining good alignment of the body is an absolute necessity to performing the *chakkar*s with perfection. Alignment of the body is achieved by engaging the abdominal muscles to hold the centre stationary. The navel area is a Kathak dancer's centre of gravity. When the centre of gravity is held properly, the upper and lower body can move freely. However, holding the centre does not mean holding the breath. Breathing normally is mastered consciously in order to perform many *chakkar*s at once. The eyes are focused at one spot in the front, and after each turn, the eyes again relocate to the same spot. This technique helps in maintaining the focus. Timing in the performance of *chakkar*s is also extremely important. A missed beat can completely jeopardize the *chakkar*s and the composition. It is

Sandhya Desai

an arduous practice to exactly initiate a *chakkar* in order to return to the front on time. Some of the paramount identifiable features in Kathak, *chakkar*s are magnificent, exhilarating, and dazzling. At the same time, they are extremely challenging and demand a great deal of practice from the students of Kathak.

Gharanas:
Schools of Kathak

THE GHARANAS OR THE DIFFERENT SCHOOLS of Kathak were instigated as a consequence of the philosophies of thousands of years of the uninterrupted discipline of *guru-shishya* tradition in spiritual and artistic practices in India.

THE *GURU-SHISHYA* LINEAGE

The *guru-shishya parampara* or lineage implied the sacred relationship between a master and a disciple. In order to understand, absorb, and assimilate the subtleties of imparted knowledge, a *shishya* (disciple) studied with a *guru* (master) in an intimate setting. This setting encouraged an atmosphere infused with dedication, reverence, trust, and positivity through which the transmission of sacred knowledge from *guru* to *shishya* took place in the most committed manner. *Guru*s were not simply teachers, but the embodiment of wisdom, truth, and knowledge. The disciples absorbed the knowledge imparted by their *guru*s with utter reverence in order to retransmit the knowledge to their own successive disciples. This was the most effective way to ensure that the advanced knowledge and insights were continuously relayed to the next generation. The relationship between a *guru* and a *shishya* was not on a mundane level; instead, it took on a spiritual overtone and was established through a formal initiation ceremony.

Another explicit aspect of this discipline was the oral tradition, where the knowledge was not written, but was passed along via the spoken word. The oral tradition was used to sharpen the minds of disciples, as it increased their capacities of attention, concentration, and contemplation. Also, it prevented erroneous learning, which usually was the result of reading a recorded document. For esoteric subject matters, such as philosophy, spirituality, and arts, written materials were merely factual and lacked in providing experiential knowledge to a learner.

In Hindustani classical music and dance, *ganda bandhan* or the initiation ceremony establishes the sacred relationship between the *guru* and the *shishya*. *Ganda* ceremony is not a mere initiation ceremony; it is a profound spiritual experience for both the guru and the disciple, and it formalizes the lifelong relationship between the two of them. The word *ganda* means 'sacred thread', and the word *bandhan* means 'binding'. In *ganda* ceremony, the *guru* ties a thread around the *shishya*'s wrist, which is a symbol of their union for music or dance. *Mauli*, the cotton thread, is dyed yellow and red. The mantras and prayers are evoked when the *guru* ties the purified thread around the *shishya*'s wrist. The guests present at the ceremony witness the auspicious bonding between the *guru* and the *shishya*. The *shishya* presents gifts to the *guru*, his family, and the distinguished guests. The ceremony culminates with a feast. The *ganda bandhan* ceremony symbolizes commitment, responsibility, and devotion for music or dance for both the *guru* and the *shishya*.

GHARANA

For thousands of years, *guru-shishya parampara* thrived in India. Gharanas in classical Indian dance and music were modelled after this tradition. The continuous transmission of knowledge from a *guru* to a *shishya* created schools of music and dance. Each school differed in expressive, artistic, creative, and technical principles. In Hindustani classical music and dance, these schools are known as gharanas. The word 'gharana' is a compound word, comprising of two words: *ghar* and *aana*. The word *ghar* means 'home' and *aana* refers to 'arrival'; therefore, gharana means 'to arrive home'. It clearly implies the home of the guru, who was the originator of that particular gharana. The names of the gharanas are acquired from the names of the city, town, or district where a gharana originated.

Each gharana has its own characteristics, and each specializes in different techniques and artistic expressions. According to musicologist David Courtney:

> In the professional sense a *Gharana* has some of the characteristics of a guild.
> It was always understood that tracing one's lineage to a major *Gharana* was
> a prerequisite for obtaining a position in royal courts. The *Gharanas* were

entrusted with the duty of maintaining a certain standard of musicianship. In the artistic sense the *Gharana* is somewhat comparable to a 'style' or 'school'. Over the years poor transportation and communication caused the various *Gharanas* to adopt their own particular approach to presentation, technique, and repertoire.[1]

In his analysis, Dr Courtney indicates that the lack of transportation and communication in India did not allow different gurus to communicate and agree on one technique or style; therefore, different styles came into place as gharanas. After the degeneration of the Mughal era, Kathak dancers dispersed to different places in India. Most of them made their livelihood in the nearby small towns and villages, and some obtained patronage from the kings and nawabs. The names of gharanas of Kathak are based on the cities where the great gurus established themselves. There are four major gharanas in Kathak: Lucknow Gharana, Jaipur Gharana, Banaras Gharana, and Raigarh Gharana.

THE LUCKNOW GHARANA

It is not surprising that Lucknow, the capital of Uttar Pradesh, India, became a major gharana of Kathak. Throughout history, art, music, dance, poetry, and architecture thrived on this cultural city's soil. The glorious richness of arts and culture seeped into every aspect of life in Lucknow after it became the capital city of Awad or Oudh. It is believed that Awadh actually was an affluent ancient city called Ayodhya, which was the capital of the kingdom Kosala. After 1350 CE, different territories of Awadh came under the rule of the Delhi Sultanate: Mughal empire, the nawabs of Awadh, the East India Company, and the British Raj. The earlier capital of Awadh was Faizabad. The fourth nawab of Awadh Nawab Asaf-ud-Daula (1748–1797) declared Lucknow the capital of Awadh in 1775 CE. At that time, Lucknow became one of India's most culturally prominent cities. The lavish and sophisticated lifestyles of the nawabs made them patrons of the arts. Music, dance, poetry, and architecture flourished during their time, and Lucknow became the cultural centre. The evenings of Lucknow permeated

---

[1] David Courtney, 'Kathak—A Classical Dance of Northern India', http://www.tarang-classical-indian-music.com/tanz_links/kathak_Gharana_eng.htm (accessed on 16 April 2018).

Pandit Birju Maharaj

with arts, music, dance, and the extravagant lifestyles of nawabs, and came to be known as Shaam-e-Awadh.

The tenth and the last nawab of Awadh Wajid Ali Shah (1822–1887) contributed much to the art of Kathak. As a result, Kathak reached its glorious peak.

Wajid Ali Shah was himself an excellent composer, dancer, poet, and theatre director. His renowned *parikhana*, which literally means a 'dwelling for nymphs', supported the dance and musical training of hundreds of young women, who were trained by the greatest gurus of that time under the royal patronage. He even built a theatre known as Qaiser Bagh Baradari, where he staged many *raha*s in Kathak style. According to scholars, he created about thirty-six different types of *raha*s that were exquisitely composed, choreographed, and staged. It is also believed that his *raha*s were inspired by the Raas Leelas, in which he acted and danced himself. Wajid Ali Shah received Hindustani vocal training under the great singers of that time, such as Ustad Basit Khan, Ustad Pyare Khan, and Ustad Jaffer Khan. Wajid Ali Shah wrote many *ghazal*s and *thumri*s under the pseudonyms Qaisar and Akhtarpiya. He is also considered the first playwright of the Hindustani Theatre. His first theatrical production *Radha Kanhaiya ka*

Kissa was greatly inspired by the Raas Leela theatre. He himself acted as Krishna in this play and wrote dance sequences in Kathak style. He studied Kathak with the great guru, Pandit Thakur Prasad ji. Wajid Ali Shah also appointed two other eminent gurus of Kathak as court dancers. These two gurus were the famed brothers Kalka Maharaj ji and Bindadin Maharaj ji. Kathak dance attained new heights of artistry and recognition during the reign of Wajid Ali Shah because of the lavish patronage that he extended to the musicians and dancers of that time. However, the seeds of Lucknow Gharana started to sprout as early as the tenth century, and the dancers of Lucknow Gharana actually migrated from Rajasthan: ' … it is also claimed by the present descendants of Kalka and Bindadin Maharaj that their forefathers migrated from a village names Jaiatna, in Jodhpur state in Rajasthan and settled down at Handia Tahsil in Allahabad district. These Kathaks belonged to Rasdhari tradition.'[2]

Ishwari Prasad Mishra is credited as the first Kathak dancer in the Lucknow Gharana lineage. After him, the knowledge was passed on from one generation to another in his family. There is a very interesting account regarding his lifelong devotion to Kathak. It is alleged that he once saw Lord Krishna in a dream and was instructed to create the *Bhagavad* of Kathak dance. *Bhagavad* is an ancient treatise that contains the highest truth about life and recounts the tales of supreme godhead, Shri Krishna. Ishwari Prasad ji tirelessly devoted his life to Kathak and worked until the age of eighty. He called Kathak dance the Natwari Nritya. Natwar is one of the many names of Krishna, which means 'the supreme actor and dancer'. Ishwari Prasad ji imparted all his knowledge to his three sons: Argu ji, Khargu ji, and Tularam ji. Ishwari Prasad ji lived till 105 years. Until the end of his life, he kept teaching the niceties of Kathak to his sons. He died from a cobra bite. His wife passed away immediately after his death. The death of their parents shocked Khargu ji and Tularam ji to the point that Khargu ji stopped dancing and Tularam ji renounced the world. Argu ji's three sons Pragas ji, Dayal ji, and Harilal ji were all expert dancers, having studied the art of Kathak with their father and grandfather. Pragas ji was also known as Prakash ji. Later, after the death of Argu ji, Prakash ji moved to Lakshmanpur (modern-day Lucknow) and became the celebrated court dancer of Nawab Asaf-ud-Daula. His incessant work for Kathak gave rise to Kathak as a principal dance form. Prakash ji's three sons, Durga Prasad ji, Thakur Prasad ji, and Maan ji, remained in Lucknow and

---

[2] Kapila Vatsyayan, *Bharata: The Natyasastra* (New Delhi: Sahitya Akademi, 1996), p. 63.

became notable court dancers. Later, Thakur Prasad ji became the guru of Nawab Wajid Ali Shah.

In Vedic tradition, there was a ceremony of making an offering to the guru both spiritually and monetarily after a disciple completed formal studies. Wajid Ali Shah followed this Hindu tradition and gifted Thakur Prasad ji a massive amount of wealth, carried in six palanquins. By this time, Kathak had reached new heights of popularity and Kathak dancers gained enormous respect. Durga Prasad ji had three sons. Not much is discussed about his son Bhairon Prasad ji; however, his sons Bindadin Maharaj ji and Kalka Prasad ji are reverently remembered for their great efforts to make Kathak one of the most important dance forms of India. In fact, through their efforts, Lucknow Gharana of Kathak started to take a concrete shape. It is accounted that Bindadin Maharaj ji's training was so concentrated that he practised the *bols Tig dha dig dig* for many years and often for ten to twelve hours a day. Bindadin Maharaj ji's contribution to the world of *thumri* is enormous. He composed hundreds of *thumris* and numerous *bhajans* and *dadras*. He even inspired Wajid Ali Shah to incorporate *thumris* in Kathak and his *rahas* productions. His command of the expressive aspects of Kathak was so firm and intense that as a consequence, *bhava* and *abhinaya* became one of the most identifiable styles of Lucknow Gharana. Kalka Prasad ji was known for his genius in the rhythmic aspects of Kathak. He, along with his brother Bindadin Maharaj ji, created a fertile atmosphere for Kathak throughout the country. They trained many disciples and performed everywhere in the country. Kalka Prasad ji's three sons, Jagannath Prasad (also called Acchan Maharaj ji), Baijnath Maharaj ji (also called Lachhu Maharaj), and Shambhu Maharaj ji are iconic figures of Kathak dance. These three brothers were trained by both their father and uncle and received rigorous training in both the expressive and rhythmic aspects of Kathak. Shambhu Maharaj ji and Lachhu Maharaj ji were also trained by their older brother, Acchan Maharaj ji. Acchan Maharaj ji was known for his authority on rhythmic aspects. His precise movements with agility and subtlety tantalized his audience. Shambhu Maharaj ji was known for his execution of *bhava*. He studied the Hindustani classical vocal music from the distinguished Ustad Rahimuddin Khan. Lachhu Maharaj ji was known for his performances of his *gats* and *gat-bhaavs*. Acchan Maharaj ji was appointed in many courts as a court dancer. He was considered the jewel of the Raigarh court. Lachhu Maharaj ji moved to Bombay (present-day Mumbai) and became the dance director for many important Hindi films. He also received the Sangeet Natak Akademi

Pandit Lachhu Maharaj

award in 1957. Sangeet Natak Akademi is India's highest national institution for music, dance, and drama. In 1952, Shambhu Maharaj ji became the head of the Kathak Dance Department at Bhartiya Kala Kendra in New Delhi. He received India's fourth highest civilian award Padma Shri in 1956. He was also awarded the Sangeet Natak Akademi Fellowship award in 1967. His two sons Rammohan ji and Krishnamohan ji also became eminent artists of Kathak.

Today, Pandit Brijmohan Mishra (also called Birju Maharaj ji), the son of Acchan Maharaj ji, is the torchbearer of Lucknow Gharana. His contributions to the Kathak field today are incomparable. He founded Kalashram in New Delhi after retiring from Kathak Kendra, New Delhi. He started working with his uncle Pandit Shambhu Maharaj ji at Kathak Kendra, when it was known as Bharatiya Kala Kendra. He studied Kathak from his father and uncles and received training in all aspects of Kathak for which they were celebrated. Pandit Birju Maharaj gave a new dimension to Kathak by creating mesmerizing conceptual and choreographic

Pandit Birju Maharaj

Pandit Shambhu Maharaj

elements in this art form. He has achieved the status of 'living legend'. He has trained many Kathak dancers, many of whom achieved very respectable status in the field of Kathak. Pandit Birju Maharaj is not only one of the greatest Kathak dancers; he has also mastered in Hindustani vocal music and percussion instrument playing. His sense of *bhava* and *tala* along with picturesque body movements enthrall his audience.

One family member of Ishwari Prasad ji carried out the task of founding, developing, and expanding the Lucknow Gharana with incredible support extended by the nawabs of Awadh. The role of *twaif*s (courtesans), who were part of the feudal society, and their *kotha*s (brothels) in the growth of this Lucknow Gharana cannot be disregarded. The lavishly decorated *kotha*s were more than brothels. They were artistic centres, where music and dance flourished. In the same way, the *twaif*s were not merely prostitutes; they were also highly trained artists. During the reign of Asaf-al-Daula, Lucknow became famous for the *twaif* culture, and it remained such until the imprisonment of Wajid Ali Shah, the last nawab of Awadh. These *twaif*s were greatly supported by the nawabs, noblemen, elites, and the artistic community. In turn, the *twaif*s contributed greatly to the fields of dance, music, theatre, and the literary arts. They preserved the art of Kathak: 'Extremely accomplished and knowledgeable in Arabic, Persian, and Urdu literature, and well-trained in Indo-Muslim musical traditions and performing arts, the tawaifs made a significant contribution to Hindustani music, dance and creative writing, and also to theatre and film.'[3]

The famous *twaif*s of that time received arduous training under the great

----

[3] Nishat Haider, 'The Tawa'ifs of Lucknow', by Café Dissensus on 15 April 2014, http://cafedissensus.com/2014/04/15/the-tawaifs-of-lucknow/ (accessed on 16 April 2018).

gurus of music and dance. Besides maintaining their flamboyant *kotha*s, the *twaif*s also performed in courts and the houses of upper-class noblemen. Their refinement in the matter of arts and entertainment fetched them substantial financial gains. The *twaif* culture declined significantly after Lucknow came under British control. They were deprived of the generous patronage they were receiving from the nawabs, and were thrown into the dark alleys of moral judgment and social disgrace. Still, the Lucknow Gharana of Kathak dance never suffered due to lack of patronage. The great exponents and practitioners of this gharana gave every single breath to resuscitate the art of Kathak during the British rule. Even during the British Raj, the Lucknow Gharana of Kathak produced many remarkable Kathak dancers. This gharana started to spread in entire North India. Today, Lucknow Gharana of Kathak is one of the major gharanas of Kathak and is practised widely throughout India.

The main characteristics of Lucknow Gharana Lucknow Gharana of Kathak is known for its lyrical movements, elegance, and sophistication. The decorative and graceful movements combined with poise makes this style very attractive. *Abhinaya* is a forte of this style. The Radha-Krishna theme is portrayed through beautiful and sensual movements, and the *shringar rasa* is brought into play at every corner. Creating mood through different *cheshta*s and *bhava*s is given prominence in this style, which makes it very expressive. Literature-oriented *thumri*s, *bhajan*s, and *ghazal*s are performed with utmost splendour. *Gat-nikas* and *gat-bhaav*s are performed brilliantly in this style, where many mythological and literary stories are conveyed through exquisite movements. *Bhav-batana* is a unique aspect of this gharana, in which many dancers sing the lyrics while performing them. The Lucknow style of Kathak developed in the courts of Muslim rulers; therefore, many Arabic and Persian words are still used in this school for different repertoires. There are some rhythmic compositions that are very specific to this gharana. Even many syllables used in *padhant* or vocalization in this gharana vary from other gharanas. Even the simple *bol*s of *ta thai thai tat* of *takar* are presented with numerous variations. *Primalu tukda*s are also used widely to show the Lasya or the graceful aspect of dance. Many performers of Lucknow Gharana still perform *salami*, which is very specific to this school. *Salami* is performed in *vilambit laya* in the beginning of the performance, in which the composition ends with a salaam, the Muslim greeting in many Arabic and Persian countries.

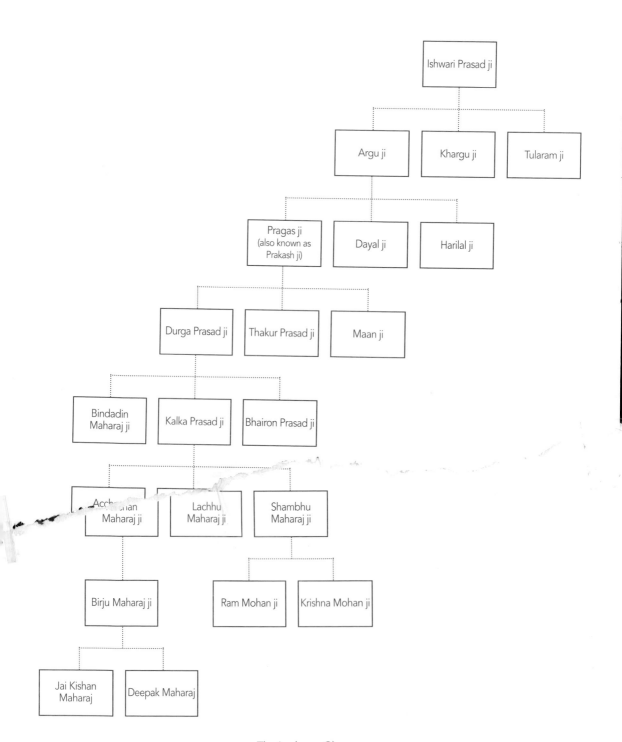

The Lucknow Gharana

*Natwari tukda*s are another important feature of this gharana. Even though this gharana developed in the Mughal courts, reverence for Krishna was always an important element of this dance form. Lord Krishna Himself supposedly danced *Natwari tukda*s. Both *nritya* and *nrtta* aspects of dance are beautifully balanced in this style. Lucknow Gharana is both stylistically and technically different from other gharanas. The pakhawaj was the main percussion instrument for Kathak in the courts. However, after the tabla-player brothers Modu Khan and Bakshu Khan moved to Lucknow from Delhi in the eighteenth century, the Lucknow or the Purab Gharana of tabla was created. At that time, Kathak dancers from Lucknow started to use tabla for accompaniment. Consequently, tabla *bol*s are used beautifully in Lucknow Gharana of Kathak. Pakhawaj *bol*s are still used in *paran*s and some other compositions of Lucknow Gharana.

In the twentieth century, many new repertoires were added in this school. By this time, Kathak had made its way among the general audience. It broke free from its confinement to the courts, parlour rooms, and *kotha*s. Dancers started to perform for larger audiences. New movements were created that were more suitable for the proscenium stage. The Lucknow Gharana of Kathak kept its roots intact, but it did change its movement vocabulary to accommodate the needs of larger stages. In this way, the Lucknow Gharana of Kathak was continuously evolving.

Some of the important past and present performers of Lucknow Gharana are: Ishwari Prasad ji, Adgu ji, Khadgu ji, Tularam ji, Prakash ji, Dayal ji, Harilal ji, Durga Prasad ji, Thakur Prasad ji, Mann ji, Bindadin Maharaj, Kalka Prasad ji, Bhairon Prasad ji, Wajid Ali Shah, Lachhu Maharaj, Shambhu Maharaj, Acchan Maharaj, Birju Maharaj, Ram Mohan Mishra, Krishna Mohan Mishra, Maya Rao, Kumudini Lakhia, Rohini Bhate, Munna Shukla, Vijay Shankar ji, Kartik Ram, Kalyan Das, Kumkum Dhar, Rani Karna, Saswati Sen, Prerna Deshpande, Arjun Mishra, Anuradha Guha, Uma Sharma, Aditi Mangaldas, Kajal Sharma, Sandhya Desai, Shovana Narayan, and Anuj Mishra.

THE JAIPUR GHARANA

If the Lucknow style of Kathak developed in the enticing and refined environment of the lavish courts of Awadh, Jaipur Gharana matured on the soil of Rajasthan, where the valiant Rajputana warriors with a double-edged dagger fought courageously against the British Raj. If the Lucknow style of Kathak was drenched with the perfumes of rose and jasmine, the Jaipur style of Kathak was soaked in the colour of saffron, the symbol of passion and heroism.

The Jaipur Gharana of Kathak flourished in the temples and the magnificent palaces of Rajput kings. Maharaja means 'king', and Rajasthan literally means 'land of maharajas'. The Rajputs were the descendants of the Kshatriya combatants of the Vedic era, and they ruled Rajasthan. They were great patrons of arts, music, dance, literature, and architecture. Kathak grew in Rajasthan mainly under their patronage.

The Jaipur Gharana is considered the oldest gharana in Kathak, which came into existence about 180 years ago. However, its roots can be traced as early as the eleventh century, since Rajasthani culture was always steeped in dance, music, and literature. Many masters were practising dance in different parts of Rajasthan. This could be why—unlike the Lucknow Gharana—the Jaipur Gharana was created by the contributions of many lineages. There were as many gharanas as gurus in Rajasthan. Later, their individual styles were consolidated into one school and became known as the Jaipur Gharana.

The Kachwaha kings, also known as the Kushwaha kings of Rajputana, wholeheartedly supported and employed dancers, musicians, painters, and poets. The honourable general of Emperor Akbar (1542–1605), Raja Man Singh (1550–1614), was the Kachwaha king of Amber, the ancient name for Jaipur. Raja Man Singh was a great benefactor of arts:

> Amritrai, a poet who was a contemporary of Raja Man Singh, composed in 1585 AD Mancharitra 2 which mentions the use of musical instruments in the palace of Amber. That the art of music, dance and drama were flourishing is borne out from the literary compositions of the period and the references found therein. Another work also named Mancharitra composed by Narottam Kavi and copied in 1640 AD by the scribe Manohar Mahatma who was in the service of Raja Jai singh refers to Raga Chitras painted on the walls of Amber palace and the *Pothikhana* collection has Mohan Kavi's Sanskrit drama *Madan Manjari* which was staged for Raja Man singh at Amber.[4]

---

[4] Sunil Kothari, *Kathak: Indian Classical Dance Art* (New Delhi: Abhinav Publications, 1989), p. 41.

Raja Man Singh was also a great devotee of Lord Krishna, and had erected a seven-storey temple of red sandstone in Vrindavan, Uttar Pradesh, for Sri Chaitanya Mahaprabhu, a great Hindu saint. Raja Man Singh had sent Vallabhdas, a great dancer from Amber, to Vrindavan to teach Raas Leela dances. The *kavitta*s and *primalu*s created by Vallabhdas are still performed by the exponents of the Jaipur Gharana. This proves that Kathak was performed in Rajasthan only as early as the sixteenth century, even though the Jaipur Gharana was not formalized at that time. These *kavitta*s and *primalu*s are the repertoires of both the ancient Raas Leela and the modern-day Jaipur Gharana. Raja Madho Singh followed the footsteps of his older brother Raja Man Singh and supported the arts of music and dance. During his reign, very important volumes on music and dance entitled *Raga Manjari* and *Nartana Nirnaya* were written by Pundrik Vitthal. Another vital volume on dance from the time of Raja Ram Singh is *Hastak Ratnavali*. Raja Ram Singh appointed many dancers in his *zenana-khana* or the establishment for ladies. These dancers were called *patura*s. The dancers who stayed at *zenana-khana* performed exclusively for the king and his family circle. There were also courtesans, expert in dance, music, and other art forms, who performed for the entire court. These courtesans were quite well respected, and many of them were even given the privilege to participate in state matters. Even outside the realm of the king's court, dance and music flourished in Rajasthan. A few temples also employed devadasis (dancing girls), who devotionally danced for gods during temple rituals. Literature of that era also confirms that Kathak was popular and this beautiful dance form inspired the poets. The poets of that time used dance vocabulary in their poems to portray the actions and reactions of their focus. Those terms remain in use in Kathak. The Ragmala paintings were also created during this era. Ragmala paintings are exquisite paintings that personify musical modes through colour, postures of subjects, mood, seasons, time of the day and night, and written verses. The depiction of *nayak*s and *nayika*s in these paintings epitomize them in Kathak costumes and postures. Amber was later renamed Jaipur after Raja Sawai Jai Singh (1688–1743), who remodelled the entire city. During the rule of Raja Sawai Jai Singh, music, dance, and other art forms reached new heights. He had formed the *gunijan khana*, or the chamber of highly gifted individuals, where the greatest dancers, musicians, artists, poets, and craftsmen practised their arts throughout the day. In the evenings, they performed at the nearby temple of Govindji, where dance became one of the most loved pursuits. All the successors of Raja Sawai Jai Singh continually supported arts. Along with the famous sand dunes of the Thar desert, charming gardens, magnificent palaces, glorious temples, and music and dance became inseparable parts of the culture of Rajasthan. Distinguished aestheticians and musicians in Rajasthan wrote many important books on art, music, and dance.

Even though, during the sixteenth and seventeenth centuries, Kathak dancers were practising Kathak in many different areas of Rajasthan, the dancers who truly carried the tradition remained mainly in the western parts of Rajasthan. They belonged largely to the Bikaner, Sujangarh, and Shekhawati regions. The family *charan*s or bards kept an account of these dancers and, through their narratives, the history of Jaipur Gharana was constructed:

> From the documents in the possession of Mohanlal ji, eldest son of the late Hanuman Prasad ji of Jaipur and on the strength of the oral history from the family bard Pratap ji, one is able to construct some plausible history of the exponents of the Jaipur Gharana. This takes us as far as one hundred and eighty years approximately.[5]

The direct lineage of Kachwahas of Jaipur came to an end by 1880. Kayam Singh (1861–1922), a nineteen-year-old soldier serving under the British order in the Tonk infantry, was adopted and renamed Sawai Madho Singh II. The *gunijan khana* continued thriving during his reign. The records of *gunijan khana* kept during Sawai Madho Singh II's reign reveal the number of dancers and musicians and their names. According to these records, there were ten male Kathak dancers and thirty-eight female dancers in *gunijan khana*. Among the male dancers, the main ones were Shyamlal ji, Natthu Lal ji, Badri Prasad ji, Chunni Lal ji, Harihar Prasad ji, Hanuman Prasad ji, and Narayan Prasad ji. Among the female dancers, Gauhar Jaan, Kamar Jaan, Sardar of Sambhar, Kamla, Dhanni Bai, Ratan, and Maina were very well known. After the dissolution of *gunijan khana*, the employed musicians and dancers relocated to different places inside and outside of Rajasthan.

The name that stands out as an originator of Jaipur Gharana is of Bhanu ji, who was a great devotee of Lord Shiva and had received training in Shiva Tandava, the dance of Lord Shiva, from a saint whose name is not identified. The vigorous and energetic Shiva Tandava is supposedly the divine dance of Lord Shiva that

---

[5] Ibid., p. 43.

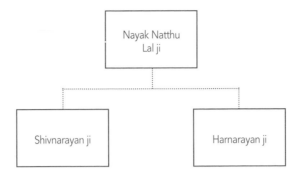

The first lineage of Jaipur Gharana

signifies the creation, preservation, and annihilation of the universe. Bhanu ji's son Malu ji and his grandsons Lalu ji and Kanu ji also had great knowledge of Shiva Tandava. Kanu ji travelled to Vrindavan to study Lasya dance, which is characterized by grace and beauty, in order to have equal authority on both the Tandava and Lasya elements of dance. Kanu ji's two sons Geedha ji and Shehja ji were also well versed in both Tandava and Lasya styles of dance. Geedha ji's five sons also studied dance. One of his sons Dulha ji settled in Jaipur. Dulha ji was also known by the name Giridhari ji.

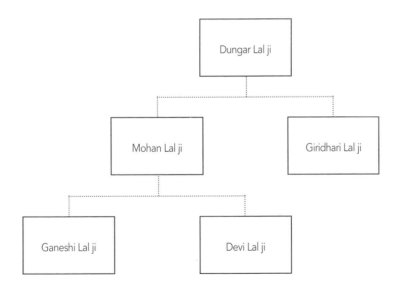

The second lineage of Jaipur Gharana

Giridhari Prasad ji had two sons, Hari Prasad ji and Hanuman Prasad ji, both of whom were employed in *gunijan khana* in Jaipur. Hari Prasad ji was celebrated for his vigorous *chakkardar parans*, and Hanuman Prasad ji was known for the grace and charm in his dance. Hari Prasad ji and Hanuman Prasad ji worked so much for Kathak that they were regarded as Hari Prasad and Hanuman Prasad Gharana. Hanuman Prasad ji was a great devotee of Lord Krishna, and his dance reflected this devotion. Hanuman Prasad ji's three sons Mohan Lal ji, Chiranji Lal ji, and Narayan Prasad ji brought Kathak to new heights. Mohan Lal ji, who was also a great vocalist and sang *dhrupad* and *dhamar* with great proficiency, moved to Khairagarh in Chhattisgarh to teach Kathak and music. Chiranji Lal ji, who was also known for his tabla-playing skills, moved to New Delhi to teach at the prestigious Gandharva Mahavidyalaya. His brother Narayan Prasad ji followed his footsteps and also taught in New Delhi at the same institute. Narayan Prasad ji performed at many different places in India and became a celebrity in the field of Kathak. His dance had poise and grandeur. He was known for handling complex *tala*s effortlessly. His *bedum paran*s and *tihai*s captured the hearts of his audience, where he performed three parts of compositions without any pause between the

Pandit Sundar Prasad

sections. His performances of *tripalli*s and *panchpalli*s were brilliant. *Tripalli*s and *panchpalli*s are the compositions in which the same *bol*s and phrases of a dance are performed three or five times, respectively, in different *laya*s. He had mastery over all different aspects of Kathak. Later, his two sons Charan Giridhar 'Chand' and Tej Prakash 'Suraj' made great names for themselves in the field of Kathak.

Hari Prasad ji and Hanuman Prasad ji's cousins Shyam Lal ji, Chunni Lal ji, Durga Prasad ji, and Govardhan ji also are known for their outstanding dancing. They all studied from Shankar Lal ji. Not much is known about Shankar Lal ji except that he, along with great dancers of his time such as Bhanu ji, Prakash ji,

Pandit Durga Lal

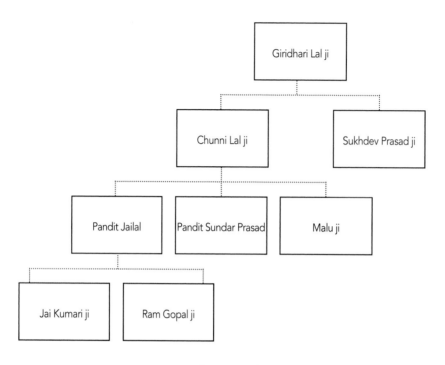

Giridhari Lal ji's family tree

Janaki Prasad ji, Sukhdeo ji, Makhan Lal ji, and Natthu Ram ji, studied dance with the great guru Maharaj Sanwal Lal ji. Shankar Lal ji was not only a brilliant dancer; he was also an extraordinary *thumri* singer. His grandson Badri Prasad ji was also very skilled in Kathak. Chunni Lal ji's two sons Jailal ji and Sundar Prasad ji earned tremendous respect in the field of dance. Their technique was outstanding even in very fast tempos. Jailal ji was also appointed at the *gunijan khana*. He was invited by Raja Chakradhar Singh at the Raigarh court, where he trained some famous dancers of Jaipur Gharana. Later in life, Jailal ji moved to Kolkata and trained many well-known dancers, including his son Ram Gopal ji and daughter Jai Kumari. Jailal ji's younger brother Sundar Prasad ji studied Jaipur Gharana of Kathak from a very early age, but later, he also studied the Lucknow Gharana with Bindadin Maharaj ji. He trained many dancers in Mumbai, New Delhi, and Madras. He was on the faculty of Bharatiya Kala Kendra, the famed music and dance institution in New Delhi. He also received the Sangeet Natak Akademi award in 1959. Jailal ji's disciple Sohan Lal ji is credited for bringing Kathak to South India.

Narayan Prasad ji's nephew Kundan Lal Gangani ji's contribution in Kathak will always be remembered. He trained many students in Baroda and later taught at Kathak Kendra, one of the greatest training centres of Kathak in New Delhi. His son Guru Rajendra Gangani is currently carrying the torch of Jaipur Gharana. Guru Rajendra Gangani is celebrated for his strength, grace, power, vocalization technique, *chakkar*s, and *laykari* in Kathak. Guru Rajendra Gangani received the Sangeet Natak Akademi Award in 2003. Kundan Lal Gangani's brother Sundar Lal ji studied with Sundar Prasad ji, Gauri Shankar ji, and Hazari Lal ji. Kundan Lal ji trained hundreds of students in Baroda, including his two sons.

Gauri Shankar ji's name is always spoken of with reverence among the Kathak dancers. He studied Kathak under his father Devilal ji, and also under Sundar Prasad ji and Shivlal ji. He is known for receiving the highest award in Berlin, Germany, for the International Dance Olympiad. He also worked with Nobel Prize winner and India's celebrated writer Rabindranath Tagore at his school at Santiniketan. Later, he established his own school of Kathak in Mumbai. He also taught at Jaipur's Kathak Kendra. Gauri Shankar ji is known for choreographing full-length dance dramas.

Another famous name of the Jaipur Gharana, who is remembered with a great deal of admiration, is of Pandit Durgalal. Pandit Durgalal was born in Rajasthan and was equally gifted in vocal music, percussion music, and Kathak. He started his training in Hindustani vocal music with his father Omkar Lal ji and studied percussion with Pandit Purushottam. Initially, Durgalal ji trained in Kathak with his older brother Devilal ji, and later studied with Sundar Prasad ji. He was awarded one of the highest civilian awards of the government of India Padma Shri, as well as Sangeet Natak Akademi awards for his contributions in the field of Kathak.

The Jaipur Gharana was also sustained by many remarkable dancers from different parts of Rajasthan. Besides Jaipur, some other states also had established *gunijan khana*, where many other great dancers of the Jaipur Gharana were employed. All these dancers had dedicated their lives to performing and teaching Kathak. Many lineages of this gharana existed in different parts of Rajasthan and, earlier, they all had their own gharanas based on their family names or the name of the guru. Later, all these separate gharanas merged into one gharana called the Jaipur Gharana.

Though there is no written record available the contemporary gurus of Jaipur Gharana maintain that a meeting of Kathakas took place in 1895 AD during the time of Maharaja Sawai Madho Singh in Jaipur to drown all the differences about the Gharanas…in this meeting exponents from luck now were also invited. It was resolved that instead of giving names to the Gharanas after the individuals, they be given name of the place….Thus the two major Gharanas came to be known by that time as Lucknow Gharana and Jaipur Gharana.[6]

The main characteristics of Jaipur Gharana

Many early dancers of Jaipur Gharana were devotees of Lord Shiva and focused on Shiva Tandava, a dance characterized by vigour, strength, power, force, and exaltation. The dynamic Kathak of Jaipur Gharana has acquired all these characteristics of Shiva Tandava. Also, Jaipur Gharana developed in the courts of Kachwaha kings who were great warriors. The heroism of these proud and courageous warriors influenced the Kathak dancers to transfer the same fortitude in their dance. Therefore, the Jaipur Gharana of dance can be described as energetic and forceful with great endurance. Even so, this gharana is not devoid of grace and beauty. Lasya dance, which is graceful and delicate in nature, also inspired the dancers of the Jaipur Gharana, the influence of which can be observed in the *that*, *kavitta*, *bhajan*, and *gat* aspects of Kathak from this gharana.

Dazzling footwork and swift pirouettes are the hallmark traits of this style. Very complex and fast footwork is performed seemingly effortlessly. The turns and pirouettes that seem faster than the moving blades of a fan are breathtaking. *Laykari* is another very important aspect of this school. Jaipur Gharana dancers dance in complex *tala*s using intricate *laykari*. The great dancers of Jaipur Gharana have complete command over *laya* and *tala*, along with an amazing sense of rhythmic subtleties. They play with different *laya*s, as if the rhythmic phrases are puzzle pieces. Because of their rhythmic wizardly, they dance extensively in *vilambit laya*, which gives them enough space between the two beats to rhythmically manipulate that space. Therefore, the rhythmic compositions of the Jaipur Gharana have characteristics of being resolute and dense. *Lambchad paran*s are the specialty of Jaipur Gharana, where the *paran*s are very long

[6] Ibid., p. 44.

and complicated. These intense *paran*s are performed with many *chakkar*s or pirouettes. *Chakkar*s are an extremely important part of Jaipur Gharana, where dancers perform many *chakkar*s in one composition. *Chakkar*s in this gharana are performed in both counterclockwise and clockwise directions.

Abhinaya in the Jaipur Gharana is projected through *bhajan*s, *vandana*s, *kavitta*s, and *gat-bhaav*. Dancers tell an entire story through movements in *gat-bhaav*. Even though *gat-bhaav*s are *lambchad* or long, the dancer takes time to portray a mythological episode in the most elaborate manner. *Kavitta*s are another identifying element of the Jaipur Gharana. *Kavitta*s are poems bound in rhythm. These *kavitta*s usually portray different gods and deities. Sometimes, a story is told through a *kavitta*. *Bhakti rasa*, *veer rasa*, and *shringar rasa* are the most portrayed *rasa*s in this gharana.

A lot of attention is given to the vocalization technique. Weighty *bol*s of pakhawaj and dynamic *bol*s of tabla are used a great deal for *padhant* by the dancers, which make the vocalization of compositions exciting and energetic. Many *bol*s of the Jaipur Gharana resemble the sounds of nature and ancient chanting. Even many body movements and the vocabulary used for those particular movements are taken from ancient treatises on dance. *Urmai*, *urap*, *tirap*, and *puhup punjari* are a few of the ancient words in the vocabulary of Jaipur Gharana dance. Another very alluring aspect of Jaipur Gharana Kathak is its repertoire of Chamatkar Nritya, which is slowly becoming a lost art. The word *chamatkar* means 'marvel' or 'amazement'. The old dancers from Jaipur Gharana performed pieces that seemed almost miraculous. Many of these dancers were experts in dancing on burning coals, executing footwork on the blade of a sword, or dancing on top of *batasha*s (sugar drop candy) without breaking them. The Gulal-chitra Nritya was very famous at one time, but it disappeared with the passage of time. In Gulal-chitra Nritya, the floor was covered by *gulal* or coloured powder with a white sheet on top. The dancers would dance on the white sheet. After their performance, they lifted the sheet and the audience could see the imprints of elephants, peacocks, flowers, or other elements of nature that were created by the dancer's feet.

The oldest gharana of Kathak, the Jaipur Gharana, is growing steadfastly even today. Many new elements such as group choreography, conceptual choreography, and maintaining the balance of *laya*, *tala*, and *bhava* are keeping this gharana as strong as ever.

Guru Kundan Lal Gangani

Some of the important past and present performers of Jaipur Gharana are: Hanuman Prasad ji, Harihar Prasad ji, Chiranji Lal ji, Pandit Mohan Lal ji, Pandit Narayan Prasad, Pandit Jailal, Pandit Sundar Prasad, Pandit Gauri Shankar, Pandit Kundan Lal Gangani, Pandit Sundar Lal Gangani, Jai Kumari ji, Pandit Ramgopal, Pandit Shiva Narayan, Hanuman Prasad ji (younger), Pandit Durga Prasad, Sohan Lal ji, Pandit Durga Lal, Charan Giridhar 'Chand', Jagdish Gangani ji, Guru Rajendra Gangani, Giridhari Maharaj ji, Kanhaiya Lal ji, Damayanti Joshi, Rajkumar Jabda, Kajal Mishra, Rohini Bhate, Roshan Kumari, Rani Karnaa, Maya Rao, Kumudini Lakhia, Puvaiya sisters, Pandit Tirath Ram Azad, Dr Puru Dadheech, Uma Sharma, Urmila Nagar, Rita Bhandari, Geetanjali Lal, Anjani Ambegaokar, Shovana Narayan, Prerana Shrimali, and Uma Dogra.

Pandit Rajendra Gangani

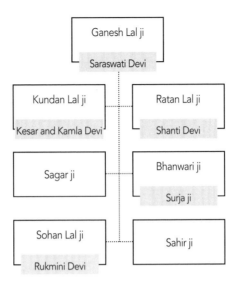

Ganesh Lal Ji's family tree (provided by Guru Rajendra Gangani)

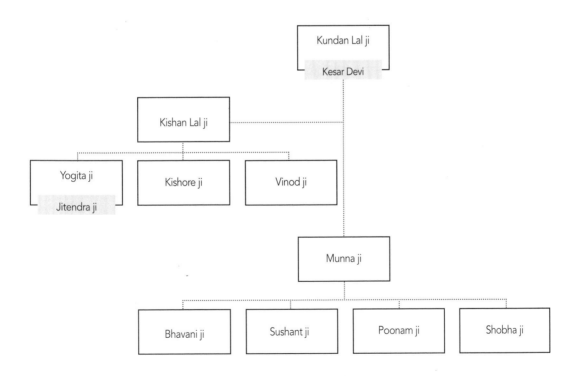

Guru Kundan Lal ji's family tree from Kesar Devi

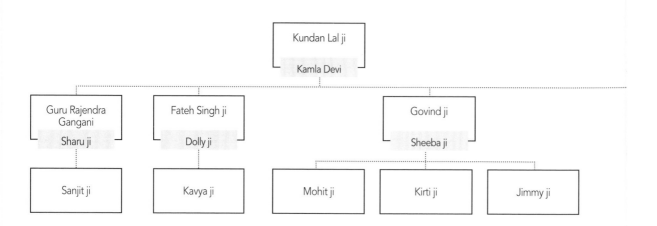

Guru Kundan Lal ji's family tree from Kamla Devi

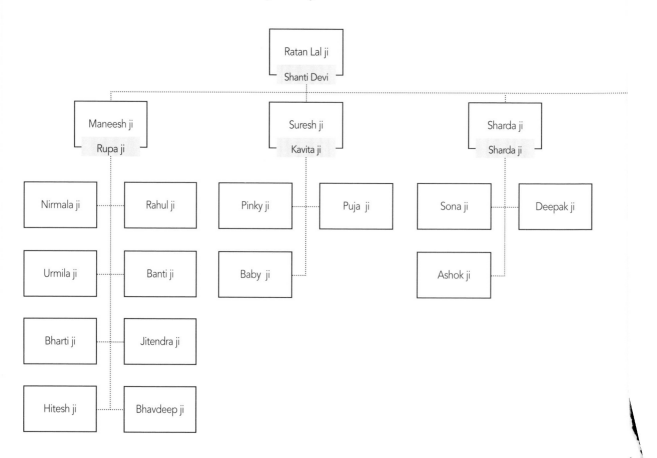

Ratan Lal ji's family tree

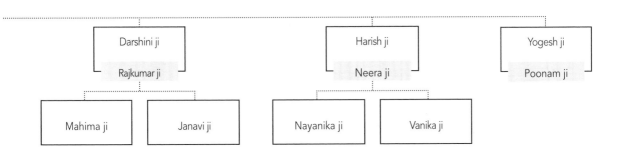

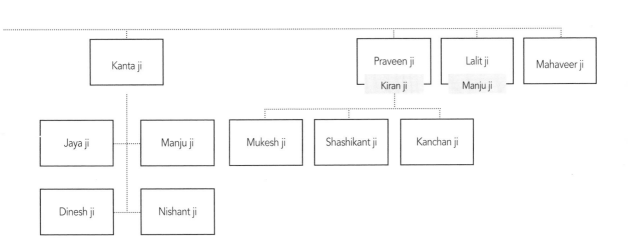

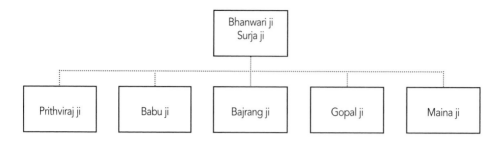

Bhanwari ji's family tree

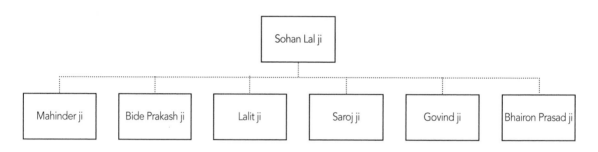

Sohan Lal ji's family tree

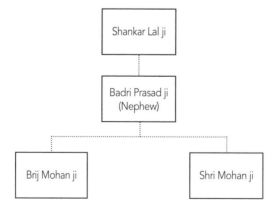

The third lineage of Jaipur Gharana

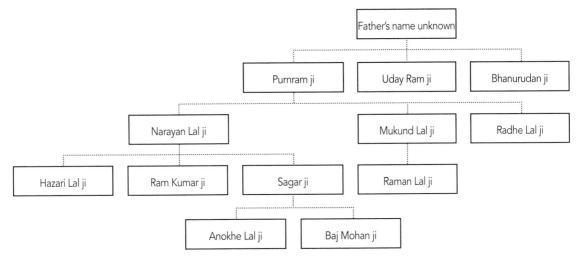

The fourth lineage of Jaipur Gharana

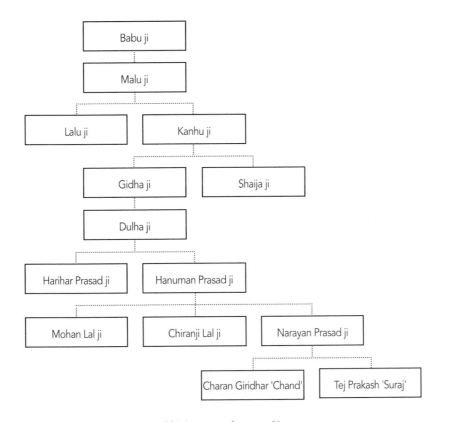

The fifth lineage of Jaipur Gharana

BANARAS GHARANA

Banaras Gharana, also known as the Janaki Prasad Gharana, originated in Rajasthan and flourished in Banaras. Janaki Prasad ji was the originator of this gharana, who settled and trained many disciples in the spiritual city of Banaras, Uttar Pradesh.

Situated at the bank of the holy Ganges River, Banaras is mentioned as Kashi in Rigveda, an ancient Hindu scripture. The word 'kashi' literally means 'the luminous city of supreme lights'. One of the oldest cities in the world, Banaras is also known as Varanasi. Many proponents of the Bhakti Movement were born in Banaras, which furthered the spiritual uniqueness of Banaras. A major pilgrimage site, Banaras is known for its beautiful temples shimmering in golden sunrises. The magical waters of the Ganges pull thousands of people to its banks in the morning. Many great sages and saints were born in Banaras, and the exponents of Bhakti Movement visited the city.

Janaki Prasad ji gravitated towards Banaras, and he moved there from Bikaner, west Rajasthan, and established the Banaras Gharana of Kathak. According to many scholars, there was a Shyamal Das Gharana in Rajasthan to which Janaki Prasad ji originally belonged. According to Sunil Kothari:

> Janaki Prasad hailed from Mailsur village in Bikaner state. In recent times the exponents of Janakiprasad Gharana have traced his genealogy, which mentions three previous generations of dancers: his father, grandfather, and great grandfather. He was born in the family of dancer Gopi-Prasad of Mailsur. Gopi Prasad had a son named Govind Prasad. His son Anand Prasad had two children. One of them was Janakiprasad and the other Chunnilal.[7]

Vidushi Sunayana Hazarilal, one of the greatest contemporary dancers of Banaras Gharana, mentions a very interesting story about Janaki Prasad ji in one of her interviews: 'The Banaras Gharana was founded by Pandit Janki Prasad. It is said that his in-laws gave him a single composition written on

----

[7] Ibid., p. 59.

a scrap of paper as dowry, expecting him to create his wealth from it. He was offended and walked away from his marriage, dedicating himself to dance.'[8]

Janaki Prasad ji had three principal disciples: Chunni Lal, Dularam, and Ganeshi Lal. Since there is no written genealogy and all this information is passed orally from generation to generation, there is ambiguity whether Chunni Lal ji, Dularam ji, and Ganeshi Lal ji were Janaki Prasad ji's brothers. Another name, Hukma Ram, appears in the genealogy of Banaras Gharana dancers. It is not clear whether Chunni Lal ji was Hukma Ram ji's son. However, every scholar agrees that Janaki Prasad ji taught Kathak to all of the said dancers.

Chunni Lal Ji's son Sabia ji studied Kathak under both his father and Janaki Prasad ji. Among the three sons of Dularam ji, Bihari Lal ji was a remarkable dancer who later moved to Bombay. He performed all over the country and danced with the eminent tabla player, Ustad Ahmed Jan Thirakwa. His second son Puran Lal ji also moved to Bombay. His third son Hira Lal ji moved to Indore and was appointed there as a court dancer.

Bihari Lal ji had three sons, who were all famous Kathak dancers: Kishan Lal ji, Mohan Lal ji, and Sohan Lal ji. Kishan Lal ji practised mainly in Bombay. Both Mohan Lal ji and Sohan Lal ji moved to Dehradun, the capital city of the state of Uttarakhand in North India, to spread the art of Kathak there. Puran Lal ji's sons Madan Lal ji and Ram Lal ji moved to Patiala in Punjab and taught Kathak there.

Among the three distinguished disciples of Janaki Prasad ji, Ganeshi Lal ji had three sons: Hanuman Prasad ji, Shiv Lal ji, and Pandit Gopal Das ji. Hanuman Prasad ji was a very famous dancer and was appointed in many courts as a court dancer. He also taught at Sangeet Bharti, Delhi. Hanuman Prasad ji was also a remarkable tabla player. He had one daughter and taught Kathak to his three grandsons—Nawal Kishor ji, Bansi Lal ji, and Omkar ji in Delhi. Ganeshi Lal ji's second son Shiv Lal ji was also trained in Kathak, but he is better known as a tabla player. According to some scholars, he was also a poet. Shiv Lal ji's three sons Sukhdev ji, Kundan Lal ji, and Durga Prasad ji studied Kathak with their father, but did not adopt Kathak as their profession. Ganeshi Lal ji's third

---

[8] Ranjana Dave, 'The Story of a Gharana', *The Hindu*, updated 15 April 2011, http://www.thehindu.com/todays-paper/tp-features/tp-fridayreview/the-story-of-a-Gharana/article1697629.ece (accessed on 16 April 2018).

son Gopal Das ji became a prominent Kathak dancer and was known as Pandit Gopal. He was a court dancer in the state of Patiala, but spent most of his time in Lahore, which is now a city in the Pakistani province of Panjab. Pandit Gopal produced many famous disciples, such as Bhure Khan and Hazari Lal ji. This celebrated dancer of the Banaras Gharana was awarded with the title of Nritya Samrat, literally translated as the Emperor of Dance. He also contributed to Indian films. Pandit Gopal is credited for bringing Kathak to Pakistan. His son Kishan Kumar also trained under the legendary master of the Lucknow Gharana, Pandit Shambhu Maharaj. Kishan Kumar ji worked in Delhi, and his son Ashok Kumar was also a Kathak dancer. One of Pandit Gopal's main disciples was Bhure Khan, also known as Ashiq Hussain. Ashiq Hussain and Hazari Lal ji devoted their lives to Kathak and produced some great disciples who, today, are carrying the responsibility of keeping this gharana alive.

Today, the Banaras Gharana is not only carried by the family members of this gharana. The gurus of this gharana worked very hard to spread the art of Kathak and produced many great disciples who became celebrated artists in their own right. The Banaras Gharana did not become as famous as the Jaipur and Lucknow gharanas, but it has created an important place for itself among the gharanas of Kathak. It also has produced some of the greatest Kathak dancers of India.

The main characteristics of Banaras Gharana The Jaipur and Lucknow gharanas of Kathak have assimilated the *bol*s or syllables of tabla and pakhawaj in their dance repertoire. Janaki Prasad ji was a purist, and he pursued using only the *natwari bol*s or dance syllables in his Kathak compositions. There are twelve distinguished *bol*s in the Natwari Nritya collection, and Banaras Gharana compositions employ these *natwari bol*s in their Kathak creations. The Banaras Gharana dance is also very graceful, and the compositions are performed in slow or moderate tempo to keep the movements precise and elegant. *Ati drut laya* is usually avoided in this style. *Chakkar*s are performed both clockwise and counterclockwise with clarity and accuracy. Pandit Gopi Krishna, one of the greatest dancers of this gharana, performed *chakkar*s on his knees. Still, *chakkar*s are not performed excessively in this style.

In *tatkar*, heels are used in a variety of different ways to mimic the *bol*s of Natwari Nritya. The *tatkar* on the heel is performed in a very artistic way with maximum control of the body. The *bol*s *tig dha dig dig* are performed with four stomps in other gharanas, but in Banaras Gharana, they are performed with six stomps. The *bol*s progress gradually, both in speed and multiplicity. Some of the body postures also differ from other gharanas, and special attention is given to the 'back to the audience' movements and body lines. Also, floor movements are utilized during the execution of *thaat*s. The Banaras Gharana was inspired by the traits of the two cities where it developed. It integrates the quality of valour of Bikaner, Rajasthan, and the characteristic spirituality and purity of Banaras. Janaki Prasad ji was also very well versed in Sanskrit. Perhaps, this is the reason that this gharana has maintained the spirituality and devotion of Hindu culture. *Bhajan*s, *pad*s, *vandana*s, and *thumri*s are presented exquisitely by the dancers of this gharana. The Banaras Gharana delves so beautifully into the poetic and devotional aspects of Kathak that the impressions of the Vaishnav tradition of bhakti is very apparent in the repertoire. Although the primary artists of this gharana migrated to Banaras from Rajasthan, this gharana developed its own personality and appears to be very different from the Jaipur Gharana in body movements, vocabulary, and execution of movements.

Some of the important past and present performers of Banaras Gharana are: Janaki Prasad ji, Dulha Ram ji, Ganeshilal ji, Chunni Lal ji, Bihari Lal ji, Hira Lal ji, Puran Lal ji, Hanuman Prasad ji, Shiv Lal and Gopal ji, Nawal Kishore, Bansidhar ji, Omkar Prasad ji, Sukhdev ji, Durga Prasad ji, Kundan Lal ji, Krishna Kumar, Pandit Sandeep Kumar Songra, Sitara Devi, and Gopi Krishna.

RAIGARH GHARANA

The Raigarh Gharana of Kathak did not enjoy the recognition that other gharanas did; nevertheless, it occupies an important place among the gharanas of Kathak. Raigarh Gharana originated in the princely state of Raigarh in the early twentieth century. The early history of Raigarh is not established because of the lack of documented evidence. Some historical sources suggest that Maharaja Madan Singh, who originally belonged to the Bairagarh village of Chanda district, established the first kingdom of Raigarh. After Maharaja Madan Singh, many other kings ruled Raigarh. One of these rulers, Maharaja Bhupdev Singh, was very fond of music, dance, and literature, and became a great patron of arts. Other rulers after Raja Bhupdev Singh also supported arts; however, it was during the reign of Maharaja Chakradhar Singh (1905–1947) that the arts flourished to the highest degree in Raigarh.

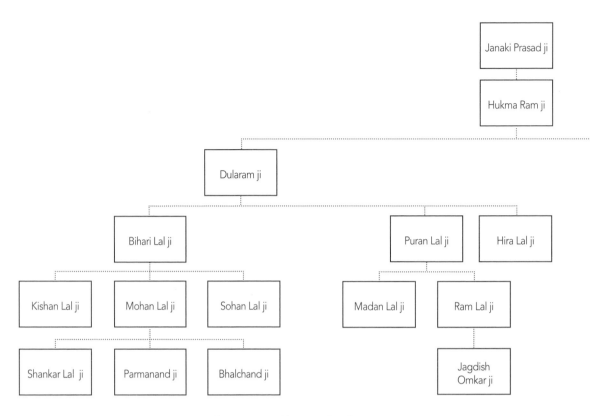

The Banaras Gharana family tree

Maharaja Chakradhar Singh himself was a musician and an author. He employed and supported many celebrity musicians and dancers in his court. He had an excellent lingual command of Sanskrit, Hindi, Oriya, and Urdu. He authored many books on music, dance, and literature, such as *Alkapuri Tilasmi, Bairagadiya Rajkumar, Jashe Pharhad, Kavya Kanan, Mayachakra, Muraj Paran Pushpakar, Mrignayani, Nartan Sarvaswam, Nigare Pharhad, Prem ke Teer, Raag Ratna Manjusha, Ramyaras, Ratnahar, Taal Tayonidhi,* and *Taalbal Pushpakar.* Some of these books concern *tala, bol*s, and classical dance. Maharaja Chakradhar was also known for organizing music and dance conferences to which he invited eminent artists of India.

Great Kathak dancers belonging to both Jaipur and Lucknow gharanas, such as Pandit Jagannath Prasad, Pandit Kalka Prasad, Pandit Acchan Maharaj, Pandit Shambhu Maharaj, and Pandit Jai Lal, received patronage in the court of Maharaja Chakradhar Singh. Even the dancers of Banaras Gharana graced

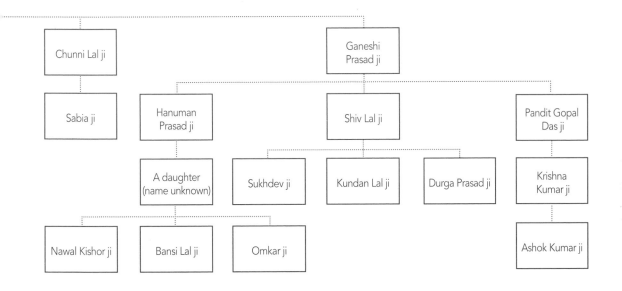

his court. Since Maharaja Chakradhar Singh himself was a tabla and pakhawaj player, he took great interest in Kathak and even accompanied some famous dancers of India. According to some scholars, he was not only a musician but also a dancer. He assimilated the characteristics of both Jaipur and Lucknow gharanas of Kathak and created a new gharana which was acknowledged as the Raigarh Gharana of Kathak. Maharaja Chakradhar Singh is credited for arranging the first All India Music Conference in Allahabad, Uttar Pradesh, in 1938. He presented sixty artists, who formed his team, at this conference.

Many times, Maharaja Chakradhar Singh accompanied Pandit Kartik Ram, an exponent of Raigarh Gharana of Kathak, on tabla. One of the most memorable programmes was the conference held to welcome Lord Linlithgow, the viceroy of India, in 1939, when Maharaja Chakradhar Singh mesmerized the audience with his tabla accompaniment with Kartik Kalyan ji. He was awarded the honour of Sangeet Samrat or the Emperor of Music by the viceroy. His contribution to the world of Kathak is immense, and the credit for the formation of Raigarh Gharana goes to him.

After Maharaja Chakradhar Singh's death in 1947, his son Raja Lalit Kumar Singh became the king of Raigarh, and he ruled this princely state until it was incorporated into the Union of India in December 1947. Maharaja Chakradhar Singh's contributions to music, dance, and literature were honoured by the music academy founded after him.

Pandit Kartik Ram and Kalyan, the two main court dancers who studied with Chunni Lal ji and Shivnarain ji, continued the tradition of Raigarh Gharana and trained many students, including Kartik Ram ji's son Ram Lal ji. Many of the students of Kartik Ram ji became celebrated dancers of India. The Raigarh Gharana struggled for a long time to be accepted as a proper gharana. Today, there is no doubt that this gharana has produced some exceptional dancers and has added to the repertoire of Kathak dance.

The main characteristics of Raigarh Gharana

The Raigarh Gharana is a beautiful combination of different gharanas. The movements of other gharanas were not merely combined in this one. Instead, it took inspiration from other gharanas and created a new and unique movement vocabulary. The dancers of this gharana start their performance in *ati vilambit laya* (very slow speed), which, because of its slowness, gives chance to dancers to execute movement vocabulary with much deliberation. At the same time, *ati vilambit* is a difficult *laya* to carry out, since the space between two beats is significant. One cycle of a *tala* takes a long time to complete. Special compositions were created in Raigarh Gharana to dance effectively in *ati vilambit laya*.

The Raigarh Gharana dancers also utilize the *joda bols*, the *bols* that, like a pair, are set in corresponding arrangement. Sometimes, there are *joda* or paired *tihai*s, *tukda*s, and *paran*s that complement each other. *Laykari* is an important part of Raigarh Gharana. Maharaja Chakradhar Singh was an exponent of tabla and pakhawaj, and he created the *tala chakra* which is still utilized by the dancers of Raigarh Gharana. Alpana Shukla Vajpeyi, who teaches at Chakradhar Nritya Kendra, discusses the *tala chakra* created by Maharaja Chakradhar Singh in one of her interviews:

[Singh] also created the *Tala Chakra*, a circular diagrammatic form of the *Tala avartan*. Another distinctive feature of his art was that he made rhythmic patterns and gave them thematic names, such as *Megh Pushp*, *Chamak Bijli*,

Brahma Beej, Dal Badal Paran....These are all *bandishes* (compositions) of tabla, pakhawaj and dance. (The *bols* themselves don't have a meaning but he selected those with the appropriate sound to bring out the theme.)[9]

The thematic use of rhythm sets the Raigarh Gharana apart. This can be observed in their variety of *chaals* in *gat* in respect of the theme of *gat* that is being depicted. In addition to a thematic approach to rhythm, a new body movement vocabulary, *abhinaya*, is also treated in a very sophisticated way in Raigarh Gharana. *Thumris* are performed with grace and poise.

Some of the important past and present performers of the Raigarh Gharana are: Pandit Kartikram, Pandit Kalyan Das Mahant, Pandit Phirtu Maharaj, Pandit Barmanlal, Pandit Ramlal, Ram Murti Vaishnav, Dr Bhagwan Das Manik Mahant, Vasanti Vaishnav, Sunnel Vaishnav, Dr Jyoti Bakshi, Dr Neeta Geharwal, Saridhdha Chaudhari, V. Anuradha Singh, Alpana Vajpeyi, Suchitra Harmalakar, Chetana Jyotishi, Dr Vijya Sharma, and Dr Srishti Gupta.

SIGNIFICANCE OF GHARANAS IN PRESENT DAY

Gharanas are lineages that remain true to a particular dance style. They are the bond between the gurus and disciples either through relationship or an apprenticeship. Gharanas adhere to their own principles and philosophies regarding dance, which affects a dancer's beliefs about dance as well as their performance and teaching styles. Each gharana specializes in certain aspects of Kathak. The technique, rhythmic aspects, and the subject matter for *abhinaya* are relatively the same in every gharana; however, the way of presenting them as well as their comparative importance in repertoire differ in each gharana.

Since gharanas are recognized through certain specializations in dance, the question arises whether it is important to specialize in one gharana. Some dancers believe in specializing in one gharana in order to teach and perform in depth with full concentration on certain aspects of Kathak that a particular gharana propagates. Others believe that interactions with other gharanas brings diversity to their teaching and performance.

....

[9] Anjana Rajan, 'Rise of Raigarh', *The Hindu*, http://www.thehindu.com/features/friday-review/dance/rise-of-raigarh/article3657624.ece (accessed 17 April 2018).

Group Choreography: Rajendra Gangani, Bhaswati Mishra,
and Arjun Mishra (standing from left to right); Prerna Shrimali, Veronique Azan,
and Abha Bhatnagar Roy (sitting from left to right)

The collaborative approach in gharanas has stemmed from today's globalization process, wherein learning Kathak is no longer limited to oral teaching. Modern technology such as recording devices and remote/online teaching has made music and dance accessible to everyone. At the same time, it can hamper deep understanding that results from the personal, face-to-face environment of traditional instruction. Many students move from one guru or gharana to another without going through the material in depth. In today's world, very few dancers are dedicated to one gharana and have expertise in it. For others, the boundaries of gharanas are disappearing. It is understandable that in today's world, gharanas have started to merge because of technological advances and demands of the modern lifestyle. Nonetheless, looking at the Kathak performances today, it seems even more necessary that students study in depth the art of Kathak with competent gurus. Delving into another gharana will make sense only when the essentials of one gharana have been mastered.

Application of Music
in Kathak

HINDUSTANI SANGEET OR NORTH INDIAN classical music complements the art of Kathak, where dance and music together express the same artistic vision. Many genres of Hindustani sangeet, such as *thumri* and *tarana*, have contributed greatly to the expansion of Kathak repertoire. Similarly, dance has inspired the classical and semi-classical music of North India. Many musical compositions use the *bol*s of dance. The expressions and themes of dance have also been incorporated in music by Hindustani classical musicians. Dance is an art form that moves in both time and space. The choreographic aspects of dance relate to space, whereas the time aspect of dance is engaged with music. Music plays a vital role in Kathak, and uncompromising understanding of music is expected from the dancers. This is why the exponents of Kathak go through the rigorous training of both vocal and percussion music.

Many scholars have speculated that Kathak was earlier accompanied by the ancient instruments, such as the pakhawaj and *manjira*. Now all types of Indian instruments are used: *avanaddh vadya* (percussion), *tantu vadya* (strings), *sushir vadya* (winds), and *ghan vadya* (metal/wooden instruments). The pakhawaj and tabla are two types of *avanaddh vadya* associated with Kathak dance. They are membranophones in which the sounds are produced from the vibrations created by striking tightly stretched membranes.

The pakhawaj is a barrel-shaped drum that has two heads, one on each end of the barrel. The left end has the bass tone and the right end has the treble tone. The main body is made of wood. It belongs to the family of ancient *paksa vadya* or two-sided instruments. Many derivatives of *paksa vadya*, such as the mridangam, mardala, and pakhawaj are in use today. The pakhawaj has a deep, resonating, mellow sound, which is the most desirable for *dhrupad* style of singing. *Dhrupad* developed

Pakhawaj, a North Indian
classical drum

Tabla

at the same time during the Mughal period when Kathak was also evolving as a full-fledged dance form. The pakhawaj became the main instrument for Kathak's rich rhythmic repertoires. After the tabla was invented, it became the favourite instrument for Kathak dancers because of its expressive and mesmerizing sounds, which perfectly matched the mood of Kathak.

The tabla is used as a percussive instrument, primarily in Hindustani classical music, that produces different sounds by way of a vibrating stretched membrane. It consists of two small drums known as *dayan* and *bayan*. *Dayan* is the right-hand treble drum, and *bayan* is the left-hand bass drum. There is no clear evidence of when tabla was created. Carvings found in the Bhaja Caves (circa 200 BCE) in Maharashtra depict a woman playing an instrument resembling a tabla, which demonstrates that tabla did have some ancient predecessor. According to some scholars, tabla was created by the thirteenth-century court musician/poet Amir Khusrow. According to others, an eighteenth-century musician from Delhi Darbar known as Sidar Khan Dhari invented the tabla. In *The History of the Tabla*, Arjun Mandaiker writes:

> Most likely no single person was totally responsible for creating the tabla and diverse influences led to the development of its physical structure and musical repertoire. What is certain is that the tabla fuses Arabic, Turkish and Persian influences with indigenous Indian drums. In fact, the name tabla originates from 'tabl' the Arabic term for 'drum'. The dholak and pakhavaj seem to be early forms of the tabla.[1]

[1] Arjun Mandaiker, 'The History of the Tabla', 22 October 2013, http://www.desiblitz.com/content/history-tabla (accessed on 16 April 2018).

Ragmala painting of Sarang Ragini, 1605

Ragmala Painting series in realistic style
made by artist Navin R. Soni from Bhuj-India

Today, most Kathak dancers prefer the tabla as their main accompaniment. Many dancers use both pakhawaj and tabla for their performances and, in that case, compositions containing pakhawaj *bol*s are played by a pakhawaj player and tabla *bol*s are played by a tabla player. Sometimes, the selection of a *tala* used in a performance also determines the choice of the percussion instrument. Pakhawaj is more appropriate for heavy and sombre *tala*s. The versatile sounds of tabla are suitable for almost every *tala*.

The *nrtta ang* of Kathak requires a fixed melody or a *lehra* to keep the *avartan*s of a *tala*. For example, for *teental's* sixteen beats, the *lehra* will be a fixed melody of sixteen beats composed in a way that the *sum*, *tali*s, and *khali* of *teental* are strongly emphasized. That particular melody, which is woven in a raga, is repeated over and over for dancers to perform their *nrtta* aspects. *Lehra* measures and regulates the time in dance. The tempo of *lehra* is determined by a dancer, depending on the *laya* in which they execute their compositions. The melodies of *lehra* are set in Hindustani ragas.

A raga is a melodic structure upon which the entire Hindustani classical music rests. Loosely translated, a raga is a scale or a set of four or more musical notes. These notes appear in different order in the compositions of different ragas and have characteristic musical designs according to a mood of a raga. Each raga is unique and conveys a certain mood. The musicians improvise a raga in various ways, following the rules of its basic structure, in order to express a *rasa* or a sentiment.

Traditionally, each raga is linked with a time of a day or a season. It is alleged that when sung or played at its assigned time, the emotions of ragas are heightened and deeply touch the hearts of the musician as well as the audience. The word 'raga' derives from a Sanskrit root word *ranj*, meaning 'to colour'. Ragas colour the minds and hearts of the listeners with certain moods and emotions through musical notes. Ragas have been personified both in literature and Ragmala

Asavari Ragini, Ragmala, 1610 (A lady charms snakes in a rocky landscape)

Goda Raga, the 'son' of Megha Raga, Ragmala, 1710

Ragmala Painting of Dhanasri Ragini, Rajasthan

Malasri Ragini from a Ragmala series

Bhairavi Ragini (Two women worship Shiva in
a lotus-filled lake)

Ragmala Khambhavati Ragini,
Golconda, 1750

Nata Ragini, wife of Bhairava Raga,
Ragmala paintings, 1762

Vasant Ragini, Ragmala, Kota,
Rajasthan, 1770

paintings. Around the fourteenth century CE, the nature of ragas was expressed through verses for dhyana or meditation. Later, the Ragmala paintings were created to visually interpret the ragas as divine beings. These paintings depict ragas along with their female counterparts called raginis, their male offspring called *ragaputra*s, and their female offspring called *ragaputri*s. The ragas and raginis are represented by their colours and moods and the verses that describe their emotions, time, and season to be performed.

The use of *lehra* bound in a certain raga provides an emotional overtone to the performance of Kathak. Competent Kathak dancers carefully choose a raga for the *lehra* accompaniment, which appropriately supports the mood of the performance. Traditionally, *lehra* is played on a sarangi or sitar. Both instruments fall under the category of chordophones, where the sounds are produced from the vibrations of strings.

A sarangi is a *vitat* or a stringed instrument. It is a bowed, gut-strung instrument with a short neck. The origin of the sarangi is much debated. Many believe that the etymology of the word 'sarangi' has Sanskrit origins, and is made up to two Sanskrit words—*saar* and *ang*. The word *saar* means 'summation' and the word *ang* means 'form'. Therefore, sarangi is an instrument which is an abridgement of all musical forms. Others believe that the word sarangi has Persian origins and is made up of two words—*seh* and *rangi*. The word *seh* refers to number three, and *rangi* means 'colourful'. Therefore, sarangi is an instrument with three strings to represent colourful music. Some also believe that sarangi is a compound word made up of two words: *sou* or hundred, and *rangi* or colours, since a musician on the sarangi can generate hundreds of musical nuances and emotions. The sarangi has the flexibility to imitate human voice and all the tones that human vocal chords can produce. Carved from a single wedge of *tun* or red cedar wood, the fretless sarangi has three or four playing strings and thirty-five sympathetic strings. The sarangi is a very difficult instrument to play, since the strings are not pressed by the finger, but the resonating sounds are produced by sliding the fingernails alongside the strings.

Sarangi, 1865

Sitar is another very melodious and mesmerizing *tantu vadya*, or an instrument from the lute family, and is used for *lehra* in Kathak. It is a long-necked plucked instrument. Some believe that the sitar is a derivative of ancient Indian instrument called veena. Others believe that it is an offshoot of a Persian instrument known as *sehtar* or the instrument with three strings. The sitar developed and prospered around the sixteenth and seventeenth centuries in the Mughal courts of India. It has a beautiful musical amalgamation of both the Hindu and Muslim cultures. The sitar has a spherical body made from a gourd, on which a long hollow wooden neck is placed. The neck holds twenty curved metal frets, tuning pegs, and metal strings. A sitar has between eighteen and twenty strings—there are five to seven melody strings, one or two drone strings for rhythmic stresses, and about thirteen *tarab tar*s or sympathetic strings that run under the frets. The frets are tied to the neck and can be moved to adjust to the notes of a raga. The strings are plucked using the right hand with a *mizrab*, a wire finger plectrum. The left hand is used to create melody by light pressure and, sometimes, dragging the main string outwards with the middle and index finger. The gourd, which rests on the floor, serves as the main resonating chamber of the sitar. Some sitar players use an additional resonator gourd, which can be attached to the top part of the sitar's long neck. The sound of the sitar is enthralling and, perhaps, this is why the Indian instrumental field is dominated by sitar players. The sitar is also a favourite instrument of Kathak dancers and is used in Kathak both for the purpose of playing *lehra* and to enhance the sentiments of choreographic pieces.

Among the *sushir vadya*s or the wind instruments, harmonium holds a very important place in Kathak. The free reed instrument harmonium is also called a *peti* or a *baja*.

The harmonium was introduced in India by missionaries during the British rule in the nineteenth century. At that time, it was mostly a pedal-pumped instrument and was extremely popular in both the United States and Europe. It was modified to be used as an accompaniment for the Hindustani classical music. In present-day Kathak and North Indian music, handheld harmoniums are used. The pedal-pumped harmonium enabled a musician to play melody with one hand and harmony with another. Because Indian music is melody based, the hand-pumped harmonium better suited the needs

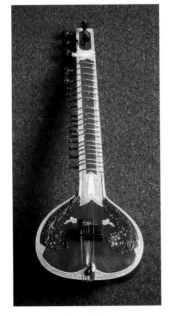

Miraj Sitar

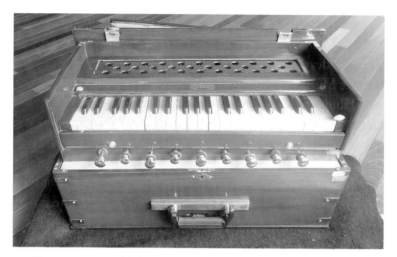
Three octave portable harmonium with triple reeds and nine air stops

of Indian musicians. Moreover, Indian music is performed while seated on the floor, and the handheld harmonium allowed the harmonium player to sit on the floor with his fellow musicians. A modern-day Indian harmonium is a small organ with a bellow, which is pumped for air in order for sound to materialize. It consists of a wooden box, keyboard, keys, reeds, reed board, stops, scale changer, coupler, and a bellow. Most harmoniums have thirty-nine keys producing notes in three octaves. The reeds are made of metal and they vibrate when air is bellowed into the instrument. The coupler is a double-key function, which means that when one key is pressed, the corresponding key in a different octave depresses automatically. Both the main stops and the drone stops control the flow of air in a harmonium. The harmonium is one of the most popular instruments in Hindustani classical music because of its tonal quality. Kathak dancers use the harmonium for *lehra* accompaniment as well as for choreographic compositions. The sustained sound of the harmonium suits the mood of Kathak dance.

One of the oldest instruments in the world, the bansuri is a type of flute which is a transverse or side-blown *sushir vadya* of India. This ancient flute is associated with Lord Krishna, who is known as a master flute player and a dancer. Since Kathak is inspired by the Raas Leelas of Krishna, Krishna's hypnotic, divine instrument, the bansuri, has found an important place in Kathak dance. The word bansuri means 'a bamboo that produces melodious sounds'. It is an aerophone made of a thin-walled, hollow, single piece of bamboo of varying length. The bansuri was more of a folk instrument until Pandit Pannalal Ghosh (1911–1960) modified it to make it suitable for Hindustani classical music. This great bansuri maestro experimented with many aspects of the instrument, such as the length, the number of holes, and its bore. A bore is the interior chamber of the bansuri through which the air flows. The bore affects the resonance of sound and the length of a bansuri affects its pitch. Because of Pandit Pannalal Ghosh's diligent efforts, bansuri found a respectable place in Hindustani classical music. In Kathak, the bansuri is rarely used as the only *lehra* accompaniment. However, it is used freely and widely in the musical compositions of Kathak.

The *ghana vadya*s such as gongs and bells are used mostly as ambient sounds in order to bring out the mood of the choreography or the story being told by a dancer. These are idiophones—the sounds are produced from the vibrating body of the instruments. The *ghungru* worn around a Kathak dancer's ankles is also a *ghana vadya*. Sometimes, the ancient instrument *manjira* or small hand-cymbals is also used to record time in Kathak.

Globalization has scattered Kathak dancers in different parts of the world. In some parts of the world, it is not always easy to find Indian musicians, and hiring many musicians to travel from afar can be costly. Therefore, the practice of performing to recorded music sometimes becomes necessary for a Kathak dancer. Also, the dance dramas based on Kathak dance require more than one instrument. Many different types of Indian instruments are used for recorded music to make the recordings more appealing and to bring out the emotions of the choreography. Sarod, santoor, *surbahar*, *dilruba*, *esraj*, *swarmandal*, Indian violin, Indian mandolin, tanpura, and *kashta-tarang* are but a few instruments that are used widely both for the recorded music and the choreographies based on narratives.

A 23-inch-long flute often used in concerts

Padhant or the recitation of *nrtta bol*s to accompany a dancer is an important part of the music of Kathak. Typically, the dancers themselves vocalize the *bol*s of a composition before performing it. Once the dancer starts to perform the composition, the *padhant*

Padhant by Pandit Rajendra Gangani

aspect is taken over by someone else who is well versed in the compositions to which the dancer is performing.

Vocal music is another indispensible aspect that makes a performance of Kathak complete. Many expressional compositions of Kathak, such as *vandana, thumri, stuti, ghazal,* and *bhajan* are inspired by the vocal repertoire of Hindustani classical music. A competent vocalist is absolutely crucial for a Kathak performance.

The dynamic art of *upaj* or improvisation in Kathak requires a dancer's thorough understanding of *laya, tala,* and *abhinaya.* It also calls for a remarkable mental and emotional connection between the musicians and the dancer. Therefore, the musicians are treated as co-performers rather than accompanists. The percussionists and vocalists do not simply follow a dancer; they engage in active interaction with him/her. Similarly, expert Kathak dancers also become part of the Kathak orchestra, since they recite the *bol*s and sing the verses of their *abhinaya* pieces. The boundary between dance and music recedes during a Kathak performance. This makes a Kathak performance with live music both dazzling and poignant.

Sadhana:
The Mindful Practice

SADHANA IN INDIAN DANCE and music means 'the practice to achieve perfection'. The word 'sadhana' derives from the Sanskrit root word *sadh*, which means 'to attain'. It is a conscious practice to access and adopt the deepest aspects of music and dance. The concept of sadhana is also applied in yoga and other spiritual practices, and goes beyond the ideas of training and practising. It is a path of ego transcendence, wherein the practitioner becomes one with the subject being practised. Students on the path of sadhana are *sadhak*s. Gurus who already have achieved their aspirations are called the siddhas, and the means that are important to reach to goal are *sadhan*s. That for which the sadhana is done is *sadhya*. The end outcome of sadhana is to achieve *sadhya* and to be able to do a *kriya* or action that can be carried out with precision.

The concept of sadhana in Indian music and dance has come from the ancient Indian spiritual practices. Sadhana is diligently carried out throughout the physical and mental practices. In yoga, the first recommendation for a worthy sadhana, after mastering the physical postures, is pratyahara. In pratyahara, a *sadhak* must control the *indriya*s, or senses, so that the sadhana is done with absolute concentration. Many Kathak dancers practise yoga and meditation in order to have better focus. It also facilitates the effortless internalization of the subject being practised. In the *dharana* stage of sadhana, the mind retains knowledge without any force. The word *dharana* means 'to hold'. The mind holds the insights and awareness gained from sadhana effortlessly. When the state of *dharana* matures and is established in the mind, it becomes dhyana or 'contemplation'. Dhyana is an essential aspect where a *sadhak* deliberates and reflects upon the learned subject matter. Finally, samadhi is meditation, where the dancer acquires the meditative state. Pratyahara, *dharana*, dhyana, and samadhi happen on a mental level, after the *sadhak* has acquired adeptness at the physical level.

The serious Kathak dancers and the gurus of Kathak greatly honour their sadhana. In Kathak, dance movements are first learned and practised at the physical level, when students learn the techniques of Kathak. Afterwards, they practise mental sadhana to go beyond the physical techniques. This is where the dance becomes artistry rather than just a skill or talent. Sadhana is very important for all performing art forms that employ the art of improvisation. Improvisation is intuitive and involves journeying into the soul, which, according to Indian artists, is possible only with internal practices of pratyahara, *dharana*, dhyana, and samadhi. Improvisation is an important part of Kathak. Students of Kathak must engage a commitment into internal sadhana in order to find the flow in which they can hear their heart's voice.

The ultimate goal of Indian dance is *rasabhivyakti*, which evokes emotions through facial expressions, body movements, and hand gestures. This is where dance breaks itself free from mere athleticism. In order to evoke a *rasa*, a dancer needs to internalize the learned movements through sadhana and become one with their dance, which in turn allows them to emote a theme or a mood. This is when the emotions presented by a dancer become so alive that the audience can relish them.

In Kathak, the old masters used to practice their footwork on sand at the bank of a river. Dancing on sand took a lot of energy and strengthened the muscles of the legs. Sometimes, they would dip their feet in ice-cold water while practising. This not only endowed them with strong footwork, but also allowed them to engage in their sadhana with concentration and discipline. It has been accounted that Pandit Bindadin Maharaj practised just one *bol* of dance for many years for ten hours a day. Many great Kathak dancers have been observed using their hands and feet to keep *laya* even during deep sleep. All other aspects of Kathak, such as body movements, *abhinaya*, *laya*, *tala*, and *padhant* are mastered only through concentrated sadhana.

Aasana and *samay* for sadhana are also considered very important. *Aasana* is having the same place for practice, and *samay* is setting aside the same time every day when the sadhana is performed. *Aasana*, or the place of the practice, is considered sacred and is always kept immaculately clean. *Samay* or the scheduled pattern of practising every day at the same time not only aids in regulation and discipline, but also encourages in maintaining the momentum of sadhana. Learned material is just a tiny seed that grows when the luminous sunshine of physical sadhana encourages its growth. It expands and enlarges into a shady, fruit-bearing tree when the mental sadhana is integrated into this growth process. A very important condition for true sadhana is humility, which is achieved by transcending one's ego, where the *sadhak* is not important; only the sadhana and the *sadhya* are important.

Sadhana is also called *abhyasa*, which is a repeated practice with concentration and reflection. The great saint-poet Kabir Das wrote that by continuous practice, even an unintelligent being can become insightful—*karat karat abhyas te, jadmati haut sujaan, rasri aawat jaat te, sil par parat nisaan* (*abhyasa* can be compared to a soft rope, which leaves a mark even on a stone if rubbed on it every day).

With the Mughal influence on North Indian music and dance, the term *riyaaz* for practising became prevalent among the musicians and dancers. The word *riyaaz* is derived from an Arabic word *riyazat*—a process of achievement, which is nothing else than digging constantly in the sacred land of the heart where the precious water of knowledge is hidden. Surely, only after much digging, sweet water is found at that depth. However, this metaphorical digging is to be done with care and attention. One of the greatest Sufi classical musicians of India, Hazrat Inayat Khan, elaborates on this subject:

> Digging is not enough. Love and devotion, no doubt, help to bring out frequent merits hidden in the soul, as the qualities of sincerity, thankfulness, and gentleness, all things which produce a harmonious atmosphere, and all things which bring men in tune with life. But it is possible that in this process of digging one may only reach mud and lose patience. So dismay, discontentment may follow and man may withdraw himself from further pursuit. It is the patient pursuit which will bring the water from the depth of the ground.[1]

The first stage is setting an intention, which is the beginning of a dancer's artistic journey. The second stage is preparation, which is *riyaaz*. During *riyaaz* or

----

[1] 'Volume VIII—The Art of Being, The Privilege of Being Human, Chapter VII, Truth', The Spiritual Message of Hazrat Inayat Khan, http://wahiduddin.net/mv2/VIII/VIII_2_7. htm (accessed on 16 April 2018).

practice, one needs to be attentive and should practice with single-mindedness, without distraction. Inner composure is another important factor in *riyaaz*, where the practice should be only for the sake of practice and without attachment to the idea of materialistic gain from it. This process of *riyaaz* is an end in itself. Finally, *riyaaz* should be done with humility and patience.

Chillah is a kind of *riyaaz*, the completion of which is a dream for every professional musician and dancer. *Chillah* is a forty-day intense *riyaaz*, during which the *sadhak* stays in an isolated place called *chilla-khana* and any contact from the outside world is prohibited. With minimum time for sleep and restricted diet, *chillah* is performed in demanding circumstances. During these forty days, the *riyaaz* becomes the *sadhak's* greatest friend and changes the inner state of a soul. The concept of forty days has been given importance in many different cultures. The inspiration of forty days of intense *riyaaz* comes from the state of an embryo in a womb. It is believed that the fertilized embryo stays in that state for forty days and, thereafter, each development and transformation of a human in the womb takes another forty days.

If followed, the philosophy of sadhana, *abhyasa*, and *riyaaz* produces great results in Kathak. Kathak is a complete art form in itself, which comprises many facets such as body movements, intricate footwork, *abhinaya*, complex *laya* and *tala*, and *padhant*. Creating compositions spontaneously requires great knowledge of all aspects of Kathak, which can be mastered only through sadhana. A Kathak dancer also needs to cultivate *bahumukhi pratibha* or multifaceted talent. The great masters of Kathak train in vocal music, instrumental music, poetry, painting, and the dramatic arts. Sadhana of other art forms helps a Kathak dancer to become a complete artist. One also needs to realize that learning and sadhana never stop. They are lifelong pursuits.

Prastuti:
Performance of Kathak

BHARATA IN HIS *NATYASHASTRA* suggested an elaborate invocation to divine powers in order to purify the stage, environment, and the minds and hearts of performers and spectators. He called this detailed ritual *purvarang*, or an overture before a performance, which he instructed to be undertaken before any stage performance. Bharata Muni has prescribed many building blocks of a *purvarang*, some of which are performed behind a curtain and others on the stage in front of the audience. Traditionally, the *purvarang* started with various activities behind the curtain. During the pratyahara, all musical instruments were carried to the stage and were situated at their predetermined places. *Avatarana* followed, when the singers placed themselves on the stage to commence *arambha* or the rehearsal of the chorus. During *asravana*, *vaktrapani*, and *parighattana*, wind and string instruments were tuned. During *margasarita*, all instruments rehearsed together, followed by *asarita*, when the percussion instruments were introduced. All of these activities were performed to receive benediction from different deities. The curtain opened with the presentation of *gitavidhi* to pay tribute to the gods. During *utthapana*, the percussionists played their instruments for the *sutradhara*, the commentator and director of the play. The *sutradhara* recited the *nandi* stanzas for invocation and placed the banner of Lord Indra on the stage for protection. The *purvarang*, performed prior to a theatrical production, was a very elaborate ritual. This ritual prepared the performers psychologically, mentally, and emotionally to get immersed in their intended presentation.

Today, in Kathak performances, the *purvarang* is not observed in exactly the same way Bharata instructed it to be implemented. Yet, the essence of *purvarang* can be detected in the preliminary proceedings of a traditional Kathak performance. There are a few important rituals that are practised by Kathak dancers behind the curtains before the actual presentation starts. These rituals commence as soon as the dancer and the musicians enter the auditorium. Any footwear is left outside the stage and dancers bow to the stage in reverence. After spacing and marking the stage mentally, the next step is dressing for the performance. Application of make-up, styling the hair, and putting on costumes have a direct impact on the cognitive process. Kathak dancers treat the entire process of dressing up with reverence as to transform ordinary thoughts into artistic energy, which is later transmitted to the audience during their performance. This is also the time for the dancers to immerse themselves in the thought process directly related to their performance, since a traditional Kathak performance pushes the mental, emotional, and physical capabilities of a dancer to their limits. The great maestros of Kathak do not choreograph their solo Kathak performances. Most of their performances are drawn from compositions they have memorized. They also improvise on stage. The time spent in the green room is well-utilized by these maestros, where they consciously indulge in the process of memory organization and make important artistic decisions regarding their performance. Tying the *ghungru*s around the ankles is another ritual in which the dancers silently venerate their *ghungru*s and, at the same time, ask the universe for blessings. *Bhumi namaskar* is carried out when the curtain is closed. *Bhumi namaskar* is an act of honouring the deities, surroundings, the stage, fellow musicians, the guru, and the audience. It is done with a short sequence of dance movements that flow into one another. In fact, *bhumi namaskar* is performed before every Kathak practice session. Finally, the dancer completes *milna* or the meeting with the musicians. A general outline of a performance is discussed at that time, and an appropriate *lehra* for the *nrtta* aspect of the dance is chosen.

Rituals are also performed in front of the audience. The instruments are meticulously tuned in front of audience, which sets the mood for the performance. An astute audience can decipher the raga in which the first choreography of the evening will be presented just by listening to the tuning. After the tuning, the tabla player plays a composition, while the dancer takes a position in the wings backstage. This introductory percussive composition features complicated *bol*s of tabla in intricate *laya*s with an extensive *tihai*. Often, this introductory tabla playing is two to five minutes long. If both a tabla player and a pakhawaj player are present on stage, they both play compositions from the repertoire of their instruments, either separately or together. This ritual bears a resemblance to Bharata's *utthapana* part of *purvarang*. Bharata Muni suggested the ritual of *utthapana* to magnetize the attention of the audience with the power of percussion music. In Kathak presentations, the short performance by a percussionist not only catches the attention of the audience, but it also introduces the percussionist who is considered a co-performer rather than just an accompanist.

Bharata has given a lot of emphasis on the performance of the invocation to gods and deities at the beginning of a performance, which is still followed in a traditional Kathak presentation. Kathak dancers perform a *vandana, stuti*, or a *shloka* as an invocation piece after coming on stage and bowing to the audience, followed by the execution of *nrtta* part of Kathak. In the *nrtta* aspect, dancers present *that, aamad, paran-aamad, natwari tukda*s, *todas, paran, primalu, chakkardar paran, gat, tatkar, palta*s, and all other technical aspects of Kathak in different *laya*s. A Kathak performance starts with *vilambit laya* and ends in *drut laya*. The compositions are chosen according to the gharana of Kathak being represented. Dancers from the Lucknow Gharana sometimes perform *salami* or namaskar in *vilambit laya* at the commencement of a *nrtta* presentation. Dancers from Jaipur Gharana start their *nrtta* presentation with a *chala*, in which they execute *laykari* through footwork in *vilambit laya* to set the mood for the entire performance. Also, the *prakar*s (varieties) of compositions are performed in *vilambit laya*. Different varieties of footwork and complex compositions such as *tripalli, chaupalli, panchpalli*, and *lambchad paran* are executed. The presentation of the *nrtta* is interactive; the dancer relates with the audience through *padhant* or recitation of *bol*s. Sometimes, the dancers also strike up meaningful conversations with the musicians and the audience. This feature of a Kathak presentation was more animated when Kathak was performed for a small gathering in grand parlour settings. The *nrtta* portion of a Kathak presentation is electrifying and displays the virtuosity of a dancer. It is also very demanding physically, mentally, and emotionally, especially if the programme is not preset. A dancer is required to have exceptional command on *laya, padhant*, and body movements to execute a stimulating *nrtta* aspect of Kathak. *Farmaishi* compositions are presented for the knowledgeable audience. Spellbinding footwork and dazzling pirouettes are used to make the performance exciting.

Another exhilarating component of Kathak is *sawal jawab* or *jugalbandi*, which is performed at the end of the *nrtta* performance and during which a stimulating dialogue takes place between the dancer and the percussionist. During this exchange, the initial longer phrase of the dialogue gets shorter and shorter as the *sawal jawab* progresses until, at one point, both artists meet and perform together at a very high speed. The *sawal jawab* ends with a *tihai*. The *sawal jawab* is different from the Western call and response, in which one musician presents a phrase and the other responds to it with another phrase that seems like a direct commentary on the first presented phrase. Unlike call and response, in *sawal jawab*, the same phrase is performed by both the dancer and the percussionist. Usually the percussionist offers a phrase, which the dancer presents in the exact manner with footwork. The level of difficulty increases as the phrases start to become shorter and shorter. Sometimes, the call and response technique also happens between the Kathak dancer and the percussionist during the *that* and *aamad* section in *vilambit laya*, where a rhythmic theme is improvised by the two in call and response manner. The *sawal jawab* has its own charm, and it creates an invigorating experience for the audience.

A dancer needs to have tremendous strength and stamina, since the *nrtta* presentation of Kathak is extremely arduous at the physical level and tends to be long in duration. Also, concentrating on *laya* while performing complicated compositions takes up a lot of mental energy. As Mihaly Csikszentmihalyi states, a dancer needs to be in 'the flow' or 'the zone'. In positive psychology, the flow is the mental state where a person is single-mindedly engaged in an activity and experiences a positive and energized alignment with what one is doing. Being in the flow, a person experiences rapturous joy: 'Flow is being completely involved in an activity for its own sake. The ego falls away. Time flies, every action, movement, and thought follows inevitably from the previous one, like playing jazz. Your whole being is involved, and you are using your skills to the utmost.'[1]

Great masters of Kathak dance have been known for being in the flow or the zone, where they either single-mindedly access the information from their memory or improvise at the spur of the moment and execute it with complete involvement. During this process of being in the flow, the great masters also achieve what Bharata called the *sadharanikaran* or the universalization of emotions, when attainment of oneness with the audience is achieved. The zone and *sadharanikaran* are also attained during the *nritya* and *natya* aspects of a performance.

[1] Mihaly Csikszentmihalyi, Brain Channels, Thinker of the Year Award 2000, 'Flow Theory', http://www.brainchannels.com/thinker/mihaly.html (accessed on 16 April 2018).

In *nritya* and *natya*, an enhanced emotional experience is given more prominence, where the *gat-bhaav, thumri, bhajan*, and *ghazal* are performed in accordance with the *rasa* theory. Usually, dancers perform *gat-bhaav* to end their *nrtta* performance. *Nritya ang* is a blend of *nrtta* and *natya. Kavitta*s and *gat-bhaav*s are used to tell a story or emphasize a particular character. The *bol batana* of *thumri* also incorporates both *nritya* and *natya* aspects. According to Bharata, *natya* and *nritya* are performed to evoke a *rasa*, which is formed through *bhava*s. In *thumri*s, the *mukhabhinaya* or facial expressions are so important that many times a dancer just sits in a position and projects a *bhava* through hand gestures and facial expressions. The *upaj* or improvisation is a unique characteristic of a Kathak performance, presented through expressions, movement vocabulary, and rhythmic variations. The notion of improvisation was first mentioned by Sharangdeva in the thirteenth century. It is not clear whether Indian music was improvised prior to that time:

> In Indian pre-modern theoretical sources, there is no explicit theorizing of the concept of improvisation. But there are indications in treatises such as the 13th century Sangeet Ratnakar, by Sharangdeva, that certain aspects of performance were the responsibility of the performer rather than of the composer; though of course the performer and composer were ideally the same person.[2]

Great Kathak maestros find immense gratification in taking on the responsibility of improvising certain aspects of their performance. *Upaj* mostly takes the form of structured improvisation in Kathak as opposed to free improvisation. Free improvisation has no stated rules, whereas, in Kathak, structure is given in terms of rules and types of compositions. During *upaj*, dancers make a decision on stage regarding which composition they are going to present, and sometimes perform them with spontaneous movement vocabulary.

When it comes to rhythmic permutations, *upaj* unfolds extemporaneously against the backdrop of a chosen *tala*. In footwork section, dancers create rhythms that are unpremeditated and delve into different rhythmic permutations and variations, which requires tremendous knowledge and practice of *laykari*. The *abhinaya* segment of Kathak gives great improvisational scope and freedom to an

---

[2] Laudan Nooshin and Richard Widdess, 'Improvisation in Iranian and Indian Music', https://eprints.soas.ac.uk/5430/1/NooshinWiddess1.pdf (accessed on 16 April 2018).

artist. Many maestros of Kathak sing the *thumri* while dancing on the lyrics and the intended meaning of it, and use the improvisation techniques of both the *bol banao* and *bol batana*. *Bol banao* is the improvisation of text syllables of a *thumri* by singing it with different melodic motifs. *Bol batana* is the improvisation of different *bhavas* of a *thumri* through *abhinaya*. The great dancers, through improvisation, also elaborate on the meaning of a *thumri*, and sometimes even go out of the context to reveal different meanings of the lyrics through *abhinaya*. All other compositions that fall into the category of *nritya ang* of Kathak, such as *gat-bhaav*, *bhajan*, and *ghazal*, among others, give tremendous opportunity and inspiration to a dancer to improvise spontaneously.

Many scholars, musicians, and dancers prefer the term 'elaboration' instead of improvisation, since the *tala*s, *abhinaya*, compositions, and movement vocabulary of dance is already taught to dancers, and they just elaborate on what is already learned. Still, to generate their own compositions spontaneously, or to add their own personality to existing compositions by embellishing the mood, rhythms, and movements, dancers have to go beyond what they have already learned:

> Intensive practice is required, extending over years, before this material is mastered and the student can begin to go beyond it....Traditional teaching methods might therefore be thought to promote imitation and memorization rather than improvisation. Yet alongside formal training, students regularly hear their teachers perform, and thus learn how far an accomplished artist can spontaneously transform memorized material in performance.[3]

The entire North Indian music and dance system is based on a pedagogy that allows the students to excel in such a way that the art of improvisation is achievable. In the first phase of this method, students blindly imitate their gurus by watching every move and listening to every word. In the second phase, the memorization of taught material is accomplished. In the third phase, students assimilate the taught material. In the fourth phase, the detailed analysis and assessment of the taught material is carried out. Finally, in the fifth phase, the creative personality of a student emerges through creative improvisation processes.

Traditionally, the Kathak dancers did not perform a choreographed

[3] Ibid.

programme. Inspired by their audience and the atmosphere as well as their frame of mind during a performance, the dancers improvised on the stage. In today's world, the organization of Kathak performances has changed considerably because of the requirements of a proscenium stage and the needs of the audience. Also, today, many practitioners of Kathak dance do not train the way students once did under the *guru-shishya parampara*. As a result, the art of improvisation is getting lost in Kathak performances. Many dancers today maintain the 'fourth wall' on the stage and perform their choreographed pieces. The *upaj* happens when the masters of Kathak demolish the fourth wall and inspire their audiences with their personal creative and artistic touches.

Another important aspect of Kathak performance is that the dancers make the full decision regarding the length of their dance pieces. Kathak is traditionally a solo art form, giving dancers complete freedom to choose their dance repertoire to be performed. Today, duets and group performances have come into play, which necessitate the need for choreography. In choreographed pieces, dancers cannot deviate from a set routine, which results in a performance with no room for improvisation. However, written notation for the choreographic pieces has still not become part of Kathak, so even the group choreography is stored in the memory of each of the dancers.

Kathak ballet, as it was identified in the past, is another remarkably appealing facet of Kathak performance. Today, Kathak ballets are called Kathak dance dramas. The word 'Kathak' is derived from the Sanskrit *katha*, meaning 'the art of storytelling', and the practitioners of Kathak were the *kathakar*s who narrated mythological and religious stories through dance, drama, and music. It is no surprise that even modern Kathak dancers became fascinated by dance dramas, since they provide great scope for storytelling. In dance dramas in Kathak style, theatrical traditions are blended with the movements, music, and different repertoires of Kathak. Dance dramas in Kathak allow group productions in which many Kathak dancers can participate in the same performance. The theatrical presentations of Raas Leela and other folk theatres of North India as well as Wajid Ali Shaha's *raha*s presentations have definitely inspired today's Kathak dance dramas. Wajid Ali Shah mentioned thirty-six types of *raha*s in his book *Bani*. *Raha*s were brilliant productions, synthesizing theatre, lyrical compositions, expressive movements of Kathak, and stirring poetry in a single presentation. Wajid Ali Shah's famous *raha Radha Kanhaiya ka Kissa* featured many characters and was indeed a production that gave concrete definition to

Contemporary Kathak—Natya Stem Dance Kampani

Kathak dance dramas. All theatrical productions of Wajid Ali Shah, including the famous *Inder Sabha*, was presented in a dance-drama style. Lila Sokhey, popularly known as Madame Menaka, who rose to prominence in 1930s, is a celebrated figure in Kathak dance for introducing and developing the new world of Kathak ballets. She studied Kathak with Pandit Sitaram Misra, Maharaj Baidyanath Misra, and Guru Ram Dutt Mishra, the great masters of the Lucknow Gharana. She also went through training in Kathakali and Manipuri, the other classical dance forms of India. The presentations of her three Kathak ballets *Deva Vijaya Nritya*, *Krishna Leela*, and *Manaka Lasyam* that she choreographed after 1935 earned her international renown. Her Kathak ballets introduced the art of stage crafting, innovative music, orchestra, and costuming in Kathak.

> Menaka introduced expert choreography into Kathak and skillfully used its enchanting foot rhythm with intricate timing, its Abhinaya enriched by extensive use of mime, expressive of emotions and incidents, and its anghara and Karana, the beautiful body and arm movements to make it an exquisite medium of drama. She made duets, group dances and solos to tell the story of the theme continuously.[4]

....

[4] Kapila Vatsyayan, *Bharata: The Natyasastra* (New Delhi: Sahitya Akademi, 1996), p. 99.

Later, great gurus of Kathak—namely Pandit Shambhu Maharaj and Pandit Lachhu Maharaj—created many dance dramas in Kathak style. Some of their productions were based on revered Sanskrit plays and others were more contemporary. Pandit Shambhu Maharaj was the director of the Kathak department at the Shriram Bharatiya Kala Kendra in New Delhi, and he created many Kathak choreographies at the ballet wing there. After Pandit Shambhu Maharaj's death, Pandit Birju Maharaj took the responsibility of being the head of the Kathak department and enriched the world of Kathak with his choreography of magnificent Kathak dance dramas. Among many other noted dance-drama choreographers of that time, Smt. Maya Rao and Smt. Kumudini Lakhia contributed greatly to the Kathak dance dramas. Today, many choreographers are creating dance dramas on various subjects that include both traditional and contemporary themes, giving Kathak dance dramas a new dimension. Abundant, with multifaceted subject matters, innovative choreography, modern stagecraft and technology, rich music, and eye-catching costumes, dance dramas in Kathak have become a vibrant and intensely expressive aspect of Kathak dance and its performances.

Chamatkar Nritya pieces were extraordinary presentations of Kathak, which, with time, have slipped into obscurity. *Chamatkar* pieces of Kathak mesmerized the audience with astounding dancing, where the dancers performed in atypical conditions using unusual props. Dancing on different surfaces such as the rim of a metal plate or a glass, the sharp edge of a sword, on top of *batasha*s (hard candy sugar drops), on prickly needles, pieces of broken glasses, and on top of a wooden bar floating in a river—all these fall into the category of Chamatkar Nritya in Kathak. Some Kathak dancers also danced on red powder covered with a sheet, which was removed after their performance. It was spectacular to see the impression of a dancer's feet create beautiful imprints of the elements of nature in red powder, as, 'Pandit Sundar Prasad ji and Sri Khemchand Prakash [of the Jaipur Gharana] were the experts in making the imprints of an elephant [translation].'[5]

Kathak dancers also performed stunning pieces while balancing clay pots on their heads. It is reported that during the Mughal period, the court dancers danced while balancing a glass of wine on their heads. Today, hardly anyone

[5] Prem Dave, *Kathak Nritya Parampara* (Jaipur: Panchsheel Prakashan, 2004), p. 147.

Aditi Mangaldas with ensemble, show in Warsaw

performs Chamatkar Nritya, perhaps because very few dancers practised this art and then did not train enough dancers to carry on this tradition. According to some scholars, many dancers of Kathak viewed Chamatkar Nritya as a gimmick and did not want to resort to it. Even if *chamatkar* presentation of Kathak is not in practice today, it was nevertheless a part of Kathak performance repertoire at one time and may emerge again in the future.

There is a widespread notion about the traditional arts that tradition opposes experimentation (*parampara prayog ke virodh karti hai*). This has not been true for the art of Kathak. Kathak has integrated traditionalism and modernism in an extraordinary way. The modern and postmodern Kathak keeps the integrity of traditional Kathak and, at the same time, explores all new human conditions, behaviours, and emotions. The new choreographies reflect every traditional aspect of Kathak that give this art form a distinct identity. Kathak has changed only to the point where it saw a necessity to accommodate the new times and where the soul of Kathak could still revel in its truth and beauty. This is clearly evident in its performances and repertoire. The aspects of Kathak that are difficult to master and are slowly fading will come back with full force. It has happened in the past and it will happen again in the future. Those aspects of Kathak—dancing difficult compositions, the art of improvisation—are too beautiful to disappear. There always have been and always will be performers who will honour the tradition and cultivate the legacy of performing Kathak with purity and integrity.

Appendix

A FEW IMPORTANT *TALAS* (IN ALPHABETICAL ORDER)

Tala Addha Chautal
14 *matra*s, 7 *vibhag*s, 4 *tali*s, 3 *khali*s
Dhin Tirakit
X
Dhin na
2
Tun na
0
KaT Ta
3
Tirakit dhin
0
Na dhin
4
Dhin na
0

Tala Addha
16 *matra*s, 4 *vibhag*s, 3 *tali*s, 1 *khali*
Dha - dhin -
X
Dha dha Tin -
2
Ta - Tin -
0
Dha dha dhin -
3

Tala Chautal
12 *matra*s, 6 *vibhag*s, 4 *tali*s, 2 *khali*s
Dha dha
X
Din Ta
0
Tita dha
2

Din Ta
0
Tita kaTa
3
Gadi gina
4

Tala Dadra
6 *matra*s, 2 *vibhag*s, 1 *tali*, 1 *khali*
Dha dhin na
X
Dha Tu na
0

Tala Deepchandi
10 *matra*s, 4 *vibhag*s, 3 *tali*s, 1 *khali*
Dha dhin -
X
Dha dha dhin -
2

Ta Tin -
0
Dha dha dhin -

Tala Dhamar
14 *matra*s, 4 *vibhag*s, 3 *tali*s, 1 *khali*
Ka dhi ta dhi ta
X
Dha -
2
Ga di na
0
Di na Ta -
3

Tala Dhumali
8 *matra*s, 4 *vibhag*s, 3 *tali*s, 1 *khali*
Dha dhin
X
Dha Tin
2
Taka Dhin
0
Dhage Traka
3

Tala Ektal
12 *matra*s, 6 *vibhag*s, 4 *tali*s, 2 *khali*s
Dhin dhin
X
Dhage Tirakit
0
Tun na
2
KaT Ta
0
Dhage Tirakit
3
Dhin na
4

Tala Farodast
14 *matra*s, 7 *vibhag*s, 5 *tali*s, 2 *khali*s
Dhin dhin
X
Dhage Tirakit
0
Tun na
2
Kat Ta
0
Dhina kadha
3
Tirakit dhina
4
Kadha Tirakit
5

Tala Jat
8 *matra*s, 4 *vibhag*s, 3 *tali*s, 1 *khali*
Dhage dhin
X
Dhage Tin
2
Taake dhin
0
Dhage dhin
3

Tala Jhaptal
10 *matra*s, 4 *vibhag*s, 3 *tali*s, 1 *khali*
Dhin na
X
Dhin dhin na
2
Tin na
0
Dhin dhin na
3

Tala Keharwa
8 *matra*s, 2 *vibhag*s, 1 *tali*, 1 *khali*
Dha ge na Ti
X
Na ka dhi na
0

Tala Matta
18 *matra*s, 9 *vibhag*s, 6 *tali*s, 3 *khali*s
Dhin -
X
Na -
0
Dhin Tirakit
2
Dhin na
3
Tun na
0
Kat Ta
4
Tirakit dhin

5
Na dhin
6
Dhin na
0

Tala Pancham-Sawari
15 *matra*s, 4 *vibhag*s, 3 *tali*s, 1 *khali*
Dhin na dhindhin
X
Na dhindhin nadhin dhinna
2
Tikda Tinna Tirakit Tunna
0
KaTTa dhindhin nadhin dhinna
3

Tala Rupak
7 *matra*s, 3 *vibhag*s, 2 *tali*s, 1 *khali*
Tin Tin na
0
Dhin na
2
Dhin na
3

Tala Sooltal or Sulfakta
10 *matra*s, 5 *vibhag*s, 3 *tali*s, 2 *khali*s
Dha dha
X
Din Ta
0
Kit dha
2
Tete kaTa
3
Gadi gana
0

Tala Teental
16 *matra*s, 4 *vibhag*s, 3 *tali*s, 1 *khali*
Dha dhin dhin dha
X
Dha dhin dhin dha

2
Dha Tin Tin Ta
0
Ta Dhin dhin dha
3

Tala Tevra
7 *matra*s, 3 *vibhag*s, 3 *tali*s
Dha din Ta
X
Tita kaTa
2
Gadi gana
3

Tala Tilvada
16 *matra*s, 4 *vibhag*s, 3 *tali*s, 1 *khali*
Dhi Tirakita dhin dhin
X
Dha dha Tin Tin
2
Ta Tairakita dhin dhin
0
Dha dha dhin dhin
3

Tala Rudra
11 *matra*s, 8 *vibhag*s, 8 *tali*s
Dhin Tirakit
X
Dhin
2
Na
3
Tun na
4
KaT
5
Ta
6
Dhindhin
7
Nadhin dhinna
8

Table 1: *Tala Teental*

Matra	1	2	3	4	5	6	7	8	9	10	11	12	13	14	15	16
Theka	Dha	dhin	dhin	dha	Dha	dhin	dhin	dha	Dha	Tin	Tin	Ta	Ta	dhin	dhin	dha
Tala sign	X				2				0				3			

Table 2: *Tala Jhaptal*

Matra	1	2	3	4	5	6	7	8	9	10
Theka	Dhin	na	Dhin	dhin	na	Tin	na	Dhin	dhin	na
Tala sign	X		2			0		3		

Table 3: *Tala Deepchandi*

Matra	1	2	3	4	5	6	7	8	9	10	11	12	13	14
Theka	Dha	dhin	-	Dha	dha	dhin	-	Dha	Tin	-	Dha	dha	dhin	-
Tala sign	X			2				0			3			

Table 4: *Rupak Tala*

Matra	1	2	3	4	5	6	7
Theka	Tin	Tin	Na	Dhin	Na	Dhin	Na
Tala sign	0			2		3	

Table 5: *Tevra Tala*

Matra	1	2	3	4	5	6	7
Theka	Dha	din	Ta	Tita	KaTa	gadi	gina
Tala sign	X			2		3	

Table 6: An example of *theka* of *tala chautal*

Matra	1	2	3	4	5	6	7	8	9	10	11	12
Theka	Dha	dha	din	Ta	Tita	dha	din	Ta	Tita	kaTa	gadi	gina
Tala sign	X		0		2		0		3		4	

Table 7: An example of *theka* of *tala ektal*

Matra	1	2	3	4	5	6	7	8	9	10	11	12
Theka	Dhin	dhin	dhage	Tirakita	Tu	na	KaT	Ta	dhage	Tirakita	dhin	na
Tala sign	X		0		2		0		3		4	

Table 8: An example of the *theka* of *keharwa tala*

Matra	1	2	3	4	5	6	7	8
Original *Theka*	Dha	ge	na	Ti	na	ka	dhi	na
Tala sign	X				0			

Table 9: An example of *theka prakars* of *keharwa tala* through ornamentation of original *bols*

	1	2	3	4	5	6	7	8
Keharwa Prakar 1	Dha	-	Tin	-	Ta	-	dhin	-
Keharwa Prakar 2	Dhin -	dha dhin	- dhi	Naka	Tin -	Ta Tin	-Ti	na ka
Keharwa Prakar 3	Dha Trak	dhin dhin	dha dha	dhin dhin	Ta Trak	Tin Tin	dha dha	dhin dhin
Keharwa Prakar 4	Dha	dhin	dhaga	dhin	Ta	Tin	na na	Tete
Tala sign	X				0			

Table 10: An example of *gunas* in *tala teental*

	1	2	3	4
Pawguna (1:4)	1			
Adh-guna (2:4)	1 -	- -	2 -	- -
Paun-guna (3:4)	1 - -	- 2 -	- - 3	- - -
Ekguna (1:1)	1	2	3	4
Sawaguna (5:4)	1 - - - 2	- - - 3 -	- - 4 - -	- 5 - - -
Dedh-guna (6:4)	1 - - - 2 -	- - 3 - - -	4 - - - 5 -	- - 6 - - -
Paune-do-guna (7:4)	1 - - - 2 - -	- 3 - - - 4 -	- - 5 - - - 6	- - - 7 - - -
Duguna (8:4)	1 - 2 -	3 - 4 -	5 - 6 -	7 - 8 -
Sawa-do-guna (9:4)	1 - - - 2 - - - 3	- - - 4 - - - 5 -	- - 6 - - - 7 - -	- 8 - - - 9 - - -
Dhai-guna (10:4)	1 - - - 2 - - - 3 -	- - 4 - - - 5 - - -	6 - - - 7 - - - 8 -	- - 9 - - - 10 - - -
Paune-teen-guna (11:4)	1 - - - 2 - - - 3 - -	- 4 - - - 5 - - - 6 -	- - 7 - - - 8 - - - 9	- - - 10 - - - 11 - - -
Tiguna (12:4)	1 2 3	4 5 6	7 8 9	10 11 12
Chauguna (16:4)	1 2 3 4	5 6 7 8	9 10 11 12	13 14 15 16

Table 11: An example of *paun-guna*

Matra	1	2	3	4
Paun-guna (3:4)	1 - -	- 2 -	- - 3	- - -

Table 12: Types of *jatis*

Names of *Jatis*	Description	*Bols*
Tishra	Each *matra* consists of 3 beats or a multiple of 3 beats	Ta ki ta
Chatushra	Each *matra* consists of 4 beats or a multiple of 4 beats	Ta thai thai Tat
Khanda	Each *matra* consists of 5 beats or a multiple of 5 beats	Ta ka Ta ki ta
Mishra	Each *matra* consists of 7 beats or a multiple of 7 beats	Ta ki ta Ta thai thai Tat
Sankirna	Each *matra* consists of 9 beats or a multiple of 9 beats	Ta ka Ta ki ta Ta thai thai Tat

Table 13: *Tihai*

Matra	**1**	2	3	4	**5**	6	7	8	**9**	10	11	12	**13**	14	15	16
Theka	**Tig**	dha	dig	dig	thai	-	**tig**	dha	dig	dig	thai	-	**tig**	dha	dig	dig
	Thai															
Tala sign	X				2				0				3			

Table 14: *Dumdar tihai* formula 1

Matra	1	2	3	4	5	6	7	8	9	10	11	12	13	14	15	16
Tihai	1	2	3	4	dha	-	1	2	3	4	dha	-	1	2	3	4
	dha															
Tala sign	X				2				0				3			

Table 15: *Dumdar tihai* formula 2

Matra	1	2	3	4	5	6	7	8	9	10	11	12	13	14	15	16
Tihai	1	2	3	4	5	6	7	8	9	10	11	12	13	14	dha	-
	-	1	2	3	4	5	6	7	8	9	10	11	12	13	14	dha
	-	-	1	2	3	4	5	6	7	8	9	10	11	12	13	14
	Dha															
Tala sign	X				2				0				3			

Table 16: An example of *farmaishi chakkardar tihai* in *teental*

TakaTaka	TakitaTa	kaTakaTa	kitaTaka
X			
taTakaTa	kitaTaka	TakitaTa	kaTakita
0			
dha---	Takitadhikita	Takitadhikita	Takitadhikita
X			
Takitadhikita	Takitadhikita	Dha ---	TakaTaka
0			
taTakaTa	kaTakita	TakaTaki	taTakaTa
X			
Takitadhikita	Takitadhikita	Takitadhikita	Dha---
0			
dha	Takitadhikita	Takitadhikita	Takitadhikita
X			
kaTakaTa	kitaTaka	TakaTaki	taTakaTa
0			
TakitaTa	kaTakita	Takitadhikita	Takitadhikita
X			
Takitadhikita	Takitadhikita	Takitadhikita	Dha---
0			
dha			
X			

TakaTaki	taTakaTa	kaTakita	TakaTaki
2			
Takitadhikita	Takitadhikita	Takitadhikita	Takitadhikita
3			
Takitadhikita	dha--	Takitadhikita	Takitadhikita
2			
TakitaTa	kaTakaTa	kitaTaka	TakaTaki
3			
kitaTaka	TakitaTa	kaTakita	Takitadhikita
2			
Takitadhikita	Takitadhikita	Takitadhikita	Takitadhikita
3			
Takitadhikita	dha---	TakaTaka	TakitaTa
2			
kaTakita	TakaTaki	taTakaTa	kitaTaka
3			
Takitadhikita	Takitadhikita	dha---	Takitadhikita
2			
Takitadhikita	Takitadhikita	Takitadhikita	Takitadhikita
3			

Table 17: An example of *kamali chakkardar thai* in *teental*

Dha - na	dha -Ta	ki ta dha	- dhi ki	ta dha -	ka Ta ga	di gi na	Ta ki ta
X				2			
Dhi ki ta	Ta ki ta	dha Tra ka	dhi ki ta	dha Tra ka	dhi ki ta	ka Ta ga	di gi na
0				3			
dha- -	dha- -	dha- -	dha Tra ka	dhi ki ta	dha Tra ka	dhi ki ta	ka Ta ga
X				2			
di gi na	dha - -	dha - -	dha	dha Tra ka	dhi ki ta	dha Tra ka	dhi ki ta
0				3			
ka Ta ga	di gi na	dha- -	dha- -	dha- - -	- - -	dha - na	dha -Ta
X				2			
Ki ta dha	-dhi ki	ta dha -	ka Ta ga	di gi na	Ta ki ta	dhi ki ta	Ta ki ta
0				3			
dha Tra ka	dhi ki ta	dha Tra ka	dhi ki ta	ka Ta ga	di gi na	dha - -	dha- -
X				2			
dha - -	dha Tra ka	dhi ki ta	dha Tra ka	dhi ki ta	ka Ta ga	di gi na	dha - -
0				3			
dha - -	dha --	dha Tra ka	dhi ki ta	dha Tra ka	dhi ki ta	ka Ta ga	di gi na
X				2			
dha - -	dha - -	dha - -	- - -	dha - na	dha -Ta	ki ta dha	- dhi ki
0				3			
ta dha -	ka Ta ga	di gi na	Ta ki ta	dhi ki ta	Ta ki ta	dha Tra ka	dhi ki ta
X				2			
dha Tra ka	dhi ki ta	ka Ta ga	di gi na	dha - -	dha - -	dha - -	dha Tra ka
0				3			
dhi ki ta	dha tra ka	dhi ki ta	ka Ta ga	di gi na	dha - -	dha - -	dha - -
X				2			
dha Tra ka	dhi ki ta	dha Tra ka	dhi ki ta	ka Ta ga	di gi na	dha - -	dha - -
0				3			
Dha							
X							

Table 18: An example of the shape and rhythmic notation of a traditional *ginati ki tihai* in *teental*

Dha	dhin	dhin	dha	Dha	dhin	dhin	dha	Dha	tin	tin	ta	Ta	dhin	dhin	dha
12-1	23-1	234-	1234	5-12	345-	1234	5678	1234	5678	1---	12-1	23-1	234-	1234	5-12
345-	1234	5678	1234	5678	1---	12-1	23-1	234-	1234	5-12	345-	1234	5678	1234	5678
1															
X				2				0				3			

Table 19: An example of a *ginati ki tihai* with gaps

Dha	Dhin	Dhin	Dha	Dha	Dhin	Dhin	Dha	Dha	Tin	Tin	Ta	Ta	Dhin	Dhin	Dha
12-3	4-56	78-1	23-4	56-7	8123	4-56	78-1	2345	678-	1---	12-3	4-56	78-1	23-4	56-7
8123	4-56	78-1	2345	678-	1---	12-3	4-56	78-1	23-4	56-7	8123	4-56	78-1	2345	678-
1															
X				2				0				3			

Table 20: An example of the *bol*s of a *gopuchcha tihai*

Dha	Dhin	Dhin	Dha	Dha	Dhin	Dhin	Dha	Dha	Tin	Tin	Ta	Ta	Dhin	Dhin	Dha
Tig	dha	dig	dig	thai	dha	dig	dig	thai	dig	dig	thai	dig	thai	Ta tha	iTa
thai	dig	thai	Tatha	iTa	thai	dig	thai	Ta tha	iTa	thai	Tig	dha	dig	dig	Thai
dha	dig	dig	thai	dig	dig	thai	dig	thai	Ta tha	iTa	thai	dig	thai	Ta tha	iTa
thai	dig	thai	Tatha	iTa	thai	Tig	dha	dig	dig	thai	dha	dig	dig	thai	dig
dig	thai	dig	thai	Ta tha	iTa	thai	dig	thai	Tatha	ita	thai	dig	thai	Tatha	ita
Thai															
X				2				0				3			

Table 21: *Tala Teental – 16 matras*

Dha	dhin	dhin	dha	dha	dhin	dhin	dha	dha	Tin	Tin	Ta	Ta	dhin	dhin	dha
								Tigdha	digdig	thai	tigdha	Digdig	thai	Tigdha	digdig
Thai															
X				2				0				3			

Table 22: *Tala Jhaptal* – 10 matras

Dhin	Na	dhin	dhin	na	Tin	na	dhin	dhin	na
		Tigdha	digdig	thai	tigdha	digdig	thai	tigdha	digdig
Thai									
X		2			0		3		

Table 23: *Tala Ektal* – 12 matras

Dhin	dhin	dha	Trak	Tu	na	kaT	Ta	dha	Trak	dhin	na
				Tigdha	digdig	thai	tigdha	digdig	thai	Tigdha	digdig
Thai											
X		0		2		0		3		4	

Table 24: *Tala Dhamar* – 14 Matras

Ka	dhi	ta	dhi	ta	dha	-	ga	di	na	di	na	Ta	-
					Tigdha	digdig	thai	tigdha	digdig	thai	tigdha	digdig	
Thai													
X					2		0			3			

Table 25: *A tihai* for any *tala* of 4 matras

Tigdhadigdig	thai-tigdha	digdigthai-	tigdhadigdig
Thai			
X			

Table 26: *A tihai* for any *tala* of 5 matras

Ta thai thai TaT	thai---	Ta thai thai TaT	thai---	Ta thai thai TaT
Thai				
X				

Jhulan Pastime—Hindola-Raga Pahari, Kangra, c. 1790

Table 27: *A tihai for any tala of 6 matras*

Ta thai thai TaT Aa thai thai TaT	thai - - -	- - - - Ta thai thai TaT
Thai		
X		

Table 28: *A tihai for any tala of 7 matras*

Ta thai thai TaT, Aa thai thai TaT	thai - - - Ta - - -	thai - - - Ta thai thai TaT	Aa thai thai TaT thai - - -
Thai			
X			

Table 29: *A tihai for any tala of 8 matras*

Takitadhikita	Takitadhikita	dha -	Takitadhikita
Thai			
X			

Table 30: *A tihai for any tala of 9 matras*

Ta thai thai TaT	Aa thai thai TaT	Thai - - - -	- - Ta thai	Thai TaT Aa thai
Thai				
X				

Table 31: *A tihai for any tala of 10 matras*

Ta thai thai TaT	Aa thai thai TaT	thai -Ta -	thai - Ta thai	thai TaT Aa thai
Thai				
X				

Table 32: *A tihai for any tala of 11 matras*

Ta thai thai TaT	Aa thai thai TaT	thai -Ta -	thai - - -	Ta thai thai TaT
Thai				
X				

Aa thai thai TaT thai - - -	- - - -	Ta thai thai TaT Aa thai thai TaT- -

Ta - - - -thai - - - -	Ta thai thai TaT Aa thai thai TaT	thai - - -Ta - - -

Takitadhikita	dha -	Takitadhikita	Takitadhikita

Thai TaT thai -	- - - - -	Ta thai thai TaT	Aa thai thai TaT

thai TaT thai -	Ta - thai -	Ta thai thai TaT	Aa thai thai TaT	thai -Ta -

Aa thai thai TaT	thai -Ta -	thai - - -	Ta thai thai TaT	Aa thai thai TaT	thai -Ta -

Table 33: *A tihai for any tala of 12 matras*

Ta thai thai TaT	Aa thai thai TaT	thai	-	-	Ta thai thai TaT
Thai					
X					

Table 34: *A tihai for any tala of 13 matras*

Ta thai thai TaT	Aa thai thai TaT	thai TaT	thai	-	Ta thai thai TaT	Aa thai thai TaT
Thai						
X						

Table 35: *A tihai for any tala of 14 matras*

Takita	dhikita	Ta thai	thai TaT	thai -	Takita	dhikita
Thai						
X						

Table 36: *A tihai for any tala of 15 matras*

Ta thai thai TaT	Aa thai thai TaT	Ta ka dhi na	Ta ka dhi na	dha - - -	- - Ta thai	thai TaT Aa thai
Thai						
X						

Table 37: *An example of a tihai for the 7-matra rupak tala*

Tin	**Tin**	**Na**	**Dhin**
Tigdhadigdig	thai	tigdhadigdig	thai
-	tigdhadigdig	thai	tigdhadigdig
-	-	tigdhadigdig	thai
Thai			
0			1

Aa thai thai TaT	thai	-	-	Ta thai thai TaT	Aa thai thai TaT

thai TaT	thai	-	Ta thai thai TaT	Aa thai thai TaT	thai TaT

Ta thai	thai TaT	thai -	Takita	dhikita	Ta thai	thai TaT

thai TaT Ta ka	dhi na Ta ka	dhi na dha -	- - - -	Ta thai thai TaT	Aa thai thai TaT	Ta ka dhi na	Ta ka dhi na

Na	Dhin	Na
tigdhadigdig	thai	-
thai	tigdhadigdig	thai
tigdhadigdig	thai	tigdhadigdig
	2	

Table 38: A *tihai* after 14 and 3/4 *matras*

Dha dhin dhin dha	dha dhin dhin dha	dha Tin Tin Ta	Ta dhin - - - 1 2 1 2 1
2			
X	2	0	3

Table 39: A *tihai* after 13 and 1/4 *matras*

Dha dhin dhin dha	dha dhin dhin dha	dha Tin Tin Ta	Ta dhin - 1 2 - 1 2 - 1
2			
X	2	0	3

Table 40: A *tihai* after 13 and ¾ *matras*

Dha dhin dhin dha	dha dhin dhin dha	dha Tin Tin Ta	Ta - - - 1 2 - - 1 2 - - 1
2			
X	2	0	3

Table 41: A *tihai* from the 13th *matra*

Dha dhin dhin dha	dha dhin dhin dha	dha Tin Tin Ta	1234 5-12 345- 1234
5			
X	2	0	3

Table 42: A *tihai* from the 12th *matra*

Dha dhin dhin dha	dha dhin dhin dha	dha Tin Tin 1234	5-1- 1234 5-1- 1234
5			
X	2	0	3

Table 43: A *tihai* from the 11th *matra*

Dha dhin dhin dha	dha dhin dhin dha	dha Tin 1234 5- - -	- -12 345- - - - - 1234
5			
X	2	0	3

Table 44: A *tihai* from the 10th *matra*

Dha dhin dhin dha	dha dhin dhin dha	dha 1234 5--- ----	1234 5--- ---- 1234
5			
X	2	0	3

Table 45: A *tihai* from the 9th *matra*

Dha dhin dhin dha	dha dhin dhin dha	1234 5-12 3--- 1234	5-12 3--- 1234 5-12
5			
X	2	0	3

Table 46: A *tihai* from the 8th *matra*

Dha dhin dhin dha	dha dhin dhin 1234	5-12 3-12 345- 123-	1234 5-12 3-12 3-12
5			
X	2	0	3

Table 47: A *tihai* from the 7th *matra*

Dha dhin dhin dha	dha dhin 1234 5-12	3-12 345- 123- 1234	5-12 3--- 123- --12
5			
X	2	0	3

Table 48: A *tihai* from the 6th *matra*

Dha dhin dhin dha	dha 1234 5-12 3-12	345- 123- 1234 5-12	3--- --12 3--- --12
5			
X	2	0	3

Table 49: A *tihai* from the 5th *matra*

Dha dhin dhin dha	1234 5-12 3-12 345-	123- 1234 5-12 3---	---- 123- ---- --12
5			
X	2	0	3

Table 50: A *tihai* from the 4th *matra*

Dha dhin dhin 1234	5-12 3-12 3-12 3-12	345- 123- 123- 123-	1234 5-12 3-12 3-12
3			
X	2	0	3

Table 51: A *tihai* from the 3rd *matra*

Dha dhin 1234 5-12	3-12 3-12 3--- 1234	5-12 3-12 3-12 3---	1234 5-12 3-12 3-12
3			
X	2	0	3

Table 52: A *tihai* from the 2nd *matra*

Dha	1234	5-12	3-12	3-12	3---	--12	345-	123-	123-	123-	----	1234	5-12	3-12	3-12
3															
X				2				0				3			

Table 53: A *tihai* from the 1st *matra*

1234	5678	1-2-	3-4-	5-12	3-12	3456	781-	2-3-	4-5-	123-	1234	5678	1-2-	3-4-	5-12
3															
X				2				0				3			

Table 54: *Tatkar* of *teental* with 8 *matras*

Theka	Dha	dhin	dhin	dha	Dha	dhin	dhin	dha	Dha	tin	tin	ta	Ta	dhin	dhin	dha
Tatkar	Ta	-	thai	-	thai	-	TaT	-	Aa	-	thai	-	thai	-	TaT	-
Tala-sign	X				2				0				3			
Footwork	Right	-	left	-	right	-	left	-	left	-	right	-	left	-	right	-

Table 55: *Tatkar* in *teental* in a *barabar ki laya*, *duguna*, *tiguna*, and *chauguna*

Barabar ki laya	Ta thai thai TaT	Aa thai thai TaT	Ta thai thai TaT	Aa thai thai TaT
Duguna	Ta thai thai TaT	Ta thai thai TaT	Ta thai thai TaT	Ta thai thai TaT
	Aa thai thai TaT	Aa thai thai TaT	Aa thai thai TaT	Aa thai thai TaT
Tiguna	Ta thai thai	Aa thai thai	Ta thai thai	Aa thai thai
	TaT Aa thai	TaT Ta thai	TaT Aa thai	TaT Ta thai
	thai TaT Ta	thai TaT Aa	thai TaT Ta	thai TaT Aa
	thai thai TaT	thai thai TaT	thai thai TaT	thai thai TaT
Chauguna	Ta thai thai TaT	Ta thai thai TaT	Ta thai thai TaT	Ta thai thai TaT
	Aa thai thai TaT	Aa thai thai TaT	Aa thai thai TaT	Aa thai thai TaT
	Ta thai thai TaT	Ta thai thai TaT	Ta thai thai TaT	Ta thai thai TaT
	Aa thai thai TaT	Aa thai thai TaT	Aa thai thai TaT	Aa thai thai TaT
	X	2	0	3

Table 56: *Tatkar ke prakar* in *teental*

Matras	1	2	3	4	5	6	7	8
Prakar 1	TaT -	Ta thai	thai TaT	TaT -	Aa thai	thai TaT	Ta thai	thai TaT
Prakar 2	Ta ki	ta Ta	ki ta	dhi na	Ta ki	ta Ta	ki ta	dhi na
Prakar 3	Dig dig	Ta dig	dig Ta	dig dig	Ta thai	thai TaT	Aa thai	thai TaT
Prakar 4	Ta Traka	dhin na	Ta thai	thai TaT	Aa Traka	dhin na	Aa thai	thai TaT
Prakar 5	Ta ka	Ta ka	Ta ka	Ta ka	Ta -	Traka -	dhin -	na -
Prakar 6	Kir dhin	- na	aa dhin	dhin na	na dhin	dhin na	na dhin	dhin na
Tala sign	X				2			
Matras	9	10	11	12	13	14	15	16
1 contd.	TaT -	Ta thai	thai TaT	TaT-	Aa thai	thai TaT	Ta thai	thai TaT
2 contd.	Ta ki	ta Ta	ki ta	dhi na	Ta ki	ta Ta	ki ta	dhi na
3 contd.	Dig dig	Ta dig	dig Ta	dig dig	Ta thai	thai TaT	Aa thai	thai TaT
4 contd.	Ta Traka	dhin na	Ta thai	thai TaT	Aa Traka	dhin na	Aa thai	thai TaT
5 contd.	Ta ka	Ta ka	Ta ka	Ta ka	Aa -	Traka -	dhin -	na -
6 contd.	Kir dhin	- na	na dhin	dhin na	na dhin	dhin na	na dhin	dhin na
Tala sign	0				3			

Table 57: An example of *paltas* of *tatkar* in *teental*

Matras	1	2	3	4	5	6	7	8
Palta 1	TaT-	TaT -	Ta thai	thai TaT	Aa thai	thai TaT	Ta thai	thai TaT
Palta 2	TaT-	TaT -	TaT -	Ta thai	thai TaT	Aa thai	thai TaT	TaT -
Palta 3	TaT-	TaT -	TaT -	TaT -	Ta thai	thai TaT	Aa thai	Thai TaT
Palta 4	TaT -	TaT -	TaT -	TaT -	TaT -	Ta thai	thai TaT	Aa thai
Palta 5	TaT -	TaT -	TaT -	TaT -	TaT -	TaT -	Ta thai	thai TaT
Palta 6	TaT-	TaT -	TaT -	TaT -	TaT -	TaT -	TaT -	Ta thai
Palta 7	TaT -	TaT -	TaT -	TaT -	TaT -	TaT -	TaT -	TaT -
Tihai	TaT -	Ta thai	thai TaT	TaT -	Aa thai	thai TaT	TaT -	Ta thai
	Ta thai	thai TaT	Aa thai	thai TaT	thai -	- -	TaT -	Ta thai
	Aa thai	thai TaT	Ta thai	thai TaT	Aa thai	thai TaT	Ta thai	thai TaT
	Aa thai	thai TaT	TaT -	Ta thai	Thai TaT	TaT -	Aa thai	thai TaT
	Thai							
	X				2			
Matras	9	10	11	12	13	14	15	16
1 cont.	TaT -	TaT -	Aa thai	thai TaT	Ta thai	thai TaT	Aa thai	thai TaT
2 cont.	Ta thai	thai TaT	TaT -	Aa thai	Thai TaT	TaT -	Ta thai	thai TaT
3 cont.	TaT -	Ta thai	thai TaT	TaT -	Aa thai	thai TaT	Ta thai	thai TaT
4 cont.	thai TaT	TaT -	Ta thai	thai TaT	Aa thai	thai TaT	Ta thai	thai TaT
5 cont.	Aa thai	Thai TaT	Ta thai	thai TaT	Aa thai	thai TaT	Ta thai	thai TaT
6 cont.	thai TaT	TaT -	Aa thai	thai TaT	TaT -	Ta thai	thai TaT	TaT -
7 cont.	Tat -	Ta thai	thai TaT	TaT -	Aa thai	thai TaT	Ta thai	thai TaT
Tihai cont.	thai TaT	TaT -	Aa thai	thai TaT	Ta thai	thai TaT	Aa thai	thai TaT
	thai TaT	TaT -	Aa thai	thai TaT	TaT -	Ta thai	thai TaT	TaT -
	Aa thai	thai TaT	thai	- - -	TaT -	Ta thai	thai Tat	TaT -
	Ta thai	thai TaT	Aa thai	thai TaT	Ta thai	thai TaT	Aa thai	thai TaT
	0				3			

Table 58: An Example of a *ladi* in *teental*

1	2	3	4	5	6	7	8	9	10	11	12	13	14	15	16
Taki	taTa	kita	dhin	Taki	taTa	kita	dhin	Taki	taTa	kita	dhin	Taki	taTa	kita	dhin
Taka	dhin	Taka	dhin	Taki	taTa	kita	dhin	Taki	taTa	kita	dhin	Taki	taTa	kita	dhin
Taka	dhin	Taka	dhin	Taki	taTa	kita	dhin	Taka	dhin	Taka	dhin	Taki	taTa	kita	dhin
Taka	dhin	Taka	dhin	Taka	dhin	Taka	dhin	Taka	dhin	Taka	dhin	Taki	taTa	kita	dhin
Taka	dhin	Taki	taTa	Kita	Taki	taTa	kita	Taki	taTa	kita	dhin	Taki	taTa	kita	dhin
Taki	taTa	kita	dhin	dha	dhin	dha	dhin	Taki	taTa	kita	dhin	Taki	taTa	kita	dhin
Taki	taTa	kita	dhin	dhin	dhin	dhin	dhin	Taki	taTa	kita	dhin	Taki	taTa	kita	dhin
Taki	taTa	kita	Taka	dhin	Taka	dhin	Taka	Taki	taTa	kita	dhin	Taki	taTa	kita	dhin
Tihai:															
Taka	dhin	Taka	dhin	Taka	dhin	Taka	dhin	Taki	tadhi	kita	Taki	tadhi	kita	Taki	tadhi
kita	Taki	tadhi	kita	dha	-	Taka	dhin	Taka	dhin	Taka	dhin	Taka	dhin	Taki	tadhi
kita	Taki	tadhi	kita	Taki	tadhi	kita	Taki	tadhi	kita	dha	-	Taka	dhin	Taka	dhin
Taka	dhin	Taka	dhin	Taki	tadhi	kita	Taki	tadhi	kita	Taki	tadhi	kita	Taki	tadhi	kita
dha															
X				2				0				3			

Table 59: An example of a simple *chala* in *teental* from Jaipur Gharana

Theka	**Dha**	**Dhin**	**Dhin**	**Dha**
Theme	Ta---	dha---	Ta-ki-	ta-Ta-
Variation 1	Ta---	dha---	Ta-ki-	ta-Ta-
Variation 2	Ta---	dha---	Ta-ki-	ta-Ta-
Variation 3	Ta---	Ta-ki-	ta-Ta-	---dha
Variation 4	Ta---	dha---	Ta-ki-	ta-Ta-
Variation 5	Ta---	dha---	Ta-ki-	ta-Ta-
Variation 6	Ta-dha-	-Takita	Ta-dha-	-Takita
Variation 7	Dhadhadhadha	-Takita dhikita	Dhadhadhadha	-Takita dhikita
Variation 8	Dhadhadhadha	dhadhadhadha	Takitadhikitataki	tadhikitadha-dha-
Tihai	Ta-dha-Takita-	TakitadhikitaTaka	TakitadhikitaTaka	TakitadhikitadhaTi
	dha -TakaTakitadhi	kitadhaTidha - - -	dha- - - dha-Taka	Takitadhi kitadhaTi
	dha			
Tala sign	X			
Theka	**Dha**	**Tin**	**Tin**	**Ta**
Theme	Ta---	dha---	Ta-ki-	ta-Ta-
Variation 1	Ta---	dha--	Ta-ki-	ta-Ta-
Variation 2	Ta---	dha---	Ta-ki-	ta-Ta-
Variation 3	Ki-ta-	Ta-ka-	Ta- ki-	ta-Ta-
Variation 4	Ta---	dha---	Ta-ki-	ta-Ta-
Variation 5	dha-Taka	TakaTaki	Tadhikita	Ta-dha-
Variation 6	Ta-dha-	-Takita	Ta-dha-	-Takita
Variation 7	dhadhadhadha	--Takitadhikita	dhadhadhadha	--Takitadhikita
Variation 8	dhadhadhadha	dhadhadhadha	TakitadhikitaTaki	tadhikitadha-dha-
Tihai	TakitadhikitadhaTi	dha - - -dha - - -	dha-------	Ta-dha-Takita-
	TakitadhikitaTaka	TakitadhikitadhaTi	dha - - - dha - - -	dha TakaTakitadhi
Tala sign	0			

Dha	Dhin	Dhin	Dha
dha---	Ta-dha-	---Ta	dha---
-- dha-	-- Ta-	ka-Ta-	ki-ta-
dha---	--Ta-	ka-Ta-	ki-ta-
---Ta	ki-ta-	dha-dha-	dha-Ta-
dha---	TakaTaka	Takitadhi	kitaTaka
dha---	TakaTaka	Takitadhi	kitaTa-
Ta-dha-	-Takita	Ta-dha-	-Takita
Dhadhadhadha	-Takita dhikita	Dhadhadhadha	-Takita dhikita
Dhadhadhadha	dhadha dhadha	Takitadhikitataki	tadhikitadha-dha-
dha- - -dha- - -	dha-TakaTakitadhi	kitadhaTidha - - -	dha- - - dha-Taka
dha - - -dha - - -	dha- - - - - - -	Ta-dha-Takita-	TakitadhikitaTaka

2

Ta	Dhin	Dhin	Dha
dha---	Ta-dha-	---Ta	dha---
dha---	Ta-dha-	---Ta	dha---
dha---	Ta-dha-	---Ta	dha---
dha---	Ta-dha-	---Ta	dha---
dha---	Ta-dha-	---Ta	dha---
TakaTaka	Takitadhi	kitaTa-	dha---
Ta-dha-	-Takita	Ta-dha-	-Takita
Dhadhadhadha	--Takitadhikita	dhadhadhadha	--Takitadhikita
dhadhadhadha	dhadhadhadha	TakitadhikitaTaki	tadhikitadha-dha-
TakitadhikitaTaka	TakitadhikitaTaka	TakitadhikitadhaTi	dha - - - dha - - -
kitadhaTidha - - -	dha- - - dha-Taka	Takitadhi kitadhaTi	dha - - -dha - - -

3

Table 60: *Vajan* in *teental* in *barabar ki laya*

Dha	Dhin	Dhin	Dha	Dha	Dhin	Dhin	Dha	Dha	Tin	Tin	Ta	Ta	Dhin	Dhin	Dha
Ta	thai	thai	TaT	Aa	thai	thai	TaT	Ta	thai	thai	TaT	Aa	thai	thai	**TaT**
Ta	thai	thai	TaT	Aa	thai	thai	TaT	Ta	thai	thai	TaT	Aa	thai	**thai**	TaT
Ta	thai	thai	TaT	Aa	thai	thai	TaT	Ta	thai	thai	TaT	Aa	**thai**	thai	TaT
Ta	thai	thai	TaT	Aa	thai	thai	TaT	Ta	thai	thai	TaT	**Aa**	thai	thai	TaT
Ta	thai	thai	TaT	Aa	thai	thai	TaT	Ta	thai	thai	**TaT**	Aa	thai	thai	TaT
Ta	thai	thai	TaT	Aa	thai	thai	TaT	Ta	thai	**thai**	TaT	Aa	thai	thai	TaT
Ta	thai	thai	TaT	Aa	thai	thai	TaT	Ta	**thai**	thai	TaT	Aa	thai	thai	TaT
Ta	thai	thai	TaT	Aa	thai	thai	TaT	**Ta**	thai	thai	TaT	Aa	thai	thai	TaT
Ta	thai	thai	TaT	Aa	thai	thai	**TaT**	Ta	thai	thai	TaT	Aa	thai	thai	TaT
Ta	thai	thai	TaT	Aa	thai	**thai**	TaT	Ta	thai	thai	TaT	Aa	thai	thai	TaT
Ta	thai	thai	TaT	Aa	**thai**	thai	TaT	Ta	thai	thai	TaT	Aa	thai	thai	TaT
Ta	thai	thai	TaT	**Aa**	thai	thai	TaT	Ta	thai	thai	TaT	Aa	thai	thai	TaT
Ta	thai	thai	**TaT**	Aa	thai	thai	TaT	Ta	thai	thai	TaT	Aa	thai	thai	TaT
Ta	thai	**thai**	TaT	Aa	thai	thai	TaT	Ta	thai	thai	TaT	Aa	thai	thai	TaT
Ta	**thai**	thai	TaT	Aa	thai	thai	TaT	Ta	thai	thai	TaT	Aa	thai	thai	TaT
Ta	thai	thai	TaT	Aa	thai	thai	TaT	Ta	thai	thai	TaT	Aa	thai	thai	TaT

Table 61: A traditional *vajan ki baant* in *teental*

Theka	**Dha**	**dhin**	**dhin**	**dha**	**Dha**	**dhin**	**dhin**	**dha**	**Dha**	**Tin**	**Tin**	**Ta**	**Ta**	**dhin**	**dhin**	**Dha**
Variation 1	**Ta**	thai	thai	TaT	Aa	thai	thai	TaT	**Ta**	thai	thai	TaT	Aa	thai	thai	TaT
Variation 2	**Ta**	thai	thai	TaT	**Aa**	thai	thai	TaT	Ta	thai	thai	TaT	Aa	thai	thai	TaT
Variation 3	**Ta**	thai	thai	TaT	**Aa**	thai	thai	TaT	**Ta**	thai	thai	TaT	Aa	thai	thai	TaT
Variation 4	Ta	**thai**	thai	TaT	Aa	thai	**thai**	TaT	Ta	**thai**	thai	TaT	Aa	thai	**thai**	TaT
Variation 5	Ta	thai	**thai**	TaT	Aa	**thai**	thai	TaT	Ta	thai	**thai**	TaT	Aa	**thai**	thai	TaT
Variation 6	**Ta**	**thai**	thai	TaT	Aa	thai	thai	TaT	**Ta**	**thai**	thai	TaT	Aa	thai	thai	TaT
Variation 7	**Ta**	thai	**thai**	TaT	Aa	thai	thai	TaT	**Ta**	thai	**thai**	TaT	Aa	thai	thai	TaT
Variation 8	**Ta**	thai	**thai**	TaT	**Aa**	thai	**thai**	TaT	**Ta**	thai	**thai**	TaT	**Aa**	thai	**thai**	TaT
Variation 9	**Ta**	thai	thai	TaT	Aa	**thai**	thai	TaT	Ta	thai	**thai**	TaT	Aa	thai	thai	**TaT**
	Ta	thai	thai	TaT	**Aa**	thai	thai	TaT	**Ta**	thai	thai	TaT	**Aa**	thai	thai	TaT
Tihai	**Ta**	thai	thai	TaT	Aa	**thai**	thai	TaT	Ta	thai	**thai**	TaT	Aa	thai	thai	**TaT**
	TaT-	--	Ta	thai	thai	TaT	TaT-	--	**TaT**	--	**Aa**	thai	thai	TaT	TaT	--
	TaT	--	**TaT**	--	**Ta**	thai	thai	TaT	thai	Ta	**thai**	**Ta**	thai	thai	TaT	Aa
	thai	thai	TaT	Ta	thai	**thai**	TaT	Aa	thai	thai	**TaT**	**TaT**	--	**Ta**	thai	thai
	TaT	TaT	--	**TaT**	--	**Aa**	thai	thai	TaT	TaT	--	TaT	--	**TaT**	--	**Ta**
	thai	thai	TaT	thai	Ta	**thai**	**Ta**	thai	thai	TaT	Aa	**thai**	thai	TaT	Ta	thai
	thai	TaT	Aa	thai	thai	**TaT**	**TaT**	--	**Ta**	thai	thai	TaT	TaT	--	**TaT**	--
	Aa	thai	thai	TaT	TaT	--	TaT	--	**TaT**	--	**Ta**	thai	thai	TaT	thai	ta
	Thai															
	X				2				0				3			

Table 62: An example of footwork with *dum kriya* in *teental*

Theka	**Dha**	**dhin**	**dhin**	**dha**	**Dha**	**dhin**	**dhin**	**dha**
Variation 1	-	thai	thai	TaT	-	thai	thai	TaT
Variation 2	Ta	thai	thai	-	Aa	thai	thai	-
Variation 3	-	-	thai	TaT	-	-	thai	TaT
Variation 4	Ta	-	thai	TaT	Aa	-	thai	TaT
Variation 5	Ta	thai	-	TaT	Aa	thai	-	TaT
Variation 6	-	-	thai	TaT	Aa	thai	-	-
Variation 7	Ta	-	thai	-	Aa	thai	thai	-
Tatkar (double speed)	Ta thai	thai TaT	Aa thai	thai TaT	Ta thai	thai TaT	Aa thai	thai TaT
Tihai	Ta	thai	-	Ta	thai	-	Ta thai	thai TaT
	-	Ta thai	thai TaT	thai	Ta	thai	Ta	thai
	Thai							
	X				2			

Table 63: An example of footwork with *aujhad kriya* and *uran* in *teental*

Theka	**Dha**	**dhin**	**dhin**	**dha**	**Dha**	**dhin**	**dhin**	**dha**
Aujhad	Ta	thai	-	TaT	Aa	thai	thai	-
	Thai							
	X				2			

Dha	Tin	Tin	Ta	Ta	dhin	dhin	dha
-	thai	thai	TaT	-	thai	thai	TaT
Ta	thai	thai	-	Aa	thai	thai	-
-	-	thai	TaT	-	-	thai	TaT
Ta	-	thai	TaT	Aa	-	thai	TaT
Ta	thai	-	TaT	Aa	thai	-	TaT
-	-	thai	TaT	Aa	thai	-	-
Ta	-	thai	TaT	Aa	thai	thai	-
Ta thai	thai TaT	Aa thai	thai TaT	Ta thai	thai TaT	Aa thai	thai TaT
thai	Ta	Thai	Ta	thai	-	Ta	thai
-	Ta	thai	-	Ta thai	thai TaT	thai	Ta
0				3			

Dha	Tin	Tin	Ta	Ta	dhin	dhin	dha
-	-	-	-	Ta dha - -	dha Tita dha -	dha TirkitaTaka	TatirkitTaka
0				3			

Table 64: *Khade per ki tatkar*

Theka	**Dha**	**dhin**	**dhin**	**dha**	**Dha**	**dhin**	**dhin**	**dha**
Variation 1	Kir dhin	- na	na dhin	dhin na	na dhin	dhin na	na dhin	dhin na
Variation 2	Kir dhin	- na	na dhin	dhin na	Kir dhin	- na	na dhin	dhin na
Variation 3	Kir dhin	- na	kir dhin	- na	kir dhin	- na	na dhin	dhin na
Variation 4	Kir dhin	- na	kir dhin	- na	dhin na	dhin na	na dhin	dhin na
Variation 5	Kir dhin	kir dhin	kir dhin	dha -	na dhin	dhin na	na dhin	dhin na
Variation 6	Kir dhin	dha kir	dhin dha	kir dhin	na dhin	dhin na	na dhin	dhin na
Tihai	Kir dhin	dha kir	dhin dha	kir dhin	na dhin	dhin na	na dhin	dhin na
	dhin na	na dhin	dhin na	na dhin	dhin na	dha -	kir dhin	dha kir
	dha							
	X				2			

Table 65: *Ghungru ki tatkar*

Theka	**Dha**	**dhin**	**dhin**	**dha**	**Dha**	**dhin**	**dhin**	**dha**
Variation 1	Dig dig	Ta dig	dig Ta	dig dig	dig dig	Ta dig	dig Ta	dig dig
Variation 2	Ta dig	dig Ta	dig dig	dig dig	dig dig	Ta dig	dig Ta	dig dig
Variation 3	Ta dig	dig Ta	dig dig	dig dig	Ta dig	dig Ta	dig dig	dig dig
Variation 4	Dig dig	dig dig	dig dig	Ta-	dig dig	Ta dig	dig Ta	dig dig
Variation 5	Dig dig	- dig	dig -	dig dig	dig dig	Ta dig	dig Ta	dig dig
Variation 6	Dig dig	dig dig	- -	dig dig	dig dig	- dig	dig -	dig dig
Variation 7	Dig dig	dig dig	dig dig	dig dig	dig dig	Ta dig	dig Ta	dig dig
Tihai	Dig dig	Ta dig	dig Ta	dig dig	Ta -	- -	dig dig	Ta dig
	Ta							
	X				2			

Dha	Tin	Tin	Ta	Ta	dhin	dhin	dha
kir dhin	- na	na dhin	dhin na	na dhin	dhin na	na dhin	dhin na
kir dhin	- na	na dhin	dhin na	na dhin	dhin na	na dhin	dhin na
Kir dhin	- na	kir dhin	- na	kir dhin	- na	na dhin	dhin na
Kir dhin	- na	kir dhin	- na	dhin na	dhin na	na dhin	dhin na
Kir dhin	kir dhin	kir dhin	Ta -	na dhin	dhin na	na dhin	dhin na
kir dhin	Ta kir	Dhin Ta	kir dhin	na dhin	dhin na	na dhin	dhin na
na dhin	na dhin	dha -	kir dhin	dha kir	dhin dha	kir dhin	na dhin
dhin dha	kir dhin	na dhin	dhin na	na dhin	dhin na	na dhin	dhin na
0				3			

Dha	Tin	Tin	Ta	Ta	dhin	dhin	dha
dig dig	Ta dig	dig Ta	dig dig	dig dig	Ta dig	dig Ta	dig dig
Ta dig	dig Ta	dig dig	dig dig	dig dig	Ta dig	dig Ta	dig dig
Ta dig	dig Ta	dig dig	dig dig	dig dig	Ta dig	dig Ta	dig dig
dig dig	dig dig	dig dig	Ta-	dig dig	Ta dig	dig Ta	dig dig
dig dig	- dig	dig -	dig dig	dig dig	Ta dig	dig Ta	dig dig
dig dig	dig dig	- -	dig dig	dig dig	- dig	dig -	dig dig
dig dig	dig dig	dig dig	dig dig	dig dig	Ta dig	dig Ta	dig dig
dig Ta	dig dig	Ta -	- -	dig dig	Ta dig	dig Ta	dig dig
0				3			

Table 66: Krishna Kavitta

Baja	tata	-l	mir	dan-	ga mu	ra li	dhu na
ta na	na na	su ga	-ndha	Mana	bhaya	uma-	nga-
na -	- -	- -	Krish	Na -	Krish	na -	Krish
na							
X				2			

Table 67: Ganesh Kavitta

Gan	gan	gan	pati	gaja	mukh	man	dal
Tat	Tat	thai	-	jai	jag	van	dan
Vigh	naha	ran	shubh	karan	dhage	nadha	ge-
dadi	gina	thai-	Tharu	nga-	Tharu	nga-	dadi
Thai							
X				2			

Table 68: Kaliya Daman Kavitta

Gen-d	khe-lat	hirat	firatat	karat	chalbal	kariri	deh me
pahunch	ga-ye-	na-gin	yon-se	kahan	laa-ge	uthao	naa-g
paa-l	la-la-	hamko	aavatah	taras	tumpe	hanste	hanste
uth ke	de-kha-	kro-dh	se-maa-	ri-phu	nka-r-	sanana	nana phun
nee-l	baranan	bhaye la	ge-do-	yu-ddha	karne -	jahatak	jhatjhat
khee-nch	karle-	aa-ye	jamuna-	dhaa-r	me---	fanana	na upar
tramTa	Ta Thai-	nirat	tattat	karan	la-ge-	saa-nw	re-go-
charana	na-na-	par pra	bhu- ke	vinati	kar kah	ne- la	gin---
haa-g	la-la-	na-gin	ion-ki-	te-r	sun kar	na-g	ji- ko-
kaa-r	mach gayee	na-nd	ba-ba-	magan	bhaye jab	ma-ya	sho-da-
ya-n	ko---	guna para	bhu-ke-	ga--i	ga-i ke	na--ch	na-ch ke
bhaye-	na---	ra---	yan---	dha	-	magan	bhaye-
ra---	yan---	dha	-	magan	bhaye-	bhaye-	magan
Dha							
X				2			

Ta-	dhala	-nga	duma	Kita	Taka	da di	gi na
Ni ra	ta ka	ra ta	Krish	Na -	Krish	na -	Krish
Na -	- -	- -	Krish	Na -	Krish	na -	Krish
0				3			

ghit	ghir	ghit	ghir	ghit	ghir	thun	thun
va-	kratu	-nd	dha	ni	dha	ta	--
dhum	kita	dhum	kita	Tharu	nga-	Tharu	nga-
gina	thai-	Tharu	nga-	Tharu	nga-	dadi	gina
0				3			

koo-d	ga-ye-	maa-r	go-ta-	naa-g	ji-ke-	paa-s	jab tab
de-v	ko---	na--gi	nyan tab	chamak	uththi	tum ho	baa-l go
krishna	bo-le-	naa-g	nathan	aa-yo-	main---	naa-g	ji-ne-
kaa-r	ki- jab	gu-nj	dhwani	cha- ga	yee---	krishna	ji-tab
patak	pat pat	naa-g	ji-ko-	naa-th	liyo--	naa-th	se-tab
charana	nanadhar	nadigdig na	digdigdigdig	thodigdig tho	digdigdigdig	tramta	ta thai -
pa-l	la-la-	tarara	rararara	na-gi	ni-yan-	kaa-np	uththi -
abhun	ja-nu-	tumho	krishnava	ta--r	prabhu ji	hamko	deo su
de-di	yo---	bhu-mi	braj me	dhu-m	mach gayee	krishna	jaijai
karat	aa-rti	mo-ti	yan ke	thaa-l	bhar bhar	de-t	na-ra-
magan	bhaye-	bhaye-	magan	bhaye-	bhaye –	magan	bhaye-
bhaye-	magan	bhaye-	bhaye-	magan	bhaye-	bhaye-	na---
bhaye-	bhaye-	magan	bhaye-	bhaye-	na---	ra---	yan---
0				3			

List of Illustrations and Figures

Jhulan Pastime—Hindola-Raga Pahari,
Kangra, c. 1790 313

FIGURES

Illustration Credits

Ananda Natanam, the cosmic dance of Shiva, released into the public domain by its author, Manu. hotmail at English Wikipedia, Wikimedia Commons.

Sas Bahu Temple, Eklingji, Dennis Jarvis, Creative Commons Attribution-Share Alike 2.0 Generic license, Wikimedia Commons.

Râgmâlâ-Serie, Szene: Vasanta Râginî (Frühling), Krishna tanzt zur Musik zweier Mädchen, Indischer Maler um 1660, The Yorck Project: 10.000 Meisterwerke der Malerei. DVD-ROM, 2002. ISBN 3936122202. Distributed by DIRECTMEDIA Publishing GmbH, Wikimedia Commons.

Deutsch: Râgmâlâ-Serie, Szene: Krishna mit seiner Flöte, Indischer Maler um 1740, The Yorck Project: 10.000 Meisterwerke der Malerei. DVD-ROM, 2002. ISBN 3936122202. Distributed by DIRECTMEDIA Publishing GmbH, licensed under the GNU Free Documentation License, Wikimedia Commons.

Râgmâlâ-Serie, Szene: Krishna in der Schaukel, The Yorck Project: 10.000 Meisterwerke der Malerei. DVD-ROM, 2002. ISBN 3936122202. Distributed by DIRECTMEDIA Publishing GmbH, collection of reproductions compiled by The Yorck Project. Compilation copyright is held by Zenodot Verlagsgesellschaft mbH and licensed under the GNU Free Documentation License, Wikimedia Commons.

Yashoda adorning Krishna with ornaments, oil painting on canvas by Raja Ravi Varma—Huzur Mahadi Palace, Thanjavur, Tamilnadu. Public domain work of art, Wikimedia Commons.

Râgmâlâ series, scene: Krishna steals milk, Indischer Maler um 1660, The Yorck Project: 10.000 Meisterwerke der Malerei. DVD-ROM, 2002. ISBN 3936122202. Distributed by DIRECTMEDIA Publishing GmbH, Wikimedia Commons.

Krishna dances over the subdued Kaliya Naag in river Yamuna, while his wives are praying to Krishna for his mercy. Also seen on the banks are people of Gokula, Krishna's father Nanda Baba and his brother Balarama. From a Bhagavata Purana manuscript, c.1640, Indischer Maler um 1640, The Yorck Project: 10.000 Meisterwerke der Malerei. DVD-ROM, 2002. ISBN 3936122202. Distributed by DIRECTMEDIA Publishing GmbH, Wikimedia Commons.

Krishna und der Berg Govardhân, Shahadin, The Yorck Project: 10.000 Meisterwerke der Malerei. DVD-ROM, 2002. ISBN 3936122202. Distributed by DIRECTMEDIA Publishing GmbH, Wikimedia Commons.

Pandit Rajendra Gangani in Krishna pose, from the collection of Pandit Rajendra Gangani.

Pandit Rajendra Gangani in Nataraja pose, from the collection of Pandit Rajendra Gangani.

Danse Kathak, Sharmila Sharma et Rajendra Kumar Gangani et leurs musiciens samedi 24 Novembre 2007 au musée Guimet (Paris), author: Jean-Pierre Dalbéra Paris, France, The Creative Commons Attribution 2.0 Generic license, Wikimedia Commons.

Bharatnatyam different facial expressions, author: Suyash Dwivedi, The Creative Commons Attribution-Share Alike 4.0 International license, Wikimedia Commons.

An expressive pose in Kuchipudi dance by Yashoda Thakur, author: P Das Arayil from Cheruthuruthy, The Creative Commons Attribution-Share Alike 2.0 Generic, Wikimedia Commons.

Nandini Ghosal performing Odissi at the Coffman Memorial Union in the University, author: Bala Sivakumar from Seattle, The Creative Commons Attribution-Share Alike 2.0 Generic, Wikimedia Commons.

Divya Nedungadi, mohiniyattam mohini attam mohiniattam, author: Mohiniyattom, The Creative Commons Attribution-Share Alike 3.0 Unported license, Wikimedia Commons.

Kalamandalam, K G Vasudevan Nair, author: Mullookkaaran. The Creative Commons Attribution-Share Alike 4.0 International license, Wikimedia Commons.

Bimbavati Devi (Manipuri), author: Jean-Pierre Dalbéra from Paris, France, The Creative Commons Attribution 2.0 Generic license, Wikimedia Commons.

Krishnakahi Kashyap performing Sattriya dance, Sattriyadance critic, The Creative Commons Attribution-Share Alike 3.0 Unported license, Wikimedia Commons.

Unknown, author: Pradeep Adwani, Creative Commons Attribution-Share Alike 3.0 Unported license, GNU Free Documentation License, Wikimedia Commons.

Guru Dr Maya Rao. From the collection of Madhu Nataraj, Founder Director of Natya Stem Dance Kampani, photographer: Govind Vidyarti.

Replica of 'Dancing Girl' of Mohenjodaro at Chhatrapati Shivaji Maharaj Vastu Sangrahalaya in Mumbai, Joe Ravi, license CC-BY-SA 3.0, The Creative Commons Attribution-Share Alike 3.0 Unported, Wikimedia Commons.

Carte de l'expansion moghole en Inde, author: Nataraja at French Wikipedia, The Creative Commons Attribution-Share Alike 3.0 Unported license, Wikimedia Commons.

Raas Leela of Lord Krishna, author: Raj441977, The Creative Commons Attribution-Share Alike 4.0 International license, Wikimedia Commons.

Amir Khusrow surrounded by young men. Miniature from a manuscript of Majlis AlUsshak by Husayn Bayqarah. Anonymous artist from Bokhara, PD-US, Wikimedia Commons. Русский: Амир Хосров Дехлеви и юноши. Миниатюра из «Маджлис ал-Ушшак» Хусейна Байкара. Рукопись ИВ АН УзССР, 65, л. 68. English: Late 1600s or early 1700s.

Akbar and Tansen visit Swami Haridas in Vrindavan. Swami Haridas is to the right, playing the lute; Akbar is to the left, dressed as a common man; Tansen is in the middle, listening to Haridas. Jaipur-Kishangarh mixed style, c.1750, unknown painter in Rajasthani miniature style, public domain work of art, PD-US, Wikimedia Commons.

Wajid Ali Shah, an engraving from 1872 (also published in the Illustrated London News, 1857), public domain work of art, PD-US, Wikimedia Commons, Source: http://www.columbia.edu/itc/mealac/ pritchett/00routesdata/1800_1899/ avadh_late/vajidalishah/vajidalishah. html.

A photograph of two dancing girls, by K L Brajbasi & Co., Patna, 1910. Author: K L Brajbasi & Co. From: Frederic Courtland Penfield: East of Suez. Ceylon, India, China and Japan. New York: The Century Co. 1907. Retrieved from: http://www.gutenberg.org/ files/27260/27260-h/27260-h.htm, Wikimedia Commons.

A Calcutta nautch dancer from Frederic Courtland Penfield, East of Suez, *Ceylon, India, China and Japan.* New York: The Century Co. 1907. Retrieved from: http://www.gutenberg.org/ files/27260/27260-h/27260-h.htm, PD-US, Wikimedia Commons.

Studio portrait of a 'Mohammedan dancing girl', Jaipur, 1890. Source: ebay, June 2011, http:// www.columbia.edu/itc/mealac/ pritchett/00routesdata/1800_1899/ women/nautchphotos/nautchphotos. html, author unknown, Wikimedia Commons.

Dancers: Abha Bhatnagar Roy, Prerna Shrimali, and Veronique Azan (standing from left to right); Bhaswati Mishra and Arjun Mishra (sitting). Photographer: Avinash Pasricha, from the collection of Abha Bhatnagar Roy—Kathak dancer, New York.

Kathak Dance Drama 'Shavan Atah-Kim' by Kadamb, choreographer: Kumudini Lakhia, Sangeet Natak Akademi.

Saswati Sen, Sangeet Natak Akademi.

Pandit Rajendra Gangani, Sangeet Natak Akademi.

Pandit Rajendra Gangani, Sangeet Natak Akademi.

Saswati Sen, Sangeet Natak Akademi.

The three humours in Ayurveda and the five great elements that they are composed of. Author: Krishnavedala, The Creative Commons CC0 1.0 Universal Public Domain Dedication, Wikimedia Commons.

Pandit Rajendra Gangani, from the collection of Pandit Rajendra Gangani.

Pandit Rajendra Gangani, Sangeet Natak Akademi.

Saswati Sen, Sangeet Natak Akademi.

Uma Sharma, Sangeet Natak Akademi.

Rohini Bhate, Sangeet Natak Akademi.

Niketa Patel—Moghul Costume (*Aharya Abhinaya*), from the collection of photographer Vivek Desai.

Hetvi Desai—Kathak Jewellery (*Aharya Abhinaya*), from the collection of photographer Vivek Desai.

Hetvi Desai, from the collection of photographer Vivek Desai.

Hemant Panwar and Vaishali Panwar, from the collection of Hemant and Vaishali Panwar, Canada.

Kathak solo performance, Suyash Dwivedi, Creative Commons Attribution- Share Alike 4.0 International license, Wikimedia Commons.

Ghungru. Author: Kadiv, Creative Commons Attribution-Share Alike 3.0 Unported license, Wikimedia Commons.

Pandit Rajendra Gangani, Sangeet Natak Akademi.

Pandit Rajendra Gangani, Sangeet Natak Akademi.

Prerna Shrimali, Sangeet Natak Akademi.

Pandit Rajendra Gangani, Sangeet Natak Akademi.

Sunayana Hazarilal, Sangeet Natak Akademi.

Pandit Rajendra Gangani, Sangeet Natak Akademi.

Vasaka Sajja Nayika, artist unknown, dated between 1680 and 1700, Brooklyn Museum Collection, PD-US, Wikimedia Commons.

Independent Heroine (*Swadhinpatika*), *Nayika* Painting Appended to a Ragmala (Garland of Melodies), c.1650, The Los Angeles County Museum of Art www.lacma.org, accession no. M.73.2.9, Wikimedia Commons.

Anxious Heroine (*Utkanthita*), *Nayika* Painting Appended to a Ragmala (Garland of Melodies), c.1650, Los Angeles County Museum of Art, www.lacma.org, accession no. M.73.2.10, Wikimedia Commons.

Khandita Nayika, artist unknown, dated between 1790 and 1830, A. Augustus Healy Fund and the Frank L. Babbott Fund, Online Collection of Brooklyn Museum; Photo: Brooklyn Museum, 36.251_IMLS_SL2.jpg, Wikimedia Commons.

Deceived Heroine (*Vipralabdha*), *Nayika* Painting Appended to a Ragmala (Garland of Melodies), c.1650, Los Angeles County Museum of Art www.lacma.org, accession no. M.73.2.5, Wikimedia Commons.

Displeased Heroine (*Kalahantarita*), *Nayika* Painting Appended to a Ragmala (Garland of Melodies), c.1650, Los Angeles County Museum of Art www.lacma.org, accession no. M.73.2.3, Wikimedia Commons.

Forlorn Heroine (*Proshitapriyatama*), *Nayika* Painting Appended to a Ragmala (Garland of Melodies), c.1650, Los Angeles County Museum of Art www.lacma.org, accession no. M.73.2.4, Wikimedia Commons.

Abhisarika Nayika ('The Heroine Going to Meet Her Lover at an Appointed Place'), c.1800, author: Mola Ram. Opaque watercolour and gold on paper. One of the paintings in the Ross-Coomaraswamy collection at MFA. Description from the MFA website: 'Night scene: a woman walks between two groups of trees. She looks down over her shoulder at a golden anklet, which has apparently just fallen off. Several snakes appear at her feet, including one which has wrapped itself around the base of a tree at the right. Above there is a multi-forked bolt of lightning. Attribution to Mola Ram of Garhwal was made by a descendant of the artist, Balak Ram Sah.'

Sum Position—Pandit Rajendra Gangani, from the collection of Pandit Rajendra Gangani.

Footwork—Pandit Rajendra Gangani, from the collection Pandit Rajendra Gangani.

Madhu Nataraj, from the collection of Madhu Nataraj, Founder Director of Natya Stem Dance Kampani, photographer: Shamanth Patil.

Guru Dr Maya Rao, from the collection of Madhu Nataraj, Founder Director of Natya Stem Dance Kampani. Photographer: Govind Vidyarti.

Guru Dr Maya Rao, from the collection of Madhu Nataraj, Founder Director

of Natya Stem Dance Kampani.
Photographer: Govind Vidyarti.

Vandana—Pandit Rajendra Gangani,
from the collection of Pandit Rajendra
Gangani.

Sandhya Desai, from the collection of
Sandhya Desai.

Pandit Birju Maharaj, Sangeet Natak
Akademi.

Pandit Lachhu Maharaj, Sangeet Natak
Akademi.

Pandit Birju Maharaj, Sangeet Natak
Akademi.

Pandit Shambhu Maharaj, Sangeet Natak
Akademi.

Pandit Sundar Prasad, Sangeet Natak
Akademi.

Pandit Durga Lal, Sangeet Natak Akademi.

Pandit Durga Lal, Sangeet Natak Akademi.

Guru Kundan Lal Gangani, from the
collection of Abha Bhatnagar Roy—
Kathak dancer, New York.

Guru Kundan Lal Gangani, from the
collection of Abha Bhatnagar Roy—
Kathak dancer, New York.

Pandit Rajendra Gangani, Sangeet Natak
Akademi.

Group Choreography: Rajendra Gangani,
Bhaswati Mishra, and Arjun Mishra
(standing from left to right); Prerna
Shrimali, Veronique Azan, and Abha
Bhatnagar Roy (sitting from left to
right). Photographer: Avinash Pasricha.
Source: Abha Bhatnagar Roy—Kathak
dancer, New York.

Pakhawaj, a North Indian classical drum.
Author: Anunaad Singh, the Creative
Commons Attribution-Share Alike 2.0
Generic license, Wikimedia Commons.

Tabla, professional tabla from Pakrashi,
the Creative Commons Attribution-
Share Alike 3.0 Unported license,
Wikimedia Commons.

Ragmala Painting of Sarang Ragini,
1605. Opaque watercolour on
paper, Chawand, Mewar, India,
V&A Museum, Nasiruddin, public
domain in India, Wikimedia Commons.

Ragmala Painting series in realistic
style made by artist Navin R. Soni
from Bhuj-India, Artist Navin Soni,
the Creative Commons Attribution-
Share Alike 4.0 International license,
Wikimedia Commons.

Ragmala Painting of Asavari Ragini, 1610
(A lady charms snakes in a rocky
landscape), dated 1610). Source:
V&A, Nasiruddin, PD-US, Wikimedia
Commons.

Ragmala Painting of Goda Raga, the `son'
of Megha Raga, 1710. V&A, public
domain in India, Wikimedia Commons.

Ragmala Painting of Dhanasri Ragini,
Rajasthan, Rajput period, c. 1690,
Kimbell Art Museum, PD-US,
Wikimedia Commons.

Ragmala Painting of Malasri Ragini, 1640.
Freer Gallery of Art, AAFfqdm9D55Scw
at Google Cultural Institute, accession
no. F1924.7, PD-US, Wikimedia
Commons.

Ragmala Painting of Bhairavi Ragini, 1610
(Two women worship Shiva in a lotus-
filled lake), unknown artist, sub-imperial
Mughal style, British Museum, PD-US,
Wikimedia Commons.

Ragmala Painting of Khambhavati Ragini,
Golconda, 1750, Deccan School, PD-
US, Wikimedia Commons.

Ragmala Painting of Nata Ragini, wife of
Bhairava Raga, 1762. Bhimsen, PD-US,
Wikimedia Commons.

Ragmala Painting of Vasant Ragini, Kota, Rajasthan, 1770, Art Gallery of New South Wales, http://www.artgallery. nsw.gov.au/collection/works/82.1997/, accession no. 82.1997, PD-US, Wikimedia Commons.

Sarangi, c.1865. Metropolitan Museum of Art, Gift of Miss Alice Getty, 1946, Creative Commons CC0 1.0 Universal Public Domain Dedication., Wikimedia Commons.

Miraj Sitar, author: Jan Kraus, public domain, Wikimedia Commons.

Three octave portable harmonium with triple reeds and nine air stops, author: Niranjan Arminius, source: Harmonium_20151009, The Creative Commons Attribution-Share Alike 2.0 Generic license, Wikimedia Commons.

A 23-inch-long flute often used in concerts, author: Betelgeuse, Creative Commons Attribution-Share Alike 3.0 Unported license, Wikimedia Commons.

Padhant by Pandit Rajendra Gangani, from the collection of Pandit Rajendra Gangani.

Contemporary Kathak—Natya Stem Dance Kampani, from the collection of Madhu Nataraj, Founder Director of Natya Stem Dance Kampani. Photographer: PeeVee (Venkatesan Perumal).

Aditi Mangaldas with ensemble, show in Warsaw, author: Dobromila, GNU Free Documentation License, Wikimedia Commons.

Jhulan Pastime—Hindola-Raga Pahari, Kangra, c. 1790, http://www.harekrsna. com/sun/features/12-11/features2312. htm,1 January 1790, Wikimedia Commons.

References

BOOKS AND MAGAZINES

Bandlamudi, Lakshmi. *Dialogics of Self, The Mahabharata and Culture: The History of Understanding and Understanding of History*. UK and USA: Anthem Press, 2010.

Banerji, Projesh. *Kathak Dance through Ages*. New Delhi: Cosmos Publications, 1982.

Bhatnagar, Ved. *Shringar—The Ras Raj: A Classical Indian View*. Delhi: Abhinav Publications, 2011.

Capra, Fritjof. *The Tao of Physics: An Exploration of the Parallels between Modern Physics and Eastern Mysticism*. Massachusetts, USA: Shambhala Publications, 1991.

Dave, Prem. *Kathak Nritya Parampara*. Jaipur: Panchsheel Prakashan, 2004.

Garg, Laxmi Narayan. *Kathak Nritya*. Hathras: Sangeet Karyalaya, 1994.

Gupta, Ganapatichandra. *Sahityik Nibandh*. Allahabad: Lokbharti Prakashan, 1990.

Kothari, Sunil. *Kathak: Indian Classical Dance Art*. New Delhi: Abhinav Publications, 1989.

Maharaj, Pandit Birju. *Ang Kavya*. New Delhi: Har-Anand Publications Pvt. Ltd., 2002.

Marchand, Peter. *The Yoga of the Nine Emotions: The Tantric Practice of Rasa Sadhana*. Vermont, US: Destiny Books, 2006.

Massey, Reginald. *India's Kathak Dance: Past, Present, Future*. New Delhi: Abhinav Publications, 1999.

Meyer-Dinkgräfe, Daniel. *Approaches to Acting: Past and Present*. New York: Bloomsbury Continuum, 2001.

Narayan, Shovana. *Kathak (Dances of India Series)*. New Delhi: Wisdom Tree, 2004.

Rangacharya, Adya. *Introduction to Bharata's Natyasastra*. New Delhi: Munshiram Manoharlal Publishers Pvt. Ltd., 1966.

Sastri, Babu Lal Shukla. *Natyashastra of Bharat Muni* (Part 1–4). Varanasi: Chaukhambha Sanskrit Sansthan, 2009.

Sharma, Bhagwatsharan. *Tala Ank*. Hathras: Sangeet Karyalaya, year: n.a.

Sharma, Prem Lata. 'The Origin of Thumari'. In *Aspects of Indian Music*. Delhi: Publications Division, Ministry of Information and Broadcasting, Government of India, 2006.

Singh, Thakur Jaideva. *Bharatiya Sangeet ka Itihaas*. Calcutta: Sangeet Research Academy, 1994.

Vatsyayan, Kapila. *Bharata: The Natyasastra*. New Delhi: Sahitya Akademi, 1996.

Watts, Nigel. *The Way of Love*. London: Thorsons, 1999.

Zarrilli, Phillip. *Kathakali Dance-Drama: Where Gods and Demons Come to Play*. London: Routledge, 2000.

WEBSITES

'A General Introduction to Lasya and Dance Traditions', http://shodhganga.inflibnet.ac.in/bitstream/10603/25592/9/09_chapter%201.pdf (accessed on 12 April 2018).

Ananth, Ambika. 'Shringara—The Raja Rasa', issue 18 (March–April 2018), http://www.museindia.com/Home/AuthorContentDataView, *Muse India* (accessed on 13 April 2018).

Capra, Fritjof. 'Shiva's Cosmic Dance at CERN.' 20 June 2004, http://www.fritjofcapra.net/shivas-cosmic-dance-at-cern/ (accessed on 12 April 2018).

Centre for Cultural Resources and Training, http://ccrtindia.gov.in/kathak.php (accessed on 13 April 2018).

Clayton, Martin. 'Metre and Tal in North Indian Music', https://www.researchgate.net/profile/Martin_Clayton/publication/265654904_METRE_AND_TAL_IN_NORTH_INDIAN_MUSIC/links/54b91ba00cf28faced626e41/METRE-AND-TAL-IN-NORTH-INDIAN-MUSIC.pdf (accessed on 16 April 2018).

Courtney, David. 'Kathak—A Classical Dance of Northern India', http://www.tarang-classical-indian-music.com/tanz_links/kathak_*Gharana*_eng.htm (accessed on 16 April 2018).

Courtney, David. 'The Tawaif, The Anti-nautch movement, and the Development of North Indian Classical Music, Part 3 – Evolution of the Will to End the Tawaifs', https://chandrakantha.com/articles/tawaif/3_the_will.html (accessed on 19 April 2018).

Courtney, 'The Tawaif, The Anti-Nautch movement, and the Development of North Indian Classical Music, Part 5 – The Anti-Nautch Movement', https://chandrakantha.com/articles/tawaif/5_anti_nautch_movement.html (accessed on 19 April 2018).

Crossley-Holland, Peter. 'Rhythm'. Encyclopaedia Britannica. Last updated on 31 May 2002, https://www.britannica.com/art/rhythm-music (accessed on 16 April 2018).

Csikszentmihalyi, Mihaly. Brain Channels, Thinker of the Year Award 2000, 'Flow Theory', http://www.brainchannels.com/thinker/mihaly.html (accessed on 16 April 2018).

Dave, Ranjana. 'The Story of a Gharana'. *The Hindu*. Updated on 15 April 2011, http://www.thehindu.com/todays-paper/tp-features/tp-fridayreview/the-story-of-a-*Gharana*/article1697629.ece (accessed on 16 April 2018).

Franz, Paris. Decoded = {Past}. 'The Emperor Akbar: Mughal Patron of the Arts'. 13 Sep. 2013, http://decodedpast.com/the-emperor-akbar-mughal-patron-of-the-arts/ (accessed on 13 April 2018).

'Girls performing a Kathak Dance' (Aurangzeb period), United Kingdom of Great Britain and Northern Ireland, http://colnect.com/en/stamps/stamp/3453-Girls_performing_a_Kathak_Dance_Aurangzeb_period-Greetings_Stamps_-_Art-United_Kingdom_of_Great_Britain_Northern_Ireland (accessed on 18 April 2018).

Hine, Phil. 'Rasa Theory'. Enfolding.org, http://enfolding.org/wikis-4/tantra-wikiwikis-4tantra-wiki/tantra_essays/rasa-theory/ (accessed on 13 April 2018).

Haider, Nishat. 'The Tawa'ifs of Lucknow'. Café Dissensus. 15 April 2014, http://cafedissensus.com/2014/04/15/the-tawaifs-of-lucknow/ (accessed on 16 April 2018).

'Indian Dramatic Tradition', uploaded by anjumvyas on 17 Aug 2014, https://www.scribd.com/document/237009086/Indian-Dramatic-Tradition (accessed on 24 April 2018).

Kersenboom, Saskia. 'Ananda's Tandava: "The Dance of Shiva" Reconsidered'. The Free Library by Farlex, Marg, A Magazine of the Arts. 1 March 2011, https://www.thefreelibrary.com/ndava%3A+%22The+Dance+of+Shiva%22+reconsidered.-a0253862093 (accessed on 12 April 2018).

Kher, Geetika Kaw. 'A Glimpse into Abhinavagupta's Ideas on Aesthetics', http://shaivism.net/abhinavagupta/4.html (accessed on 13 April 2018).

Krishnan. 'Krishna, Human Manifestation of God'. Wednesday, 13 June 2007, http://blog1gk.blogspot.com/2007/06/krishna-human-manifestation-of-god.html (accessed on 12 April 2018).

Magar, Shiva. 'Communication in Eastern and Western Perspectives', 16 December 2010, http://shivamagar.wordpress.com/2010/12/16/communication-in-eastern-and-western-perspectives/ (accessed on 13 April 2018).

Malkar, Anjali. 'Tarana—An Aesthetic Musical Thought Beyond Words', http://www.shadjamadhyam.com/tarana (accessed on 16 April 2018).

Mandaiker, Arjun. 'The History of the Tabla', 22 October 2013, http://www.desiblitz.com/content/history-tabla (accessed on 16 April 2018).

Mason, David. 'Introduction to Theatre in India: Rasa', http://www.yavanika.org/theatreinindia/?page_id=446 (accessed on 13 April 2018).

Mayer, John D. 'Emotions—How To Understand, Identify and Release Your Emotions.' The Home of Vibrational Health, http://www.mkprojects.com/pf_emotions.html (accessed on 16 April 2018).

Narayan, Shovana. 'Kinetics of Cultural Synthesis in Performing Arts.' Explore Rural India, Heritage and Development 2(2) (2014), http://www.itrhd.com/magazine/volume2-issue2-july-2014.pdf (accessed on 13 April 2018).

Narayan, Shovana. 'The Origin and Evaluation of Kathak in Delhi'. Yumpu, https://www.yumpu.com/en/document/view/45426585/the-origin-and-evolution-of-kathak-in-delhi-delhi-heritage-city/8 (accessed on 13 April 2018).

'Navarasa: An Embodiment of Indian Art'. IHC Visual Arts Gallery, http://archive.is/XZ0hY (accessed on 19 April 2018).

Nevile, Pran. 'Nautch Girls: Sahibs Danced to Their Tune, Excerpted from Stories from the Raj: Sahibs, Memsahibs and Others'. Spectrum. The Tribune. 25 July 2004, http://www.tribuneindia.com/2004/20040725/spectrum/main1.htm (accessed 13 April 2018).

No Fear Shakespeare: King Lear. Act 4, scene 6, http://nfs.sparknotes.com/lear/page_244.html (accessed on 16 April 2018).

Nooshin, Laudan and Richard Widdess. 'Improvisation in Iranian and Indian Music', https://eprints.soas.ac.uk/5430/1/NooshinWiddess1.pdf (accessed on 16 April 2018).

Nupur Global Dance Academy, http://www.learnkathak.com/index.php?option=com_content&view=article&id=16&Itemid=14 (accessed on 13 April 2018).

Pande, Alka. 'Ashtanayika: The Messengers of Love', The Stainless Gallery, Matters of Art, http://mattersofart.blogspot.in/2008/12/ashtanayika-messengers-of-love.html (accessed on 16 April 2018).

Phadke, Parimal. 'Concept of Naayaka in Bharata's Natyasastra', http://www.narthaki.com/info/articles/art128.html (accessed on 16 April 2018).

Poet Seers. 'Bhakti Poets', site developed by members of the Sri Chinmoy Centre, http://www.poetseers.org/poets/bhakti-poets/ (accessed 13 April 2018).

Rajagopalan, Jayashree. *Aharya Abhinaya–A Study*, http://www.jayashreerajagopalan.com/download/Synopsis_of_Thesis_Aharya_Abhinaya.pdf (accessed on 16 April 2018).

Rajagopal, Jayashree. 'Rasa Theory with Reference to Bharata's Natyasastra', http://www.shadjamadhyam.com/*rasa*_theory_with_reference_to_bharatas_natyashastra (accessed on 13 April 2018).

Rajan, Anjana. 'Rise of Raigarh'. *The Hindu*, http://www.thehindu.com/features/friday-review/dance/rise-of-raigarh/article3657624.ece (accessed 17 April 2018).

Rath, Chintamani. 'A Grammar of the Tihai'. Essay written in August 1989, Appendices in March 2008, http://www.ragaculture.com/tihai.html (accessed on 16 April 2018).

'Laya and Tala', https://www.ragaculture.com/laya_and_tala.html (accessed on 2 May 2018).

'Rumi Love and Ecstasy Poems', http://peacefulrivers.homestead.com/rumilove.html (accessed on 16 April 2018).

Sangeet Natak Akademi, http://sangeetnatak.gov.in/sna/introduction.php, Sangeet Natak Akademi introduction page (accessed on 19 April 2018).

Sankaranarayanan, S. 'Sangeet Natak Akademi'. *Sruti: India's Premier Magazine for Performing Arts*, http://www.sruti.com/index.php?route=archives/heritage_details&hId=50 (accessed on 19 April 2018).

Sanyal, Ritwik and Richard Widdess. 'Dhrupad: Tradition and Performance in Indian Music'. SOAS Musicology Series. Hampshire, England, and Burlington, VT: Ashgate, 2004, https://ipfs.io/ipfs/QmXoypizjW3WknFiJnKLwHCnL72vedxjQkDDP1mXWo6uco/wiki/Dhrupad.html (accessed on 16 April 2018).

Sethumadhavan T.N. 'Bhagavad Gita–Chap 11 (Part-1) Vishwaroopa Darshana Yogah—Yoga of the Vision of the Universal Form'. May 2011, http://www.esamskriti.com/essay-chapters/Bhagavad-Gita--Chap-11-(Part-1)-Vishwaroopa-Darshana-Yogah--Yoga-of-the-Vision-of-the-Universal-Form-1.aspx (accessed on 12 April 2018).

Shahriari, Shahriar. 'Hafiz-e-Shirazi'. 2012, http://www.hafizonlove.com/divan/01/032.htm (accessed on 16 April 2018).

Shyamdas. 'The Ashta Chaap Poets and their Bhava'. Excerpt from 'Krishna's Inner Circle: The Ashta Chhap Poets' by Shyamdas, http://shyamdas.com/2010/07/01/the-ashta-chaap-poets-and-their-bhava-2/ (accessed on 13 April 2018).

Srinivas, C.S. 'Significance of *Rasa* and *Abhinaya* Techniques in Bharata's *Natyasastra*.' *IOSR Journal of Humanities and Social Science* (IOSR-JHSS) 19, no. 5 (2014) Ver. IV, http://iosrjournals.org/iosr-jhss/papers/Vol19-issue5/Version-4/E019542529.pdf (accessed on 17 April 2018).

'Vedic Recitation, Rhythms and Metrical Forms'. Gurubodh: Fragrance of Love and Light. September–October 2005, https://greenopia.in/live/gurujinarayana/wp-content/uploads/2017/06/Vedic-Recitation-Rhythms-and-Metrical-Forms.pdf (accessed on 17 April 2018).

'Volume VIII—The Art of Being, The Privilege of Being Human, Chapter VII, Truth'. The Spiritual Message of Hazrat Inayat Khan, http://wahiduddin.net/mv2/VIII/VIII_2_7.htm (accessed on 16 April 2018).

Walker, Margaret. 'Revival and Reinvention in India's *Kathak* Dance', https://journals.lib.unb.ca/index.php/MC/article/view/20234/23336 (accessed on 19 April 2018).

NEWSPAPER ARTICLE

Narayan, Shovana. 'Forgotten Page of History'. *Spectrum. The Tribune.* Sunday, 28 September 2008.

Further Readings

Bapodara, Ramesh. *Tabla Handbook*. Ahmedabad: Ashtachhap Kirtan Sangeet Vidyapith, 2006.

Bhatnagar, Chaya. *Bharat ke Shastriya Nritya*. Delhi: Young Man and Company, 1981.

Clayton, Martin. *Time in Indian Music, Rhythm, Metre, and Form in North Indian Rag Performance (Oxford Monographs on Music)*. New York: Oxford University Press, 2000.

Deva, B.C. *Musical Instruments*. Delhi: National Book Trust, 1977.

Khokar, Ashish Mohan. *Classical Dance*. New Delhi: Rupa Co., 2004.

Rangacharya, Adya. *The Natyashastra, English Translation with Critical Notes*. New Delhi: Munshiram Manoharlal Publishers Pvt. Ltd., 1984.

Saxena, S.K. *The Winged Form, Aesthetical Essays on Hindustani Rhythm*. New Delhi: Sangeet Natak Akademy, 1979.

Sharma, Prem Lata, ed. *Sarangdeva and His Sangita-Ratnakara*. Delhi: Sangeet Natak Akademi, 1998.

Acknowledgements

I WOULD LIKE TO EXPRESS MY GRATITUDE to all those who have made my journey of writing this book possible. The book has greatly benefitted directly and indirectly from all those who contributed to my life as a Kathak dancer.

I am very grateful to my parents Dr Kamla Kanodia and Sri Banwari Lal Kanodia, who first introduced me to the field of classical Indian music and dance. If not for them, I would not have known that divine magic existed on this earth in the form of dance and music.

Each and every day, I am so grateful to my gurus and to the art of Kathak, which has revolutionized my life. I am immensely grateful to Fattan Khan Saheb (my first guru), Vidushi Maya Rao, Guru Rajendra Gangani, and Vidushi Sandhya Desai for handing me the knowledge of Kathak. In this journey, they all became my adored family. Heartfelt thanks to my gurus Pandit Subhankar Banerjee and Pandit Debashish Bhattacharya, who have patiently exposed me to the art of tabla and raga music. I studied the basics of tabla as well as many aspects of *laykari* from Pandit Subhankar Banerjee in order to strengthen the *tala* and *laya* aspects of my Kathak performances.

I am extremely grateful to my friend Abhik Mukherjee, who also became my teacher in many ways and has shown me ways to enhance my artistic understanding. It is almost impossible to list all my other friends and colleagues who have been my inspiration and have taught me a lot about arts and life—I think of them all the time and always feel grateful and fortunate to share this planet with them.

I am so thankful to my daughter Eshani, the love of my life, for her continual encouragement and being a supportive witness of my artistic journey.

My sisters Alka Aashlesha and Gareema Geetika, who are also artists, have always inspired and motivated me. I am so grateful to them for their unwavering support in my artistic and personal journey. Thanks to my brother Vidyut Ranjan, who is a businessman with inherent artistic talent. I am especially thankful to Kapilas Bhuyan and Dr Dinanath Pathy, who encouraged me to write this book. I am truly moved and inspired by the artistic work that Dr Dinanath Pathy produced in his lifetime.

When I moved to the United States in the late 1980s, I was discouraged to see that there was no Kathak dance programme in the State of Connecticut. I am so very thankful to Gita Agrawal and Giri Agrawal for their help in starting my first Kathak dance school in Connecticut and for their efforts in establishing me as a performer. How can I thank the organizations Connecticut Commission on Culture and Tourism, Arts for Learning, Trinity College, Charter Oak Cultural Center, Vallabhdham Temple, and Hindu Cultural Center, which supported me in my efforts of preserving the art of Kathak in the State of Connecticut, USA? I couldn't have sustained my artistic life without their help. I am also thankful to Gita Desai, who believed in me for her film *Raga Unveiled*. Working on *Raga Unveiled* as a creative support, I learned tremendously about the art of classical Indian music and dance. During the making of that film, I also met the stalwarts of Indian dance and music, whose artistry and philosophy on arts deeply affected me. In fact, the seed of writing this book started to germinate in my mind during the shooting of that film.

I am especially thankful to my Kathak students and their amazingly supportive parents who bring so much joy in my life. Because of them, my life is artistically beautiful each and every day.

I would also like to extend my sincere thanks to Helen Acharya and the library of Sangeet Natak Akademi for aiding me in my research for this book.

I am extremely thankful to my editor Pamela Adelman, who has helped me with the continuity and revisions of this book. Pamela is one of the most patient and accommodating people I have ever met.

Finally, many thanks to my readers. Living so far away from India, for me, Kathak has been the greatest link to my roots. This book is the result of my sadhana and my steadfast passion for Kathak. I hope my readers will benefit from this book and will forgive me for any shortcomings in this effort. As we say in the music and dance field in India: if my readers like this book, the credit goes to my gurus and all the people who became the guiding lights in my life; if my readers find any lack in this book, the fault is mine.

There are some books available on Kathak in English, which are brilliantly written and provide the cultural, historical, and philosophical perspectives on Kathak. However, there are hardly any books in English that provide detailed insight into the compositions and repertoires of Kathak dance. I have tried to present both proven methods and rare equations for creating complex Kathak compositions in this book. My experiences as a Kathak dancer and my research work in the areas of this dance form compelled me to write this book. I have tried my best to do justice to the knowledge, which was so affectionately handed to me by my gurus.

Writing this book has changed me both as a person and as a dancer. While researching the ancient theories on Indian dance, I felt deeply connected to my roots, which in turn gave me a profound sense of belongingness. Dance has now become for me a place where we remain silent and can even listen to the unsung songs of life. And now, my striving in dance is only about how I can become a conduit for the inherent human sentiments to be expressed—to be who I am. I have started to feel that the world is so mysterious and beautiful because I am blessed with the gifts of dance and music. Through this book, I hope to become a channel to share my blessings with my readers and make them understand that the art of Kathak takes us within, where the truth exists, and we can have a heartfelt communion with our higher selves.

Index

performers, 262
Janaki Prasad Gharana
    Jayadeva, 268
jati-bhed, 142, 146
jatis, 165, 181–82, 211; see
    also tishra, chatushra,
    khanda, mishra, and
    sankirna jatis
jhaptal, 171, 195; see also
    tala jhaptal
jhoola, 226
jhoomar, 120
jivas, 29
jnana shakti, 17
joda bols, 274
jugalbandi, 293

K
kaal, 160–62; see also
    sukshma kaal and sthula
    kaal
Kachwaha kings, 252, 254,
    260
kahaga, 52
kahub, 52
kaivad prabandh, 233
kajri, 223, 226
kala, 161, 165; also see
    vardhamaana kala and
    nashta kala
kalahantarita nayika, 149,
    150
kalapa, 42
kalapaka, 112
kalaripayattu, 44
Kalidas, 56, 153
Kalika Tandava, 19
Kaliya Daman, 218, 332
Kalpa Sūtra, 52
kama, 94
kamali chakkardar parans,
    211
Kamasutra (Vatsyayana), 53
karanas, 18, 35, 92, 111–
    12, 298

karuna rasa, 98, 102
katha, 44, 49, 51–2, 55, 297
Kathak,
    meaning, 55
    dexterity of graceful
    hand movements in,
    114
    in Independent India,
    78–84
    in Mughal Courts,
    65–70
    during Mughal era, 57
    origin, 51–7
    pada bhangimas or feet
    positions in, 115
    post-Mughal period,
    70–2
    Tandava ang, 62
    vachik abhinaya, 116–17
    vocalizations and
    terminology, 62
Kathakali, 44–5
    costume and make-up
    of, 44–7
    orchestra of, 45
    sampradayams, 45
Kathakars, 11, 23, 49, 53,
    60, 64, 213, 297
Kathak Nritya Parampara
    (Dr Prem Dave), 61
Kathak repertoire, 60–2,
    136, 199, 277
kathika, 52
katthya, 52
Kavi, Chidambara, 54
kavitta, 134, 216–19, 253,
    261, 295
Kedara, 158
keharwa tala, 177
Kerala Kalamandalam, 46
Keshavdas, 137, 147–48
khade per ki tatkar, 205–
    206, 330–31
khanapuri, 173
khanda jati, 112, 165, 169

Khan, Pyar, 71
Khan, Ustad Hafiz Ali, 82
khandani Kathak dancers, 79
khandani Kathak masters,
    83
khandita nayika, 149
Khrumba Bhangi Pareng,
    47
Khusrow, Amir, 66–7, 229,
    233, 278
khyal gayaki, 67
kinkini, 123, 154
koshas, 12, 86–7, 89–90
kothas, 79, 248
koti, 120
Krishna, 22–6, 27, 28–9,
    59–63, 64, 65, 95, 108,
    138–39, 209, 211,
    213–19, 222, 231–32,
    245, 251, 284
    stories associated with
    Lord Krishna, 23–9,
    61–3, 64
krishna-abhisarika nayika,
    150
Krishna kavitta, 217
Krishnanattam, 44
kriyas, 13, 160–61, 163–65,
    199–200, 204, 287; see
    also shashabd kriyas and
    nishabd kriyas
kriya chatur, 138
kriya shakti, 17
kriya vidagdha, 145
Kuchipudi, 40–2
Kurukshetra, 25
kushilavs, 32, 53
Kushwaha kings of
    Rajputana, 252
kuwar laya, 180

L
Lachhu Maharaj, 81, 246,
    247, 251, 299
ladi, 136, 203

Riti Kaal, 137–38, 216
riyaaz, 289–90
Roy, Abha Bhatnagar, *80, 276*
Rudra Tandava, 19

S
Sabdakalpadruma, 54
sabha bhava, 130
sadhana, 287–90
sadhak, 287–90
sadharanikaran, 12, 103–104, 294
sadhya, 287, 289
Saguna Bhakti, 60
Sahitya Darpana, 137, 143
sahridayata, 103–104
salaam, 207, 249
salami, 207, 249, 293
sama laya, 183, 192
Sama Veda, 129
Samagana, 160
samadhi, 18, 287–88
samanya abhinaya, 36, 127–28
samay, 288
Sama Yati, 166
samhara, 17
sampravriddha, 138–39
sanchari bhavas, 91–2, 112
Sandhya Tandava, 19
sangeet, 54, 135, 172, 277
Sangeet Natak Akademi, 39–40, 48, 79, 81, 246–47, 258–59,
Sangeet Ratnakara, 18, 39, 54, 56–7
Sankardev, Srimanta, 48
sankirna jati, 165, 183, 306
Sankuka, Sri, 104, 127
santoor, 285
sarangi, 282
Saraswati, 19
sari, 120
sarod, 285
sashabd kriya, 163

Sattriya, 48–9
instruments accompanying, 48–9
repertoires, 49
sattva, 88, 125–26, 128
sattvika bhavas, 91–3
*sattvik abhinaya*s, 117, 125–28, 213
Satyam, Guru Vempati Chinna, 42
sawaguna, 180
sawal jawab, 293–94
seedha chakkar, 238
sehtar, 283
Sen, Saswati, *81, 83, 109,* 251
Sabdakalpadruma, 54
Shabdartha Chintamani, 54
shabd or *bol bhava*, 130
shadmargas, 162–63
Shah, Wajid Ali, 71–3, 223–24, 244–46, 297–98
Shah Jahan, Emperor, 68–9
Shaivite, 18, 42
Shakti, 17, 20–1, 24
Shambhu Maharaj, 81, 117, 246–47, *248,* 251, 272, 299
shamashan, 19, 99
shankhini, 146
shankh, 26–7
shanta rasa, 100–101, 104
Sharangdeva, 18, 39, 54, 56, 295
Shastri, Guru Vedantam Lakshminarayana, 41–2
Shastriya Nritya, 40
shayars, 228
shers, 227
Shiva, Lord, 15–22, 24, 46, 96, 99–100, 102–103, 130, 135, 172, 254
shlokas, 232–33
Shori Mian, 223

Shribhatta Devacharya, 63, 235
Shrimali, Prerna, *80, 132,* 262, *276*
shringar, 52, 94
shringar rasa, 94–5, 97, 102, 138, 140, 147, 153, 155, 176, 208–209, 224–26, 249, 261
Shriram Bharatiya Kala Kendra, 81, 299
shristi, 17
Shuddhadvaita, 60
shukla-abhisarika nayika, 150
shukla-paksha nakshatra, 52
shushka-aksharas, 233
Shyamal Das Gharana, 268
Siddhanta Kaumudi, 52, 54
Siddheshwari Devi, 82
siddhis, 12, 88–9
Singh, King Chandrakirti, 47
Singh, Raja Madho, 253
Singh, Raja Man, 252–53
Singh, Raja Ram, 253
Singh, Raja Sawai Jai, 253
sitar, 282–83
South Indian classical dance forms
Bharatnatyam, 40–2
Dasi Attam, 40–1
Kathakali, 44–5
Kuchipudi, 41–2
Mohiniattam, 45–6
Sadir Natyam, 40–1
Srimad Bhagavata Maha Purana, 60
Sri Sankuka, 104, 127
Sriram Bharatiya Kala Kendra, 82
sthanaka, 112
sthayi bhavas, 91, 93, 112, 117
sthiti, 17